AF539394

POPULATION AND SOCIETY

Dr. Prem Lata

RANDOM PUBLICATIONS
NEW DELHI - 110 002 (INDIA)

Population and Society

ISBN 978-93-51117-33-9

Published in 2015 in India by
RANDOM PUBLICATIONS
4376-A/4B, Gali Murari Lal, Ansari Road
New Delhi-110 002
Phone: +9111-43580356, 23289044
E-mail: randomexports@gmail.com; sales@randompublications.com; info@randompublications.com

Reprinted 2025

Type Setting by: Friends Media, Delhi-110089
Digitally Printed at: Replika Press Pvt. Ltd.

Preface

Throughout history, populations have grown slowly despite high birth rates, due to the population-reducing effects of war, plagues and high infant mortality. During the 750 years before the Industrial Revolution, the world's population increased very slowly, remaining under 250 million. Global human population growth is around 75 million annually, or 1.1% per year. The global population has grown from 1 billion in 1800 to 7 billion in 2012. It is expected to keep growing to reach between 9 and 12 billion people by the end of the century. In 1800 only 3% of the world's population lived in cities. By the 20th century's close, 47% did so. In 1950, there were 83 cities with populations exceeding one million; but by 2007, this had risen to 468 agglomerations of more than one million. If the trend continues, the world's urban population will double every 38 years, according to researchers. The UN forecasts that today's urban population of 3.2 billion will rise to nearly 5 billion by 2030, when three out of five people will live in cities.

Population growth is a two-edge sword. In the short term, growth reflects good times, but if maintained for any period of time, increasing numbers put pressure on resources, especially food production. In the world of nature, rapid growth in the numbers of any species soon leads to a population implosion, as the carrying capacity of the local environment is exceeded. At the level of countries, and even the world, changes in population size have an important effect on the environmental and related challenges facing all of the world's inhabitants. Some countries experience negative population growth, especially in Eastern Europe mainly due to low fertility rates, high death rates and emigration. In Southern Africa, growth is slowing due to the high number of HIV-related deaths. Some Western Europe countries might also encounter negative population growth. Japan's population began decreasing in 2005. The United Nations Population Division expects world population to peak at over 10 billion at the end of the 21st century but Sanjeev Sanyal has argued that global fertility will fall below replacement rates in the 2020s and that world population will peak below 9 billion by 2050 followed by a long decline. Human overpopulation occurs if the number of people in a group exceeds the carrying capacity of a region occupied by that group. Overpopulation can further be viewed, in a long term perspective, as existing when a population can't be maintained without the rapid depletion of non-renewable resources or without the degradation of the capacity of the environment to give support to the population. The recent rapid increase in human population over the past three centuries has raised concerns that the planet may not be able to sustain present or larger numbers of inhabitants. The InterAcademy Panel Statement on Population Growth, circa 1994, has stated that many environmental problems, such as rising levels of atmospheric carbon dioxide, global warming, and pollution, are aggravated by the population expansion. Other problems associated with overpopulation include the increased demand for resources such as fresh water and food, starvation and malnutrition, consumption of natural resources faster than the rate of regeneration, and a deterioration in living conditions. Wealthy, but highly populated territories like Britain remain in situations in which they rely on food imports from overseas.

This text book will be used as the standard and most up-to-date text on population and society for courses across the social sciences.

I thank all members of my team who have helped in the preparation of the book. My special thanks go to "Random Publications" who have published the book.

— Dr. Prem Lata

Contents

Chapter 1

Human Population

History of Population Growth

The human population has gone through a number of periods of growth since the dawn of civilization in the Holocene period, around 10,000 BCE. The beginning of civilization coincides with the final receding of glacial ice following the end of the last glacial period.

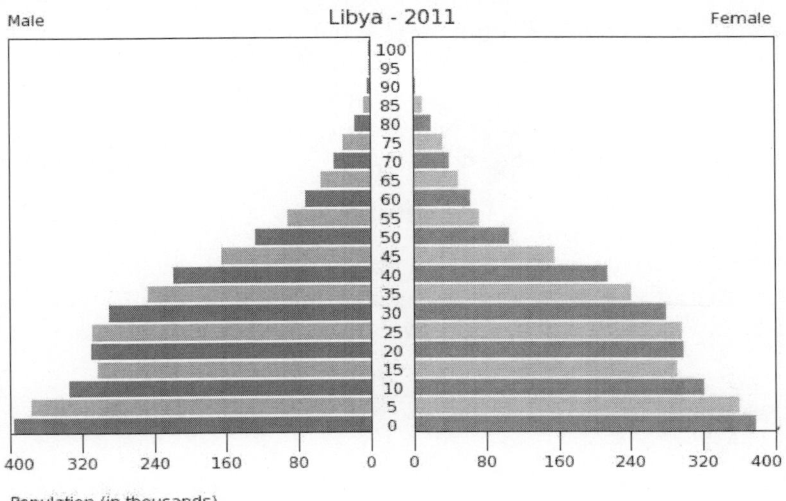

Figure: *A population pyramid based on the 2011 Libyan population.*

It is estimated that about 1,000,000 people, subsisting on hunting and foraging, inhabited the Earth in the period before the neolithic revolution, when human activity shifted away from hunter-gathering and towards very primitive farming. Around 8000 BCE, at the dawn of agriculture, the population of the world was approximately 5 million. The next several millennia saw minimal changes in the population, with a steady growth beginning in 1000 BCE, and a peak of between 200 and 300 million people in 1 BCE.

The Plague of Justinian caused Europe's population to drop by around 50% between 541 and the 8th century. Steady growth resumed in 800 CE. However, growth was again disrupted by frequent plagues; most notably, the Black Death during the 14th century. The effects of the Black Death are thought to have reduced the world's population, then at an estimated 450 million, to between 350 and 375 million by 1400. The population of Europe stood at over 70 million in 1340; these levels did not return until 200 years later. England's population reached an estimated 5.6 million in 1650, up from an estimated 2.6 million in 1500. New crops from the Americas via the Spanish colonizers in the 16th century contributed to the population growth.

In other parts of the globe, China's population at the founding of the Ming dynasty in 1368 stood close to 60 million, approaching 150 million by the end of the dynasty in 1644. The population of the Americas in 1500 may have been between 50 and 100 million.

Encounters between European explorers and populations in the rest of the world often introduced local epidemics of extraordinary virulence. Archaeological evidence indicates that the death of around 90% of the Native American population of the New World was caused by Old World diseases such as smallpox, measles, and influenza. Over the centuries, the Europeans had developed high degrees of immunity to these diseases, while the indigenous peoples had no such immunity.

After the start of the Industrial Revolution, during the 18th century, the rate of population growth began to increase. By the end of the century, the world's population was estimated at just under 1 billion. At the turn of the 20th century, the world's population was roughly 1.6 billion. By 1940, this figure had increased to 2.3 billion.

***Table:** Population Growth 1990–2009 (%)*

World	28.8%
Africa	58.4%
Middle East	53.4%
Asia	36.9%
Latin America	32.0%
OECD North America	25.1%
OECD Europe	9.9%
OECD Pacific	9.5%
Non-OECD Europe and Eurasia	-2.7%

Dramatic growth beginning in 1950 (above 1.8% per year) coincided with greatly increased food production as a result of the industrialisation of agriculture brought about by the Green Revolution. The rate of human population growth peaked in 1964, at about 2.2% per year. For example, Indonesia's population grew from 97 million in 1961 to 237.6 million in 2010, a 145% increase in 49 years. In India, the population grew from 361.1 million people in 1951 to just over 1.2 billion by 2011, a 235% increase in 60 years. Some people are concerned that the recent sharp population rises in many countries in Sub-Saharan Africa, the Middle East, South Asia and South East Asia is creating problems such as increased demand for resources, especially for the less fortunate countries. The population of Chad has, for example, ultimately grown from 6,279,921 in 1993 to 10,329,208 in 2009. Vietnam, Mexico, Nigeria, Egypt, Ethiopia and the DRC are witnessing a similar growth in population. The situation is most acute in northern, western and central Africa. Refugees from places like Sudan have further strained the resources of neighbouring states like Chad and Egypt. The nation is also host to roughly 255,000 refugees from Sudan's Darfur region, and about 77,000 refugees from the Central African Republic, whilst approximately 188,000 Chadians have been displaced by their own civil war and famines, have either fled to either the Sudan, the Niger or, more recently, Libya.

Projections of Population Growth

Continent	*Projected 2050 population*
Africa	1.9 billion
Asia	5.2 billion
Europe	674 million
Latin America and Caribbean	765 million
North America	448 million

According to projections, the world population will continue to grow until at least 2050, with the population reaching 9 billion in 2040, and some predictions putting the population in 2050 as high as 11 billion. Walter Greiling projected in the 1950s that world population would reach a peak of about nine billion, in the 21st century, and then stop growing, after a readjustment of the Third World and a sanitation of the tropics. Recent extrapolations from available figures for population growth show that the population of Earth will stop increasing around 2070.

According to the United Nations' World Population Prospects report:

- The world population is currently growing by approximately 74 million people per year. Current United Nations predictions estimate that the world population will reach 9.0 billion around 2050, assuming a decrease in average fertility rate from 2.5 down to 2.0.
- Almost all growth will take place in the less developed regions, where today's 5.3 billion population of underdeveloped countries is expected to increase to 7.8 billion in 2050. By contrast, the population of the more developed regions will remain mostly unchanged, at 1.2 billion. An exception is the United States population, which is expected to increase by 44% from 2008 to 2050.
- In 2000–2005, the average world fertility was 2.65 children per woman, about half the level in 1950–1955 (5 children per woman). In the medium variant, global fertility is projected to decline further to 2.05 children per woman.
- During 2005–2050, nine countries are expected to account for half of the world's projected population increase: India, Pakistan, Nigeria, Democratic Republic of the Congo, Bangladesh, Uganda, United States, Ethiopia, and China, listed according to the size of their contribution to population growth. China would be higher still in this list were it not for its one-child policy.
- Global life expectancy at birth is expected to continue rising from 65 years in 2000–2005 to 75 years in 2045–2050. In the more developed regions, the projection is to 82 years by 2050. Among the least developed countries, where life expectancy today is just under 50 years, it is expected to increase to 66 years by 2045–2050.
- The population of 51 countries or areas is expected to be lower in 2050 than in 2005.
- During 2005–2050, the net number of international migrants to more developed regions is projected to be 98 million. Because deaths are projected to exceed births in the more developed regions by 73 million during 2005–2050, population growth in those regions will largely be due to international migration.
- In 2000–2005, net migration in 28 countries either prevented population decline or doubled at least the contribution of natural increase (births minus deaths) to population growth.

- Birth rates are now falling in a small percentage of developing countries, while the actual populations in many developed countries would fall without immigration.

Demographic Transition

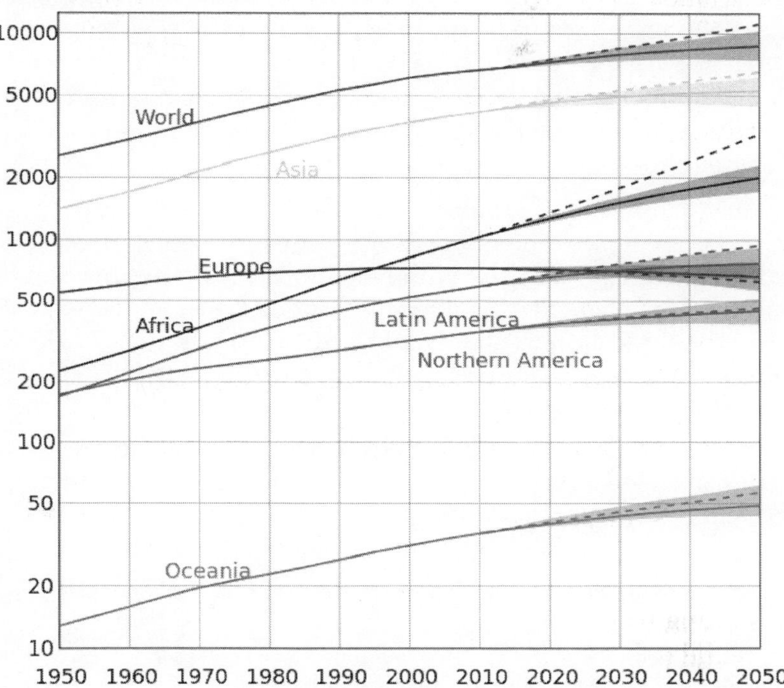

Figure: *United Nation's population projections by location*

The theory of demographic transition held that, after the standard of living and life expectancy increase, family sizes and birth rates decline. However, as new data has become available, it has been observed that after a certain level of development the fertility increases again. This means that both the worry the theory generated about aging populations and the complacency it bred regarding the future environmental impact of population growth are misguided.

Factors cited in the old theory included such social factors as later ages of marriage, the growing desire of many women in such settings to seek careers outside child rearing and domestic work, and the decreased need of children in industrialized settings. The latter factor stems from the fact that children perform a great deal of work in small-scale agricultural societies, and work less in industrial ones; it has been cited to explain the decline in birth rates in industrializing regions.

Another version of demographic transition is proposed by anthropologist Virginia Abernethy in her book *Population Politics*, where she claims that the demographic transition occurs primarily in nations where women enjoy a special status. In strongly patriarchal nations, where she claims women enjoy few special rights, a high standard of living tends to result in population growth. Many countries have high population growth rates but lower total fertility rates because high population growth in the past skewed the age demographic towards a young age, so the population still rises as the more numerous younger generation approaches maturity.

"Demographic entrapment" is a concept developed by Maurice King, Honorary Research Fellow at the University of Leeds, who posits that this phenomenon occurs when a country has a population larger than its carrying capacity, no possibility of migration, and exports too little to be able to import food. This will cause starvation. He claims that for example many sub-Saharan nations are or will become stuck in demographic entrapment, instead of having a demographic transition.

For the world as a whole, the number of children born per woman decreased from 5.02 to 2.65 between 1950 and 2005. A breakdown by region is as follows:

- Europe – 2.66 to 1.41
- North America – 3.47 to 1.99
- Oceania – 3.87 to 2.30
- Central America – 6.38 to 2.66
- South America – 5.75 to 2.49
- Asia (excluding Middle East) – 5.85 to 2.43
- Middle East & North Africa – 6.99 to 3.37
- Sub-Saharan Africa – 6.7 to 5.53

Excluding the observed reversal in fertility decrease for high development, the projected world number of children born per woman for 2050 would be around 2.05. Only the Middle East & North Africa (2.09) and Sub-Saharan Africa (2.61) would then have numbers greater than 2.05.

Sub-replacement Fertility

Sub-replacement fertility is a total fertility rate (TFR) that (if sustained) leads to each new generation being less populous than the previous one in a given area. In developed countriessub-replacement fertility is any rate below approximately 2.1 children born per woman, but the threshold can be as high as 3.4 in some developing countries because of higher mortality rates. Taken globally, the total fertility rate at replacement was 2.33 children per woman in 2003. This can be "translated" as 2 children per woman to replace the parents, plus a "third of a child" to make up for the higher probability of boys being born, and early mortality prior to the end of their fertile life. Replacement level fertility in terms of the net reproduction rate (NRR) is exactly one, because the NRR takes both mortality rates and sex ratios at birth into account. Today about 42% of the world population lives in nations with sub-replacement fertility. Nonetheless most of these countries still have growing populations due to immigration, population momentum and increase of the life expectancy. This includes most nations of Europe, Canada, Australia, Russia, Iran, Tunisia, China, Japan, and many others. The countries or areas that have the lowest fertility are Hong Kong, Macau, Singapore, Taiwan, Ukraine and Lithuania. Only a few countries have low enough or sustained sub-replacement fertility (sometimes combined with other population factors like emigration) to have population decline, such as Japan, Germany, Lithuania, and Ukraine.

Causes

There have been a number of explanations for the general decline in fertility rates in much of the world, and the true explanation is almost certainly a combination of different factors.

Higher Education

The fact that more people are going to colleges and universities, and are working to obtain more post-graduate degrees there, along with the soaring costs of education, have contributed greatly to postponing marriage in many cases, and bearing children at all, or fewer numbers of children. And the fact that the number of women getting higher education has increased has contributed to fewer of them getting married younger, if at all. In the US, for example, females make up more than half of all college students, which is a reversal from a few decades back.

Economic Development

The growth of wealth and human development are related to this phenomenon. High costs of living and job insecurity can make it difficult for young people to marry and start families.

Urbanization

The increase of urbanization around the world is considered by some a central cause. In recent times, residents of urban areas tend to have fewer children than people in rural areas,. The need for extra labour from children on farms does not apply to urban-dwellers. Cities tend to have higher property prices, making a large family more expensive, especially in those societies where each child is now expected to have his own bedroom, rather than sharing with siblings as was the case until recently. Rural areas also tend to be more conservative with less contraception and abortion than urban areas.

Contraception

Changes in contraception are also an important cause, and one that has seen dramatic changes in the last few generations. Legalization, and widespread acceptance, of contraception in the developed world is a large factor in decreased fertility levels. A systematic review, however, came to the result that European fertility rates do not seem to be decreased significantly by availability of contraception. The other way around, the same review also stated that government support of assisted reproductive technology is beneficial for families, but its effect on total fertility rate in Europe is extremely small.

Female Social Role

Growing female participation in the work force has led to many women delaying or deciding against having children, or to not have as many. A longer pursuit of education also delays marriages. Greater access to contraception and abortion, and greater proclivity of women to use them, also has reduced rates.

Other social changes both separate and related to feminism also have played a role. Bearing children is regarded as less of a social duty than it once was in many societies. Women's social status increasingly correlates with their work or behaviour as consumers rather than from their role as mothers. Indeed having a large family is often socially deprecated, being associated with lower status groups.

Government Policies

Some governments (e.g. those of China and India) have launched programmes to reduce fertility rates and curb population growth.

Religiosity

There are those who have pointed to the religiosity of the United States with its somewhat higher overall fertility rates as evidence of the influence of religion and human fertility. Religious groups, such as Latter-Day Saints (Mormons) and Amish sects in the US, as well as among ultra orthodox Jews in Israel, very likely point to a high probability that the beliefs among certain religious groups, with their correspondingly higher fertility rates, indicate a causal effect among certain, though certainly not among all religious groups.

Some others, though, claim that religiosity has been found to have virtually no causal relationship to fertility rates.

Tempo Effect

In the conventionally reported measure of TFR, the *period* TFR (based on the level of fertility or number of births in a *given* year), there is a statistical effect called the tempo effect which makes it a misleading measure of overall (life cycle) fertility. Specifically, if the age of childbearing increases – but assuming that the total number of births over a life cycle remains unchanged – then while this increase is happening, the measured TFR is lower (the births happen in a later year), but when the age of childbearing stops increasing the TFR increase, due to these births catching up. For illustration, if in the past women always had 1 child at the age of 20 (TFR of 1), but suddenly in the year 2000 all women born in 1980 or later postponed having children until age 30, there would suddenly be no births for 10 years (TFR of 0), and then 10 years later (2010) it would suddenly jump back up (TFR of 1) (assuming flat population structure, no deaths, etc.), even though the life cycle TFR was always 1.

Thus, period TFR reflects not only life cycle TFR, but also timing effects, and these effects are conflated in a simple period TFR number. Life cycle TFR is unambiguous, and strict measure of life cycle fertility are not affected by this effect (e.g., counting the average children that have been born to all women who cease child-bearing in a given year (via menopause, sterilization, death, etc.)), but are lagging statistics because they require women to cease child-bearing before they are counted. Thus, adjusted measures of TFR – period TFR, adjusted for timing – are proposed instead to give a more accurate measure of life cycle fertility, without needing to wait until women have definitively ceased bearing children.

Thus, if age of childbearing is increasing *and* life cycle fertility is decreasing, period TFR will initially overstate the decline, and then may have a spurious increase even if life cycle fertility is actually still declining. This is computed to be the case in Spain in the period 1980–2002, for instance.

John Bongaarts and Griffith Feeney have suggested that this tempo effect is driving the decline of measured fertility rate in the developed world. Taking tempo changes into account, adjusted birth rates for a number of European countries are higher than the conventional TFR. A particularly strong example is the Czech Republic in the period 1992–2002, which witnessed a steady rise in childbearing age, hence the period TFR dropped sharply, overstating the decline in life cycle fertility.

Partnership Instability

Another explanation for falling fertility could be a reduction in the frequency of sex in populations with low birth rates. For example, according to a survey published by the Japanese Family Planning Association in March 2007, a record 39.7 per cent of Japanese citizens aged 16–49 had not had sex for more than a month. [2] A study came to the result that instability of modern partnerships is a major cause of European sub-replacement fertility.

Also, a number of sociologists and demographers have pointed out that among those who co-habit, without marrying, are now usually likely to have fewer children than those who are married, due to the lack of commitment in the male/female relationship. This uncertainty induces a 'wait and see' approach in many cases, especially on the part of the female.

Effects

Sub-replacement fertility does not immediately translate into a population decline because of population momentum: recently high fertility rates produce a disproportionately young population, and younger populations have higher birth rates. This is why some nations with sub-replacement fertility still have a growing population, because a relatively large fraction of their population are still of child-bearing age. But if the fertility trend is sustained (and not compensated by immigration), it results in population ageing and population decline. This is forecast for most of the countries of Europe and East Asia.

Current estimates expect the world's total fertility rate to fall below replacement levels by 2050, although population momentum will continue to increase global population for several generations beyond that. The promise of eventual population decline helps reduce concerns of overpopulation, but many believe the Earth's carrying capacity has already been exceeded and that even a stable population would not be sustainable.

Some believe that not only this (apparent) economic depression we have entered, but the 'Great Depression' of the 1930's (and beyond?) may be, and may have been, the result of a decline in birthrates overall. Clarence L. Barber, an economist at the University of Manitoba, pointed out how demand for housing in the US, for example, began to decline in 1926, due to a decline in 'household formation' (marriage), due, he believed, to the effects of World War I upon society. In early 1929, US housing demand declined precipitously. And, of course, the stock market crash followed in October of that same year.

Even though the overall world population continues to "grow", it is more at the 'back end' than the 'front end' that this is occurring. That is, more people are kept alive than in the past due to improved nutrition, more refrigeration and better sanitation worldwide, as well as health care advances, from vaccines to antibiotics, and many other advances in medications and in different improvements in health care. Certainly, in advanced nations, few groups would be considered to be "breeding like rabbits". The 'baby boom' (1946-1964) in the US, was likely, if Barber's hunches are correct, more of a return to birthrates closer to historical norms, like those of the first decade of the 20th century (but the 'baby boom' of 1946-1964 were still lower than the 1900-1910 period), with birth dearths both before and since making the so-called "baby boom" appear so big.

Sub-replacement fertility can also change social relations in a society. Fewer children, combined with lower infant mortality has made the death of children a far greater tragedy in the modern world than it was just fifty years ago. Having many families with only one or two children also reduces greatly the number of siblings, aunts and uncles, making this 'demographic winter' much of the world is in not only 'colder', but also much lonelier. This may be the reason that Europeans, overall, appear more reluctant to send their sons to war, including Russians to Afghanistan and Chechnya, than Americans have been (even though US fertility rates are, in some comparisons, only marginally higher).

Population aging poses an economic cost on societies, as the number of elderly retirees rises in relation to the number of young workers. This has been raised as a political issue in France, Germany, and the United States, where many people have advocated policy changes to encourage higher fertility and immigration rates. In France, payments to couples who have children have increased birthrates.

Forecast

Some European governments, fearful of a future pensions crisis, have developed natalist policies to attempt to encourage more women to have children. Measures include increasing tax allowances for working parents, improving child-care provision, reducing working hours/weekend working in female-dominated professions such as healthcare and a stricter enforcement of anti-discrimination measures to prevent professional women's promotion prospects being hindered when they take time off work to care for children. Over recent years, the fertility rate has increased to around 2.0 in France and 1.8 in Britain and some other northern European countries, but the role of population policies in these trends is debated.

Attempts to increase the fertility rate among working women bring difficult political dilemmas: how far to alter traditional working practices so that women who are juggling work and child-raising responsibilities are not disadvantaged in their careers compared with men (for example, by legislating for compulsory paternity leave, flexible working and/or limiting total weekly working hours for men as well as women) and above all the question of whether the problem of sub-replacement fertility is so serious that unmarried women should also now be encouraged to have more children.

Giving women paid maternity leave can have the unintended negative consequence of dissuading employers from hiring women because they may fear having to pay a pregnant woman wages for a job she isn't doing. This may increase the gender-wage gap, the income disparity between men and women in the labour force. This disincentive can be ameliorated by giving parental leave to both men and women. Germany's family minister Ursula von der Leyen has stated that the slight increase in Germany, Italy, and other European countries with low fertility might be the first small steps to an eventual reversal. Although the increase will so far not counter an expected population decline it will however slow it down. European analysts hope, with the help of government incentives and large-scale change towards family-friendly policies, to stall the population decline and reverse it by around 2030, expecting that most of Europe will have a slight natural increase by then. C. D. Howe Institute, for example, tries to demonstrate that immigration can not be used to effectively counter population ageing.

Cases of Fertility Rate Increases in Individual Countries

United States: While almost all of the developed world, and many other nations, have seen plummeting fertility rates over the last twenty years, the United States' rates have remained stable and even slightly increased. This is largely due to the high fertility rate among communities such as Hispanics, but it is also because the fertility rate among non-Hispanic whites in the US, after falling to about 1.6 in the 1970s and early 1980s, had increased and is now around 1.9-2.0, or slightly below replacement level, rather than collapsing to the 1.3-1.5 level common in Europe.

New England has a rate similar to most Western European countries, while the South, Midwest, and border states have fertility rates considerably higher than replacement. States where The Church of Jesus Christ of Latter-day Saints has a strong presence, most notably Utah, also have higher-than-replacement fertility rates, especially among the LDS population. Heaton and Goodman (1985) found that LDS women average about one child more than women in other religious groups.

Other Developed Countries

Some other developed countries are also experiencing an increase in their birth rate, including France, which recorded a TFR of over 2.00 in 2008, Australia, where the birth rate rose from 1.73 in 2001 to 1.93 in 2007 and New Zealand, where the TFR was 2.2 in 2008. A few developed countries have never had sub-replacement fertility for reasons that are unique to the particular country. One example of that is Israel, where the growing Arab and religious Jewish populations (mostly Haredim) have high fertility rates, and the aliyah of Jews from the diaspora also contributes to Israel's population growth.

Carrying Capacity

The carrying capacity of a biological species in an environment is the maximum population size of the species that the environment can sustain indefinitely, given the food, habitat, water and other necessities available in the environment. In population biology, carrying capacity is defined as the environment's maximal load, which is different from the concept of population equilibrium.

For the human population, more complex variables such as sanitation and medical care are sometimes considered as part of the necessary establishment. As population density increases, birth rate often decreases and death rate typically increases. The difference between the birth rate and the death rate is the "natural increase". The carrying capacity could support a positive natural increase, or could require a negative natural increase. Thus, the carrying capacity is the number of individuals an environment can support without significant negative impacts to the given organism and its environment. Below carrying capacity, populations typically increase, while above, they typically decrease. A factor that keeps population size at equilibrium is known as a regulating factor. Population size decreases above carrying capacity due to a range of factors depending on the species concerned, but can include insufficient space, food supply, or sunlight. The carrying capacity of an environment may vary for different species and may change over time due to a variety of factors, including: food availability, water supply, environmental conditions and living space.

The origins of the term carrying capacity are uncertain with researchers variously stating that it was used "in the context of international shipping" or that it was first used during 19th Century laboratory experiments with micro-organisms. A recent review finds the first use of the term in an 1845 report by the US Secretary of State to the Senate.

Examples

One of the world's best-studied predator-prey relationships is the moose and wolf population of Isle Royale National Park [1] in Lake Superior. Without the wolves, the moose would overgraze the island's vegetation. Without the moose, the wolves would die. The first scientists who studied the issue thought that the wolves would eventually overpopulate and kill all the moose calves, then die from famine. This has not occurred as inbreeding, disease and environmental factors have limited the wolf population naturally.

Easter Island has been cited as an example of a human population crash. When fewer than 100 humans first arrived, the island was covered with trees with a large variety of food types. In 1722, the island was visited by Jacob Roggeveen, who estimated a population of 2000 to 3000 inhabitants with very few trees, "a rich soil, good climate" and "all the county was under cultivation". Half a century later, it was described as "a poor land" and "largely uncultivated". The ecological collapse which followed has been variously attributed to overpopulation, slave traders, European diseases (including a smallpox epidemic which killed so many so quickly, the dead were left unburied and a tuberculosis epidemic wiped out a quarter of the population), social upheaval and invasive species (such as the Polynesian rats which may have wiped out the ground nesting birds and eaten the palm tree seeds). Whatever the combination of factors, only 111 inhabitants were left on the island in 1877. For whatever reasons (whether Moai worship, survival, status or sheer ignorance), the question of how many humans the island could realistically support never seems to have been answered.

The Chincoteague Pony Swim [2] is a human-assisted Example.

Both herds are managed differently. The National Park Service owns and manages the Maryland herd while the Chincoteague Volunteer Fire Company owns and manages the Virginia herd. The

Virginia herd, referred to as the "Chincoteague" ponies, is allowed to graze on Chincoteague National Wildlife Refuge, through a special use permit issued by the U.S. Fish and Wildlife Service. The size of both herds is restricted to approximately 150 adult animals each in order to protect the other natural resources of the wildlife refuge.

A further example is the Island of Tarawa, where the finite amount of space is evident, especially since landfills cannot be dug to dispose of solid waste, due to constraints in the subsurface rock and lack of topographic elevations. With colonial influence and an abundance of food (relative to life before the year 1850), the population has expanded to the extent that overpopulation is transparently present.

Mathematics

The Lotka-Volterra equations are simple mathematical model of population dynamics which show how in a closed system, like that of the wolves and moose on Isle Royale, limited prey will cause the predator population to decline rapidly. An extended example can be used where multiple species are competing for the same resources, or single species feed on multiple prey.

Humans

The application of the concept of carrying capacity for the human population has been criticized for not successfully capturing the multi-layered processes between humans and the environment, which have a nature of fluidity and non-equilibrium, and that it often has a blame-the-victim framework.

Supporters of the concept argue that the idea of a finite carrying capacity is just as valid when applied to humans as when applied to any other species. Animal population size, living standards, and resource depletion vary, but the concept of carrying capacity still applies. The carrying capacity of Earth has been studied by computer simulation models like World3.

Food Supply and Consumption

Carrying capacity, at its most basic level, is about organisms and food supply, where "X" amount of humans need "Y" amount of food to survive. If the humans neither gain or lose weight in the long run, the calculation is fairly accurate. If the quantity of food is invariably equal to the "Y" amount, carrying capacity has been reached. Humans, with the need to enhance their reproductive success, understand that food supply can vary and also that other factors in the environment can alter humans' need for food. A house, for example, might mean that one does not need to eat as much to stay warm as one otherwise would. Over time, monetary transactions have replaced barter and local production, and consequently modified local human carrying capacity. However, purchases also impact regions thousands of miles away. For example, carbon dioxide from an automobile travels to the upper atmosphere. This led Paul R. Ehrlich to develop the IPAT equation

$$I = P * A * T$$

where:

I is the impact on the environment resulting from consumption

P is the population number

A is the consumption per capita (affluence)

T is the technology factor

Technology is an important factor in the dynamics of carrying capacity. For example, the Neolithic revolution increased the carrying capacity of the world relative to humans through the invention of agriculture. Currently, the use of fossil fuels has artificially increased the carrying capacity of the world by the use of stored sunlight, albeit at many other expenses. Other technological advances that have increased the carrying capacity of the world relative to humans are: polders, fertilizer, composting, greenhouses, land reclamation, and fish farming.

Agricultural capability on Earth expanded in the last quarter of the 20th century. But now there are many projections of a continuation of the decline in world agricultural capability (and hence carrying capacity) which began in the 1990s. Most conspicuously, China's food production is forecast to decline by 37% by the last half of the 21st century, placing a strain on the entire carrying capacity of the world, as China's population could expand to about 1.5 billion people by the year 2050. This reduction in China's agricultural capability (as in other world regions) is largely due to the world water crisis and especially due to mining ground-water beyond sustainable yield, which has been happening in China since the mid-20th century.

Ecological Footprint

One way to estimate human demand compared to ecosystem's carrying capacity is "Ecological Footprint" accounting. Rather than speculating about future possibilities and limitations imposed by carrying capacity constraints, Ecological Footprint accounting provides empirical, non-speculative assessments of the past. It compares historically regeneration rates (biocapacity) against historical human demand (Ecological Footprint) in the same year. One result shows that humanity's demand for 1999 exceeded the planet's biocapacity for 1999 by over 20 percent.

Resources

Overpopulation does not depend only on the size or density of the population, but on the ratio of population to available sustainable resources. It also depends on the way resources are used and distributed throughout the population. The resources to be considered when evaluating whether an ecological niche is overpopulated include clean water, clean air, food, shelter, warmth, and other resources necessary to sustain life. If the quality of human life is addressed, there may be additional resources considered, such as medical care, education, proper sewage treatment, waste disposal and energy supplies. Overpopulation places competitive stress on the basic life sustaining resources, leading to a diminished quality of life.

David Pimentel, Professor Emeritus at Cornell University, has stated that "With the imbalance growing between population numbers and vital life sustaining resources, humans must actively conserve cropland, freshwater, energy, and biological resources. There is a need to develop renewable energy resources. Humans everywhere must understand that rapid population growth damages the Earth's resources and diminishes human well-being."

These reflect the comments also of the United States Geological Survey in their paper The Future of Planet Earth: Scientific Challenges in the Coming Century. "As the global population continues to grow...people will place greater and greater demands on the resources of our planet, including mineral and energy resources, open space, water, and plant and animal resources." "Earth's natural wealth: an audit" by *New Scientist* magazine states that many of the minerals that we use for a variety of products are in danger of running out in the near future . A handful of geologists around the world have calculated the costs of new technologies in terms of the materials they use and the implications of their spreading to the developing world. All agree that the planet's booming population and rising standards of living are set to put unprecedented demands on the materials that only Earth itself can provide . Limitations on how much of these materials is available could even mean that some technologies are not worth pursuing long term.... "Virgin stocks of several metals appear inadequate to sustain the modern 'developed world' quality of life for all of Earth's people under contemporary technology".

On the other hand, some researchers, such as Julian Simon and Bjorn Lomborg believe that resources exist for further population growth. In a 2010 study, they concluded that "there are not (and will never be) too many people for the planet to feed" according to The Independent. Some critics warn, this will be at a high cost to the Earth: "the technological optimists are probably correct in claiming that overall world food production can be increased substantially over the next few decades...[however] the environmental cost of what Paul R. and Anne H. Ehrlich describe as 'turning the Earth into a giant human feedlot' could be severe. A large expansion of agriculture to provide growing populations with improved diets is likely to lead to further deforestation, loss of species, soil erosion, and pollution from pesticides and fertilizer runoff as farming intensifies and new land is brought into production." Since we are intimately dependent upon the living systems of the Earth, some scientists have questioned the wisdom of further expansion.

According to the Millennium Ecosystem Assessment, a four-year research effort by 1,360 of the world's leading scientists commissioned to measure the actual value of natural resources to humans and the world, "The structure of the world's ecosystems changed more rapidly in the second half of the twentieth century than at any time in recorded human history, and virtually all of Earth's ecosystems have now been significantly transformed through human actions." "Ecosystem services, particularly food production, timber and fisheries, are important for employment and economic activity. Intensive use of ecosystems often produces the greatest short-term advantage, but excessive and unsustainable use can lead to losses in the long term. A country could cut its forests and deplete its fisheries, and this would show only as a positive gain to GDP, despite the loss of capital assets. If the full economic value of ecosystems were taken into account in decision-making, their degradation could be significantly slowed down or even reversed."

Another study by the United Nations Environment Programme (UNEP) called the Global Environment Outlook which involved 1,400 scientists and took five years to prepare comes to similar conclusions. It "found that human consumption had far outstripped available resources. Each person on Earth now requires a third more land to supply his or her needs than the planet can supply." It faults a failure to "respond to or recognise the magnitude of the challenges facing the people and the environment of the planet... 'The systematic destruction of the Earth's natural and nature-based resources has reached a point where the economic viability of economies is being challenged – and where the bill we hand to our children may prove impossible to pay'... The report's authors say its objective is 'not to present a dark and gloomy scenario, but an urgent call to action'. It warns that tackling the problems may affect the vested interests of powerful groups, and that the environment must be moved to the core of decision-making... '

Although all resources, whether mineral or other, are limited on the planet, there is a degree of self-correction whenever a scarcity or high-demand for a particular kind is experienced. For example in 1990 known reserves of many natural resources were higher, and their prices lower, than in 1970, despite higher demand and higher consumption. Whenever a price spike would occur, the market tended to correct itself whether by substituting an equivalent resource or switching to a new technology.

Fresh Water

Fresh water supplies, on which agriculture depends, are running low worldwide. This water crisis is only expected to worsen as the population increases.

Potential problems with dependence on desalination are reviewed below, however, the majority of the world's freshwater supply is contained in the polar icecaps, and underground river systems accessible through springs and wells.

Fresh water can be obtained from salt water by desalination. For example, Malta derives two thirds of its freshwater by desalination. A number of nuclear powered desalination plants exist; However, the high costs of desalination, especially for poor countries, make impractical the transport of large amounts of desalinated seawater to interiors of large countries. The cost of desalinization varies; Israel is now desalinating water for a cost of 53 cents per cubic metre, Singapore at 49 cents per cubic metre. In the United States, the cost is 81 cents per cubic metre ($3.06 for 1,000 gallons).

According to a 2004 study by Zhoua and Tolb, "one needs to lift the water by 2000 m, or transport it over more than 1600 km to get transport costs equal to the desalination costs. Desalinated water is expensive in places that are both somewhat far from the sea and somewhat high, such as Riyadh and Harare. In other places, the dominant cost is desalination, not transport. This leads to somewhat lower costs in places like Beijing, Bangkok, Zaragoza, Phoenix, and, of course, coastal cities like Tripoli."

Thus while the study is generally positive about the technology for affluent areas that are proximate to oceans, it concludes that

"Desalinated water may be a solution for some water-stress regions, but not for places that are poor, deep in the interior of a continent, or at high elevation. Unfortunately, that includes some of the places with biggest water problems." Another potential problem with desalination is the by production of saline brine, which can be a major cause of marine pollution when dumped back into the oceans at high temperatures."

The world's largest desalination plant is the Jebel Ali Desalination Plant (Phase 2) in the United Arab Emirates, which can produce 300 million cubic metres of water per year, or about 2500 gallons per second. The largest desalination plant in the US is the one at Tampa Bay, Florida, which began desalinizing 25 million gallons (95000 m^3) of water per day in December 2007. A 17 January 2008, article in the *Wall Street Journal* states, "Worldwide, 13,080 desalination plants produce more than 12 billion gallons of water a day, according to the International Desalination Association." After being desalinized at Jubail, Saudi Arabia, water is pumped 200 miles (320 km) inland though a pipeline to the capital city of Riyadh.

However, new data originating from the GRACE experiments and isotopic testing done by the IAEA show that the Nubian aquifer—which is under the largest, driest part of the earth's surface, has enough water in it to provide for "at least several centuries". In addition to this, new and highly detailed maps of the earth's underground reservoirs will be soon created from these technologies that will further allow proper budgeting of cheap water.

Food

Some scientists argue that there is enough food to support the world population, but critics dispute this, particularly if sustainability is taken into account.

However, many countries rely heavily on imports. Egypt and Iran rely on imports for 40% of their grain supply. Yemen and Israel import more than 90%. And just 6 countries – Argentina, Australia, Canada, France, Thailand and the USA – supply 90% of grain exports. In recent decades the US alone supplied almost half of world grain exports.

A 2001 United Nations report says population growth is "the main force driving increases in agricultural demand" but "most recent expert assessments are cautiously optimistic about the ability of global food production to keep up with demand for the foreseeable future (that is to say, until approximately 2030 or 2050)", assuming declining population growth rates.

However, the observed figures for 2007 show an actual increase in absolute numbers of undernourished people in the world, 923 million in 2007 versus 832 million in 1995.; the more recent FAO estimates point to an even more dramatic increase, to 1.02 billion in 2009.

Global Perspective

The amounts of natural resources in this context are not necessarily fixed, and their distribution is not necessarily a zero-sum game. For example, due to the Green Revolution and the fact that more and more land is appropriated each year from wild lands for agricultural purposes, the worldwide production of food had steadily increased up until 1995. World food production per person was considerably higher in 2005 than 1961.

As world population doubled from 3 billion to 6 billion, daily Calorie consumption in poor countries increased from 1,932 to 2,650, and the percentage of people in those countries who were malnourished fell from 45% to 18%. This suggests that Third World poverty and famine are caused by underdevelopment, not overpopulation. However, others question these statistics. From 1950 to 1984, as the Green Revolution transformed agriculture around the world, grain production increased by over 250%. The world population has grown by about four billion since the beginning of the Green Revolution and most believe that, without the Revolution, there would be greater famine and malnutrition than the UN presently documents.

The number of people who are overweight has surpassed the number who are undernourished. In a 2006 news story, MSNBC reported, "There are an estimated 800 million undernourished people and more than a billion considered overweight worldwide." The U.S. has one of the highest rates of obesity in the world.

The Food and Agriculture Organization of the United Nations states in its report *The State of Food Insecurity in the World 2006*, that while the number of undernourished people in the developing countries has declined by about three million, a smaller proportion of the populations of developing countries is undernourished today than in 1990–92: 17% against 20%. Furthermore, FAO's projections suggest that the proportion of hungry people in developing countries could be halved from 1990–92 levels to 10% by 2015. The FAO also states "We have emphasized first and foremost that reducing hunger is no longer a question of means in the hands of the global community. The world is richer today than it was ten years ago. There is more food available and still more could be produced without excessive upward pressure on prices. The knowledge and resources to reduce hunger are there.

What is lacking is sufficient political will to mobilize those resources to the benefit of the hungry."

As of 2008, the price of grain has increased due to more farming used in biofuels, world oil prices at over $100 a barrel, global population growth, climate change, loss of agricultural land to residential and industrial development, and growing consumer demand in China and India Food riots have recently taken place in many countries across the world. An epidemic of stem rust on wheat caused by race Ug99 is currently spreading across Africa and into Asia and is causing major concern. A virulent wheat disease could destroy most of the world's main wheat crops, leaving millions to starve. The fungus has spread from Africa to Iran, and may already be in Afghanistan and Pakistan.

It is becoming increasingly difficult to maintain food security in a world beset by a confluence of "peak" phenomena, namely peak oil, peak water, peak phosphorus, peak grain and peak fish. Growing populations, falling energy sources and food shortages will create the "perfect storm" by 2030, according to the UK government chief scientist. He said food reserves are at a 50-year low but the world requires 50% more energy, food and water by 2030. The world will have to produce 70% more food by 2050 to feed a projected extra 2.3 billion people, the United Nations' Food and Agriculture Organisation (FAO) warned.

Africa

In Africa, if current trends of soil degradation and population growth continue, the continent might be able to feed just 25% of its population by 2025, according to UNU's Ghana-based Institute for Natural Resources in Africa. Hunger and malnutrition kill nearly 6 million children a year, and more people are malnourished in sub-Saharan Africa this decade than in the 1990s, according to a report released by the Food and Agriculture Organization. In sub-Saharan Africa, the number of malnourished people grew to 203.5 million people in 2000–02 from 170.4 million 10 years earlier says *The State of Food Insecurity in the World* report. In 2001, 46.4% of people in sub-Saharan Africa were living in extreme poverty.

Asia

According to a 2004 article from the BBC, China, the world's most populous country, suffers from an "obesity surge". The article stated that, "Altogether, around 200 million people are thought to be overweight, 22.8% of the population, and 60 million (7.1%) obese". More recent data indicate China's grain production peaked in the mid 1990s, due to over extraction of ground-water in the North China plain.

Other Countries

Nearly half of India's children are malnourished, according to recent government data. Japan may face a food crisis that could reduce daily diets to the austere meals of the 1950s, believes a senior government adviser.

Population as a Function of Food Availability

Thinkers such as David Pimentel, a professor from Cornell University, Virginia Abernethy, Alan Thornhill, Russell Hopffenberg and author Daniel Quinn propose that like all other animals, human populations predictably grow and shrink according to their available food supply – populations grow in an abundance of food, and shrink in times of scarcity.

Proponents of this theory argue that every time food production is increased, the population grows. Some human populations throughout history support this theory. Populations of hunter-gatherers fluctuate in accordance with the amount of available food. Population increased after the Neolithic Revolution and an increased food supply. This was followed by subsequent population growth after subsequent agricultural revolutions.

Critics of this idea point out that birth rates are lowest in the developed nations, which also have the highest access to food. In fact, some developed countries have both a diminishing population and an abundant food supply. The United Nations projects that the population of 51 countries or areas, including Germany, Italy, Japan and most of the states of the former Soviet Union, is expected to be lower in 2050 than in 2005. This shows that when one limits their scope to the population living within a given political boundary, human populations do not always grow to match the available food supply. Additionally, many of these countries are major *exporters* of food. Nevertheless, on the global scale the world population is increasing, as is the net quantity of human food produced – a pattern that has been true for roughly 10,000 years, since the human development of agriculture. That some countries demonstrate negative population growth fails to discredit the theory. Food moves across borders from areas of abundance to areas of scarcity. Additionally, this hypothesis is not so simplistic as to be rejected by a single case study, as in Germany's recent population trends – clearly other factors are at work: contraceptive access, cultural norms and most importantly economic realities differ from nation to nation.

As a Result of Water Deficits

Water deficits, which are already spurring heavy grain imports in numerous smaller countries, may soon do the same in larger countries, such as China or India, if technology is not used. The water tables are falling in scores of countries (including Northern China, the US, and India) owing to widespread overdrafting beyond sustainable yields. Other countries affected include Pakistan, Iran, and Mexico.

This overdrafting is already leading to water scarcity and cutbacks in grain harvest. Even with the over pumping of its aquifers, China has developed a grain deficit. This effect has contributed in driving grain prices upward. Most of the 3 billion people projected to be added worldwide by mid-century will be born in countries already experiencing water shortages. One suggested solution is for population growth to be slowed quickly by investing heavily in female literacy and family planning services. 'Desalination is also considered a viable and effective solution to the problem of water shortages. After China and India, there is a second tier of smaller countries with large water deficits – Algeria, Egypt, Iran, Mexico, and Pakistan. Four of these already import a large share of their grain. Only Pakistan remains self-sufficient. But with a population expanding by 4 million a year, it will also soon turn to the world market for grain.

Land

The World Resources Institute states that "Agricultural conversion to croplands and managed pastures has affected some 3.3 billion [hectares] – roughly 26 percent of the land area.

All totaled, agriculture has displaced one-third of temperate and tropical forests and one-quarter of natural grasslands." Forty percent of the land area is under conversion and fragmented; less than one quarter, primarily in the Arctic and the deserts, remains intact. Usable land may become less useful through salinization, deforestation, desertification, erosion, and urban sprawl. Global warming may cause flooding of many of the most productive agricultural areas.

The development of energy sources may also require large areas, for example, the building of hydroelectric dams.

Thus, available useful land may become a limiting factor. By most estimates, at least half of cultivable land is already being farmed, and there are concerns that the remaining reserves are greatly overestimated.

High crop yield vegetables like potatoes and lettuce use less space on inedible plant parts, like stalks, husks, vines, and inedible leaves. New varieties of selectively bred and hybrid plants have larger edible parts (fruit, vegetable, grain) and smaller inedible parts; however, many of these gain of agricultural technology are now historic, and new advances are more difficult to achieve. With new technologies, it is possible to grow crops on some marginal land under certain conditions.

Aquaculture could theoretically increase available area. Hydroponics and food from bacteria and fungi, like quorn, may allow the growing of food without having to consider land quality, climate, or even available sunlight, although such a process may be very energy-intensive. Some argue that not all arable land will remain productive if used for agriculture because some marginal land can only be made to produce food by unsustainable practices likeslash-and-burn agriculture. Even with the modern techniques of agriculture, the sustainability of production is in question.

Some countries, such as the United Arab Emirates and particularly the Emirate of Dubai have constructed large artificial islands, or have created large dam and dike systems, like the Netherlands, which reclaim land from the sea to increase their total land area.

Some scientists have said that in the future, densely populated cities will use vertical farming to grow food inside skyscrapers. The notion that space is limited has been decried by skeptics, who point out that the Earth's population of roughly 6.8 billion people could comfortably inhabit an area comparable in size to the state of Texas, in the United States (about 269,000 square miles or 696,707 square kilometres). However, the impact of humanity extends over a far greater area than that required simply for habitation.

Fossil Fuels

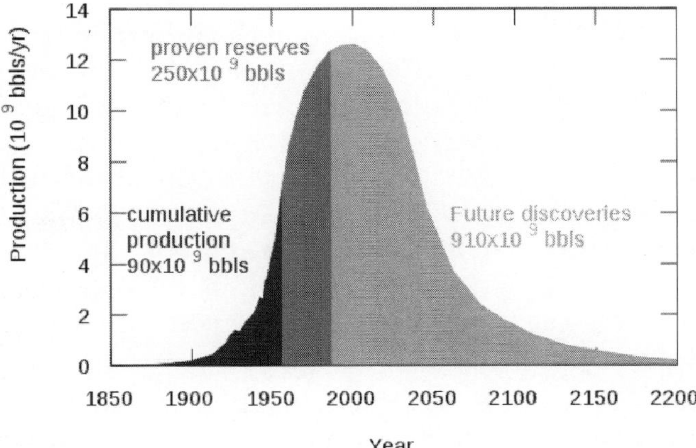

***Figure:** M. King Hubbert's prediction of world petroleum production rates. Modern agriculture is totally reliant on petroleum energy.*

Population optimists have been criticized for failing to take into account the depletion of the petroleum required for the production offertilizers and fuel for transportation, as well as other fossil fuels.

In his 1992 book *Earth in the Balance*, Al Gore wrote, "... it ought to be possible to establish a coordinated global programme to accomplish the strategic goal of completely eliminating the internal combustion engine over, say, a twenty-five-year period..." Approximately half of the oil produced in the United States is refined into gasoline for use in internal combustion engines.

Optimists counter that fossil fuels will be sufficient until the development and implementation of suitable replacement technologies—such as hydrogen or other sources of renewable energy—occurs. Methods of manufacturing fertilizers from garbage, sewage, and agricultural waste by using thermal depolymerization have been discovered.

Wealth and Poverty

The United Nations indicates that about 850 million people are malnourished or starving, and 1.1 billion people do not have access to safe drinking water. Some argue that Earth may support 6 billion people, but only if many live in misery. The proportion of the world's population living on less than $1 per day has halved in 20 years, but these are inflation-unadjusted numbers and likely misleading.

The UN Human Development Report of 1997 states: "During the last 15–20 years, more than 100 developing countries, and several Eastern European countries, have suffered from disastrous growth failures. The reductions in standard of living have been deeper and more long-lasting than what was seen in the industrialised countries during the depression in the 1930s. As a result, the income for more than one billion people has fallen below the level that was reached 10, 20 or 30 years ago". Similarly, although the proportion of "starving" people in sub-Saharan Africa has decreased, the absolute number of starving people has increased due to population growth. The percentage dropped from 38% in 1970 to 33% in 1996 and was expected to be 30% by 2010. But the region's population roughly doubled between 1970 and 1996. To keep the numbers of starving constant, the percentage would have dropped by more than half.

As of 2004, there were 108 countries in the world with more than five million people. All of these in which women have, on the average, more than 4 children in their lifetime, have a per capita GDP of less than $5000. Only in two countries with per capita GDP above 1.6 1060 do women have, on the average, more than 2 children in their lifetime: these are Israel and Saudi Arabia, with average lifetime births per woman between 2 and 4.

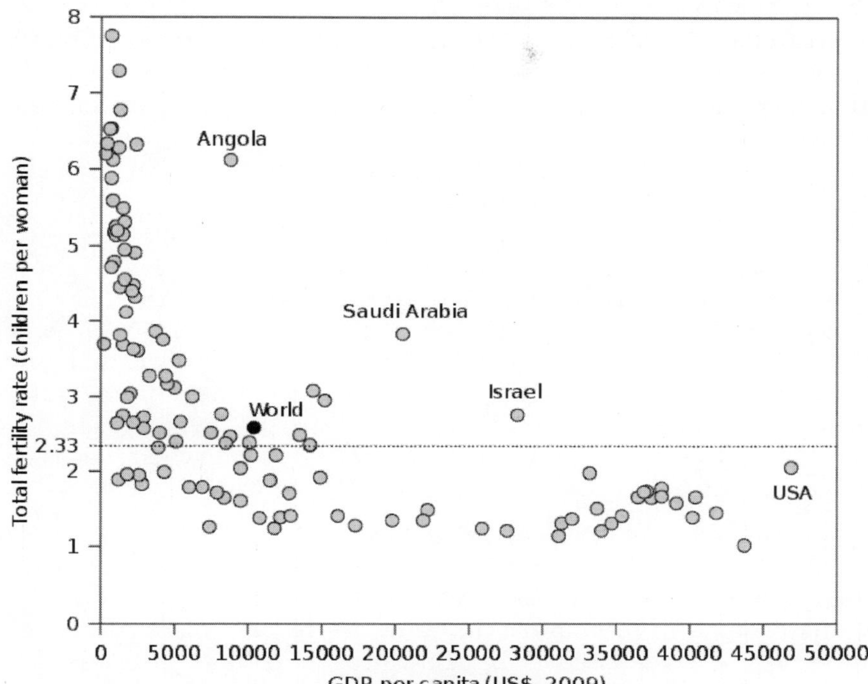

Figure: *wealth per capita graphed against fertility rate.*

As their income increases, women are liberated and tend to have fewer "quantity kids", as in two in place of six. The correlation does not imply cause and effect, and can be linked to the interplay of birth rates, death rates and economic development. Poor living conditions can also cause a very bad effect on the population; diseases such as malaria and HIV/AIDS can also contribute to this. Lack of nutrients, poor sanitation and poor health institutions. Death rate and birth rate can also have a negative effect on the population.

Environment

Overpopulation has substantially adversely impacted the environment of Earth starting at least as early as the 20th century. There are also economic consequences of this environmental degradation in the form of ecosystem service sattrition. Beyond the scientifically verifiable harm to the environment, some assert the moral right of other species to simply exist rather than become extinct.

Environmental author Jeremy Rifkin has said that "our burgeoning population and urban way of life have been purchased at the expense of vast ecosystems and habitats. ... It's no accident that as we celebrate the urbanization of the world, we are quickly approaching another historic watershed: the disappearance of the wild."

Says Peter Raven, former President of the American Association for the Advancement of Science (AAAS) in their seminal work AAAS Atlas of Population & Environment, "Where do we stand in our efforts to achieve a sustainable world? Clearly, the past half century has been a traumatic one, as the collective impact of human numbers, affluence (consumption per individual) and our choices of technology continue to exploit rapidly an increasing proportion of the world's resources at an unsustainable rate. ... During a remarkably short period of time, we have lost a quarter of the world's topsoil and a fifth of its agricultural land, altered the composition of the atmosphere profoundly, and destroyed a major proportion of our forests and other natural habitats without replacing them. Worst of all, we have driven the rate of biological extinction, the permanent loss of species, up several hundred times beyond its historical levels, and are threatened with the loss of a majority of all species by the end of the 21st century."

Further, even in countries which have both large population growth and major ecological problems, it is not necessarily true that curbing the population growth will make a major contribution towards resolving all environmental problems. However, as developing countries with high populations become more industrialized, pollution and consumption will invariably increase.

The Worldwatch Institute said the booming economies of China and India are planetary powers that are shaping the global biosphere. The report states:

The world's ecological capacity is simply insufficient to satisfy the ambitions of China, India, Japan, Europe and the United States as well as the aspirations of the rest of the world in a sustainable way

It said that if China and India were to consume as much resources per capita as United States or Japan in 2030 together they would require a full planet Earth to meet their needs. In the longterm these effects can lead to increased conflict over dwindling resources and in the worst case a Malthusian catastrophe. Many studies link population growth with emissions and the effect of climate change.

Cities

In 1800 only 3% of the world's population lived in cities. By the 20th century's close, 47% did so. In 1950, there were 83 cities with populations exceeding one million; but by 2007, this had risen to 468 agglomerations of more than one million. If the trend continues, the world's urban population will double every 38 years, according to researchers. The UN forecasts that today's urban population of 3.2 billion will rise to nearly 5 billion by 2030, when three out of five people will live in cities.

The increase will be most dramatic in the poorest and least-urbanised continents, Asia and Africa. Projections indicate that most urban growth over the next 25 years will be in developing countries. One billion people, one-sixth of the world's population, or one-third of urban population, now live in shanty towns, which are seen as "breeding grounds" for social problems such as crime, drug addiction, alcoholism, poverty and unemployment. In many poor countries, slums exhibit high rates of disease due to unsanitary conditions, malnutrition, and lack of basic health care.

In 2000, there were 18 megacities—conurbations such as Tokyo, Seoul, Mexico City, Mumbai, São Paulo and New York City – that have populations in excess of 10 million inhabitants. Greater Tokyo already has 35 million, more than the entire population of Canada (at 34.1 million).

By 2025, according to the *Far Eastern Economic Review*, Asia alone will have at least 10 hypercities, those with 20 million or more, including Jakarta (24.9 million people), Dhaka (25 million), Karachi (26.5 million), Shanghai (27 million) and Mumbai (33 million). Lagos has grown from 300,000 in 1950 to an estimated 15 million today, and the Nigerian government estimates that city will have expanded to 25 million residents by 2015. Chinese experts forecast that Chinese cities will contain 800 million people by 2020. Despite the increase in population density within cities (and the emergence of megacities), UN Habitat states in its reports that urbanization may be the best compromise in the face of global population growth. Cities concentrate human activity within limited areas, limiting the breadth of environmental damage. But this mitigating influence can only be achieved ifurban planning is significantly improved and city services are properly maintained.

Effects of Human Overpopulation

Some problems associated with or exacerbated by human overpopulation:

- Inadequate fresh water for drinking water use as well as sewage treatment and effluent discharge. Some countries, like Saudi Arabia, use energy-expensive desalination to solve the problem of water shortages.

- Depletion of natural resources, especially fossil fuels.

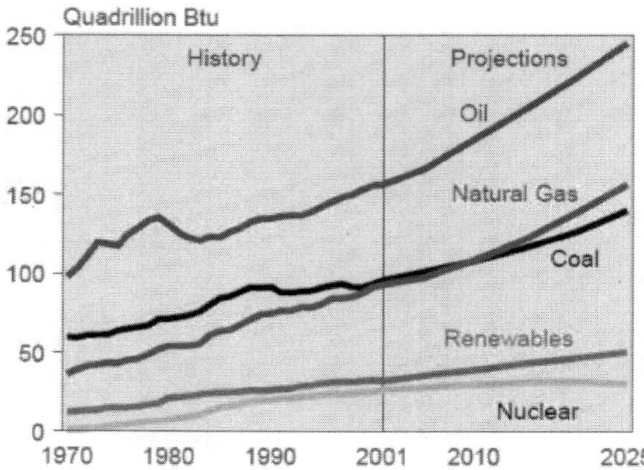

Figure: *World energy consumption & predictions, 1970–2025.*

- Increased levels of air pollution, water pollution, soil contamination and noise pollution. Once a country has industrialized and become wealthy, a combination of government regulation and technological innovation causes pollution to decline substantially, even as the population continues to grow.
- Deforestation and loss of ecosystems that sustain global atmospheric oxygen and carbon dioxide balance; about eight million hectares of forest are lost each year.
- Changes in atmospheric composition and consequent global warming.
- Irreversible loss of arable land and increases in desertification. Deforestation and desertification can be reversed by adopting property rights, and this policy is successful even while the human population continues to grow.
- Mass species extinctions from reduced habitat in tropical forests due to slash-and-burn techniques that sometimes are practiced by shifting cultivators, especially in countries with rapidly expanding rural populations; present extinction rates may be as high as 140,000 species lost per year. As of February 2011, the IUCN Red List lists a total of 801 animal species having gone extinct during recorded human history.
- High infant and child mortality. High rates of infant mortality are caused by poverty. Rich countries with high population densities have low rates of infant mortality.

- Intensive factory farming to support large populations. It results in human threats including the evolution and spread of antibiotic resistant bacteria diseases, excessive air and water pollution, and new viruses that infect humans.
- Increased chance of the emergence of new epidemics and pandemics. For many environmental and social reasons, including overcrowded living conditions, malnutrition and inadequate, inaccessible, or non-existent health care, the poor are more likely to be exposed to infectious diseases.
- Starvation, malnutrition or poor diet with ill health and diet-deficiency diseases (e.g. rickets). However, rich countries with high population densities do not have famine.
- Poverty coupled with inflation in some regions and a resulting low level of capital formation. Poverty and inflation are aggravated by bad government and bad economic policies. Many countries with high population densities have eliminated absolute poverty and keep their inflation rates very low.
- Low life expectancy in countries with fastest growing populations.
- Unhygienic living conditions for many based upon water resource depletion, discharge of raw sewage and solid waste disposal. However, this problem can be reduced with the adoption of sewers. For example, after Karachi, Pakistan installed sewers, its infant mortality rate fell substantially.
- Elevated crime rate due to drug cartels and increased theft by people stealing resources to survive.
- Conflict over scarce resources and crowding, leading to increased levels of warfare.
- Less personal freedom and more restrictive laws. Laws regulate interactions between humans. Law "serves as a primary social mediator of relations between people." The higher the population density, the more frequent such interactions become, and thus there develops a need for more laws and/or more restrictive laws to regulate these interactions. It was even speculated by Aldous Huxley in 1958 that democracy is threatened due to overpopulation, and could give rise to totalitarian style governments.

Many of these problems are addressed in the science fiction film *Soylent Green*.

Some economists, such as Thomas Sowell and Walter E. Williams argue that third world poverty and famine are caused in part by bad government and bad economic policies. Most biologists and sociologists see overpopulation as a serious threat to the quality of human life.

Overpopulation and Warfare

The hypothesis that population pressure causes increased warfare (youth bulge theory) has been recently criticized on the empirical grounds. Both studies focusing on specific historical societies and analyses of cross-cultural data have failed to find positive correlation between population density and incidence of warfare. Andrey Korotayev, in collaboration with Peter Turchin, has shown that such negative results do not falsify the population-warfare hypothesis. Population and warfare are dynamical variables, and if their interaction causes sustained oscillations, then we do not in general expect to find strong correlation between the two variables measured at the same time (that is, unlagged). Korotayev and Turchin have explored mathematically what the dynamical patterns of interaction between population and warfare (focusing on internal warfare) might be in both stateless and state societies. Next, they have tested the model predictions in several empirical case studies: early modern England, Han and Tang China, and the Roman Empire. Their empirical results have supported the population-warfare theory: Korotayev and Turchin have found that there is a tendency for population numbers and internal warfare intensity to oscillate with the same period but shifted in phase (with warfare peaks following population peaks). Furthermore, they have demonstrated that in the agrarian societies the rates of change of the two variables behave precisely as predicted by the theory: population rate of change is negatively affected by warfare intensity, while warfare rate of change is positively affected by population density.

Mitigation Measures

There are several mitigation measures that have been or can be applied to reduce the adverse impacts of overpopulation. All of these mitigations are ways to implement social norms. Overpopulation is an issue that threatens the state of the environment in the above-mentioned ways and therefore societies must make a change in order to reverse some of the environmental effects brought on by current social norms. In societies like China, the government has put policies in place that regulate the number of children allowed to a couple. Other societies have already begun to implement social marketing strategies in order to educate the public on overpopulation effects. "The intervention can be widespread and done at a low cost. A variety of print materials (flyers, brochures, fact sheets, stickers) needs to be produced and distributed throughout the communities such as at local places of worships, sporting events, local food markets, schools and at car parks (taxis / bus stands)." Such prompts work to introduce the problem so that social norms are easier to implement. Certain government policies are making it easier and more socially acceptable to use contraception and abortion methods. An example of a country whose laws and norms are hindering the global effort to slow population growth is Afghanistan. "The approval by Afghan President Hamid Karzai of the Shia Personal Status Law in March 2009 effectively destroyed Shia women's rights and freedoms in Afghanistan. Under this law, women have no right to deny their husbands sex unless they are ill, and can be denied food if they do."

Birth Regulations

Overpopulation is related to the issue of birth control; some nations, like the People's Republic of China, use strict measures to reduce birth rates. Religious and ideological opposition to birth control has been cited as a factor contributing to overpopulation and poverty. Some leaders and environmentalists (such as Ted Turner) have suggested that there is an urgent need to strictly implement a China-like one-child policy globally by the United Nations, because this would help control and reduce population gradually.

Indira Gandhi, late Prime Minister of India, implemented a forced sterilization programme in the 1970s. Officially, men with two children or more had to submit to sterilization, but many unmarried young men, political opponents and ignorant men were also believed to have been sterilized. This programme is still remembered and criticized in India, and is blamed for creating a public aversion to family planning, which hampered Government programmes for decades.

Urban designer Michael E. Arth has proposed a "choice-based, marketable birth license plan" he calls "birth credits." Birth credits would allow any woman to have as many children as she wants, as long as she buys a license for any children beyond an average allotment that would result in zero population growth (ZPG). If that allotment was determined to be one child, for example, then the first child would be free, and the market would determine what the license fee for each additional child would cost. Extra credits would expire after a certain time, so these credits could not be hoarded by speculators. The actual cost of the credits would only be a fraction of the actual cost of having and raising a child, so the credits would serve more as a wake-up call to women who might otherwise produce children without seriously considering the long term consequences to themselves or society.

Education and Empowerment

One option is to focus on education about overpopulation, family planning, and birth control methods, and to make birth-control devices like male/female condoms, pills and intrauterine devices easily available. Worldwide, nearly 40% of pregnancies are unintended (some 80 million unintended pregnancies each year). An estimated 350 million women in the poorest countries of the world either did not want their last child, do not want another child or want to space their pregnancies, but they lack access to information, affordable means and services to determine the size and spacing of their families. In the developing world, some 514,000 women die annually of complications from pregnancy and abortion, with 86% of these deaths occurring in the sub-Saharan Africa region and South Asia. Additionally, 8 million infants die, many because of malnutrition or preventable diseases, especially from lack of access to clean drinking water. In the United States, in 2001, almost half of pregnancies were unintended. Egypt announced a programme to reduce its overpopulation by family planning education and putting women in the workforce. It was announced in June 2008 by the Minister of Health and Population Hatem el-Gabali. The government has set aside 480 million Egyptian pounds (about 90 million U.S. dollars) for the programme.

Extraterrestrial Settlement

In the 1970s, Gerard O'Neill suggested building space habitats that could support 30,000 times the carrying capacity of Earth using just the asteroid belt and that the Solar System as a whole could sustain current population growth rates for a thousand years. Marshall Savage (1992, 1994) has projected a human population of five quintillion throughout the Solar System by 3000, with the majority in the asteroid belt. Freeman Dyson (1999) favours the Kuiper belt as the future home of humanity, suggesting this could happen within a few centuries. In *Mining the Sky*, John S. Lewis suggests that the resources of the solar system could support 10 quadrillion (10^{16}) people.

K. Eric Drexler, famous inventor of the futuristic concept of molecular nanotechnology, has suggested in *Engines of Creation* that colonizing space will mean breaking the Malthusian limits to growth for the human species.

It may be possible for other parts of the Solar System to be inhabited by humanity at some point in the future. Geoffrey Landis of NASA's

Glenn Research Centre in particular has pointed out that "[at] cloud-top level, Venus is the paradise planet", as one could construct aerostat habitats and floating cities there easily, based on the concept that breathable air is a lifting gas in the dense Venusian atmosphere.

Venus would, like also Saturn, Uranus, and Neptune, in the upper layers of their atmospheres, even afford a gravitation almost exactly as strong as that on Earth. Many authors, including Carl Sagan, Arthur C. Clarke, and Isaac Asimov, have argued that shipping the excess population into space is not a viable solution to human overpopulation. According to Clarke, "the population battle must be fought or won here on Earth".

The problem for these authors is not the lack of resources in space (as shown in books such as *Mining the Sky*), but the physical impracticality of shipping vast numbers of people into space to "solve" overpopulation on Earth. However, Gerard O'Neill's calculations show that Earth could offload all new population growth with a launch services industry about the same size as the current airline industry.

A hypothetical extraterrestrial colony could potentially grow organically, with most of the inhabitants being the direct descendants of the original colonists.

Population Decline

Population decline can refer to the decline in population of any organism, but this article refers to population decline in humans. It is a term usually used to describe any great reduction in a human population. It can be used to refer to long-term demographic trends, as in urban decay or rural flight, but it is also commonly employed to describe large reductions in population due to violence, disease, or other catastrophes.

Definition

Sometimes known as depopulation, population decline is the reduction over time in a region's census. It can be caused for several reasons; notable ones include sub-replacement fertility (along with limited immigration), heavy emigration, disease, famine, and war. History is replete with examples of large scale depopulations. Many wars, for example, have been accompanied by significant depopulations. Prior to the 20th century, population decline was mostly observed due to disease, starvation and/or emigration. The Black Death in Europe, the arrival of Old World diseases to the Americas, the tsetse fly invasion of the Waterberg Massif in South Africa, and the Great Irish Famine have all caused sizable population declines. In modern times, the AIDS epidemic has caused declines in the population of some African countries. Less frequently, population declines are caused by genocide or mass execution; for example, in the 1970s, the population of Cambodia underwent a period of decline due to wide-scale executions by the Khmer Rouge.

Sometimes the term under population is applied in the context of a specific economic system. It does not relate to carrying capacity, and is not a term in opposition to overpopulation, which deals with the total possible population that can be sustained by available food, water, sanitation and other infrastructure. "Under population" is usually defined as a state in which a country's population has declined too much to support its current economic system. Thus the term has nothing to do with the biological aspects of carrying capacity, but is an economic term employed to imply that the transfer payment schemes of some developed countries might fail once the population declines to a certain point. An example would be if retirees were supported through a social security system which does not invest savings, and then a large emigration movement occurred. In this case, the younger generation may not be able to support the older generation.

Changing Trends

Today, emigration and sub-replacement fertility rates as well as high death rates in the former Soviet Union and its former allies are the principal issues related to any regional population decline. However, governments can influence the speed of the decline, including measures to halt, slow or suspend decline. Among such measures include pro-birth policies and subsidies, media influence, immigration, bolstering healthcare and laws aimed at rooting out vice (lowering death rates). Such is the case in Russia and Armenia, as well as many Western European nations who have used immigration and other policies as a means of suspending or slowing population decline. Therefore although very long term trends may favour accelerating population decline, short term trends may slow decline or even reverse from decline to growth and back and so on, creating seemingly conflicting statistical data. A great example of changing trends occurring over a century is Ireland.

Statistical Misreadings

Statistical data, especially comparing only two sets of figures, can show an incorrect population trend. A nation's population could be increasing, but an one-off event could have resulted in decline and vice-versa. Nations can acquire territory or lose territory and people, consider people citizens they previously denied citizenship to, e.g.

stateless persons, indigenous people, and undocumented immigrants or long stay foreign residents.

Political instability can render an area within a nation's count unreliable for comparison.

A common misreading is due to time. Populations on the verge of decline could rise in summer and decline in winter as deaths increase in winter in cold regions, similarly, census dates over too long a time range could show a rise when a country has already tipped into decline. Therefore, numerous sets of statistics should be interpreted to get an idea of a trend.

Long Term Decline Situation

A long-term population decline is typically caused by sub-replacement fertility, coupled with a net immigration rate that fails to compensate the excess of deaths over births. A long-term decline is accompanied by population aging and creates an increase in the ratio of retirees to workers and children. When a sub-replacement fertility rate remains constant, population decline accelerates over time.

Eastern Europe and Former Soviet Republics

Population is falling due to health factors and low replacement, as well as emigration of ethnic Russians to Russia. Exceptions to this rule is in those ex-Soviet states which have a Muslim majority (Uzbekistan, Turkmenistan, Tajikistan, Kyrgyzstan, Azerbaijan) as high birth rates are traditional. Much of Eastern Europe has lost population due to migration to Western Europe. In Eastern Europe and Russia, natality fell abruptly after the end of the Soviet Union, and death rates generally rose. Together these nations occupy over 8,000,000 square miles (21,000,000 km^2) and are home to over 400 million people (less than six percent of the world population), but if current trends continue, more of the developed world and some of the developing world could join this trend.

Albania

Albania's population in 1989 recorded some 3,182,417 people, the largest for any census. Since then, its population has declined to 2,831,741 as of the October 2011 census figures. This represents a 10.5% decrease of 12.4% in total population since the peak census figure.

Armenia

Armenia's population peaked at 3,604,000 in 1991 and has continued its decline to 3,260,000 estimated in 4Q 2010. This represents a 10.5% decrease in total population since the peak census figure.

Belarus

Belarus' population peaked at 10,151,806 in 1989 Census, and then has declined to 9,467,300 in August 1, 2011. This represents a 7.2% decline since the peak census figure.

Bulgaria

Bulgaria's population has declined from a peak of 9,009,018 in 1989 and since 2001, has lost yet another 600,000 people, according to 2011 census preliminary figures to no more than 7.3 million. This represents a 23.4% decrease in total population since the peak, and a -0.82% rate in the last 10 years.

Croatia

Croatia's peak census population was 4,784,265 in 1991 and has since shrunk to 4,290,612 as of 2011. This represents a 11.5% decrease since the peak census figure.

Greece

Greece's latest census reported its population fell to 10,787,690 from 10,934,097 in 2001 census.

Japan

Though Japan has been forecast to decline in population for years, and its monthly and even annual estimates have shown a decline in the past, the 2010 census result figure was slightly higher at just above 128 million than the 2005 census and its population has yet to register a decline between census periods though shorter periods may show declines. The 2010 census figure is expected to be the long term census peak. Factors implicated in the higher figures were more Japanese returnees than expected as well as changes to the methodology of data collection. By 2060, Japan's population will shrink by 1/3 to 87 million people (from 128 million in 2012).

Hungary

Hungary's population peaked in 1980 at 10,709,000, far earlier than its Soviet cousins, and has continued its decline to under 10 million as of August 2010. This represents a decline of 7.1% since its peak, however, compared to neighbours situated to the East, the rate has been far more modest, averaging -0.23% a year over the period.

Ireland

Regarding the current area of the Republic of Ireland, the population has fluctuated dramatically. The population was 6.53 million in 1841, and dropped due to the Irish famine to under 3 million by the 1930s, and began rising, in 2011 to 4.58 million.

Latvia

When Latvia split from the Soviet Union, it had a population of 2,666,567, which was close to its peak population. The latest census recorded a population of 2,067,887 in 2011. This represents a 28.9% decline since the peak census figure. The decline is caused by both a negative population growth rate and a negative net migration rate.

Lithuania

When Lithuania split from the Soviet Union, it had a population of 3.7 million, which was close to its peak population. The latest census recorded a population of 3.05 million in 2011, down from 3.4 million in 2001. This represents a 21.3% decline since the peak census figure, and some 11.5% since 2001.

Romania

Romania's 1992 census showed 22,810,035 people, by the October 2011 census it had recorded only 19,042,936 people, a decline of over 2.6 million from the 21.68 million in 2002. It represents a decline of nearly 19.8% from the peak census figure, and a total population loss only exceeded by Russia and Ukraine.

Russia

Russia's total population is among the largest drops in numbers (but not in percentage). Its peak was 148,689,000 in 1991, while it dropped to 141,909,000 in 2009. This represents a 4.6% decrease in total population since the peak census figure. Still, the Russian government estimates an increase in the population to 143,030,106 in 2011, an increase of 0.8% in just two years. Russia's reverse population decline can be attributed to a rising birth rate, lower death rate, and continued immigration.

Serbia

Serbia recorded a peak census population of 7,576,837 in 1991, falling to 7,120,666 in the latest October 2011 census. That represents a decline of 6.4% since its peak census figure.

Ukraine

Ukraine census in 1989 resulted in 51,452,034 people, the closest known data to the peak, however than number has plummeted to 45,633,600 as of Jan 1, 2012. This represents a 12.75% decrease in total population since the peak census figure.

Declines Within Race or Ethnicity

Some large and even majority groups within a population have shown an overall decline in numbers while the total population increases. Such is the case in California, where the Non-Hispanic Whites population declined from 15.8 million to 14.95 million, meanwhile the total population increased from 33 million to over 37 million from 2000 to 2010 censuses. In Western Europe, the population of people of local origins have been in absolute decline for a number of years while total populations have shown increases.

Populations of certain ethnic groups worldwide has slowed down considerably while others have marched on. In particular, 5 groups: North American Whites (~230 million), Europeans in Europe (~700 million), Japanese (~128 million), Chinese (~1380 million), and Koreans (~73 million) population growth rates have declined sharply to very modest growth, and all these groups are expected to see population declines in the next 20–30 years, if they aren't seeing them already. Ethnic Thais (~65 million) are also expected to follow not far behind, although their cousins the ethnic Lao birth rates still in the high range.

Economic Consequences

The effects of a declining population can be adverse for an economy which has borrowed extensively for repayment by younger generations. Economically declining populations are thought to lead to deflation, which has a number of effects. However, Russia, whose economy has been rapidly growing (8.1% in 2007) even as its population is shrinking, currently has high *inflation* (12% as of late 2007). For an agricultural or mining economy the average standard of living in a declining population, at least in terms of material possessions, will tend to rise as the amount of land and resources per person will be higher.

But for many industrial economies, the opposite might be true as those economies often thrive on mortgaging the future by way of debt and retirement transfer payments that originally assumed rising tax revenues from a continually expanding population base (i.e. there would be fewer taxpayers in a declining population). However, standard of living does not necessarily correlate with quality of life, which may increase as the population declines due to presumably reduced pollution and consumption of natural resources, and the decline of social pressures and overutilization of resources that can be linked to overpopulation. There may also be reduced pressure on infrastructure, education, and other services as well.

The period immediately after the Black Death, for instance, was one of great prosperity, as people had inheritances from many different family members. However, that situation was not comparable, as it did not have a continually declining population, but rather a sudden shock, followed by population increase. Predictions of the *net* economic (and other) effects from a slow and continuous population decline (e.g. due to low fertility rates) are mainly theoretical since such a phenomenon is a relatively new and unprecedented one.

A declining population due to low fertility rates will also be accompanied by population ageing which can contribute problems for a society. This can adversely affect the quality of life for the young as an increased social and economic pressure in the sense that they have to increase per-capita output in order to support an infrastructure with costly, intensive care for the oldest among their population. The focus shifts away from the planning of future families and therefore further degrades the rate of procreation. The decade-long economic malaise of Japan and Germany in the 1990s and early 2000s is often linked to these demographic problems, though there were also several other causes. The worst case scenario is a situation where the population falls too low a level to support a current social welfare economic system, which is more likely to occur with a rapid decline than with a more gradual one.

The economies of both Japan and Germany both went into recovery around the time their populations just began to decline (2003–2006). In other words, both the total and per capita GDP in both countries grew more rapidly after 2005 than before. Russia's economy also began to grow rapidly from 1999 onward, even though its population has been shrinking since 1992-93 (the decline is now decelerating). In addition, many Eastern European countries have been experiencing similar effects to Russia. Such renewed growth calls into question the conventional wisdom that economic growth requires population growth, or that economic growth is impossible during a population decline. However, it may be argued that this renewed growth is *in spite of* population decline rather than because of it, and economic growth in these countries would potentially be greater if they were not undergoing such demographic decline. For example, Russia has become quite wealthy selling fossil fuels such as oil, which are now high-priced, and in addition, its economy has expanded from a very low nadir due to the economic crisis of the late 1990s. And although Japan and Germany have recovered somewhat from having been in a deflationary recession and stagnation, respectively, for the past decade, their recoveries seem to have been quite tepid. Both countries fell into the global recession of 2008-2009, but are now recovering once again, being among the first countries to recover.

In a country with a declining population, the growth of GDP per capita is higher than the growth of GDP. For example, Japan has a higher growth per capita than the United States, even though the US GDP growth is higher than Japan's. Even when GDP growth is zero or negative, the GDP growth per capita can still be positive (by definition) if the population is shrinking faster than the GDP.

A declining population (regardless of the cause) can also create a labour shortage, which can have a number of positive and negative effects. While some labour-intensive sectors of the economy may be hurt if the shortage is severe enough, others may adequately compensate by increased out sourcing and/or automation. Initially, the labour participation rates (which are low in many countries) can also be increased to temporarily reduce or delay the shortage. On the positive side, such a shortage increases the demand for labour, which can potentially result in a reduced unemployment rate as well as higher wages. Conversely, a high population means labour is in plentiful supply, which usually means wages will be lower. This is seen in countries like China and India.

A smaller national population can also have geo-strategic effects, but the correlation between population and power is a tenuous one. Technology and resources often play more significant roles.

National Efforts to Reverse Declining Populations

Former Russian President Vladimir Putin directed Parliament to adopt a 10-year programme to stop the sharp decline in Russia's population, principally by offering financial incentives and subsidies to encourage women to have children. Australia currently offers a $5,000 bonus for every baby plus additional fortnightly payments, a free immunization scheme and recently proposed to pay all child care costs for women who want to work. Many European countries, including France, Italy, Germany and Poland, have offered some combination of bonuses and monthly payments to families. Some Japanese localities, facing significant population loss, are offering economic incentives. Yamatsuri, a town of 7,000 just north of Tokyo, offers parents $4,600 for the birth of a child and $460 a year for 10 years. The Republic of Singapore has similar plans: $3,000 for the first child, $9,000 in cash and savings for the second; and up to $18,000 each for the third and fourth. The effectiveness of these policies is currently the subject of debate.

Paid maternity and paternity leave policies can also be used as an incentive. Sweden built up an extensive welfare state from the 1930s and onward, partly as a consequence of the debate following Crisis in the Population Question, published in 1934. Today, Sweden has generous parental leave where parents are entitled to share 16 months paid leave per child, the cost divided between both employer and State.

Alternative Concept Relative to Skills

Sometimes the concept of population decline is applied where there has been considerable ex-migration of skilled professionals. In such a case, the government may have ceased to reward or value certain skills (e.g. science, medicine and engineering), and sectors of the economy such as health care and technology may go into decline. Such characterizations have been made of Italy, Bulgaria and Russia in the period starting about 1990.

Chapter 2

Demography

Demography is the statistical study of human populations and sub-populations. It can be a very general science that can be applied to any kind of dynamic human population, that is, one that changes over time or space. It encompasses the study of the size, structure, and distribution of these populations, and spatial and/or temporal changes in them in response to birth, migration, aging and death.

Demographic analysis can be applied to whole societies or to groups defined by criteria such as education, nationality, religion and ethnicity. Institutionally, demography is usually considered a field of sociology, though there are a number of independent demography departments. Formal demography limits its object of study to the measurement of populations processes, while the broader field of social demography population studies also analyze the relationships between economic, social, cultural and biological processes influencing a population. The term demographics refers to characteristics of a population.

Data and Methods

There are two methods of data collection: direct and indirect. Direct data come from vital statistics registries that track all births and deaths as well as certain changes in legal status such as marriage, divorce, and migration (registration of place of residence). In developed countries with good registration systems (such as the United States and much of Europe), registry statistics are the best method for estimating the number of births and deaths.

A census is the other common direct method of collecting demographic data. A census is usually conducted by a national government and attempts to enumerate every person in a country. However, in contrast to vital statistics data, which are typically collected continuously and summarized on an annual basis, censuses typically occur only every 10 years or so, and thus are not usually the best source of data on births and deaths. Analyses are conducted after a census to estimate how much over or undercounting took place. These compare the sex ratios from the census data to those estimated from natural values and mortality data.

Censuses do more than just count people. They typically collect information about families or households in addition to individual characteristics such as age, sex, marital status, literacy/education, employment status, and occupation, and geographical location. They may also collect data on migration (or place of birth or of previous residence), language, religion, nationality (or ethnicity or race), and citizenship. In countries in which the vital registration system may be incomplete, the censuses are also used as a direct source of information about fertility and mortality; for example the censuses of the People's Republic of China gather information on births and deaths that occurred in the 18 months immediately preceding the census.

Indirect methods of collecting data are required in countries where full data are not available, such as is the case in much of the developing world. One of these techniques is the sister method, where survey researchers ask women how many of their sisters have died or had children and at what age. With these surveys, researchers can then indirectly estimate birth or death rates for the entire population. Other indirect methods include asking people about siblings, parents, and children.

There are a variety of demographic methods for modelling population processes. They include models of mortality (including the life table, Gompertz models, hazards models, Cox proportional hazards models, multiple decrement life tables, Brass relational logits), fertility (Hernes model, Coale-Trussell models, parity progression ratios), marriage (Singulate Mean at Marriage, Page model), disability (Sullivan's method, multistate life tables), population projections (Lee Carter, the Leslie Matrix), and population momentum (Keyfitz).

- The crude birth rate, the annual number of live births per 1,000 people.
- The general fertility rate, the annual number of live births per 1,000 women of childbearing age (often taken to be from 15 to 49 years old, but sometimes from 15 to 44).
- age-specific fertility rates, the annual number of live births per 1,000 women in particular age groups (usually age 15-19, 20-24 etc.)

- The crude death rate, the annual number of deaths per 1,000 people.
- The infant mortality rate, the annual number of deaths of children less than 1 year old per 1,000 live births.
- The expectation of life (or life expectancy), the number of years which an individual at a given age could expect to live at present mortality levels.
- The total fertility rate, the number of live births per woman completing her reproductive life, if her childbearing at each age reflected current age-specific fertility rates.
- The replacement level fertility, the average number of children a woman must have in order to replace herself with a daughter in the next generation. For example the replacement level fertility in the US is 2.11. This means that 100 women will bear 211 children, 103 of which will be females. About 3% of the alive female infants are expected to decease before they bear children, thus producing 100 women in the next generation.
- The gross reproduction rate, the number of daughters who would be born to a woman completing her reproductive life at current age-specific fertility rates.
- The net reproduction ratio is the expected number of daughters, per newborn prospective mother, who may or may not survive to and through the ages of childbearing.
- A stable population, one that has had constant crude birth and death rates for such a long period of time that the percentage of people in every age class remains constant, or equivalently, the population pyramid has an unchanging structure.
- A stationary population, one that is both stable and unchanging in size (the difference between crude birth rate and crude death rate is zero).

A stable population does not necessarily remain fixed in size. It can be expanding or shrinking.

Note that the crude death rate as defined above and applied to a whole population can give a misleading impression. For example, the number of deaths per 1,000 people can be higher for developed nations than in less-developed countries, despite standards of health being better in developed countries. This is because developed countries have proportionally more older people, who are more likely to die in a given year, so that the overall mortality rate can be higher even if the mortality rate at any given age is lower. A more complete picture of mortality is given by a life table which summarises mortality separately at each age. A life table is necessary to give a good estimate of life expectancy.

The fertility rates can also give a misleading impression that a population is growing faster than it in fact is, because measurement of fertility rates only involves the reproductive rate of women, and does not adjust for the sex ratio. For example, if a population has a total fertility rate of 4.0 but the sex ratio is 66/34 (twice as many men as women), this population is actually growing at a slower natural increase rate than would a population having a fertility rate of 3.0 and a sex ratio of 50/50. This distortion is greatest in India and Myanmar, and is present in China as well.

Basic Equation

Suppose that a country (or other entity) contains $Population_t$ persons at time t. What is the size of the population at time $t + 1$?

$$Population_{t+1} = Population_t + Naturalincrease_t + Netmigration_t$$

Natural increase from time t to $t + 1$:

$$Naturalincrease_t = Births_t - Deaths_t$$

Net migration from time t to $t + 1$:

$$Netmigration_t = Immigration_t - Emigration_t$$

This basic equation can also be applied to subpopulations. For example, the population size of ethnic groups or nationalities within a given society or country is subject to the same sources of change. However, when dealing with ethnic groups, "net migration" might have to be subdivided into physical migration and ethnic reidentification (assimilation). Individuals who change their ethnic self-labels or whose ethnic classification in government statistics changes over time may be thought of as migrating or moving from one population subcategory to another.

More generally, while the basic demographic equation holds true by definition, in practice the recording and counting of events (births, deaths, immigration, emigration) and the enumeration of the total population size are subject to error. So allowance needs to be made for error in the underlying statistics when any accounting of population size or change is made.

History

Demographic thoughts can be traced back to antiquity, and are present in many civilisations and cultures, like Ancient Greece, Rome,

India and China. In ancient Greece, this can be found in the writings of Herodotus, Thucidides, Hippocrates, Epicurus, Protagoras, Polus, Plato andAristotle. In Rome, writers and philosophers like Cicero, Seneca, Pliny the elder, Marcus Aurelius, Epictetus, Cato and Collumella also expressed important ideas on this ground.

In the Middle ages, Christian thinkers devoted much time in refuting the Classical ideas on demography. Important contributors to the field were William of Conches, Bartholomew of Lucca, William of Auvergne, William of Pagula, and Ibn Khaldun.

The *Natural and Political Observations ... upon the Bills of Mortality* (1662) of John Graunt contains a primitive form of life table. Mathematicians, such as Edmond Halley, developed the life table as the basis for life insurance mathematics. Richard Price was credited with the first textbook on life contingencies published in 1771, followed later by Augustus de Morgan, 'On the Application of Probabilities to Life Contingencies' (1838).

At the end of the 18th century, Thomas Malthus concluded that, if unchecked, populations would be subject to exponential growth. He feared that population growth would tend to outstrip growth in food production, leading to ever-increasing famine and poverty. He is seen as the intellectual father of ideas of overpopulation and the limits to growth. Later, more sophisticated and realistic models were presented by Benjamin Gompertz and Verhulst.

The period 1860-1910 can be characterized as a period of transition wherein demography emerged from statistics as a separate field of interest. This period included a panoply of international 'great demographers' like Adolphe Quételet (1796–1874), William Farr (1807–1883), Louis-Adolphe Bertillon (1821–1883) and his son Jacques (1851–1922), Joseph Körösi (1844–1906), Anders Nicolas Kaier (1838–1919), Richard Böckh (1824–1907), Wilhelm Lexis (1837–1914) and Luigi Bodio (1840–1920) contributed to the development of demography and to the toolkit of methods and techniques of demographic analysis.

Transition

Contrary to Malthus' predictions and in line with his thoughts on moral restraint, natural population growth in most developed countries has diminished to close to zero, without being held in check by famine or lack of resources, as people in developed nations have shown a tendency to have fewer children. The fall in population growth has occurred despite large rises in life expectancy in these countries. This pattern of population growth, with slow (or no) growth in pre-industrial societies, followed by fast growth as the society develops and industrializes, followed by slow growth again as it becomes more affluent, is known as the greatest demographic transition. Similar trends are now becoming visible in ever more developing countries, so that far from spiraling out of control, world population growth is expected to slow markedly in this century, coming to an eventual standstill or even declining. The change is likely to be accompanied by major shifts in the proportion of world population in particular regions. The United Nations Population Division expects the absolute number of infants and toddlers in the world to begin to fall by 2015, and the number of children under 15 by 2025.

UN projections of world population out to the year 2150 (red = high, orange = medium, green = low). The UN "medium" projection shows world population reaching an approximate equilibrium at 9 billion by 2075. Working independently, demographers at the International Institute for Applied Systems Analysis in Austria expect world population to peak at 9 billion by 2070. Throughout the 21st century, the average age of the population is likely to continue to rise.

Science of Population

Populations can change through three processes: fertility, mortality, and migration. Fertility involves the number of children that women have and is to be contrasted with fecundity (a woman's childbearing potential). Mortality is the study of the causes, consequences, and measurement of processes affecting death to members of the population. Demographers most commonly study mortality using the Life Table, a statistical device which provides information about the mortality conditions (most notably the life expectancy) in the population.

Migration refers to the movement of persons from a locality of origin to a destination place across some pre-defined, political boundary. Migration researchers do not designate movements 'migrations' unless they are somewhat permanent. Thus demographers do not consider tourists and travelers to be migrating. While demographers who study migration typically do so through census data on place of residence, indirect sources of data including tax forms and labour force surveys are also important.

Demography is today widely taught in many universities across the world, attracting students with initial training in social sciences, statistics or health studies. Being at the crossroads of several disciplines such as sociology, economics, epidemiology, geography, anthropology and history, demography offers tools to approach a large range of population issues by combining a more technical quantitative approach that represents the core of the discipline with many other methods borrowed from social or other sciences. Demographic research is conducted in universities, in research institutes as well as in statistical departments and in several international agencies. Population institutions are part of the Cicred (International Committee for Coordination of Demographic Research) network while most individual scientists engaged in demographic research are members of the International Union for the Scientific Study of Population, or a national association such as the Population Association of America in the United States, or affiliates of the Federation of Canadian Demographers in Canada.

Biodemography

Biodemography is the science dealing with the integration of biology and demography. Biodemography is a new branch of human (classical) demography concerned with understanding the complementary biological and demographic determinants of and interactions between the birth and death processes that shape individuals, cohorts and populations. The biological component brings human demography under the unifying theoretical umbrella of evolution, and the demographic component provides an analytical foundation for many of the principles upon which evolutionary theory rests including fitness, selection, structure, and change. Whereas biodemographers are concerned with birth and death processes as they relate to populations in general and to humans in particular, population biologists specializing in life history theory are interested in these processes only insofar as they relate to fitness and evolution.

For example, evolutionary biologists seldom focus on older, post-reproductives because these individuals (it is typically argued) do not contribute to fitness. In contrast, biodemographers embrace research programmes expressly designed to study individuals at ages beyond their reproductive years because information on these age classes will shed important light onlongevity and aging. The biological and demographic components of biodemography are not hierarchical but reciprocal in that both are primary windows on the world and are thus synergistic, complementary and mutually informing.

Biodemography is unique in two respects. *First*, it is one of a small number of key subdisciplines arising from the social sciences that has embraced biology such as evolutionary psychology and neuroeconomics.

However, unlike the others which focus more narrowly on biological sub-areas (neurology) or concepts (evolution), biodemography has no explicit biological boundaries. As a consequence, it is a more all-encompassing interdisciplinary concept, but maintains deep biological roots. *Second,* the hierarchical organizations that are inherent to both biology (cell, organ, individual) and demography (individual cohort, population) form a chain in which the individual serves as the link between the lower mechanistic levels, and the higher functional levels.

Biodemography is therefore ideally suited – serving as a "*looking glass*" - to complement, engage and inform research on human aging through t

Samples of Related Research in Biodemography

- The Biodemographic Determinants of Life Span
- Biodemographic Effects of Social Evolution in Honey Bees [1]
- Aging in the Wild-Medflies and Nematodes, [2]
- The Mathematical Demography of Biodemography [3]
- Biodemography of Intergenerational Transfer [4]
- Evolutionary Dynamics of Life Span [5]

Demographic Analysis

Demographic analysis includes the sets of methods that allow us to measure the dimensions and dynamics of populations. These methods have primarily been developed to study human populations, but are extended to a variety of areas where researchers want to know how populations of social actors can change across time through processes of birth, death, and migration. In the context of human biological populations, demographic analysis uses administrative records to develop an independent estimate of the population. Demographicanalysis estimates are often considered a reliable standard for judging the accuracy of the census information gathered at any time. In the labour force, demographic analysis is used to estimate sizes and flows of populations of workers; in population ecology the focus is on the birth, death and movement of firms and institutional forms. Demographic analysis is used in a wide variety of contexts. For example, it is often used in business plans, to describe the population connected to the geographic location of the business. Demographic analysis is usually abbreviated as DA. For the 2010 U.S. Census, The U.S. Census Bureau has expanded its DA categories. Also as part of the 2010 U.S. Census, DA now also includes comparative analysis between independent housing estimates, and census address lists at different key time points. Demography is the statistical and mathematical study of the size, composition, and spatial distribution of human populations and how these features change over time. Data are obtained from a census of the population and from registries: records of events like birth, deaths, migrations, marriages, divorces, diseases, and employment. To do this, there needs to be an understanding of how they are calculated and the questions they answer which are included in these four concepts: population change, standardization of population numbers, the demographic bookkeeping equation, and population composition.

Population Change

Population change is analyzed by measuring the change between one population size to another. Global population continues to rise, which makes population change an essential component to demographics. This is calculated by taking one population size minus the population size in an earlier census. The best way of measuring population change is using the intercensal percentage change. The intercensal percentage change is the absolute change in population between the censuses divided by the population size in the earlier census. Next, multiply this a hundredfold to receive a percentage. When this statistic is achieved, the population growth between two or more nations that differ in size, can be accurately measured and examined.

Standardization (of Population Numbers)

For there to be a significant comparison, numbers must be altered for the size of the population that is under study. For example, the fertility rate is calculated as the ratio of the number of births to women of childbearing age to the total number of women in this age range. If these adjustments were not made, we would not know if a nation with a higher rate of births or deaths has a population with more women of childbearing age or more births per eligible woman.

Within the category of standardization, there are two major approaches: direct standardization and indirect standardization.

Direct Standardization

Direct standardization is able to be used when the population being studied is large enough for age-specific rate is stable.

Indirect Standardization

Indirect standardization is used when a population is small enough that the number of events (births, deaths, etc.) are also small. In this case, methods must be used to produce a standardized mortality rate (SMR) or standardized incidence rate (SIR).</ref>equations on indirect and direct standardization</ref>

Demographic Bookkeeping (or balancing) Equation

Demographic bookkeeping is used in the identification of four main components of population growth during any given time interval.

The demographic bookkeeping equation is as follows:

$$P_2 = P_1 + (B - D) + (M_i - M_o)$$

The four components being studied by this equation are Population Growth (P_1, P_2), Births (B), Deaths (D), and In (M_i) and Out (M_o) Migration.

Meaning, the population at any time is equal to the earlier population plus the excess of births over deaths in the time, plus the amount of in-migration minus the amount of out-migration.

Population Composition

Population composition is the description of population defined by characteristics such as age, race, sex or marital status. These descriptions can be necessary for understanding the social dynamics from historical and comparative research. This data is often compared using a population pyramid.

Population composition is also a very important part of historical research. Information ranging back hundreds of years is not always worthwhile, because the numbers of people for which data are available may not provide the information that is important (such as population size). Lack of information on the original data-collection procedures may prevent accurate evaluation of data quality.

Demographic Analysis in Institutions and Organizations

Labour Markets: The demographic analysis of labour markets can be used to show slow population growth, population aging, and the increased importance of immigration. The U.S. Census Bureau will project that in the next 100 years, the United States will face some dramatic demographic changes. The population is expected to grow more slowly and age more rapidly than ever before and the nation will become a nation of immigrants.

This influx is projected to rise over the next century as new immigrants and their children will account for over half the U.S. population. These demographic shifts could ignite major adjustments in the economy, more specifically, in labour markets.

Turnover and in Internal Labour Markets

People decide to exit organizations for many reasons, such as, better jobs, dissatisfaction, and concerns within the family. The causes of turnover can be split into two separate factors, one linked with the culture of the organization, and the other relating to all other factors. People who do not fully accept a culture might leave voluntarily. Or, some individuals might leave because they fail to fit in and fail to change within a particular organization.

Population Ecology of Organizations

A basic definition of population ecology is a study of the distribution and abundance of organisms. As it relates to organizations and demography, organizations go through various liabilities to their continued survival. Hospitals, like all other large and complex organizations are impacted in the environment they work. For example, a study was done on the closure of acute care hospitals in Florida between a particular time. The study examined effect size, age, and niche density of these particular hospitals. A population theory says that organizational outcomes are mostly determined by environmental factors. Among several factors of the theory, there are four that apply to the hospital closure example: size, age, density of niches in which organizations operate, and density of niches in which organizations are established.

Business Organizations

Problems in which demographers may be called upon to assist business organizations are when determining the best prospective location in an area of a branch store or service outlet, predicting the demand for a new product, and to analyze certain dynamics of a company's workforce. Choosing a new location for a branch of a bank, choosing the area in which to start a new supermarket, consulting a bank loan officer that a particular location would be a beneficial site to start a car wash, and determining what shopping area would be best to buy and be redeveloped in metropolis area are types of problems in which demographers can be called upon.

Standardization is a useful demographic technique used in the analysis of a business. It can be used as an interpretive and analytic tool for the comparison of different markets.

Nonprofit Organizations

These organizations have interests about the number and characteristics of their clients so they can maximize the sale of their products, their outlook on their influence, or the ends of their power, services, and beneficial works.

Demographic Economics

Demographic economics or population economics is the application of economics to demography, the study of human populations, including size, growth, density, distribution, and vital statistics.

Analysis includes economic determinants and consequences of:

- marriage and fertility,
- the family,
- divorce,
- morbidity and life expectancy/mortality,
- dependency ratios,
- migration,
- population growth,
- population size,
- public policy, and the
- demographic transition from "population explosion" to (dynamic) stability or decline.

Other subfields include the measuring the value of life and the economics of the elderly and the handicapped and of gender, race, minorities, and non-labour discrimination. In coverage and subfields, it complements labour economics and implicates a variety of other economics subjects.

Historical Demography

Historical demography is the quantitative study of human population in the past. It is concerned both with the three basic components of population change—fertility, mortality, and migration—and with population characteristics related to those components, such as marriage, socioeconomic status, and the configuration of families.

Sources

The sources of historical demography vary according to the period under study. Paleodemography, based on the study of skeletal remains, is the primary approach for populations that precede the modern era. In the early modern period, historical demographers rely heavily on ecclesiastical records of baptisms, marriages, and burials, using methods developed by French historian Louis Henry. For the recent period - beginning in the early nineteenth century in most European countries, and later in the rest of the world - historical demographers make use of data collected by governments, including censuses and vital statistics.

History

Historical analysis has played a central role in the study of population, from Thomas Malthus in the eighteenth century to major twentieth-century demographers such as Ansley Coaleand Samuel H. Preston. The French historian Louis Henry (1911-1991) is widely credited with the development of historical demography as a distinct subfield of demography. In recent years, new research in historical demography has proliferated owing to the development of massive new population data collections, including the Demographic Data Base in Umeå, Sweden , the Historical Sample of the Netherlands , and the Integrated Public Use Microdata Series (IPUMS).

Historical Population of the World

During the period from 500 to 900 CE world population grew slowly but the growth rate accelerated between 900 and 1300 CE when the population doubled. During the 14th century, there was a fall in population associated with the Black Death that spread from Asia to Europe. This was followed by a period of restrained growth until the 18th century when world population entered a period of accelerated growth again. As previously the acceleration was more marked in the European population, due to scientific revolution and resulting inventions lowering the childbirth mortality rate. European population reached a peak growth rate of 10 per thousand per year in the second half of the 19th century.

During the 20th century, the growth rate among the European populations fell and was overtaken by a rapid acceleration in the growth rate in other continents, which reached 21 per thousand per year in the last 50 years of the millennium. Between 1900 and 2000 CE the population of the world increased by 277 %, a fourfold increase from 1.5 billion to 6 billion. The European component increased by 124 %, and the remainder by 349 %.

Linguistic Demography

Linguistic demography is the statistical study of languages among all populations. Estimating the number of speakers of a given language is not straightforward, and various estimates may diverge considerably. This is first of all due to the question of defining "language" vs. "dialect". Identification of varieties as a single language or as distinct languages is often based on ethnic, cultural, or political considerations rather than mutual intelligibility. The second difficulty is multilingualism, complicating the definition of "native language". Finally, in many countries, insufficient census data add to the difficulties.

Demolinguistics is a branch of Sociology of language observing linguistic trends as affected by population distribution and redistribution and by the status of societies.

Most Spoken Languages

The following table compares the estimates of Comrie (1998) and Weber (1997) (number of native speakers in millions). Also given are the estimates of SIL Ethnologue (2005). Comparing estimates that do not date to the same year is problematic due to the 1.14% per year growth of world population (with significant regional differences).

		Comrie (1998)	*Weber (1997)*	*SIL*
1.	Mandarin Chinese	836	1,100	1.205 (1999)
2.-4.	Hindi+Urdu	333	250	422 (2001)
	Spanish	332	300	322 (1995)
	English	322	300	309 (1984)
5.-6.	Arabic	186	200	323 (2008)
	Bengali	189	185	171 (1994)
7.-8.	Russian	170	160	145 (2000)
	Portuguese	170	160	178 (1995)
9.	Japanese	125	125	122 (1985)
10.	German	100	100	95.4 (1994)

This table shows that for the world's largest languages, it is impossible to give an estimate of the number of native speakers with a certainty better than 10% or so. Diverse but ethnically unified languages like Chinese and Arabic are particularly difficult to define, and estimates consequently show uncertainties of the order of 25%.

Nurgaliev's Law

In population dynamics, Nurgaliev's law is an equation that describes the rate of change of the size of a population at a given time, in terms of the current population size. It is a deterministic ordinary differential equation in which the rate of change is expressed as a quadratic function of the population size.

Specification

Nurgaliev's law is expressed as

$$\frac{dn}{dt} = an^2 - bn,$$

where 'n' is the size of a population, t is time measured in years, a is a half of the average probability of a birth of a male (the same for females) of a potential arbitrary parents pair within a year, b is an average probability of a death of a person within a year.

The first term is twice proportional to the half of population (number of males and number of females). The second term is responsible for death rate and has a clear and precise sense— death rates are constant in time but vary with position on the age scale (babies are at risk at birth, the middle aged are at risk of trauma, old men become ill). It is known todemographers, for example, that the probability of death within the first year of a life is precisely equal to similar probability for the 55th year of a life. Thus, in the given model, the average person dies under the same law as an unstable atomic nucleus decays.

Stability

The population has steady states at $n=0,b/a$. The state with $n=0$ is stable whereas the state with $n=b/a$ is unstable, meaning that the equation describes a population which crashes (tends to zero) when the death rate is greater than the birth rate and explodes (tends to infinity) when it is the birth rate that is greater.

Ageing

Ageing (British English) or aging (American English) is the accumulation of changes in a person over time. Ageing in humans refers to a multidimensional process of physical, psychological, and social change. Some dimensions of ageing grow and expand over time, while others decline. Reaction time, for example, may slow with age, while knowledge of world events and wisdom may expand. Research shows that even late in life, potential exists for physical, mental, and social growth and development. Ageing is an important part of all human societies reflecting the biological changes that occur, but also reflecting cultural and societal conventions. Roughly 100,000 people worldwide die each day of age-related causes.

Age is measured chronologically, and a person's birthday is often an important event. However the term "ageing" is somewhat ambiguous. Distinctions may be made between "universal ageing" (age changes that all people share) and "probabilistic ageing" (age changes that may happen to some, but not all people as they grow older including diseases such as type two diabetes).

Chronological ageing may also be distinguished from "social ageing" (cultural age-expectations of how people should act as they grow older) and "biological ageing" (an organism's physical state as it ages). There is also a distinction between "proximal ageing" (age-based effects that come about because of factors in the recent past) and "distal ageing" (age-based differences that can be traced back to a cause early in person's life, such as childhood poliomyelitis).

Differences are sometimes made between populations of elderly people. Divisions are sometimes made between the young old (65–74), the middle old (75–84) and the oldest old (85+). However problematic this is, chronological age does not correlate perfectly with functional age, i.e. two people may be of the same age, but differ in their mental and physical capacities. Each nation, government and non-government organisation has different ways of classifying age.

Population ageing is the increase in the number and proportion of older people in society. Population ageing has three possible causes: migration, longer life expectancy (decreased death rate), and decreased birth rate. Ageing has a significant impact on society. Young people tend to commit most crimes, they are more likely to push for political and social change, to develop and adopt new technologies, and to need education. Older people have different requirements from society and government as opposed to young people, and frequently differing values as well. Older people are also far more likely to vote, and in many countries the young are forbidden from voting. Thus, the aged have comparatively more political influence.

Recent scientific successes in rejuvenation and extending a lifespan of model animals (mice-2.5 times, yeast "15 times, nematodes-10 times) and discovery of variety of species (including humans of advanced ages) having negligible senescence give hope to achieve negligible senescence (cancel ageing) for younger humans, reverse ageing or at least significantly delay it. In spite of the developments mentioned above and the fact that ageing is admitted to be the major cause of mortality in developed worlds the anti-ageing and life extension research is greatly underfunded. Although human life is declared to be a basic value in many societies there is still no strong awareness and thus demand of the society to cancel human ageing. The body still technically ages after death as it still gets older from birth.

Early Observations

The first formal studies of ageing appear to be those of Muhammad ibn Yusuf al-Harawi (1582) in his book *Ainul Hayat,* published by Ibn Sina Academy of Medieval Medicine and Sciences. This book is based only on ageing and its related issues. The original manuscript of *Ainul Hayat* was scribed in 1532 by the author Muhammad ibn Yusuf al-

Harawi. Four copies of the manuscript survive and were reprinted in an edited and translated version by Hakim Syed Zillur Rahman (2007). The book discusses behavioural and lifestyle factors putatively influencing ageing including diet, environment and housing conditions. Also discussed are drugs that may increase and decrease ageing rates.

Senescence

Senescence or biological aging is the change in the biology of an organism as it ages after its maturity. Such changes range from those affecting its cells and their function to those affecting the whole organism. There are a number of hypotheses as to why senescence occurs; for example, some posit it is programmed by gene expression changes, others that it is the cumulative damage caused by biological processes. Senescence is not the inevitable fate of all organisms. A variety of organisms, including some cold-blooded animals, have negligible senescence. Whether senescence as a biological process can be slowed down, halted or even reversed, is a subject of current scientific speculation and research.

The word *senescence* is derived from the Latin word *senex*, meaning *old man*, *old age*, or *advanced in ag*

Cellular Senescence

Cellular senescence is the phenomenon by which normal diploid cells lose the ability to divide, normally after about 50 cell divisions in vitro. Some cells become senescent after fewer replication cycles as a result of DNA double strand breaks, toxins, etc. This phenomenon is also known as "replicative senescence", the "Hayflick phenomenon", or the Hayflick limit in honour of Dr. Leonard Hayflick, co-author with Paul Moorhead, of the first paper describing it in 1961. In response to DNA damage (including shortened telomeres), cells either age or self-destruct (apoptosis, programmed cell death) if the damage cannot be easily repaired. In this 'cellular suicide', the death of one cell, or more, may benefit the organism as a whole. For example, in plants the death of the water-conducting xylem cells (tracheids andvessel elements) allows the cells to function more efficiently and so deliver water to the upper parts of a plant. The ones that do not self-destruct remain until destroyed by outside forces.

Aging of the Whole Organism

Organismal senescence is the aging of whole organisms. In general, aging is characterized by the declining ability to respond to stress, increased homeostatic imbalance, and increased risk of aging-associated diseases. Death is the ultimate consequence of aging, though "old age" is not a scientifically recognized cause of death because there is always a specific proximal cause, such as cancer, heart disease, or liver failure. Aging of whole organisms is therefore a complex process that can be defined as "a progressive deterioration of physiological function, an intrinsic age-related process of loss of viability and increase in vulnerability".

Differences in maximum life span among species correspond to different "rates of aging". For example, inherited differences in the rate of aging make a mouse elderly at 3 years and a human elderly at 80 years. These genetic differences affect a variety of physiological processes, including the efficiency of DNA repair, antioxidant enzymes, and rates of free radical production.

Senescence of the organism gives rise to the Gompertz–Makeham law of mortality, which says that mortality rate rises rapidly with age.

Some animals, such as some reptiles and fish, age slowly (negligible senescence) and exhibit very long lifespans. Some even exhibit "negative senescence", in which mortality falls with age, in disagreement with the Gompertz–Makeham "law".

Whether replicative senescence (Hayflick limit) plays a causative role in organismal aging is at present an active area of investigation.

Theories of Aging

The process of senescence is complex, and may derive from a variety of different mechanisms and exist for a variety of different reasons. However, senescence is not universal, and scientific evidence suggests that cellular senescence evolved in certain species because it prevents the onset of cancer. In a few simple species, such as Hydra, senescence is negligible and cannot be detected.

All such species have no "post-mitotic" cells; they reduce the effect of damaging free radicals by cell division and dilution. They are biologically immortal but not immortal in the traditional sense as they will eventually fall prey to trauma or disease. Moreover, average lifespans can vary greatly within and between species. This suggests that both genetic and environmental factors contribute to aging.

In general, theories that explain senescence have been divided between the programmed and stochastic theories of aging. Programmed theories imply that aging is regulated by biological clocks operating throughout the lifespan. This regulation would depend on changes in gene expression that affect the systems responsible for maintenance, repair, and defence responses. The Reproductive-Cell Cycle Theory suggests that aging is caused by changes in hormonal signaling over the lifespan. Stochastic theories blame environmental impacts on living organisms that induce cumulative damage at various levels as the cause of aging, examples of which ranging from damage to DNA, damage to tissues and cells by oxygen radicals (widely known as free radicals countered by the even more well-known antioxidants), and cross-linking.

However, aging is seen as a progressive failure of homeodynamics (homeostasis) involving genes for the maintenance and repair, stochastic events leading to molecular damage and molecular heterogeneity, and chance events determining the probability of death. Since complex and interacting systems of maintenance and repair comprise the homeodynamic (old term: homeostasis) space of a biological system, aging is considered to be a progressive shrinkage of homeodynamic space mainly due to increased molecular heterogeneity.

Evolutionary Theories

A gene can be expressed at various stages of life. Therefore, natural selection can support lethal and harmful alleles, if their expression occurs after reproduction. Senescence may be the product of such selection. In addition, aging is believed to have evolved because of the increasingly smaller probability of an organism still being alive at older age, due to predation and accidents, both of which may be random and age-invariant. It is thought that strategies that result in a higher reproductive rate at a young age, but shorter overall lifespan, result in a higher lifetime reproductive success and are therefore favoured by natural selection. In essence, aging is, therefore, the result of investing resources in reproduction, rather than maintenance of the body (the "Disposable Soma" theory), in light of the fact that accidents, predation, and disease will eventually kill the organism no matter how much energy is devoted to repair of the body. Various other theories of aging exist, and are not necessarily mutually exclusive.

The geneticist J. B. S. Haldane wondered why the dominant mutation that causes Huntington's disease remained in the population, and why natural selection had not eliminated it. The onset of this neurological disease is (on average) at age 45 and is invariably fatal within 10–20 years. Haldane assumed that, in human prehistory, few survived until age 45. Since few were alive at older ages and their contribution to the next generation was therefore small relative to the large cohorts of younger age groups, the force of selection against such late-acting deleterious mutations was correspondingly small. However, if a mutation affected younger individuals, selection against it would be strong. Therefore, late-acting deleterious mutations could accumulate in populations over evolutionary time through genetic drift.

This principle has been demonstrated experimentally. And it is these later-acting deleterious mutations that are believed to allow—even cause—age-related mortality.

Peter Medawar formalised this observation in his mutation accumulation theory of aging. "The force of natural selection weakens with increasing age—even in a theoretically immortal population, provided only that it is exposed to real hazards of mortality. If a genetic disaster... happens late enough in individual life, its consequences may be completely unimportant". The 'real hazards of mortality' are, in typical circumstances, predation, disease, and accidents. So, even an immortal population, whose fertility does not decline with time, will have fewer individuals alive in older age groups. This is called 'extrinsic mortality'. Young cohorts, not depleted in numbers yet by extrinsic mortality, contribute far more to the next generation than the few remaining older cohorts, so the force of selection against late-acting deleterious mutations, which affect only these few older individuals, is very weak. The mutations may not be selected against, therefore, and may spread over evolutionary time into the population.

The major testable prediction made by this model is that species that have high extrinsic mortality in nature will age more quickly and have shorter intrinsic lifespans. This is borne out among mammals, the best-studied in terms of life history. There is a correlation among mammals between body size and lifespan, such that larger species live longer than smaller species under controlled/optimum conditions, but there are notable exceptions. For instance, many bats and rodents are of similar size, yet bats live much longer. For instance, the little brown bat, half the size of a mouse, can live 30 years in the wild. A mouse will only live 2–3 years even under optimum conditions. The explanation is that bats have fewer predators, and therefore low extrinsic mortality. More individuals survive to later ages, so the force of selection against late-acting deleterious mutations is stronger. Fewer late-acting deleterious mutations equates to slower aging and therefore a longer lifespan. Birds are also warm-blooded and are similar in size to many small mammals, yet often live 5–10 times as long. They have less predation pressure than ground-dwelling mammals. Seabirds, which, in general, have the fewest predators of all birds, live longest.

When examining the body-size vs. lifespan relationship, one also observes that predatory mammals tend to live longer than prey mammals in a controlled environment, such as a zoo or nature reserve. The explanation for the long lifespans of primates (such as humans, monkeys, and apes) relative to body size is that their intelligence, and often their sociality, help them avoid becoming prey. Being a predator, being smart, and working together all reduce extrinsic mortality.

Another evolutionary theory of aging was proposed by George C. Williams and involves antagonistic pleiotropy. A single gene may affect multiple traits. Some traits that increase fitness early in life may also have negative effects later in life. But, because many more individuals are alive at young ages than at old ages, even small positive effects early can be strongly selected for, and large negative effects later may be very weakly selected against. Williams suggested the following example: Perhaps a gene codes for calcium deposition in bones, which promotes juvenile survival and will therefore be favoured by natural selection; however, this same gene promotes calcium deposition in the arteries, causing negative effects in old age. Thus, harmful biological changes in old age may result from selection for pleiotropic genes that are beneficial early in life but harmful later on. In this case, fitness is relatively high when Fisher's reproductive value is high and relatively low when Fisher's reproductive value is low.

Gene Regulation

A number of genetic components of aging have been identified using model organisms, ranging from the simple budding yeast *Saccharomyces cerevisiae* to worms such as Caenorhabditis *elegans* and fruit flies (*Drosophila melanogaster*). Study of these organisms has revealed the presence of at least two conserved aging pathways.

One of these pathways involves the gene *Sir2*, a NAD+-dependent histone deacetylase. In yeast, Sir2 is required for genomic silencing at three loci: The yeast mating loci, the telomeres and the ribosomal DNA (rDNA). In some species of yeast, replicative aging may be partially caused by homologous recombination between rDNA repeats; excision of rDNA repeats results in the formation of extrachromosomal rDNA circles (ERCs). These ERCs replicate and preferentially segregate to the mother cell during cell division, and are believed to result in cellular senescence by titrating away (competing for) essential nuclear factors. ERCs have not been observed in other species (nor even all strains of the same yeast species) of yeast (which also display replicative senescence), and ERCs are not believed to contribute to aging in higher organisms such as humans (they have not been shown to accumulate in mammals in a similar manner to yeast). Extrachromosomal circular DNA (eccDNA) has been found in worms, flies, and humans. The origin and role of eccDNA in aging, if any, is unknown.

Despite the lack of a connection between circular DNA and aging in higher organisms, extra copies of Sir2 are capable of extending the lifespan of both worms and flies (though, in flies, this finding has not been replicated by other investigators, and the activator of Sir2 resveratrol does not reproducibly increase lifespan in either species). Whether the Sir2 homologues in higher organisms have any role in lifespan is unclear, but the human SIRT1 protein has been demonstrated to deacetylate p53, Ku70, and the forkhead family of transcription factors. SIRT1 can also regulate acetylates such as CBP/p300, and has been shown to deacetylate specific histone residues.

RAS1 and RAS2 also affect aging in yeast and have a human homologue. RAS2 over expression has been shown to extend lifespan in yeast.

Other genes regulate aging in yeast by increasing the resistance to oxidative stress. Superoxide dismutase, a protein that protects against the effects of mitochondrial free radicals, can extend yeast lifespan in stationary phase when over expressed.

In higher organisms, aging is likely to be regulated in part through the insulin/IGF-1 pathway. Mutations that affect insulin-like signaling in worms, flies, and the growth hormone/IGF1 axis in mice are associated with extended lifespan. In yeast, Sir2 activity is regulated by the nicotinamidase PNC1. PNC1 is transcriptionally upregulated under stressful conditions such ascaloric restriction, heat shock, and osmotic shock. By converting nicotinamide to niacin, nicotinamide is removed, inhibiting the activity of Sir2. A nicotinamidase found in humans, known as PBEF, may serve a similar function, and a secreted form of PBEF known as visfatin may help to regulate serum insulin levels. It is not known, however, whether these mechanisms also exist in humans, since there are obvious differences in biology between humans and model organisms.

Sir2 activity has been shown to increase under calorie restriction. Due to the lack of available glucose in the cells, more NAD+ is available and can activate Sir2. Resveratrol, a stilbenoid found in the skin of red grapes, was reported to extend the lifespan of yeast, worms, and flies (the lifespan extension in flies and worms have proved irreproducible by independent investigators). It has been shown to activate Sir2 and therefore mimics the effects of calorie restriction, if one accepts that caloric restriction is indeed dependent on Sir2.

Gene expression is imperfectly controlled, and it is possible that random fluctuations in the expression levels of many genes contribute to the aging process as suggested by a study of such genes in yeast.

Individual cells, which are genetically identical, none-the-less can have substantially different responses to outside stimuli, and markedly different lifespans, indicating the epigenetic factors play an important role in gene expression and aging as well as genetic factors. According to the GenAge database of aging-related genes there are over 700 genes associated with aging in model organisms: 555 in the soil roundworm (*Caenorhabditis elegans*), 87 in the bakers' yeast (*Saccharomyces cerevisiae*), 75 in the fruit fly (*Drosophila melanogaster*) and 68 in the mouse (*Mus musculus*). The following is a list of genes connected to longevity through research on model organisms:

Cellular Senescence

As noted above, senescence is not universal. It was once thought that senescence did not occur in single-celled organisms that reproduce through the process of cellular mitosis. Recent investigation has unveiled a more complex picture. Single cells do accumulate age-related damage. On mitosis the debris is not evenly divided between the new cells. Instead it passes to one of the cells leaving the other cell pristine. With successive generations the call population becomes a mosaic of cells with half ageless and the rest with varying degrees of senescence.

Moreover, cellular senescence is not observed in several organisms, including perennial plants, sponges, corals, and lobsters. In those species where cellular senescence is observed, cells eventually become post-mitotic when they can no longer replicate themselves through the process of cellular mitosis; i.e., cells experience *replicative senescence.* How and why some cells become post-mitotic in some species has been the subject of much research and speculation, but (as noted above) it is widely believed that cellular senescence evolved as a way to prevent the onset and spread of cancer. Somatic cells that have divided many times will have accumulated DNA mutations and would therefore be in danger of becoming cancerous if cell division continued.

Lately, the role of telomeres in cellular senescence has aroused general interest, especially with a view to the possible genetically adverse effects of cloning. The successive shortening of the chromosomal telomeres with each cell cycle is also believed to limit the number of divisions of the cell, thus contributing to aging. There have, on the other hand, also been reports that cloning could alter the shortening of telomeres. Some cells do not age and are, therefore, described as being "biologically immortal". It is theorized by some that when it is discovered exactly what allows these cells, whether it be the result of telomere lengthening or not, to divide without limit that it will be possible to genetically alter other cells to have the same capability. It is further theorized that it will eventually be possible to genetically engineer all cells in the human body to have this capability by employing gene therapy and, therefore, stop or reverse aging, effectively making the entire organism potentially immortal.

The length of the telomere strand has senescence effects, telomere shortening activate extensive alterations in alternative RNA splicing that produce senescence toxins such as progerin that degrades the tissue and makes it more susceptible to failure. Cancer cells are usually immortal. In about 85% of tumors, this evasion of cellular senescence is the result of up-activation of their telomerase genes. This simple observation suggests that reactivation of telomerase in healthy individuals could greatly increase their cancer risk.

A research team led by Darren J. Baker and Jan M. van Deursen at the Mayo Clinic in Rochester, Minn., purged all the senescent cells in mice by giving them a drug that forces the cells to self-destruct. The mice's tissues showed a major improvement in the usual burden of age-related disorders. They did not develop cataracts, avoided the usual wasting of muscle with age, and could exercise much longer on a mouse treadmill. They retained the fat layers in the skin that usually thin out with age and, in people, cause wrinkling.

Chemical Damage

One of the earliest aging theories was the *Rate of Living Hypothesis* described by Raymond Pearl in 1928 (based on earlier work by Max Rubner), which states that fast basal metabolic rate corresponds to short maximum life span.

While there may be some validity to the idea that for various types of specific damage detailed below that are by-products of metabolism, all other things being equal, a fast metabolism may reduce lifespan, in general this theory does not adequately explain the differences in lifespan either within, or between, species. Calorically-restricted animals process as much, or more, calories per gram of body mass, as their *ad libitum* fed counterparts, yet exhibit substantially longer lifespans. Similarly, metabolic rate is a poor predictor of lifespan for birds, bats and other species that, it is presumed, have reduced mortality from predation, and therefore have evolved long lifespans even in the presence of very high metabolic rates. More recently, it was shown that, when modern statistical methods for correcting for the effects of body size and phylogeny are employed, metabolic rate does not correlate with longevity in mammals or birds. (For a critique of the *Rate of Living Hypothesis*see *Living fast, dying when?*)

With respect to specific types of chemical damage caused by metabolism, it is suggested that damage to long-lived biopolymers, such as structural proteins or DNA, caused by ubiquitous chemical agents in the body such as oxygen and sugars, are in part responsible for aging. The damage can include breakage of biopolymer chains, cross-linking of biopolymers, or chemical attachment of unnatural substituents (haptens) to biopolymers.

Under normal aerobic conditions, approximately 4% of the oxygen metabolized by mitochondria is converted to superoxide ion, which can subsequently be converted to hydrogen peroxide, hydroxyl radical and eventually other reactive species including other peroxides and singlet oxygen, which can, in turn, generate free radicals capable of damaging structural proteins and DNA. Certain metal ions found in the body, such as copper and iron, may participate in the process. (In Wilson's disease, a hereditary defect that causes the body to retain copper, some of the symptoms resemble accelerated senescence.) These processes are termed *oxidative damage* and are linked to the benefits of nutritionally derived polyphenol antioxidants.

Sugars such as glucose and fructose can react with certain amino acids such as lysine and arginine and certain DNA bases such as guanine to produce sugar adducts, in a process called *glycation*. These adducts can further rearrange to form reactive species, which can then cross-link the structural proteins or DNA to similar biopolymers or other biomolecules such as non-structural proteins. People with diabetes, who have elevated blood sugar, develop senescence-associated disorders much earlier than the general population, but can delay such disorders by rigorous control of their blood sugar levels. There is evidence that sugar damage is linked to oxidant damage in a process termed *glycoxidation*.

Free radicals can damage proteins, lipids or DNA. Glycation mainly damages proteins. Damaged proteins and lipids accumulate in lysosomes as lipofuscin. Chemical damage to structural proteins can lead to loss of function; for example, damage to collagen of blood vessel walls can lead to vessel-wall stiffness and, thus, hypertension, and vessel wall thickening and reactive tissue formation (atherosclerosis); similar processes in the kidney can lead to renal failure. Damage to enzymes reduces cellular functionality. Lipid peroxidation of the inner mitochondrial membrane reduces the electric potential and the ability to generate energy. It is probably no accident that nearly all of the so-called "accelerated aging diseases" are due to defective DNA repair enzymes. It is believed that the impact of alcohol on aging can be partly explained by alcohol's activation of the HPA axis, which stimulates glucocorticoid secretion, long-term exposure to which produces symptoms of aging.

Reliability Theory

Reliability theory suggests that biological systems start their adult life with a high load of initial damage. Reliability theory is a general theory about systems failure. It allows researchers to predict the age-related failure kinetics for a system of given architecture (reliability structure) and given reliability of its components. Reliability theory predicts that even those systems that composed entirely of non-aging elements (with a constant failure rate) will nevertheless deteriorate (fail more often) with age, if these systems are redundant in irreplaceable elements. Aging, therefore, is a direct consequence of systems.

Reliability theory also predicts the late-life mortality deceleration with subsequent levelling-off, as well as the late-life mortality plateaus, as an inevitable consequence of redundancy exhaustion at extreme old ages. The theory explains why mortality rates increase exponentially with age (the Gompertz law) in many species, by taking into account the initial flaws (defects) in newly formed systems. It also explains why organisms "prefer" to die according to the Gompertz law, while technical devices usually fail according to the Weibull (power) law. Reliability theory allows to specify conditions when organisms die according to the Weibull distribution: Organisms should be relatively free of initial flaws and defects. The theory makes it possible to find a general failure law applicable to all adult and extreme old ages, where the Gompertz and the Weibull laws are just special cases of this more general failure law. The theory explains why relative differences in mortality rates of compared populations (within a given species) vanish with age (compensation law of mortality), and mortality convergence is observed due to the exhaustion of initial differences in redundancy levels.

Miscellaneous

Recently, a kind of early senescence has been alleged to be a possible unintended outcome of early cloning experiments. The issue was raised in the case of Dolly the sheep, following her death from a contagious lung disease. The claim that Dolly's early death involved premature senescence has been vigorously contested, and Dolly's creator, Dr. Ian Wilmut has expressed the view that her illness and death were probably unrelated to the fact that she was a clone.

A set of rare hereditary (genetic) disorders, each called progeria, has been known for some time. Sufferers exhibit symptoms resembling accelerated aging, including wrinkled skin. The cause of Hutchinson–Gilford progeria syndrome was reported in the journal *Nature* in May 2003. This report suggests that DNA damage, not oxidative stress, is the cause of this form of accelerated aging.

Dividing the Lifespan

An animal's life is often divided into various age ranges. However, because biological changes are slow-moving and can vary within one's own species, arbitrary dates are usually set to mark periods of life. The human divisions given below are not valid in all cultures:

- Juvenile [via infancy, childhood, preadolescence, adolescence (teenager)]: 0–19
- Early adulthood: 20–39
- Middle adulthood: 40–59
- Late adulthood: 60+

Ages can also be divided by numbers:

Term	*Age (Years, Inclusive)*
Newborn	birth to 1 month
Infant	0 to 1
Toddler	1 to 2
Preschooler	3 to 4
Child/Kid	5 to 9
Pre-Teenager	10 to 12
Teenager	13 to 19
Vicenarian	20 to 29
Tricenarian	30 to 39
Quadragenarian	40 to 49
Quinquagenarian	50 to 59
Sexagenarian	60 to 69
Septuagenarian	70 to 79
Octogenarian	80 to 89
Nonagenarian	90 to 99
Centenarian	100 to 109
Supercentenarian	110 and older

People from 13 to 19 years of age are also known as teens or teenagers. Tween or Twelvie is an American neologism referring to someone between the ages of 8 and 12. The casual terms "twentysomething", "thirtysomething", etc. are also in use to describe people by decades of age.

Cultural Variations

In some cultures (for example Serbian) there are other ways to express age: by counting years with or without including current year. For example, it could be said about the same person that he is twenty years old or that he is in the twenty-first year of his life. In Russian the former expression is generally used, the latter one has restricted usage: it is used for age of a deceased person in obituaries and for the age of an adult when it is desired to show him/her older than he/she is. (Psychologically, a woman *in her 20th year* seems older than one who is *19 years old.*)

Depending on cultural and personal philosophy, ageing can be seen as an undesirable phenomenon, reducing beauty and bringing one closer to death; or as an accumulation of wisdom, mark of survival, and a status worthy of respect. In some cases numerical age is important (whether good or bad), whereas others find the stage in life that one has reached (adulthood, independence, marriage, retirement, career success) to be more important.

East Asian age reckoning is different from that found in Western culture. Traditional Chinese culture uses a different ageing method, called *Xusui* ([†rk) with respect to common ageing which is called *Zhousui* (hTrk). In the *Xusui* method, people are born at age 1, not age 0, because conception is already considered to be the start of the life span, and another difference is the ageing day: *Xusui* grows up at the Spring Festival (aka. Chinese New Year's Day), while *Shuo An* grows up at one's birthday.

Society

Legal: There are variations in many countries as to what age a person legally becomes an adult.

Most legal systems define a specific ages for when an individual is allowed or obliged to do particular activities. These ages include voting age, drinking age, age of consent, age of majority, age of criminal responsibility, marriageable age, age of candidacy, and mandatory retirement age. Admission to a movie for instance, may depend on age according to a motion picture rating system. A bus fare might be discounted for the young or old.

Similarly in many countries in jurisprudence, the defence of infancy is a form of defence by which a defendant argues that, at the time a law was broken, they were not liable for their actions, and thus should not be held liable for a crime. Many courts recognise that defendants who are considered to be juveniles may avoid criminal prosecution on account of their age, and in borderline cases the age of the offender is often held to be a mitigating circumstance.

Economics and Marketing

The economics of ageing are also of great importance. Children and teenagers have little money of their own, but most of it is available for buying consumer goods. They also have considerable impact on how their parents spend money. Young adults are an even more valuable cohort. They often have an income but few responsibilities such as a mortgage or children. They do not yet have set buying habits and are more open to new products. The young are thus the central target of marketers.

Health Care Demand

Many societies in Western Europe and Japan have ageing populations. While the effects on society are complex, there is a concern about the impact on health care demand. The large number of suggestions in the literature for specific interventions to cope with the expected increase in demand for long-term care in ageing societies can be organised under four headings: improve system performance; redesign service delivery; support informal caregivers; and shift demographic parametres.

However, the annual growth in national health spending is not mainly due to increasing demand from ageing populations, but rather has been driven by rising incomes, costly new medical technology, a shortage of health care workers and informational asymmetries between providers and patients. Even so, it has been estimated that population ageing only explains 0.2 percentage points of the annual growth rate in medical spending of 4.3 percent since 1970. In addition, certain reforms to Medicare decreased elderly spending on home health care by 12.5 percent per year between 1996 and 2000. This would suggest that the impact of ageing populations on health care costs is not inevitable.

Impact on Prisons

As of July 2007, medical costs for a typical inmate in the United States might run an agency around $33 per day, while costs for an ageing inmate could run upwards of $100. Most State DOCs report spending more than 10 percent of the annual budget on elderly care. That is expected to rise over the next 10–20 years. Some states have talked about releasing ageing inmates early.

Cognitive Effects

Steady decline in many cognitive processes is seen across the lifespan, accelerating from the twenties or thirties. Research has focused in particular on memory and ageing, and has found decline in many types of memory with ageing, but not in semantic memory or general knowledge such as vocabulary definitions, which typically increases or remains steady until the late adulthood. Early studies on changes in cognition with age generally found declines in intelligence in the elderly, but studies were cross-sectional rather than longitudinal and thus results may be an artefact of cohort rather than a true example of decline. However, longitudinal studies could be confounded due to prior test experience. Intelligence may decline with age, though the rate may vary depending on the type, and may in fact remain steady throughout most of the lifespan, dropping suddenly only as people near the end of their lives. Individual variations in rate of cognitive decline may therefore be explained in terms of people having different lengths of life. There are changes to the brain: though neuron loss is minor after 20 years of age there is a 10% reduction each decade in the total length of the brain's myelinated axons.

Coping and well-being

Psychologists have examined coping skills in the elderly. Various factors, such as social support, religion and spirituality, active engagement with life and having an internal locus of control have been proposed as being beneficial in helping people to cope with stressful life events in later life. Social support and personal control are possibly the two most important factors that predict well-being, morbidity and mortality in adults. Other factors that may link to well-being and quality of life in the elderly include social relationships (possibly relationships with pets as well as humans), and health.

Individuals in different wings in the same retirement home have demonstrated a lower risk of mortality and higher alertness and self-rated health in the wing where residents had greater control over their environment, though personal control may have less impact on specific measures of health. Social control, perceptions of how much influence one has over one's social relationships, shows support as amoderator variable for the relationship between social support and perceived health in the elderly, and may positively influence coping in the elderly.

Religion

Religion has been an important factor used by the elderly in coping with the demands of later life, and appears more often than other forms of coping later in life. Religious commitment may also be associated with reduced mortality, though religiosity is a multidimensional variable; while participation in religious activities in the sense of participation in formal and organised rituals may decline, it may become a more informal, but still important aspect of life such as through personal or private prayer.

Self-rated Health

Self-ratings of health, the beliefs in one's own health as excellent, fair or poor, has been correlated with well-being and mortality in the elderly; positive ratings are linked to high well-being and reduced mortality. Various reasons have been proposed for this association; people who are objectively healthy may naturally rate their health better than that of their ill counterparts, though this link has been observed even in studies which have controlled for socioeconomic status, psychological functioning and health status. This finding is generally stronger for men than women, though the pattern between genders is not universal across all studies, and some results suggest sex-based differences only appear in certain age groups, for certain causes of mortality and within a specific sub-set of self-ratings of health.

Retirement: Retirement, a common transition faced by the elderly, may have both positive and negative consequences.

Societal Impact

Of the roughly 150,000 people who die each day across the globe, about two thirds – 100,000 per day – die of age-related causes. In industrialised nations, the proportion is much higher, reaching 90%. Societal ageing refers to the demographic ageing of populations and societies. Cultural differences in attitudes to ageing have been studied.

Emotional Improvement

Given the physical and cognitive declines seen in ageing, a surprising finding is that emotional experience improves with age. Older adults are better at regulating their emotions and experience negative affect less frequently than younger adults and show a positivity effect in their attention and memory. The emotional improvements show up in longitudinal studies as well as in cross-sectional studies and so cannot be entirely due to only the happier individuals surviving.

Successful Ageing

The concept of *successful ageing* can be traced back to the 1950s, and popularised in the 1980s. Previous research into ageing exaggerated the extent to which health disabilities, such as diabetes or osteoporosis, could be attributed exclusively to age, and research in gerontology exaggerated the homogeneity of samples of elderly people.

Successful Ageing Consists of Three Components:

1. Low probability of disease or disability;

2. High cognitive and physical function capacity;
3. Active engagement with life.

A greater number of people self-report successful ageing than those that strictly meet these criteria.

Successful ageing may be viewed an interdisciplinary concept, spanning both psychology and sociology, where it is seen as the transaction between society and individuals across the life span with specific focus on the later years of life. The terms "healthy ageing" "optimal ageing" have been proposed as alternatives to successful ageing.

Six Suggested Dimensions of Successful Ageing Include:

1. No physical disability over the age of 75 as rated by a physician;
2. Good subjective health assessment (i.e. good self-ratings of one's health);
3. Length of undisabled life;
4. Good mental health;
5. Objective social support;
6. Self-rated life satisfaction in eight domains, namely marriage, income-related work, children, friendship and social contacts, hobbies, community service activities, religion and recreation/ sports.

Theories

Biological theories: At present, the biological basis of ageing is unknown. Most scientists agree that substantial variability exists in the rates of ageing across different species, and that this to a large extent is genetically based. In model organisms and laboratory settings, researchers have been able to demonstrate that selected alterations in specific genes can extend lifespan (quite substantially in nematodes, less so in fruit flies, and less again in mice). Even in the relatively simple and short-lived organisms, the mechanism of ageing remain to be elucidated. Less is known about mammalian ageing, in part due to the much longer lives in even small mammals such as the mouse (around 3 years).

The US National Institute on Aging currently funds an intervention testing programme, whereby investigators nominate compounds (based on specific molecular ageing theories) to have evaluated with respect to their effects on lifespan and age-related biomarkers in outbred mice. Previous age-related testing in mammals has proved largely irreproducible, because of small numbers of animals, and lax mouse husbandry conditions. The intervention testing programme aims to address this by conducting parallel experiments at three internationally recognised mouse ageing-centres, the Barshop Institute at UTHSCSA, the University of Michigan at Ann Arbor and the Jackson Laboratory.

Many have argued that life-span, like other phenotypes, is selected.

- Evolutionary Theories: Enquiry into the evolution of ageing aims to explain why almost all living things weaken and die with age. Exceptions such as rockfish, turtles, and naked molerat are highly informative.
- Telomere Theory: Telomeres (structures at the ends of chromosomes) have experimentally been shown to shorten with each successive cell division. Shortened telomeres activate a mechanism that prevents further cell multiplication. This may be particularly limit in tissues such as bone marrow and the arterial lining where cell division occurs repeatedly throughout life . Importantly though, mice lacking telomerase enzyme do not show a dramatically reduced lifespan, invalidating at least simple versions of the telomere theory of ageing. Mice may be an exception for the theory, as they have long hypervariable telomeres, prolonging the period after which telomere shortening would affect life-span. But wild mouse strains do not, and telomere length in these breeds is unrelated to lifespan
- Reproductive-Cell Cycle Theory: The idea that ageing is regulated by reproductive hormones that act in an antagonistic pleiotropic manner via cell cycle signalling, promoting growth and development early in life in order to achieve reproduction, but later in life, in a futile attempt to maintain reproduction, become dysregulated and drive senescence (dyosis).

Some theories suggest that ageing is a disease. Two examples are

- DNA Damage Theory of Ageing: Known causes of cancer (radiation, chemical and viral) account for about 30% of the total cancer burden and for about 30% of the total DNA damage. DNA damage causes the cells to stop dividing or induce apoptosis, often affecting stem cell pools and hence hindering regeneration. DNA damage is thought to be the common pathway causing both cancer and ageing. It seems unlikely that the estimates of the DNA damage due to radiation and chemical causes has been significantly underestimated. Viral infection would appear to be the most likely cause of the other 70% of DNA damage especially in cells that are not exposed to smoking and sun light. It has been argued, too, that intrinsic causes of DNA damage are more important drivers of ageing.

- Autoimmune Theory: The idea that ageing results from an increase in autoantibodies that attack the body's tissues. A number of diseases associated with ageing, such as atrophic gastritis and Hashimoto's thyroiditis, are probably autoimmune in this way. While inflammation is very much evident in old mammals, even SCID mice in SPF colonies still experience senescence.

Genetic Theories

Many theories suggest that ageing results from the accumulation of damage to DNA in the cell, or organ. Since DNA is the formative basis of cell structure and function, damage to the DNA molecule, or genes, can lead to its loss of integrity and early cell death.

Examples include:

- Accumulative-Waste Theory: The biological theory of ageing that points to a buildup of cells of waste products that presumably interferes with metabolism.
- Wear-and-Tear Theory: The very general idea that changes associated with ageing are the result of chance damage that accumulates over time.
- Somatic Mutation Theory: The biological theory that ageing results from damage to the genetic integrity of the body's cells.
- Error Accumulation Theory: The idea that ageing results from chance events that escape proof reading mechanisms, which gradually damages the genetic code.

Some have argued that ageing is programmed: that an internal clock detects a time to end investing in the organism, leading to death. This ageing-Clock Theory suggests, as in a clock, an ageing sequence is built into the operation of the nervous or endocrine system of the body. In rapidly dividing cells the shortening of the telomeres would provide such a clock. This idea is in contradiction with the evolutionary based theory of ageing.

- Cross-Linkage Theory: The idea that ageing results from accumulation of cross-linked compounds that interfere with normal cell function.
- Free-Radical Theory: The idea that free radicals (unstable and highly reactive organic molecules), or more generally reactive oxygen species or oxidative stress create damage that gives rise to symptoms we recognise as ageing.
- Reliability theory of ageing and longevity: A general theory about systems failure. It allows researchers to predict the age-

related failure kinetics for a system of given architecture (reliability structure) and given reliability of its components. Reliability theory predicts that even those systems that are entirely composed of non-ageing elements (with a constant failure rate) will nevertheless deteriorate (fail more often) with age, if these systems are redundant in irreplaceable elements. Ageing, therefore, is a direct consequence of systems redundancy. Reliability theory also predicts the late-life mortality deceleration with subsequent levelling-off, as well as the late-life mortality plateaus, as an inevitable consequence of redundancy exhaustion at extreme old ages. The theory explains why mortality rates increase exponentially with age (the Gompertz law) in many species, by taking into account the initial flaws (defects) in newly formed systems. It also explains why organisms "prefer" to die according to the Gompertz law, while technical devices usually fail according to the Weibull (power) law. Reliability theory allows to specify conditions when organisms die according to the Weibull distribution: organisms should be relatively free of initial flaws and defects. The theory makes it possible to find a general failure law applicable to all adult and extreme old ages, where the Gompertz and the Weibull laws are just special cases of this more general failure law. The theory explains why relative differences in mortality rates of compared populations (within a given species) vanish with age (compensation law of mortality), and mortality convergence is observed due to the exhaustion of initial differences in redundancy levels.

- Mitohormesis: It has been known since the 1930s that restricting calories while maintaining adequate amounts of other nutrients can extend lifespan in laboratory animals. Recently, Michael Ristow's group has provided evidence for the theory that this effect is due to increased formation of free radicals within the mitochondria causing a secondary induction of increased antioxidant defence capacity.
- Misrepair-Accumulation Theory: Wang et al. suggest that ageing is the result of the accumulation of "Misrepair". Important in this theory is to distinguish among "damage" which means a newly emerging defect BEFORE any reparation has taken place, and "Misrepair" which describes the remaining defective structure AFTER (incorrect) repair.

Chapter 3

Religious Views on Birth Control

Religious adherents vary widely in their views on birth control. This can be true even between different branches of one faith, as in the case of Judaism. Some religious believers find that their own opinions of the use of birth control differ from the beliefs espoused by the leaders of their faith, and many grapple with the ethical dilemma of correct action versus personal circumstance and choice.

Christianity

Among Christian denominations today there are a large variety of positions towards contraception. The Roman Catholic Church has disallowed artificial contraception for as far back as one can historically trace. Contraception was also officially disallowed by non-Catholic Christians until 1930 when the Anglican Communion changed its policy. Soon after, most Protestant groups came to accept the use of modern contraceptives as a matter of Biblically allowable freedom of conscience.

Roman Catholicism

The Catholic Church is opposed to artificial contraception and orgasmic acts outside of the context of marital intercourse. This belief dates back to the first centuries of Christianity. Such acts are considered intrinsically disordered because of the belief that all licit sexual acts must be both unitive (express love), and procreative (open to procreation). The only form of birth control permitted is abstinence. Modern scientific methods of "periodic abstinence" such as natural family planning (NFP) were counted as a form of abstinence by Pope Paul VI in his 1968 encyclical *Humanae Vitae.* The following is the condemnation of contraception:

Therefore We base Our words on the first principles of a human and Christian doctrine of marriage when We are obliged once more to declare that the direct interruption of the generative process already begun and, above all, all direct abortion, even for therapeutic reasons, are to be absolutely excluded as lawful means of regulating the number of children. Equally to be condemned, as the magisterium of the Church has affirmed on many occasions, is direct sterilization, whether of the man or of the woman, whether permanent or temporary. Similarly excluded is any action which either before, at the moment of, or after sexual intercourse, is specifically intended to prevent procreation—whether as an end or as a means.

A number of other documents provide more insight into the Church's position on contraception. The commission appointed to study the question in the years leading up to *Humanae Vitae* issued two unofficial reports, a so-called "majority report" which attempted to express reasons the Catholic Church could change its teaching on contraception, and a "minority report" which explains the reasons for upholding the traditional Christian view on contraception. In 1997, the Vatican released a document entitled "Vademecum for Confessors" (2:4) which states "[t]he Church has always taught the intrinsic evil of contraception." Furthermore, many Church Fathers condemned the use of contraception. The 1987 document Donum Vitae opposes in-vitro fertilization on grounds that it is harmful to embryos. Later on, the 2008 instruction Dignitas Personae denounces embryonic manipulations and new methods of contraception.

Many Western Catholics have voiced significant disagreement with the Church's stance on contraception. Many Catholics use contraceptive methods other than those officially sanctioned by the church.

Protestantism

Author and *Family Life Today* radio host Dennis Rainey suggests four categories as useful in understanding current Protestant attitudes concerning birth control. These are the "children in abundance" group, such as Quiverfull adherents who view all birth control and natural family planning as wrong; the "children in managed abundance" group, which accept only natural family planning; the "children in moderation" group which accepts prudent use of a wide range of contraceptives; and, the "no children" group which sees itself as within their Biblical rights to define their lives around non-natal concerns. Meanwhile, Protestant movements such as Focus on the Family view contraception use outside of marriage as encouragement to promiscuity. Sex is a powerful drive, and for most of human history it was firmly linked to marriage and childbearing. Only relatively recently has the act of sex commonly been divorced from marriage and procreation. Modern contraceptive inventions have given many an exaggerated sense of safety and prompted more people than ever before to move sexual expression outside the marriage boundary.

Hinduism

There is no ban on birth control in Hinduism. Some Hindu scriptures include advice on what a couple should do to promote conception—thus providing contraceptive advice to those who want it. However most Hindus accept that there is a duty to have a family during the householder stage of life, and so are unlikely to use contraception to avoid having children altogether. The Dharma (doctrine of the religious and moral codes of Hindus) emphasizes the need to act for the sake of the good of the world.

Some Hindus, therefore, believe that producing more children than the environment can support goes against this Hindu code. Although fertility is important, conceiving more children than can be supported is treated as violating the *Ahimsa* (nonviolent rule of conduct). Because India has such a large and dense population, much of the discussion of birth control has focused on the environmental issue of overpopulation rather than more personal ethics, and birth control is not a major ethical issue.

Islam

The Qur'an does not make any explicit statements about the morality of contraception, but contains statements encouraging procreation. The prophet Muhammad also is reported to have said "marry and procreate".

Coitus interruptus, a primitive form of birth control, was a known practice at the time of Muhammad, and his companions engaged in it. Muhammad knew about this, but did not prohibit it. Umar and Ali, the second and fourth of the Rashidun caliphs, respectively, defended the practice.

Muslims scholars have extended the example of coitus interruptus, by analogy, to declaring permissible other forms of contraception, subject to three conditions:

1. As offspring are the right of both the husband and the wife, the birth control method should be used with both parties' consent.
2. The method should not cause permanent sterility.
3. The method should not otherwise harm the body.

Judaism

The Jewish view on birth control currently varies between the Orthodox, Conservative, and Reform branches of Judaism. Among Orthodox Judaism, use of birth control has been considered only acceptable for use in certain circumstances, for example, when the couple already has two children. Conservative Judaism, while generally encouraging its members to follow the traditional Jewish views on birth control has been more willing to allow greater exceptions regarding its use to fit better within modern society. Reform Judaism has generally been the most liberal with regard to birth control allowing individual followers to use their own judgment in what, if any, birth control methods they might wish to employ. It should also be noted that Jews who follow *halakha* based on the Talmudic tradition of law will not have sex during the 11-14 days after a women begins menstruating. This precludes them from utilizing some forms of "natural birth control" such as the "Calendar-based contraceptive methods" which are relatively unobjectionable to other religious groups.

When Orthodox Jewish couples contemplate the use of contraceptives, they generally consult a rabbi who evaluates the need for the intervention and which method is preferable from a*halachic* point of view.

Other Religions

Most other religions do not engage in this discussion; for example, Sikhs have no objection to birth control, and in Buddhism there is no widely recognized policy on birth control. Neopagans almost universally embrace birth control both as a way to safely enjoy a positive natural experience, and as exercise of feminine empowerment.

Cultural Attitudes

According to Peter Mulira, "Reproduction in Africa is a cultural issue in which large families are seen as a source of free labour and wealth."

Many nations in Western Europe today would have declining populations if it were not for international immigration. The feminist movement has affected change in Western society, including education; and the reproductive rights of women to make individual decisions on pregnancy (including access to contraceptives and abortion).

A number of nations today are experiencing population decline. Growing female participation in the work force and greater numbers of women going into further education has led to many women delaying or deciding against having children, or to not have as many. In Eastern Europe and Russia, natality fell abruptly after the end of the Soviet

Union. The World Bank issued a report predicting that between 2007 and 2027 the populations of Georgia and Ukraine will decrease by 17% and 24% respectively.

Sex Education

Many teenagers, most commonly in developed countries, receive some form of sex education in school. What information should be provided in such programmes is hotly contested, especially in the United States and United Kingdom. Topics include reproductive anatomy, human sexual behaviour, information on sexually transmitted diseases (STDs), social aspects of sexual interaction, negotiating skills intended to help teens follow through with a decision to remain abstinent or to use birth control during sex, and information on birth control methods.

One type of sex education programme used in some more conservative areas of the United States is called abstinence-only education, and it generally promotes complete sexual abstinence until marriage. The programmes do not encourage birth control, often provide inaccurate information about contraceptives and sexuality, stress failure rates of condoms and other contraceptives, and teach strategies for avoiding sexually intimate situations. Advocates of abstinence-only education believe that the programmes will result in decreased rates of teenage pregnancy and STD infection.

Abstinence-only sex education programmes show an increase in the rates of pregnancy and STDs of a teenage population in randomized controlled trials. Professional medical organizations, including the AMA, AAP, ACOG, APHA, APA, and Society for Adolescent Medicine, support comprehensive sex education (providing abstinence and contraceptive information) and oppose the sole use of abstinence-only sex education.

Arguments Against Misconceptions of Birth Control

Modern misconceptions and urban legends have given rise to false claims. Below are the arguments against those false claims.

- The suggestion that douching with any substance immediately following intercourse works as a contraceptive is untrue. While it may seem like a sensible idea to try to wash the ejaculate out of the vagina, it is not likely to be effective. Due to the nature of the fluids and the structure of the female reproductive tract, douching most likely actually spreads semen further towards the uterus. Some slight spermicidal effect may occur if the douche solution is particularly acidic, but overall it is not scientifically observed to be a reliably effective method.

Douching is neither a contraceptive nor a preventative measure against STDs or other infections.

- It is untrue that a female cannot become pregnant as a result of the first time she engages in sexual intercourse.
- While women are usually less fertile for the first few days of menstruation, it is a myth that a woman absolutely cannot get pregnant if she has sex during her period.
- Having sex in a hot tub does not prevent pregnancy, but may contribute to vaginal infections.
- There is no evidence that any particular sexual position is more likely to lead to conception and no sexual position prevents pregnancy. Having sex while standing up or with a woman on top will not keep the sperm from entering the uterus. The force of ejaculation, the contractions of the uterus caused by prostaglandins in the semen, as well as ability of the sperm to swim overrides gravity.
- Urinating after sex does not prevent pregnancy and is not a form of birth control, although it is often advised anyway to help prevent urinary tract infections.
- Toothpaste cannot be used as an effective contraceptive.
- Though intrauterine devices (IUDs) are popular in many parts of the world, many people in the United States believe they are dangerous, probably in large part due to the widely publicized health risks associated with an IUD model called the Dalkon Shield. In reality, the most recent models of the IUD, ParaGard and Mirena, are both extremely safe and effective.

Comparison of Birth Control Methods

Comparison of birth control methods Different types of birth control methods have large differences in effectiveness, actions required of users, and side effects.

Ease of Use

Different methods require different actions of users. Barrier methods, spermicides, and coitus interruptus must be used at every act of intercourse. The male condom may not be applied until the man achieves an erection. Barriers such as diaphragms, caps, the contraceptive sponge, and female condoms may be placed several hours before intercourse begins (note that when using the female condom the penis must be guided into place when initiating intercourse). The female condom should be removed before arising. The other female barrier methods must be left in place for several hours after sex. Spermicides, depending on the form, may be applied several minutes to an hour before intercourse begins. The lactational amenorrhea method (LAM) requires breast feeding at least every four to six hours.

Fertility awareness-based methods require some action every day to monitor and record fertility signs. Oral contraceptives require some action every day. Other hormonal methods require less frequent action - weekly for the patch, twice a month for vaginal ring, monthly for combined injectable contraceptive, and every twelve weeks for the injection Depo-Provera. With IUDs, female or male sterilization, and hormone implant there is "little or nothing to do" post initial procedure; there is nothing to put in place before intercourse to prevent pregnancy Implants, such as Implanon, provide effective birth control for three years without any user action between insertion and removal of the implant. Insertion and removal of the Implant involves a minor surgical procedure. Intrauterine methods require clinic visits for installation and removal or replacement (if desired) only once every several years (5-12), depending on the device. Sterilization is a one-time, permanent procedure - after the success of surgery is verified (for vasectomy), no action is usually required of users.

User Dependence

Different methods require different levels of diligence by users. Methods with little or nothing to do or remember, or that require a clinic visit less than once per year are said to be *non-user dependent, forgettable* or *top-tier* methods. Intrauterine methods, implants and sterilization fall into this category. For methods that are not user dependent, the actual and perfect-use failure rates are very similar.

Many hormonal methods of birth control, and LAM require a moderate level of thoughtfulness. For many hormonal methods, clinic visits must be made every three months to a year to renew the prescription. The pill must be taken every day, the patch must be reapplied weekly, or the ring must be replaced monthly. Injections are required every 12 weeks. The rules for LAM must be followed every day. Both LAM and hormonal methods provide a reduced level of protection against pregnancy if they are occasionally used incorrectly (rarely going longer than 4–6 hours between breast feeds, a late pill or injection, or forgetting to replace a patch or ring on time). The actual failure rates for LAM and hormonal methods are somewhat higher than the perfect-use failure rates.

Higher levels of user commitment are required for other methods. Barrier methods, coitus interruptus, and spermicides must be used at every act of intercourse. Fertility awareness-based methods may require daily tracking of the menstrual cycle. The actual failure rates for these methods may be much higher than the perfect-use failure rates.

Side Effects

Different forms of birth control have different potential side effects. Not all, or even most, users will experience side effects from a method. The less effective the method, the greater the risk of the side-effects associated with pregnancy. Minimal or no other side effects are possible with coitus interruptus, fertility awareness-based, and LAM. Some forms of periodic abstinence encourage examination of the cervix; insertion of the fingers into the vagina to perform this examination may cause changes in the vaginal environment. Following the rules for LAM may delay a woman's first post-partum menstruation beyond what would be expected from different breast feeding practices.

Barrier methods have a risk of allergic reaction. Users sensitive to latex may use barriers made of less allergenic materials - polyurethane condoms, or silicone diaphragms, for example. Barrier methods are also often combined with spermicides, which have possible side effects of genital irritation, vaginal infection, and urinary tract infection.

Sterilization procedures are generally considered to have low risk of side effects, though some persons and organizations disagree. Female sterilization is a more significant operation than vasectomy, and has greater risks; in industrialized nations, mortality is 4 per 100,000 tubal ligations, versus 0.1 per 100,000 vasectomies.

After IUD insertion, users may experience irregular periods in the first 3–6 months with Mirena, and sometimes heavier periods and worse menstrual cramps with ParaGard. However, "ninety-nine percent of IUD users are pleased with them". A positive characteristic of IUD's is that fertility and the ability to become pregnant returns quickly once the IUD is removed.

Because of their systemic nature, hormonal methods have the largest number of possible side effects. Birth control pills are associated with lower desire and arousal scores when compared with other contraceptives.

Sexually Transmitted Disease Prevention

Male and female condoms provide significant protection against sexually transmitted diseases (STD) when used consistently and correctly. They also provide some protection against cervical cancer. Condoms are often recommended as an adjunct to more effective birth control methods (such as IUD) in situations where STD protection is also desired. Other barrier methods, such as diaphragm may provide limited protection against infections in the upper genital tract. Other methods provide little or no protection against sexually transmitted diseases.

Effectiveness Calculation

Failure rates may be calculated by either the Pearl index or a life table method. A "perfect-use" rate is where any rules of the method are rigorously followed, and (if applicable) the method is used at every act of intercourse.

Actual failure rates are higher than perfect-use rates for a variety of reasons:

- mistakes on the part of those providing instructions on how to use the method
- mistakes on the part of the method's users
- conscious user non-compliance with method.
- insurance providers sometimes impede access to medications (e.g. require prescription refills on a monthly basis).

For instance, someone using oral forms of hormonal birth control might be given incorrect information by a health care provider as to the frequency of intake, or for some reason not take the pill one or several days, or not go to the pharmacy on time to renew the prescription, or the pharmacy might be unwilling to provide enough pills to cover an extended absence.

Effectiveness of Various Methods

The table below colour codes the typical-use and perfect-use failure rates, where the failure rate is measured as the expected number of pregnancies per year per 100 women using the method: In the User action required column, items that are *non-user dependent* (require action once per year or less) also have a blue background.

Some methods may be used simultaneously for higher effectiveness rates. For example, using condoms with spermicides the estimated perfect use failure rate would be comparable to the perfect use failure rate of the implant. However, mathematically combining the rates to estimate the effectiveness of combined methods can be inaccurate, as the effectiveness of each method is not necessarily independent, except in the perfect case.

If a method is known or suspected to have been ineffective, such as a condom breaking, emergency contraception (ECP) may be taken up to 72 to 120 hours after sexual intercourse. Emergency contraception should be taken shortly before or as soon after intercourse as possible, as its efficacy decreases with increasing delay. Although ECP is considered an emergency measure, levonorgestrel ECP taken shortly before sex may be used as a primary method for woman who have sex only a few times a year and want a hormonal method, but don't want to take hormones all the time. Failure rate of repeated or regular use of LNG ECP is similar to rate for those using a barrier method.

Table Notes

1. The pregnancy rate applies until the user reaches six months postpartum, or until menstruation resumes, whichever comes first. If menstruation occurs earlier than six months postpartum, the method is no longer effective. For users for whom menstruation does not occur within the six months: after six months postpartum, the method becomes less effective.
2. ^[a b] In the effectiveness study of Lea's Shield, 84% of participants were parous. The unadjusted pregnancy rate in the six-month study was 8.7% among spermicide users and 12.9% among non-spermicide users. No pregnancies occurred among nulliparous users of the Lea's Shield. Assuming the effectiveness ratio of nulliparous to parous users is the same for the Lea's Shield as for the Prentif cervical cap and the Today contraceptive sponge, the unadjusted six-month pregnancy rate would be 2.2% for spermicide users and 2.9% for those who used the device without spermicide.
3. *Nulliparous* refers to those who have *not* given birth.
4. *Parous* refers to those who *have* given birth.
5. No formal studies meet the standards of *Contraceptive Technology* for determining typical effectiveness. The typical effectiveness listed here is from the CDC's National Survey of Family Growth, which grouped symptoms-based methods together with calendar-based methods. See Fertility awareness#Effectiveness.
6. The term "fertility awareness" is sometimes used interchangeably with the term "natural family planning" (NFP), though NFP usually refers to use of periodic abstinence in accordance with Catholic beliefs.
7. Users may observe one or more of the three primary fertility signs. Basal body temperature (BBT) and cervical position are checked once per day. Cervical mucus is checked before each

urination, and vaginal sensation is observed throughout the day. The observed sign or signs are recorded once per day.

Cost and Cost-effectiveness

Family planning is among the most cost-effective of all health interventions. Costs of contraceptives include method costs (including supplies, office visits, training), cost of method failure (ectopic pregnancy, spontaneous abortion, induced abortion, birth, child care expenses) and cost of side effects. Contraception saves money by reducing unintended pregnancies and reducing transmission of sexually transmitted infections.

The most significant cost in birth control is the cost of failure to prevent pregnancy. Childbirth is expensive and risky, and raising a child takes a tremendous investment of time, energy and money. For example the average cost of a birth in the US is over $9,000 (cost to health plan, 2007 dollars). The US Department of Agriculture estimates that it costs $196,000 to $393,000 to raise a child from birth to age 17. (Depends on household income, total inflation adjusted estimated expenditure in 2007 dollars) By comparison, in the US, method related costs vary from nothing to about $1,000 for a year or more of reversible contraception.

The IUD is the least expensive long-term reversible form of birth control. An IUD usually only costs money initially for examination and insertion, and typically remains costless until removal, up to 5 to 12 years later, depending on the device chosen. In their 2012 publication, Planned Parenthood estimated that in the United States "the cost for the medical exam, the IUD, the insertion of the IUD, and follow-up visits to your health care provider can range from $500 to $1,000". During the initial five years, vasectomy is comparable in cost to the IUD. Vasectomy is much less expensive and safer than tubal ligation.

Not using contraceptives is the most expensive option. While in that case there are no method related costs, it has the highest failure rate, and thus the highest failure related costs. Even if one only considers medical costs relating to preconception care and birth, any method of contraception saves money compared to using no method.

The most effective and the most cost effective methods are long-acting methods. Unfortunately these methods often have significant up-front costs, requiring the user to pay a portion of these costs prevents some from using more effective methods.

Contraception saves money for the public health system and insurers. Many governments and insurers subsidize the costs of contraception. For example, U.S. Department of Health and Human Services clinics may offer reduced cost office visits, including vasectomy and IUD birth control protection.

Beginning of Pregnancy Controversy

Controversy over the beginning of pregnancy usually occurs in the context of the abortion debate. Depending on where pregnancy is considered to begin, some methods of birth control or infertility treatment might be considered abortifacient. The controversy is not primarily a scientific issue since knowledge of human reproduction and development has become very refined, but rather is primarily a linguistic and definitional question. The issue may also have social, medical, political and legal ramifications, but only if one equates the "beginning of pregnancy" with the "beginning of an individual human being's life".

Definitions of Pregnancy Beginning

Traditionally, doctors have measured pregnancy from a number of convenient points, including the day of last menstruation, ovulation, fertilization, implantation and chemical detection. This has led to some confusion about the precise length of human pregnancy, as each measuring point yields a different figure.

At its 2004 Annual Meeting, The American Medical Association passed a resolution in favour of making "Plan B" emergency contraception available over-the-counter, and one of the claims in the resolution was that hormonal contraception that may affect implantation "cannot terminate an established pregnancy."

Similarly, the British Medical Association has defined an "established pregnancy" as beginning at implantation. The legal definition in the United Kingdom is not clear. Other definitions exist. The American Heritage Stedman's Medical Dictionary defines "pregnancy" as "from conception until birth." Definitions like this may add to a lay person's confusion, as "conception" in a medical context may be defined as implantation but in lay terms may mean either fertilization or implantation. Whether conception refers to fertilization or implantation would seemingly even impact "established pregnancies" such as an ectopic pregnancy. If conception is defined as at implantation, ectopic pregnancies could not be called pregnancies. However, some medical professionals who oppose birth control, including prominent member of Focus on the Family Walter Larimore, have argued that the medical definition of conception should include fertilization.

Finally, the standard historical method of counting the duration of pregnancy begins from the last menstruation and this remains common with doctors, hospitals, and medical companies. This system is convenient because it is easy to determine when the last menstrual period was, while both fertilization and implantation occur out of sight. An interesting consequence is that the dating of pregnancy measured this way begins two weeks before ovulation.

Legal Implications

In August 2008 the U.S. Department of Health and Human Services proposed a regulation to protect certain actions of health workers: refusal to provide patient services that the health workers believe to be abortifacient. The ban on discrimination against these employees would apply to all organizations that receive grant money from HHS. A draft version leaked in July proposed that the U.S. federal government define abortion as including "termination of [human] life... before... implantation." The official proposal dropped the definition of abortion, instead leaving it to the objecting individual to define abortion for him- or herself. Groups on both sides of the controversy believe the ban is intended to allow health workers to refuse to dispense IUDs and hormonal contraceptives, including emergency contraception. It has drawn widespread criticism from major medical and health groups.

History

In the past, pregnancy has been defined in terms of conception. For example, *Webster's Dictionary* defined "pregnant" (or "pregnancy") as "having conceived" (or "the state of a female who has conceived"), in its 1828 and 1913 editions. However, in the absence of an accurate understanding of human development, early notions about the timing and process of conception were often vague.

Both the 1828 and 1913 editions of *Webster's Dictionary* said that to "conceive" meant "to receive into the womb and ... begin the formation of the embryo." It was mentioned in the Quran +1400 years ago in Surat Al-Mu'minun [23:14]] that *((Then We made the sperm-drop into a clinging clot, and We made the clot into a lump [of flesh], and We made [from] the lump, bones, and We covered the bones with flesh; then We developed him into another creation. So blessed is Allah , the best of creators))* However most references say that it was only in 1875 that Oskar Hertwig discovered that fertilization includes the penetration of a spermatozoon into an ovum. Thus, the term "conception" was in use long before the details of fertilization were discovered. By 1966, a more precise meaning of the word "conception" could be found in common-use dictionaries: the formation of a viablezygote.

In 1959, Dr. Bent Boving suggested that the word "conception" should be associated with the process of implantation instead of fertilization. Some thought was given to possible societal consequences, as evidenced by Boving's statement that "the social advantage of being considered to prevent conception rather than to destroy an established pregnancy could depend on something so simple as a prudent habit of speech." In 1965, the American College of Obstetricians and Gynecologists (ACOG) adopted Boving's definition: "conception is the implantation of a fertilized ovum."

The 1965 ACOG definition was imprecise because, by the time it implants, the zygote is called a blastocyst, so it was clarified in 1972 to "Conception is the implantation of the blastocyst." Some dictionaries continue to use the definition of conception as the formation of a viable zygote.

Birth Control – Mechanism of Action

Birth control methods usually prevent fertilization. This cannot be seen as abortifacient because, by any of the above definitions, pregnancy has not started. However, some methods might have a secondary effect of preventing implantation, thus allowing the zygote to die. Those who define pregnancy from fertilization subsequently may conclude that the agents should be considered abortifacients. Speculation about post-fertilization mechanisms is widespread, even appearing on patient information inserts for hormonal contraception, but there is no clinical support. One small study, using fourteen women, might be considered as providing evidence of such an effect for IUDs and a study of the combined oral contraceptive pill has been proposed.

Possibly Affected Methods

- Hormonal contraception, including emergency contraception, are known to be effective at preventing ovulation. Some scientists believe hormonal methods may have a secondary effect of interfering with implantation of embryos.
- Intrauterine devices (IUDs) have been proven to have strong spermicidal and ovicidal effects; the current medical consensus is that this is the only way in which they work. Still, a few physicians have suggested they may have a secondary effect of interfering with the development of pre-implanted embryos; this secondary effect is considered more plausible when the IUD is used as emergency contraception.
- The lactational amenorrhea method works primarily by preventing ovulation, but is also known to cause luteal phase

defect (LPD). LPD is believed to interfere with the implantation of embryos.

- Natural Family Planning (NFP) methods are intended to prevent fertilization through avoiding intercourse during fertile periods. Luc Bovens argues that, under an assumption that the age of gametes has an effect on embryo viability, errors in NFP method result in the occurrence of lower-viability embryos. This is intended to be an ethical thought experiment; Bovens states that his assumption "is not backed up by empirical evidence, but does have a certain plausibility." His argument is controversial. The age of gametes at the time of fertilization has been shown to have no effect on miscarriage rates in most cases, but is a significant risk factor where there is history of miscarriage. Age of gametes at the time of fertilization has been shown to have no effect on low birth weight or preterm delivery.

Viability and Established Pregnancy

A related issue that comes up in this debate is how often fertilization leads to an established, viable pregnancy. Current research suggests that fertilized embryos naturally fail to implant some 30% to 60% of the time. Of those that do implant, about 25% suffer early pregnancy loss by the sixth week LMP (after the woman's Last Menstrual Period), and an additional 7% miscarry or are stillborn. As a result, even without the use of birth control, between 50% and 70% of zygotes never result in established pregnancies, much less birth.

Ethics of Preventing Implantation

The intention of a woman to prevent pregnancy is an important factor in whether or not the act of contraception is seen as abortive by some pro-life groups. Hormonal contraceptives have a possible effect of preventing implantation of a blastocyst, as discussed previously. Use of these drugs with the intention of preventing pregnancy is seen by some pro-life groups as immoral. This is because of the possibility of causing the end of a new human life. However, hormonal contraception can also be used as a treatment for various medical conditions. When implantation prevention is unintentionally caused as a side effect of medical treatment, such pro-life groups do not consider the practice to be immoral, citing the bioethical principle of double effect. Likewise, when a hormonal contraceptive is used with the intention of preventing fertilisation, the intended reduction in implantation failures, miscarriages and deaths from childbearing may outweigh the possibility that the method might cause some implantation failures.

A related application of the principle of double effect is breast feeding. Breast feeding greatly suppresses ovulation, but eventually an ovum is released. Luteal phase defect, caused by breast feeding, makes the uterine lining hostile to implantation and as such may prevent implantation after fertilization. Some pro-choice groups have expressed concern that the movement to recognize hormonal contraceptives as abortifacient will also cause breast feeding to be considered an abortion method.

Detectable Pregnancy

A protein called early pregnancy factor (EPF) is detectable in a woman's blood within 48 hours of ovulation if fertilization has occurred. However, testing for EPF is time consuming and expensive; most early pregnancy tests detect human chorionic gonadotropin (hCG), a hormone that is not secreted until after implantation. Defining pregnancy as beginning at implantation thus makes pregnancy a condition that can be easily tested for.

Philosophical Issues

The distinction in ethical value between existing persons and potential future persons has been questioned. Subsequently, it has been argued that contraception and even the decision not to procreate at all could be regarded as immoral on a similar basis as abortion. In this sense, beginning of pregnancy may not necessarily be equated with where it is ethically right or wrong to assist or intervene. In a consequentialistic point of view, an assisting or intervening action may be regarded as basically equivalent whether it is performed before, during or after the creation of a human being, because the end result would basically be the same, that is, the existence or non-existence of that human being.

Biirth Control Sabotage

Birth control sabotage, or reproductive coercion, refers to efforts to manipulate another person's use of birth control or to undermine efforts to prevent an unwanted pregnancy. Examples include replacing birth control pills with fakes, puncturing condoms and diaphragms, or threats and violence to prevent an individual's attempted use of birth control. A related concept, Contraceptive fraud is intentional misrepresentation regarding the use of or need for birth control. The sabotage or fraud may be practiced by either sexual partner, or by a third party.

Domestic Violence

Birth control sabotage is frequently associated with physical or sexual violence, and is a contributor to high pregnancy rates, especially teenage pregnancy rates, among abused, disadvantaged women and teenagers.

Studies on the birth control sabotage performed by males against female partners have indicated a strong correlation between domestic violence and birth control sabotage. These studies have identified two main classes of the phenomenon:

- Verbal sabotage: verbal or emotional pressure not to use birth control or to become pregnant.
- Bahavioural sabotage: the use of force to have unprotected sexual intercourse or not to use birth control.

Compulsory Sterilization

Compulsory sterilization (or sterilisation), also known as forced sterilization (or sterilisation), programmes are government policies which attempt to force people to undergo surgical sterilization. In the first half of the 20th century, several such programmes were instituted in countries around the world, usually as part of eugenics programmes intended to prevent the reproduction and multiplication of members of the population considered to be carriers of defective genetic traits. Widespread or systematic forced sterilization has been recognized as a crime against humanity by the Rome Statute in the Explanatory Memorandum. This memorandum also defines the jurisdiction of the International Criminal Court. Despite international agreement concerning the inhumanity and illegality of forced sterilization, it has been suggested that Government of Uzbekistan continues to pursue such programmes.

In countries providing for a procedure to legally recognize sex change, surgical sterilization usually is a pre-condition for such recognition. The procedure consist of surgical removal of reproductive organs (orchiectomy, oophorectomy, hysterectomy, bilateral adnexectomy) leading to irreversible loss of reproductive functions. This should be recognized as compulsory sterilization too because people going through the process do not usually have freedom of choice to undergo the procedure or not.

By Country

Canada: Two Canadian provinces (Alberta and British Columbia) performed compulsory sterilization programmes with eugenic aims. Canadian compulsory sterilization operated via the same overall mechanisms of institutionalization, judgement, and surgery as the American system. However, one notable difference is in the treatment of non-insane criminals. Canadian legislation never allowed for punitive sterilization of inmates.

Czechoslovakia and the Czech Republic

Czechoslovakia carried out a policy to sterilize some Roma women, starting in 1973. In various cases the sterilization was agreed upon, often in exchange for social welfare benefits or was given by the lack of education. The dissidents of the Charter 77 denounced it in 1977–78 as a "genocide", but the practice continued through the Velvet Revolution of 1989. A 2005 report by the Czech government's independent ombudsman, Otakar Motejl, identified dozens of cases of coercive sterilization between 1979 and 2001, and called for criminal investigations and possible prosecution against several health care workers and administrators.

Germany

One of the first acts by Adolf Hitler after achieving total control over the German state was to pass the Law for the Prevention of Hereditarily Diseased Offspring (*Gesetz zur Verhütung erbkranken Nachwuchses*) in July 1933. The law was signed in by Hitler himself, and over 200 eugenic courts were created specifically as a result of the law. Under the German law, all doctors in the Reich were required to report patients of theirs who were mentally retarded, mentally ill (including schizophrenia and manic depression), epileptic, blind, deaf, or physically deformed, and a steep monetary penalty was imposed for any patients who were not properly reported. Individuals suffering from alcoholism or Huntington's Disease could also be sterilized. The individual's case was then presented in front of a court of Naziofficials and public health officers who would review their medical records, take testimony from friends and colleagues, and eventually decide whether or not to order a sterilization operation performed on the individual, using force if necessary. Though not explicitly covered by the law, 400 mixed-race "Rhineland Bastards" were also sterilized beginning in 1937.

By the end of World War II, over 400,000 individuals were sterilized under the German law and its revisions, most within its first four years of being enacted. When the issue of compulsory sterilization was brought up at the Nuremberg trials after the war, many Nazis defended their actions on the matter by indicating that it was the United States itself from whom they had taken inspiration. The Nazis had many other eugenics-inspired racial policies, including their "euthanasia" programme in which around 70,000 people institutionalized or suffering from birth defects were killed.

Japan

In the first part of the Showa era, Japanese governments promoted increasing the number of healthy Japanese, while simultaneously decreasing the number of people suffering mental retardation, disability, genetic disease and other conditions that led to inferiority in the Japanese gene pool.

The *Leprosy Prevention laws* of 1907, 1931 and 1953, permitted the segregation of patients in sanitariums where forced abortions and sterilization were common and authorized punishment of patients "disturbing peace". Under the colonial Korean *Leprosy prevention ordinance*, Korean patients were also subjected to hard labour.

The *Race Eugenic Protection Law* was submitted from 1934 to 1938 to the Diet. After four amendments, this draft was promulgated as a *National Eugenic Law* in 1940 by the Konoegovernment. According to Matsubara Yoko, from 1940 to 1945, sterilization was done to 454 Japanese persons under this law.

According to the *Eugenic Protection Law* (1948), sterilization could be enforced on criminals "with genetic predisposition to commit crime", patients with genetic diseases such as total colour-blindness, hemophilia, albinism and ichthyosis, and mental affections such as schizophrenia, manic-depression and epilepsy. The mental sicknesses were added in 1952.

India

India's state of emergency between 1975 and 1977 included a family planning initiative that began in April 1976 through which the government hoped to lower India's ever increasing population. This programme used propaganda and monetary incentives to convince citizens to get sterilized. People who agreed to get sterilized would receive land, housing, and money or loans.

Because of this programme, thousands of men received vasectomies and even more women received tubal ligations. However, the programme focused more on sterilizing women than men. An article in The New York Times entitled "For Sterilization, Target Is Women" states, "There were 114,426 vasectomies in India in 2002-03, and 4.6 million tubal ligations, the analogous operation on women, though ligation is a more complicated operation." Despite the fact that sterilizing men is a more simple procedure, the government still chose to focus on sterilizing women instead. Son of the Prime Minister at the time Indira Gandhi, Sanjay Gandhi was largely blamed for what turned out to be a failed programme. A strong backlash against any initiative associated with family planning followed the highly controversial programme, which continues into the 21st century.

China

In 1978, Chinese authorities became concerned with the possibility of a baby boom that the country could not handle, and they initialized the one-child policy. In order to effectively deal with the complex issues surrounding childbirth, the Chinese government placed great emphasis on family planning. Because this was such an important matter, the government felt it needed to be standardized and so to this end laws were introduced in 2002. These laws uphold the basic tenets of what was previously put into practice, outlining the rights of the individuals and outlining what the Chinese government can and cannot do to enforce policy.

However, recently accusations have been raised from groups such as Amnesty International, who have claimed that practices of compulsory sterilization have been occurring for people who have already reached their one child quota. These practices run contrary to the stated principles of the law, and seem to differ on a local level. An especially egregious example, according to Amnesty International, has been occurring in Puning City, Guangdong Province. The stated goal of the sterilization drive in this city in China was to meet with family planning targets that were outlined by the government in the Population and Family Planning Law of 2002. This drive, also known as the Iron Fist Campaign, also is said to have used coercive methods in order to ensure that close to 10,000 women were sterilized, including detaining elderly family members.

The Chinese Government does not seem to be unaware of these discrepancies in policy implementation on a local level. For example, The National Population and Family Planning Commission put forth in a statement that, "Some persons concerned in a few counties and townships of Linyi did commit practices that violated law and infringed upon legitimate rights and interests of citizens while conducting family planning work." This statement comes in reference to some charges of forced sterilization and abortions in Linyi city of Shandong Province. However, it remains unclear to what extent the government has prosecuted or disciplined the officials in charge of family planning in the country.

Peru

In Peru, President Alberto Fujimori (in office from 1990–2000) has been accused of genocide and crimes against humanity as a result of a sterilization programme put in place by his administration. Peru put in place a programme of forced sterilizations against indigenous people (essentially the Quechuas and the Aymaras), in the name of a "public health plan", presented July 28, 1995. The plan was principally financed using funds from USAID (36 million dollars), the Nippon Foundation, and later, the United Nations Population Fund (UNFPA).

On September 9, 1995, Fujimori presented a Bill that would revise the "General Law of Population", in order to allow sterilization. Several contraceptive methods were also legalized, all measures that were strongly opposed by the Roman Catholic Church, as well as the Catholic organization Opus Dei. In February 1996, the World Health Organization (WHO) itself congratulated Fujimori for his plan to control demographic growth.

On February 25, 1998, a representative for USAID testified before the U.S. government's House International Relations Committee, to address controversy surrounding Peru's programme. He indicated that the government of Peru was making important changes to the programme, in order to:

- Discontinue their campaigns in tubal ligations and vasectomies.
- Make clear to health workers that there are no provider targets for voluntary surgical contraception or any other method of contraception.
- Implement a comprehensive monitoring programme to ensure compliance with family planning norms and informed consent procedures.
- Welcome Ombudsman Office investigations of complaints received and respond to any additional complaints that are submitted as a result of the public request for any additional concerns.
- Implement a 72 hour "waiting period" for people who choose tubal ligation or vasectomy. This waiting period will occur between the second counseling session and surgery.
- Require health facilities to be certified as appropriate for performing surgical contraception as a means to ensure that no operations are done in makeshift or substandard facilities.

In September 2001, Minister of Health Luis Solari launched a special commission into the activities of the Voluntary Surgical Contraception, initiating a Parliamentary commission tasked with enquiring into the "irregularities" of the programme, and to put it on an acceptable footing. In July 2002, its Final Report ordered by the

Minister of Health revealed that between 1995 and 2000, 331,600 women were sterilized, while 25,590 men submitted to vasectomies. The plan, which had the objective of diminishing the number of births in areas of poverty within Peru, was essentially directed at the indigenous people living in deprived areas (areas often involved in internal conflicts with the Peruvian government, as with the Shining Path guerilla group). Deputy Dora Núñez Dávila made the accusation in September 2003 that 400,000 indigenous people were sterilized during the 1990s. Documents proved that President Fujimori was informed, each month, of the number of sterilizations done, by his former Ministers of Health, Eduardo Yong Motta (1994–96), Marino Costa Bauer (1996–1999) and Alejandro Aguinaga (1999–2000). A study by sociologist Giulia Tamayo, *Nada Personal* (in English: Nothing Personal), showed that doctors were required to meet quotas. According to *Le Monde diplomatique*, "tubal ligation festivals" were organized through programme publicity campaigns, held in the *pueblos jóvenes* (in English: shantytowns). In 1996 there were, according to official statistics, 81,762 tubal ligations performed on women, with a peak being reached the following year, with 109,689 ligatures, then only 25,995 in 1998.

On October 21, 2011, Peru's Attorney General José Bardales decided to reopen an investigation into the cases, which had been halted in 2009 under the statute of limitations, after the Inter-American Commission on Human Rights ruled that Peru's sterilization programme involved crimes against humanity, which are not time-limited.

Sweden

In 1997, following the publication of articles by Maciej Zaremba in the *Dagens Nyheter* daily, widespread attention was given to the fact that Sweden once operated a strong sterilization programme, which was active primarily from the mid 1930s until the 1970s. A governmental commission was set up, and finished its inquiry in 2000.

The eugenistic legislation was enacted in 1934 and was formally abolished in 1976. According to the 2000 governmental report, 21,000 were estimated to have been forcibly sterilized, 6,000 were coerced into a 'voluntary' sterilization while the nature of a further 4,000 cases could not be determined. However, the 40,000 or so socio-medical cases are contested, and Zaremba and others argue that they were more in the interest of society than individual women. The Swedish state subsequently paid out damages to victims who contacted the authorities and asked for compensation.

The programme included all known criteria for sterilization, including a loosely phrased "social" indiciation. In 1922 the State Institute of Racial Biology was founded in Uppsala and in 1927 Parliament began to deal with the first legal provisions on sterilisation. A new draft was produced in 1932, already taking into account sterilisation for general socio-prophylactic reasons, and even without the consent of the person concerned. The draft was adopted in 1934. Another law, passed in 1941, was more far reaching, included a social indication and did not include any age of consent limit.

From 1950, the number of eugenic sterilisations under the 1941 legal provisions gradually decreased. It is possible but not proven that the Swedish sterilizations targeted travellers. These were sometimes viewed as a separate race or ethnic group. The Swedish Racial Hygiene Society had been founded in Stockholm in 1909, and the 1934 works by Alva and Gunnar Myrdal was very significant in promoting the eugenic tendencies in practical politics. The authors theorized that the best solution for the Swedish welfare state ("folkhem") was to prevent at the outset the hereditary transfer of undesirable characteristics that caused the individual affected to become sooner or later a burden on society. The authors therefore proposed a "corrective social reform" under which sterilisation was to prevent "unviable individuals" from spreading their undesirable traits.

In Sweden, sterilization is only compulsory before sex change. This last compulsory sterilization has been criticized by several political parties in Sweden. The Christian Democrats is the only party in the Parliament of Sweden that is in favour of keeping compulsory sterilization.

Switzerland

In October 1999, Margrith von Felten suggested to the National Council of Switzerland in the form of a general proposal to adopt legal regulations that would enable reparation for persons sterilised against their will. According to the proposal, reparation was to be provided to persons who had undergone the intervention without their consent or who had consented to sterilisation under coercion. According to Margrith von Felten:

The history of eugenics in Switzerland remains insufficiently explored. Research programmes are in progress. However, individual studies and facts are already available. For example:

The report of the Institute for the History of Medicine and Public Health "Mental Disability and Sexuality. Legal Sterilisation in the Vaud Canton between 1928 and 1985" points out that coercive sterilisations took place until the 1980s. The act on coercive sterilisations of the Vaud Canton was the first law of this kind in the European context.

Hans Wolfgang Maier, head of the Psychiatric Clinic in Zurich pointed out in a report from the beginning of the century that 70% to 80% of terminations were linked to sterilisation by doctors. In the period from 1929 to 1931, 480 women and 15 men were sterilised in Zurich in connection with termination.

Following agreements between doctors and authorities such as the 1934 "Directive For Surgical Sterilisation" of the Medical Association in Basle, eugenic indication to sterilisation was recognised as admissible.

A statistical evaluation of the sterilisations performed in the Basle women's hospital between 1920 and 1934 shows a remarkable increase in sterilisations for a psychiatric indication after 1929 and a steep increase in 1934, when a coercive sterilisation act came into effect in nearby National Socialist Germany. A study by the Swiss Nursing School in Zurich, published in 1991, documents that 24 mentally-disabled women aged between 17 and 25 years were sterilised between 1980 and 1987. Of these 24 sterilisations, just one took place at the young woman's request.

Having evaluated sources primarily from the 1930s (psychiatric files, official directives, court files, etc.), historians have documented that the requirement for free consent to sterilisation was in most of cases not satisfied. Authorities obtained the "consent" required by the law partly by persuasion, and partly by enforcing it through coercion and threats. Thus the recipients of social benefits were threatened with removal of the benefits, women were exposed to a choice between placement in an institution or sterilisation, and abortions were permitted only when women simultaneously consented to sterilisation.

More than fifty years after ending the National Socialist dictatorship in Germany, in which racial murder, euthanasia and coerced sterilisations belonged to the political programme, it is clear that eugenics, with its idea of "life unworthy of life" and "racial purity" permeated even democratic countries. The idea that a "healthy nation" should be achieved through targeted medical/social measures was designed and politically implemented in many European countries and in the U.S.A in the first half of this century. It is a policy incomparable with the inconceivable horrors of the Nazi rule; yet it is clear that authorities and the medical community were guilty of the methods and measures applied, i.e. coerced sterilisations, prohibitions of marriages and child removals – serious violations of human rights. Switzerland refused, however, to vote a reparations Act.

United States

The United States was the first country to concertedly undertake compulsory sterilization programmes for the purpose of eugenics. The heads of the programme were avid believers in eugenics and frequently argued for their programme. It was shut down due to ethical problems. The principal targets of the American programme were the mentally retarded and the mentally ill, but also targeted under many state laws were the deaf, the blind, people with epilepsy, and the physically deformed. According to the activist Angela Davis, Native Americans, as well as African-American women were sterilized against their will in many states, often without their knowledge while they were in a hospital for other reasons (e.g. childbirth). Some sterilizations took place in prisons and other penal institutions, targeting criminality, but they were in the relative minority. In the end, over 65,000 individuals were sterilized in 33 states under state compulsory sterilization programmes in the United States.

The first state to introduce a compulsory sterilization bill was Michigan, in 1897 but the proposed law failed to garner enough votes by legislators to be adopted. Eight years later Pennsylvania's state legislators passed a sterilization bill that was vetoed by the governor.Indiana became the first state to enact sterilization legislation in 1907, followed closely by Washington and California in 1909. Sterilization rates across the country were relatively low (California being the sole exception) until the 1927 Supreme Court case *Buck v. Bell* which legitimized the forced sterilization of patients at a Virginia home for the mentally retarded. The number of sterilizations performed per year increased until another Supreme Court case, *Skinner v. Oklahoma,* 1942, complicated the legal situation by ruling against sterilization of criminals if the equal protection clause of the constitution was violated. That is, if sterilization was to be performed, then it could not exempt white-collar criminals.

Most sterilization laws could be divided into three main categories of motivations: *eugenic* (concerned with heredity), *therapeutic* (part of an even-then obscure medical theory that sterilization would lead to vitality), or *punitive* (as a punishment for criminals), though of course these motivations could be combined in practice and theory (sterilization of criminals could be both punitive and eugenic, for example). *Buck v. Bell* asserted only that eugenic sterilization was constitutional, whereas *Skinner v. Oklahoma* ruled specifically against punitive sterilization. Most operations only worked to prevent reproduction (such as severing the *vas deferens* in males), though some states (Oregon and North Dakota in particular) had laws which called for the use of castration. In general, most sterilizations were performed under *eugenic* statutes, in state-run psychiatric hospitals and homes for the mentally disabled. There was never a federal sterilization statute, though eugenicist Harry H. Laughlin, whose state-level "Model Eugenical Sterilization Law" was the basis of the statute affirmed in *Buck v. Bell,* proposed the structure of one in 1922.

After World War II, public opinion towards eugenics and sterilization programmes became more negative in the light of the connection with the genocidal policies of Nazi Germany, though a significant number of sterilizations continued in a few states until the early 1960s. The Oregon Board of Eugenics, later renamed the Board of Social Protection, existed until 1983, with the last forcible sterilization occurring in 1981. The U.S. commonwealth Puerto Rico had a sterilization programme as well. Some states continued to have sterilization laws on the books for much longer after that, though they were rarely if ever used. California sterilized more than any other state by a wide margin, and was responsible for over a third of all sterilization operations. Information about the California sterilization programme was produced into book form and widely disseminated by eugenicists E.S. Gosney and Paul B. Popenoe, which was said by the government of Adolf Hitler to be of key importance in proving that large-scale compulsory sterilization programmes were feasible. In recent years, the governors of many states have made public apologies for their past programmes beginning with Virginia and followed by Oregon and California. None have offered to compensate those sterilized, however, citing that few are likely still living (and would of course have no affected offspring) and that inadequate records remain by which to verify them. At least one compensation case, *Poe v. Lynchburg Training School & Hospital* (1981), was filed in the courts on the grounds that the sterilization law was unconstitutional. It was rejected because the law was no longer in effect at the time of the filing. However, the petitioners were granted some compensation as the stipulations of the law itself, which required informing the patients about their operations, had not been carried out in many cases.

The 27 states where sterilization laws remained on the books (though not all were still in use) in 1956 were: Arizona, California, Connecticut, Delaware, Georgia, Idaho, Indiana, Iowa, Kansas, Maine, Michigan, Minnesota, Mississippi, Montana, Nebraska, New

Hampshire, North Carolina, North Dakota, Oklahoma, Oregon, South Carolina, South Dakota, Utah, Vermont, Virginia, West Virginia, Wisconsin.

Uzbekistan

According to reports, as of 2012 forced and coerced sterilization are current Government policy in Uzbekistan for women with two or three children, as a means of imposing population control and to improve maternal mortality rates. In November 2007 a report by the United Nations Committee Against Torture reported that "the large number of cases of forced sterilization and removal of reproductive organs of women at reproductive age after their first or second pregnancy indicate that the Uzbek government is trying to control the birth rate in the country" and noted that such actions were not against the national Criminal Code, in response to which the Uzbek delegation to the associated conference was "puzzled by the suggestion of forced sterilization, and could not see how this could be forced."

Reports of forced sterilizations, hysterectomies and IUD insertions first emerged in 2005, although it is reported that the practice originated in the late 1990s, with reports of a secret degree dating from 2000. The current policy was allegedly instituted by Islam Karimov under Presidential Decree PP-1096, *On additional measures to protect the health of the mother and child, the formation of a healthy generation* which came into force in 2009. In 2005 Deputy Health Minister Assomidin Ismoilov confirmed that doctors in Uzbekistan were being held responsible for increased birth rates.

Puerto Rico

The United States, the Puerto Rican government, and the medical community began a programme for the mass sterilization of women in Puerto Rico. By 1965, one-third of the female population had been sterilized and Puerto Rican women continued to use female sterilization as a form of birth control due to a lack of knowledge of the irreversible effects. Sterilization was so common that Puerto Rican women labeled it "la operacion", or the operation. The government continued with their plan as stated in a report dated November 1973. The report, entitled "Opportunities for Education, Employment, and Training", was written by an economic policy group backed by the governor of Puerto Rico. This report explains alternatives for decreasing the Puerto Rican working class and a high unemployment rate was noted in the report as Puerto Rico's main problem.

The Puerto Rican government and population was suffering from economic problems, high unemployment rate, and poverty during the

1920's. The United States blamed overpopulation for these problems. Contraception was illegal in the Puerto Rican colony which was largely due to the main religion of Puerto Rico: Catholocism. The Catholic Church teachings state that contraception and sterilization are sins against nature. Therefore, any form of contraception was illegal in Puerto Rico before the late 1930's. In 1937, the United States made contraceptives legal, initiating their plan for population control. A private organization opened twenty-three birth control clinics in 1937 and a bill was signed eliminating the laws making the advertisement of contraceptives and pregnancy prevention services a felony. Another 160 private and public birth control clinics were opened after another bill was signed authorizing the "Commissioner of Health in Puerto Rico to regulate the teaching and dissemination of eugenic principles, including contraception, to health centres and maternal hospitals". Soon after, the United States government passed Law #136 which made sterilization legal for other than strictly medical reasons and advocated picking out the "unfit".

Other Countries

Eugenics programmes including forced sterilization existed in most Northern European countries, as well as other more or less Protestant countries. Some programmes, such as Canada's and Sweden's, lasted well into the 1970s. Other countries that had notably active sterilization programmes include Denmark, Norway, Finland, Estonia, Switzerland, Iceland, and some countries in Latin America (including Panama). In the United Kingdom, Home Secretary Winston Churchill introduced a bill that included forced sterilization. Writer G. K. Chesterton led a successful effort to defeat that clause of the 1913 Mental Deficiency Act.

According to some testimonies, the Soviet Union allegedly imposed forced sterilization on female workers deported from Romania to Soviet labour camps. This is said to have occurred after World War II, when Romania was supposed to supply a reconstruction workforce (according to the armistice convention). However, no court decisions or formal investigations of these allegations are known for the moment.

Conscience Clause (Medical)

Conscience clauses are clauses in laws in some parts of the United States which permit pharmacists, physicians, and other providers of health care not to provide certain medical services for reasons of religion or conscience. Those who choose not to provide services may not be disciplined or discriminated against. The provision is most frequently enacted in connection with issues relating to reproduction, such as abortion, sterilization, contraception, and stem cell based treatments, but may include any phase of patient care.

Responses

Health care providers opposed to abortion or contraception support the clauses because they believe that disciplinary or legal action for refusing to perform services obliges providers to supply services which their moral or religious principles forbid. Reproductive rights organizations, such as Planned Parenthood and NARAL Pro-Choice America, oppose the provision because they maintain that pharmacists, doctors, and hospitals have a professional duty to fulfill patients' legal medical needs, regardless of their own ethical stances. Opponents see conscience clauses as an attempt to limit reproductive rights in lieu of bans struck down by Supreme Court rulings such as Roe v. Wade.

History

The earliest national conscience clause law in the United States, which was enacted immediately following the Supreme Court's decision in Roe v. Wade, applied only to abortion and sterilization. It was sponsored by Senator Frank Church of Idaho. The Church Amendment, passed by the Senate on a vote of 92-1, exempted private hospitals receiving federal funds under the Hill-Burton Act, Medicare and Medicaid from any requirement to provide abortions or sterilizations when they objected on "the basis of religious beliefs or moral convictions." Nearly every state enacted similar legislation by the end of the decade—often with the support of legislators who otherwise supported abortion rights. Supreme Court Justice Harry Blackmun, the author of Roe vs. Wade, endorsed such clauses "appropriate protection" for individual physicians and denominational hospital.

Conscience clauses have been adopted by a number of U.S. states. including Arkansas, Illinois, Indiana, Iowa, Kansas, Kentucky, Louisiana, Maine, Maryland, Massachusetts, Michigan, Mississippi, Pennsylvania, and South Dakota. There are some recent comprehensive reviews of federal and state conscience clause laws across the United States and in select other countries.

The Obama administration has proposed reversing recent additions to the conscience clause enacted by the Bush administration.

Informed Consent

An informed consent clause, although allowing medical professionals not to perform procedures against their conscience, does not allow professionals to give fraudulent information to deter a patient from obtaining such a procedure (such as lying about the risks involved in an abortion to deter one from obtaining one) in order to impose one's belief using deception. These principles were reaffirmed in the Utah Supreme Court's decision in *Wood v. University of Utah Medical Centre* (2002). Commenting on the case, bioethicst Jacob Appel of New York University wrote that "if only a small number of physicians intentionally or negligently withhold information from their patients significant damage is done to the medical profession as a whole" because "pregnant women will no longer know whether to trust their doctors."

Corporate Policy

Some pharmacies in U.S. jurisdictions with conscience clauses, including CVS and Target, allow pharmacists to choose, without penalty, not to dispense birth control pills. Target requires the objecting pharmacist to recommend another Target location that will dispense the medication.

Catholic Doctrine

The conscience clause is widely invoked in Catholic universities, hospitals, and agencies because the Catholic Church opposes abortion, contraceptives, sterilization, and embryonic stem cell treatments. Opponents of related FOCA legislation have interpreted the possible end of the conscience clause as a demand to either "do abortions or close." Archbishop Dolan has said, ""In effect, the president is saying we have a year to figure out how to violate our consciences." However, conscience clauses are sometimes interpreted differently and their use will often depend on the given context.

Contraceptive Implant

A contraceptive implant is a birth control device inserted under the skin by a doctor. The implant is among the most effective birth control methods. After it is inserted it prevents pregnancy by releasing hormones that prevent ovaries from releasing eggs and by thickening cervical mucous. The implant can prevent pregnancy for up to three years. Though it protects against pregnancy, it does not protect against STIs. The costs for implantation range. Brands include:

- Norplant and Jadelle (Norplant II)
- Implanon
- Sino-implant (II) marketed as Zarin, Femplant and Trust
- Nexplanon Implanon replacement
- It is easier to insert than Implanon®.

- It contains barium, which means that it will show up on an X-ray. This may be useful to locate it if it cannot be felt in the future.

Side Effects

Positive:

- It does not interrupt heat of the moment sex
- Women have fewer, lighter periods
- Lasts for up to 3 years, don't have to take it daily
- Can be used while breast feeding
- May lessen typical PMS symptoms

Negative:

For many women, these are not a problem. It is always possible to remove the implant and switch to another form of birth control if the side effects become a problem.

- Irregular bleeding for the first 6–12 months
- Less common: change in appetite, depression, headache, nausea, nervousness, sore breasts.

Chapter 4

Population Policy: Authoritarianism vs. Cooperation

"In politics," said Samuel Taylor Coleridge in 1830, "what begins in fear usually ends in folly." Coleridge is not my favourite poet, but he was, I think, right to point to the blunders we commit out of fear. Something of a folly — indeed more than a folly — is, I shall argue, happening right now through frightened reaction to population growth. Despite noticeable deceleration in recent years, the rates of population increase remain quite high in many parts of the world, and there is an understandable interest in finding ways of bringing down these rates as soon as possible.

This concern calls for serious reflection on what might be the best response to "the population problem." But critical reflection is precisely the response that is missing when policymakers in different parts of the world rush to take direct control of birth decisions of families through authoritarian intervention. There have been several moves in that direction recently — most famously in China, but also in India and elsewhere. This essay is an attempt to examine the issues raised by authoritarian approaches to the population problem and a comparison of those approaches with that of working through cooperation.

There are many complexities in assessing the seriousness of the population problem, and in arriving at sensible policies to be followed. There are enormous diversities of understanding that divide the general public as well as specialists who write on this subject. There are, in fact, two distinct battlegrounds. The first area of disagreement concerns the seriousness of the population problem, covering such issues as the reading of the pressure of population, the possibility of catastrophe that may be generated, the impact of population growth on the growth of incomes and on other economic and social variables, and so on. The second area concerns the effectiveness of different influences through which population growth rates may come down in those countries and regions where they are currently very high. The pros and cons of authoritarian intervention, with which I am mainly concerned here, belong to this second area.

Fundamental Dichotomy

The arguments in the case for and against authoritarian intervention relate to a basic attitudinal difference on the merits of the decisions that the family itself makes. There is, on the one side, an approach reflecting disparagement, which sees the family's decisions as either seriously undisciplined or incurably biassed, and often very wrong for the society as a whole and perhaps even for the respective families themselves. Arguing for a forceful and compulsive intervention from outside the family is a short step from this premise.

In contrast, an alternative approach sees the family's decision-making ability to be basically fine, even though adverse circumstances and external necessities may strongly constrain these decisions. There might, of course, be some divergences between social costs and private ones, but those who take a favourable view of people's ability to think and decide in a socially concerned way tend to expect that these divergences can be much reduced through reflections on social responsibility and the emergence of communal norms on family size. There is also the possibility of reducing the gap between private and social costs through correcting the imperfections of the market and making the prices faced by individuals reflect the social impact of their decisions more fully. It is, of course, true that governmental intervention in the markets and prices can be an indirect route to coercion, especially when the individuals are left with very few real options. But the corrections envisaged are usually much more moderate than that, in a way that would still leave much of the decision-making to the people themselves. In this general approach, the route to rational family planning lies in supporting and empowering those whose lives and responsible agency are most directly involved, and reflecting to them more fully the social consequences of their own decisions.

There is, however, a source of tension in this approach arising from conflicts and inequalities within the family, and this issue will be rather important in the analysis presented here. There can be a clash of interests between male and female members of the family, particularly given their typically asymmetric roles in child care. There can also be tensions between the different age groups and generations, particularly in a "joint family" — for example, the mother-in-law can be much more keen on a larger number of grandchildren than the daughter-in-law, who has to bear much of the burden of this achievement. In examining the intrusion of an outside bureaucracy into the affairs of the family, we must not overlook the divisions and internal tensions within the family. The route of cooperation involves the voluntary collaboration of adult family members in general, but particularly of those whose agency and well-being are most directly involved in these decisions — typically the young women who bear and, to a great extent, rear the children.

In its pure form, the cooperative approach contrasts sharply with the authoritarian one, and the battle between the two schools of thought can be seen plentifully in the literature on this subject. In practice, the contrast tends to be much less sharp and often quite a bit blurred. Nevertheless, various forms of coercion can be seen fairly clearly in the field of birth control in many countries. Sometimes coercion takes a direct form — for example, in the "one child policy" and other legal restrictions in contemporary China, and during Mrs. Indira Gandhi's "emergency period" in India in the mid-1970s. Quite often, however, that route is indirectly pursued, for example through regulations that disqualify parents of more than the specified number children from receiving public benefits of certain kinds, such as housing or government jobs. This has occurred in several countries, including China and some north Indian states. Sometimes the process chosen is "tied" services, whereby public medical attention is offered along with fairly forceful advocacy of birth control. Another form of effective coercion involves the use of uninformed consent of women, when the nature and consequences of the procedure to be used are not fully explained to the participating women. Another variant involves giving financial incentives for sterilization in circumstances that make them quite irresistible for impoverished people. I shall discuss the issue of coercion in its more frank form, but some of the arguments would apply to more concealed and less extreme forms of compulsion as well.

While the collaborative approach works, in general, through the empowerment of the persons directly involved and through increasing their effective freedom, the coercive strategy works through ordering them around and through reducing their freedom to decide. The two outlooks, in their pure forms, could not be further apart.

A Classic Debate

It may be useful to begin with a brief examination of a 200-year-old dispute between Malthus and Condorcet which relates closely to the contrasting approaches just outlined. Even though Malthus is credited with having provided the pioneering analysis of the possibility that population may tend to grow too fast, it was in fact Condorcet, the French mathematician and great Enlightenment thinker, who first presented the core of the scenario that underlies the "Malthusian" analysis of the population problem. Condorcet aired his questions thus:

> But in this progress of industry and happiness, each generation will be called to more extended enjoyments, and in consequence, by the physical constitution of the human frame, to an increase in the number of individuals. Must not there arrive a period then, when these laws, equally necessary, shall counteract each other? When the increase of the number of men surpasses their means of subsistence, the necessary result must be either a continual diminution of happiness and population, a movement truly retrograde, or, at least, a kind of oscillation between good and evil? In societies arrived at this term, will not this oscillation be a constantly subsisting cause of periodical misery?

Malthus took to this analysis of Condorcet, and quoted it with great approval in his famous Essay on population, published in 1798: "Mr. Condorcet's picture of what may be expected to happen when the number of men shall surpass the means of their subsistence is justly drawn." What Malthus did not like was the "solution" that Condorcet foresaw to the diagnosed problem, namely a cooperative response through the reasoned agency of the people themselves. Condorcet predicted the emergence of new norms of smaller family size based on "the progress of reason." He anticipated a time when "the absurd prejudices of superstition will have ceased to corrupt and degrade the moral code by its harsh doctrines," and when people "will know that, if they have a duty towards those who are not yet born, that duty is not to give them existence but to give them happiness." This type of reasoning, buttressed by the expansion of education, especially female education (of which Condorcet was one of the earliest and most vocal advocates) would lead, Condorcet thought, to lower fertility rates and smaller families, which people would choose voluntarily, "rather than foolishly to encumber the world with useless and wretched beings."

Malthus thought this most unlikely. In general, he saw little chance of solving social problems through reasoned decisions by the families involved. As far as the population problem itself was concerned, he was convinced of the inevitability of population outrunning food supply, and in this context, took the limits of food production to be relatively inflexible. And, most relevantly for the topic at hand, Malthus was particularly sceptical of voluntary family planning. While he did refer to "moral restraint" as an alternative way of reducing the pressure of population — alternative, that is, to misery and elevated mortality — he saw little real prospect that such restraint would work voluntarily. His conclusion was that "there is no reason whatever to suppose that anything beside the difficulty of procuring in adequate plenty the necessaries of life should either indispose this greater number of persons to marry early, or disable them from rearing in health the largest families."

It was because of this disbelief in the voluntary route that Malthus identified the need for — indeed the dominance of — a coercive reduction in population growth rates. He thought this would come from natural causes, that is, from what we can call the compulsion of nature. The fall in living standards resulting from population growth would not only increase mortality rates dramatically (what Malthus called "positive checks"), but would also force people, through economic penury, to have smaller families. The basic link in the argument is Malthus's conviction that population growth rate cannot be effectively pulled down by "anything beside the difficulty of procuring in adequate plenty the necessaries of life."

Scepticism about the family's ability to make sensible decisions about fertility can take us in a variety of directions. It led Malthus to oppose the public relief of poverty. Malthus saw the English "poor laws" as contributing greatly to population growth, and having the effect of depressing "the general condition of the poor." The reduction of population growth — through a lower birth rate in addition to an increased death rate — was nature's way of keeping the numbers in check, and public policy could not enhance the human condition, nor make this coercive reduction of birth rate be replaced by a reasoned cooperation of the families themselves.

That tradition of distrusting the voluntary route and of looking for some "solution" that coerces the families to have a smaller number of children has been a characteristic feature of a group of Malthusians and neo-Malthusians over the last two centuries. Sometimes the advocacy of compulsion is simple and straightforward — as in the official Chinese statements on the governmental policy of "one child family" — while in other writings some attempt is made to undermine the issue of coercion by questioning the appropriateness of that diagnosis because of uncertainty as to what "coercion" might mean. There is, without doubt, some uncertainty here, and formally Garrett Hardin is right to point out that "the word 'coercion' is not completely transparent" and that there is an "ambiguity" here. But the end result of that line of reasoning can be, as it often is, to lose the distinction between (1) a big dose of governmental bullying to make people do what they are extremely unwilling to do, and (2) inducing them to take note of the consequences of their own actions, including making corrections of market imperfections when necessary.

Indeed, the classic debate between Condorcet and Malthus remains very relevant today, and as Paul Kennedy has remarked, "This debate between optimists [Godwin, Condorcet] and pessimists [Malthus] has, in one form or another, been with us since then," and "it is even more pertinent today than when Malthus composed his Essay." The contrasting attitudes of coercive and cooperative solutions of the population problem in contemporary arguments relate quite closely to this classical debate.

As a matter of fact, the history of the world since that Malthus-Condorcet debate has not given much comfort to Malthus's point of view. Fertility rates have come down sharply with social and economic development. Some things "beside the difficulty of procuring in adequate plenty the necessaries of life" have made people choose radically smaller families, and the actual scenario — whether in the West or in the successfully developing regions in the rest of the world — has not been far from the one anticipated by Condorcet. The areas where fertility rates are high today are the poorer countries not yet experiencing much development, particularly those that are socially backward in terms of basic education (especially female education), health care, life expectancy, and women's empowerment.

Nevertheless, there has been quite a revival of Malthusian thinking in the recent years. Even the fear that the food supply is about to fall behind the growth of world population has been persistently aired, despite the continual increase in food per head in the world as a whole and in the major underdeveloped regions in particular. It is especially worth noting that the persistent increase in food supply per head has occurred despite a sharply falling relative price of food in the international market (with the consequent reduction in the economic incentive to produce more food). It is not surprising that some of the sharpest increases in food supply per head have occurred in countries such as China and India where the domestic production is less influenced by international prices of food.

There are different forms of neo-Malthusian worries that can be found plentifully in the literature — related to food supply, environmental deterioration, residential overcrowding, etc. — but what characterizes the shared basic approach is distrust in the reasoned agency of people to bring about a change in the circumstances leading to the anticipated threats. While some of the threats are wildly exaggerated — especially in the case of the fear of the food supply running out — many of the concerns are by no means dismissable — particularly in regard to some strains on global and local environment. What is at issue is not the case for worrying about these prospects, which is a sensible thing to do; indeed, Condorcet had done it himself, in that famous passage which was used by Malthus to found his alarmist thesis. What is less sensible is to jump to the conclusion that coercion rather than cooperation is needed to respond to these worrying possibilities.

It is a question of the approach to be taken in understanding how the population issue can be best addressed within the powers of reasoned agency of the people, rather than opting prematurely for a bureaucratic and authoritarian "solution."

The argument for expanding knowledge and opportunity of family planning methods does, of course, remain strong in the poorer countries in the world. This priority is a part of the commitment to expand the freedom of the family to decide on its reproductive behaviour; it is not a component of coercion. Nevertheless, the question can be — and has been — posed as to whether that process would be further helped by actually coercing people to reduce the family size. I shall turn to that question presently, but before that I shall have to consider some general arguments for state intervention in reproductive decisions, which need not be based on Malthusian presumptions.

Consequences, Autonomy, and Family Decisions

The advocacy of force in changing the family's decisions on the number of offspring has sometimes come from modern economists, including the great Swedish economic theorist Knut Wicksell, who combined neo-Malthusian beliefs about the tendency towards overpopulation with elaborate theorization regarding the size of "the optimum population." The general approach of "optimum population" need not, however, be based on Malthusian empirical presumptions, and can be combined with any set of consistent empirical assumptions. Indeed, the idea of the best population size for the society can even be made to incorporate our concern about the processes that may be used to influence reproductive behaviour (starting from any given social state), in addition to the narrowly defined "end results." However, much of the extensive literature on optimum population makes rather simple ethical assumptions that give little room for the importance of freedom and autonomy, and treats decisions about family planning in much the same way as the choice of any other economic or social variable, where the process of decision making is not given anything other than derivative significance.

In this framework, the usual arguments based on "externalities," distributional equity, or informational limitation can be easily unleashed to make out an immediate case for direct intervention by the state in the family's personal decisions about the number of children to have. A family's decision to have one more child could influence the interest — or for that matter the sense of propriety — of other people, and this can yield an "externality" based argument for the state to intervene in the reproductive behaviour of the family. It is precisely this easy translation of interventionist arguments, from standard cost-benefit analysis, that needs close scrutiny in the context of family planning. The subject matter does make a difference.

First, family planning is an intensely private subject in which — to borrow a phrase from John Stuart Mill — there is "no parity" between the family's own direct involvement in its reproductive behaviour, and that of others whose interests or susceptibilities may be indirectly influenced by this family's behaviour. As Jacques Drèze has noted, "We must recognise that, for most of us, 'adding a new person to the world' is first and foremost adding a new person to the family." Furthermore, family planning consists of actions and decisions that are by their very nature deeply intimate, and involve choices in which others need not be given a prima facie say.

Reproductive behaviour is thus a matter that immediately and decisively forms a part of the personal lives of the family members, particularly of the mother — or of the potential mother. This is not an argument to ignore all else, but that "all else" has to be very powerfully contrary to outweigh the general presumption in favour of leaving reproductive behaviour to the family in general and to the woman in particular.

Second, the usual procedures of cost-benefit analysis proceed on the assumption of the preferences of the individuals involved being "fixed" — in particular, uninfluenced by the decision under scrutiny. But, again as Jacques Drèze notes, "The decision to have a child is a decision to change the nature of a family," and it is "a decision about extending love to an as yet unknown person and sharing that person's fate, with all its uncertainties and promise." The standard fixed-preference reasoning misses out on a "recognition of what procreation is about." Once again, this is not a reason to dismiss the possibility that there could nevertheless be a good ground for intervention in reproductive behaviour, but it is an argument for being cautious, and in particular for resisting the temptation to make mechanical translation of interventionist arguments based on fixed-preference models to the field of procreation.

It is reasonable to accept the possibility that there must be some kind of a threshold of influence on other people's interests beyond which state intervention in personal lives might well be plausible. Only a drastic libertarian would reject that possibility without further examination, and we need not embrace that position. But there is a much wider consensus on the need to avoid authoritarian intervention in matters as intimate and personal as reproductive behaviour. In particular, it is not a matter just of fine-tuning conventionally defined costs and benefits: comparing the "costs" to the family members resulting from the violation of their reproductive freedom (given their preferences) with the "benefits" to others (given their interests and desires) that would result from that violation. There are reasons to see the problem rather differently. There are, in particular, grounds to question the status of coercion as a mechanical remedy for "externalities," when the decisions involved are central to personal life, and thus require us to consider the importance of elementary autonomy, personal liberty, and the contingency of our preferences.

Much would thus depend on how disastrous we think a further increase in population might be and how immediate the danger is. I have tried to examine these issues elsewhere both in the global context and specifically for countries in the so-called "Third World." It appears that the dangers, especially in the short run and at the global level, are much exaggerated. But there are certainly reasons for concern in the long run at the global level, and even in the reasonably short run for some local environmental issues. In order to resist the case for coercion, it is not necessary to dispute these worries and apprehensions. It is important, however, to seek a less breathless remedy that pays attention to issues of long-run sustainability as well as the exact process through which the reduction of population growth takes place.

Women's Agency: A Foundational Linkage

This brings us back to the contrast between the coercive and cooperative routes. Do we have any reason to believe that the coercive route would be much more effective and faster than the cooperative route that relies on the agency of the people directly involved? How does the issue of speed relate to the problem of sustainability of what is achieved? Are there indirect effects of coercion that have to be considered in assessing the case for it? I shall address these issues presently, but before that I must examine a basic relationship between women's well-being and their agency that is central to the problem of fertility.

One of the most important facts about fertility and family size is that the lives that are most battered by over-frequent child birth are those of the women who bear these children. This is especially so in the poorer and less developed economies in the world. It is not only the case that at least half a million women die every year from maternity-related causes through afflictions that are entirely preventable, but also hundreds of millions of women are shackled involuntarily to a life of much drudgery and little freedom because of incessant child bearing and rearing.

The impact of persistent child bearing on the freedom and well-being of young women can be very severely negative in the developing countries. The significance of this aspect of the problem requires us to look beyond the family as a decision unit to the specific part that women, particularly young women, may play — or may be allowed to play — in the making of these reproductive decisions. The nature of this role not only includes the power and control that young women may have over these decisions, but also the substantive opportunities they have to consider these problems with adequate assurance, independence, and knowledge.

Women's Empowerment and its Determinants

Over the last couple of decades, the importance of women's power and agency has become more widely recognized, partly as a result of a broadening of the women's movements in developing countries. The focus of attention has moved beyond working towards achieving better treatment for women — a more "square deal" — to noting the importance of women's agency. This relates to a clearer understanding of the role of women as active agents of change — as the dynamic promoters of social transformations that can alter the lives of both women and men. The reach of that agency can be very extensive indeed, and it does of course inter alia include the possibility of reasoned decisions about fertility.

There are different means through which a change in the decisional power of women may come about. The route that has received most attention in the context of fertility decisions is the impact of literacy and schooling of women, partly because of its intuitive plausibility (even Condorcet had pointed to this link 200 years ago), but largely because of the extensive statistical evidence linking women's education (including literacy) and the lowering of fertility, across different countries in the world. Other factors considered include, among others, the involvement of women in so-called "gainful" activities outside the home, the opportunity of women to earn an independent income, the property rights of women, and the general status and standing of women in the social culture.

These connections have been observed within India as well, and the statistical relations between (1) women's education and women's opportunity to earn an outside income, on the one hand, and (2) lower fertility rates, on the other, have been confirmed by several empirical investigations. The most recent — and perhaps the most extensive — study of this connection is provided by an important statistical contribution by Jean Drèze, Anne-Catherine Guio, and Mamta Murthi, dealing with data from the different districts of India in 1981 (the latest year for which adequately detailed data are available). Among all the variables included in the analysis presented by Drèze, Guio, and Murthi, the only ones that have a statistically significant effect on fertility are female literacy and female labour-force participation. The importance of women's agency emerges forcefully from this analysis, especially in comparison with the weaker effects of variables relating to general economic progress.

The powerful evidence in favour of these statistical relations has to be distinguished from the social and cultural accounting of these influences, including the common account — not implausible in itself — that both education and outside earning increase a woman's autonomy. There are indeed many different ways in which school education may enhance a young woman's decisional power within the family: through its effect on her social standing, her ability to be independent, her power to articulate, her knowledge of the outside world, her skill in influencing group decisions, and so on. Similar linkages can be suggested for the impact of outside earning on a young woman's decisional control. But plausibility at this general level must not be identified with taking these connections as established. Contrary arguments, disputing these links, can — and have — also been presented, and this is a subject of much controversy in India at this time. More sophisticated ways of characterizing women's autonomy have been suggested, with a more complex linkage to the fertility issue. Some have questioned whether female schooling does, in fact, enhance women's autonomy. Alternative explanations of the observed statistical relations between women's education and lower fertility have also been suggested — for example, the possibility that men who want a smaller number of children may prefer to marry educated women.

It has also been argued that the role of school education as a force for social change may have been oversold. This line of reasoning has a special appeal to many people in positions of influence and power in India, given the predilection of Indian upper classes to dismiss the importance of schooling for the lower order. Not only is school education, especially of girls, one of the most neglected social objectives in India, the Indian upper classes have a long record of being extremely suspicious of the value of basic education for the masses. Despite the promise made by the Indian political leaders before independence to make India fully literate with great rapidity, things have moved with remarkable slowness in this field, in contrast with speedy expansion of governmental commitment in many other areas. Even today only half the adult Indian population is literate, and two-thirds of the women remain absolutely illiterate. The upper class politicians who make up the bulk of the leadership of the major political parties in India — both in office and in opposition — seem to find it perfectly bearable that a default of this magnitude has been allowed to occur and that it is not being remedied with any speed.

The general value of women's education is a much broader subject than its role in enhancing female autonomy or in reducing fertility — potentially important as these connections might be. Female education can still be one of the most important priorities in Indian social change, even if the scepticism about its role in strengthening the autonomy of young women, or in reducing fertility rates, were to be entirely vindicated.

This has to be asserted with some force, given the history of neglect of school education — especially of girls — in India, and given the social forces that sustain that neglect — and which tend to welcome, with open arms, any ground for scepticism regarding the importance of school education for the masses. Having said this, it cannot, of course, be denied that the questions being raised are serious and deserve careful scrutiny. However, if the scepticism were to be sustained, it would not be adequate merely to dispute the standard "story" that goes with the widely observed statistical relations; it would be also necessary to provide empirically confirmable, and not just speculative, alternative explanations of the observed statistical links, especially between female education and fertility.

If this complex issue were to be pursued more fully, it would also be important to distinguish between different aspects of this problem. In particular, it would be necessary to pursue the distinction between:

(1) women's power to make decisions in different fields (fertility decisions constitute one field among many — autonomy covers other areas as well);

(2) women's direct decision-making roles vis-à-vis the influencing that can occur through more indirect routes;

(3) the power of younger women — whose lives are most directly affected by fertility decisions — vis-à-vis older women in the family;

(4) the congruence and conflicts of interests and opinions within the family which may make the independent agency of younger women less or more crucial; and

(5) women's absolute power to decide on these matters vis-à-vis their relative power compared with others in the family (or outside it).

However, for the purpose of the arguments presented here, it is not crucial to resolve all these different issues. Nor is it necessary to determine exactly how — and precisely the extent to which — women's education (or outside employment, or property rights, or political participation) will influence women's autonomy or the fertility rates. There is ample evidence to indicate that fertility rates tend to come down quite sharply when some of these predisposing social conditions are changed. The important point to note is that authoritarian intervention and bureaucratic denial of reproductive freedom are not the only routes to lower fertility, and reduction can occur with shifts in decisional procedures within the family.

The case of Kerala, the most socially advanced state in India, is particularly worth noting here, because of its remarkable success in fertility reduction based on women's agency. While the total fertility rate (a measure of the average number of children born per woman) for India as a whole is still as high as 3.7, Kerala fertility has now fallen below the "replacement level" to 1.8 — even lower than China's fertility rate of 2.0. There is considerable evidence that Kerala's high level of female education has been particularly influential in bringing about the decline in birth rate, from 44 per thousand in 1951-61 to 18 by 1991.29 Furthermore, the importance of female agency roles and literacy in the reduction of mortality rates leads to another, more indirect, route through which women's agency — including female literacy — may have helped to reduce birth rates: via reducing mortality rates. Kerala also has some other favourable features for women's empowerment and agency, including a greater recognition, by legal tradition, of women's property rights for a substantial and influential part of the community.

What Does Coercion Achieve?

Coercive measures are often advocated for reducing fertility rates in the poorer countries. They have received attention in international debates and have been favoured by some population pressure groups. That route was explicitly rejected at the International Conference on Population and Development at Cairo last year, but that rejection has not made the issue go away. Coercion persists in various forms (not least in India), and it figures, directly or indirectly, in a great many proposals that address the population problem.

In the context of discussing the imperative need to reduce birth rates in the world, China's achievement in cutting down fertility rates over a short period through rather Draconian measures receives understandable admiration. It is often suggested, by particular pressure groups, that India should emulate China in this important area. The fear of an impending crisis makes many policy advocates seek forceful measures in the Third World for coercing people to have fewer children, and despite criticism from diverse quarters, including women's groups, China's attempts in that direction have received much attention and praise. A comparison of China's and India's experiences is thus of direct relevance to the current topic.

Fairly Draconian measures have certainly been used in China to force the birth rate down. Coercive methods such as the "one child policy" have been tried in large parts of China since the reforms of 1979. Also, the government often refuses to offer housing and related benefits to families with too many children — thus penalizing the children as well as the dissident adults. By 1992 the Chinese birth rate had fallen sharply to 19 per thousand, compared with 29 per thousand in India, and 37 per thousand for the average of poor countries other than China and India. China's total fertility rate is now 2.0, just below the "replacement level" of around 2.1, and much below India's 3.7 and the weighted average of 4.9 for low-income countries other than China and India.

How good a solution is this to the population problem? There are several problems to consider here. First, the lack of freedom associated with this approach is a major social loss in itself. Human rights groups and women's organizations in particular have been especially concerned with the lack of reproductive freedom involved in any coercive system.

Second, aside from the fundamental issue of individual freedom, there are specific consequences to consider in evaluating compulsory birth control. Coercion works by making people do things they would not freely choose to do; if they would have done something anyway, there would be no need to coerce them. The social consequences of such compulsion, including the ways in which an unwilling population tends to react when it is coerced, can often be quite terrible. For example, the demands for a "one child family" can lead to the neglect — or worse — of infants, thereby increasing the infant mortality rate. Also, in a country with a strong preference for male children — a characteristic shared by China with India and many other countries in Asia and North Africa — a policy of allowing only one child per family can easily be particularly detrimental for girls; for example, in the form of fatal neglect of female children. This, it appears, is exactly what has happened on a fairly large scale in China.

Third, it is not by any means clear how much additional reduction in the fertility rate has actually been achieved through these coercive methods. It is reasonable to accept that many of China's longstanding social and economic programmes have been valuable in reducing fertility, including those that have expanded education (for women as well as men), made health care more generally available, provided more job opportunities for women, and stimulated rapid economic growth. These factors would themselves have tended to help in the reduction in the birth rate, and it is not clear how much "extra lowering" of fertility rates has been achieved in China through compulsion. For example, we can check how many countries in the world which match (or outmatch) China in life expectancy achievements, female literacy rates, and female participation in the labour force actually have a higher fertility rate than China does. Comparing all the countries in the world for which data are given in the World Development Report 1994, there are only three such countries: Jamaica (2.7), Thailand (2.2), and Sweden (2.1) — and the fertility rates of two of them are not materially different from China's figure of 2.0. It is thus not really clear what the extra contribution of coercion is in reducing fertility in China. The authoritarian admirers of China give it too little credit for its cooperative and supportive programmes, while falling for premature admiration of its coercive practices.

This is not to deny that China has, in fact, achieved something in its birth control programme that India has not been able to do. In terms of national averages, it is easy to see that China with its low fertility rate of 2.0 has got population growth under control in a way that India, with its average fertility of 3.7, simply has not achieved. The point to note here is that we would expect the fertility rate to be much lower in China given its higher percentage of female literacy (almost twice as high as India's), higher life expectancy (nearly 10 years more), larger female involvement in gainful employment (three-quarters more, in terms of share of the total labour force), and so on. The question to ask, therefore, is the difficult "counterfactual" one of the likely results that would have been observed in India had it done more in these supportive areas, to expand the possibility of cooperative reduction of fertility rates. This is, of course, a highly speculative question, but perhaps not entirely, since there are areas within India that have done much more than the Indian average.

In particular, the state of Kerala does provide an interesting comparison with China, since it too enjoys high levels of basic education, health care, and so on. Kerala's birth rate of 18 per thousand is actually lower than China's 19 per thousand, and this has been achieved without any compulsion by the state. Kerala's fertility rate is 1.8 for 1991, compared with China's 2.0 for 1992. This is in line with what we could expect through progress in factors that help voluntary reduction in birth rates. Kerala has a higher adult female literacy rate (86 per cent) than China (68 per cent). In fact, the female literacy rate is higher in Kerala than in every single province in China. Also, in comparison with male and female life expectancies at birth in China of 68 and 71 years, the 1991 figures for Kerala's life expectancy are 69 and 74 years, respectively. Further, women have played an important role in Kerala's economic and political life, and historically, also in property relations and educational movements.

It is also worth noting that since Kerala's low fertility has been achieved voluntarily, there is no sign of the adverse effects that were noted in the case of China — for example, heightened female infant mortality and widespread abortion of female foetuses. Kerala's infant mortality rate (16 for girls, 17 for boys) is much lower than China's (33 for girls, 28 for boys), even though both regions had similar infant mortality rates around the time of the introduction of the one-child policy in China. Further, while in China the infant mortality rate is lower for males (28) than for females (33), in Kerala the opposite is the case, much in line with what is observed in the more advanced countries.

It is also necessary to examine the claim in support of compulsory birth control programmes that the speed with which fertility rates can be cut down through coercive means is very high; in contrast, the voluntary processes are expected to be inherently slower. The world, we are told, does not have the time to spare. But this piece of generalization is not supported by Kerala's experience either. Its birth rate has fallen from 44 per thousand in the 1950s to 18 by 1991 — a decline no less fast than that in China. It could, of course, be argued that looking at this very long period does not do justice to the effectiveness of the "one-child family" and other coercive policies that were introduced in 1979, and that we ought really to compare what has happened between 1979 and now.

Kerala, in fact, had a higher fertility rate than China in 1979 (3.0 as opposed to China's 2.8), and by 1991 its fertility rate of 1.8 is as much below China's 2.0 as it had been above it in 1979. Despite the added "advantage" of the one-child policy and other coercive measures, the Chinese fertility rate seems to have fallen more slowly than in Kerala.

Another Indian state, Tamil Nadu, had an even faster fall, from 3.5 in 1979 to 2.2 in 1991. Tamil Nadu has had an active, but cooperative, family planning programme, and it could use for this purpose a comparative good position in terms of social achievements within India: the third highest literacy rate among the major Indian states, high female participation in gainful employment, and low infant mortality (also third among major states in both respects). Coercion of the type employed in China has not been used either in Tamil Nadu or in Kerala, and both have achieved much faster declines in fertility than China has achieved since it introduced the "one child policy" and the related measures.

Within India, contrasts between the records of Indian states offer some further insights on this subject. While Kerala and Tamil Nadu have radically reduced fertility rates, other states in the so-called "northern heartland" (such as Uttar Pradesh, Bihar, Madhya Pradesh, and Rajasthan) have much lower levels of education, especially female education, and of general health care. These states all have high fertility rates — between 4.4 and 5.1.39 This is in spite of a persistent tendency in those states to use heavy-handed methods of family planning, including some coercion (in contrast with the more "collaborative" approach used in Kerala and Tamil Nadu). The regional contrasts within India strongly argue for collaboration (based inter alia on the active and educated participation of women), as opposed to coercion.

The Temptations of Coercion

While India has managed, with a few exceptions, to escape falling for the enticement of seeking to coerce its way to success in the field of family planning, it is clear that this prospect greatly attracts many activists in India. In the middle 1970s, the government of India, under Indira Gandhi's leadership, tried a good deal of compulsion in this field. The northern states, as was mentioned earlier, have various regulations and conventions that force family control measures, particularly in the irreversible form of sterilization, often of women.

Even when coercion is not part of official policy, the government's firm insistence on "meeting the family-planning targets" often leads administrators and health-care personnel at different levels to resort to all kinds of pressure tactics that come close to compulsion. Examples of such tactics include verbal threats, making sterilization a condition of eligibility for anti-poverty programmes, depriving mothers of more than two children of maternity benefits, reserving certain kinds of health care services to persons who have been sterilized, and forbidding persons who have more than two children from contesting panchayat elections.

It is quite extraordinary that the last measure — recently introduced in Rajasthan and Haryana — has been widely praised, even though it involves a strong violation not only of personal liberty but also of basic democratic rights. Even the government's draft National Population Policy, despite placing emphasis on the need to reject coercive methods, gives support to this measure as one means of meeting the overriding goal of bringing the total fertility rate down to 2.1 by the year 2010. There is a strong possibility of the proposed measure being adopted at the all-India level, and extended to diverse forms of political participation going beyond the contesting of panchayat elections. Indeed, there is proposed legislation now in the Indian parliament that would bar anyone from holding national or state office if he or she has more than two children. The patent unfairness of this proposed regulation has been pointed out by many critics — including its effect of debarring large numbers of leaders of less privileged sections of the Indian community and operating particularly against rural leaders — but the legislation has not yet been withdrawn. The lesson that fertility reduction calls for cooperation and collaboration, rather than compulsion and coercion, has not been at all learned.

The point is sometimes made that in a poor country, it is a mistake to worry too much about the unacceptability of coercion — a luxury that only the rich countries can afford. It is not obvious what this argument is based on. The people who suffer most from these coercive measures are often among the poorest and least privileged in the society. The regulations and the way they are operated are also particularly punitive with respect to women's exercise of reproductive freedom. For example, the assembling of poorer women in sterilization camps, through various kinds of pressures, is a practice of remarkable barbarity and injustice practiced in many rural societies in north India, as the deadline for meeting "sterilization targets" approaches.

It is not clear how the acceptability of coercion to a poor population can be tested except through democratic confrontation. While that testing has not occurred in China, it was indeed attempted in India during "the emergency period" in the seventies when compulsory birth control was tried by Mrs. Gandhi's government, along with suspending various legal rights and civil liberties. The policy of coercion in general — including that in birth control — was overwhelmingly defeated in the general elections that followed. The impoverished electorate of India showed no less interest in voting against authoritarian extremism than it takes in protesting against economic and social inequality. Furthermore, voluntary birth-control programmes in India received, as family-planning experts have noted, a severe set-back from that brief programme of compulsory sterilization, since people had become deeply suspicious of the entire family-planning movement. Aside from having little immediate impact on fertility rates, the coercive measures of the emergency period were, in fact, followed by a long period of stagnation in the birth rate, which only ended in 1985.

Since the advocacy of coercion, in different forms, has been growing in India, it is important to emphasize that it achieves little and destroys a lot. It does not seem to work faster than what can happen through the cooperative route, and its other consequences, including side effects, can be quite horrendous. The alternative is to facilitate ways of relying on those whose well-being and agency are most directly involved, particularly young women. This has worked elsewhere, and there is no reason why it will not work in India as well.

To some extent, it is already happening in some parts of India, and these parts are being a lot more successful than the states which are falling for coercive measures. Cooperation can contribute something that coercion cannot provide.

Abortion Law and the Unregulated Business of Female Sex-Selective Abortions in India

The recent media glare on the proliferating practice of female sex-selective abortions is distinctively pro-life-highlighting the disproportionate number of female foetuses aborted. The July 2007 episode of 'We the people' aired on a popular current affairs channel is the most recent instance. The pro-life tone of the current debate is a slippery slope in that respecting the rights of the female child also questions the reproductive choices that women seeking abortions (abortion-seekers) make. This naturally has led to a concern expressed by feminist scholars that the pro-life emphasis may actually undermine the legalisation of abortion itself and thereby diminish reproductive choice(Menon 2004). Interestingly, medical practitioners involved in the debate also take the same view, albeit for different reasons, one of them being profit. However, profits seldom feature in the heated pro-choice/pro-life debate and consequently the evidence that since liberalisation, sex-determination and sex-selective abortions have become big business grossing Rs. 5 billion, according to some estimates. This economic aspect is overlooked in the contemporary debate.

Liberalisation or the process by which tariff barriers between the Indian and the global market for reproductive services are dismantled, give women greater access to sex-determination technology. It is not surprising therefore, that it has also thrown up opportunities for the business of abortions to flourish, and indeed it has. However, profits from abortion represent only one aspect of the possibly, irreversible changes that liberalisation brings about in its wake.

In 2001, India recorded the lowest inter-census growth rate for the past fifty years. A phenomenon widely believed to account for this slow down is the rapidly decreasing female to male child sex ratio, attributed mainly to a significant upward trend in female sex-selective abortions. Population control is a welfare goal of the state and with liberalisation, markets seem to be successfully achieving goals that state-sponsored, birth control policies have failed to achieve. This raises the issue of the extent to which markets should co-opt the welfare functions of the state.

Activists working in the field of reproductive rights have constantly cited the norm 'son preference' as the reason behind the recent upward trend in the practice of female sex –selective abortions. Thus apart from increasing the profits of medical practitioners and going some way in slowing down population growth, markets are also fulfilling the social demand for sons. A demand that requires repeated female sex-selective abortions. This questions the supposed gender-neutral foundations of the market economy.

In addition to overlooking profits, the pro-life/pro-choice debate also overlooks the systemic changes engendered by liberalising the market for reproductive services. In contrast to the individualism inherent in the pro-choice/pro-life debate, this paper argues that the upward trend in sex-selective abortions reveals a systemic problem that can be represented as follows.

The upward trend in female sex-selective abortions: repeated abortions increases profit, fulfils a social demand for sons and furthers a welfare goal: population control, can be represented as a systemic problem. The problem is not entirely about whether (abortion-seekers) are making the right reproductive choices by choosing to abort female foetuses or about the lives of the female foetuses aborted, but about systemic features of the legal, economic and political framework that engender a need for repeated sex-selective abortions. However, this is at a cost. The social (sons), political (welfare goals) and economic (profits) needs are fulfilled at a significant (and unaccounted) cost to maternal health – maternal mortality in India, is the second highest in the world: 22 per cent due to abortions of which 12 per cent are illegal. According to some estimates, this translates into about 660 thousand women dying every year, illegally, even though abortions have been legalised for nearly 30 years (Menon 2004). Further, the upward trend in female sex-selective abortions fulfils disparate needs as described above, and thereby obscures scrutiny of the birth control policies of the state. These erasures or silences in the contemporary debate around the issue form the context in which this paper examines the legal framework that regulates abortions and pre-natal, sex-determination technology (abortion law).

The practice, female foeticide or femicide is a two-stage process. The first stage involves the determination of the sex of the foetus in one of three ways: amniocentesis, chorionic villus sampling, or ultrasonography. The second stage consists of the therapeutic abortion (Patel,1996). Since 1971, abortion law in India was framed with a view to reduce population growth. In the absence or inadequate provision of abortion services by the state, abortion-seekers overwhelmingly access the market for reproductive services to determine foetal sex and to undergo sex-selective abortions.

The following section specifies the problem of sex-selective abortions. This is followed by an analysis of the Medical Termination of Pregnancy Act, 1971. Section four contextualises the preceding legal analysis within the ongoing project of economic liberalisation. This is followed by an analysis of the Pre-Conception and Pre-Natal Diagnostic (Prevention of Misuse) Act 2001. Section 6 sets out the conceptual framework that links the proliferating business of sex-selective abortions with the social demand for sons. This is followed by conclusions.

Female Sex-Selective Abortions: Specifying a Problem

This section sets out the evidence to support the claim that the current increase in female sex-selective abortions is significant and specifies the characteristic features of the current trend. The current trend was inter alia established in a large (1.1 million households) survey in the *Lancet* and published in 2006. It revealed a direct correlation between prenatal sex determination, sex-selective abortions and declining Child Sex Ratio (CSR). (*Lancet* 212)

The CSR is calculated as the number of girls per 1000 boys in the 0-6 age group. Since more boys than girls are born the world over under normal circumstances, there should normally be 950 girls to every 1000 boys. Anything below this indicates that girls are being killed either before or soon after they are born.

In 1991, there were 945 girls to every 1000 boys. However, by 2001, the number of girls in this ratio had fallen to 927. Based on conservative assumptions, the results of the *Lancet* survey established that the practice accounts for about 0.5 million missing female births yearly, translating over the past 2 decades into the abortion of some 10 million female foetuses.' Under natural circumstances, given equal care, girls survive better than boys and so a CSR of 950 girls to 1000 boys usually evens out to about 1005 girls to 1000 boys. The CSR then remains more or less the same through the next few decades and given equal treatment, women are generally even better survivors than men.

For an earlier period, Sen's 'missing women' revealed the widespread practice of female infanticide (Sen, 1992). It appeared that until the 1980's, girl children usually died after they were born not while they were in the womb. By 2001, analysis of the census data show that, though more girl babies are surviving, as by then the adult sex ratio had improved marginally and the female child mortality rate had gone down. However, there was significant evidence that there was a drastic and unprecedented decline in the female babies being born. The declining CSR has characteristic features that indicate an overlap with liberalisation of the market for reproductive services as follows.

In addition, to establishing a link between declining CSR to increased female sex-selective abortions, the *Lancet* survey also identified women with one or two female children as being at high risk of undergoing sex-selective abortions. The category high risk indicates that access to sex-determination technology is required repeatedly and that abortion-seekers (and their families) have to co-operate with medical practitioners to ensure repeated access. Thus, the medical practitioner (and through her increased access to sex-determination technology) seem to be playing a pivotal role in the recent trend. The centrality of the medical practitioner distinguishes this trend from the earlier reported practice of female infanticide, where traditionally village midwives instead of medical practitioners were involved and the practice itself required no access to sex-determination technology.

The second characteristic of declining CSR is its extensive geographic and demographic spread. Geographically, female infanticide was (and still is) prevalent in particular identifiable areas. In a state sponsored survey (in 1995) of rural households in Tamil Nadu, a southern Indian state, of the records of the Primary Health Centres revealed a "female infanticide belt" which accounted for "practically 70 per cent of all female infanticide" (Aravamudan 2007, 24). Further, the practice was confined to identifiable castes in the country, The same 1995 survey revealed that female infanticide was "prevalent among thirty-five 'self-ascribed' caste groups...the Kallars and Gounders, because of their 'numerical and social' dominance were believed to have initiated and legitimised the practice, which gained widespread acceptability especially among the poor."

In contrast, the CSR has declined and significantly across the entire country. In certain states, the CSR had decreased by more than 50 points in 10 years. In Gurdaspur in Punjab for instance, there were just 729 girls to 1000 boys. In Mehsana, in Gujarat the figure stood at 752, in Salem in Tamil Nadu, it was 763 and in Ambala in Haryana 772. At the bottom of the ladder was Shahjahanpur a district in Uttar Pradesh with a CSR of 678 (Aravamudan 2007, 44). In 1991, there were no areas in India where there were less than 800 girls to 1000 boys but by the 2001 census, four states fell below a CSR of 800.

Another significant change is in its class distribution, in that unlike female infanticide, declining CSR is not confined to any lower socio-economic class with low literacy or to rural areas. The 2001 census co-related the practice of prenatal sex-determination followed by selective abortion of female foetuses and socio-economic class. This revealed that CSR's are skewed in higher socio-economic classes and urban areas. South-west Delhi, one of the wealthier districts of the capital New Delhi, for instance, recorded a drastic fall from 904 girls to 1000 boys in 1991 to 845 girls in 2001. This situation has further deteriorated since the census figures were published. The capital city now ranks third lowest after Punjab and Haryana (Aravamudan 2007, 45). This trend was also seen in Chandigarh, Punjab where in the rural areas the number of girls in the CSR was 852 while in the urban areas the number fell to 844. There is also evidence that sex-selective abortions are not isolated, rural phenomena (like female infanticide was) but is fast becoming a proliferating, urban practice. In 1991, there were 948 girls to every 1000 boys in the rural areas. This was close to the benchmark figure. By 2001, this had come down to 934. Meanwhile, the number of girls in urban CSR has fallen from 935 to 903, almost doubling the fall in rural areas. (Aravamudan 2007, 46) The trends reveal that overall the CSR declined more in affluent urban areas where literacy rates are high than in poor areas with low literacy (Aravamudan 2007, 9). Apart from evidence of the widespread practice of sex-selective abortions, another characteristic is that 'the deficit in the number of girls born as second children is more than twice as great in educated than in illiterate mothers' (*Lancet,* 216).

An examination of evidence relating to declining CSR establishes that the medical practitioners play a pivotal role in the current upward trend in female sex-selective abortions. Medical practitioners continue to offer repeated access to sex-determination technology and continue to perform repeated and frequent sex-selective abortions.

This evidence indicates that though both the services are illegal (this is discussed in more detail later), the business of sex-selective abortions flourishes. This combined with the demographic indicators (urbanity, class and literacy) not only makes the problem profoundly economic but also indicates it as one that must be understood in the larger context of economic liberalisation. The pivotal role of the medical practitioner raises concerns about the robustness of the reproductive choices that abortion-seekers make. Are they exercising agency and are these choices autonomous etc.? The following section analyses the law legalising abortions to show that the choices that abortion-seekers make are subject to population control: a larger welfare goal of the state. This reduces the scope of their choices when compared with situations in which their choices are not similarly subject to a larger goal.

The Medical Termination of Pregnancy Act: Engendering a need for Repeated Abortions

This section analyses the Act legalising abortions: the Medical Termination of Pregnancy Act, 1971 (MTP). It clarifies how the Act engenders a need for repeated abortions and how this is fulfilled in its implementation. Briefly, the MTP sets out the conditions under which an abortion-seeker is entitled to an abortion. Only a medical practitioner can make a decision about whether an abortion-seeker fulfils the pre-conditions for a legal abortion. This section begins by specifying the rights that abortion-seekers have under the MTP and then discusses how the law is implemented.

'Reduction in Population Growth'-the overriding, welfare goal of the state, justified in the public good, was the reason why abortion was legalised in 1971. The MTP does not give abortion-seekers a pre-emptory right to an abortion. A pre-emptory right is a right that will trump all other rights (Human Rights is one example of pre-emptive rights). In contrast the MTP makes population control, a consideration that will trump the right of an abortion-seeker to an abortion. Consequently, abortion-seekers cannot avoid giving an explanation set out in the MTP to avail of an abortion. She cannot simply state that it is an unwanted pregnancy. She is required to fulfil the conditions listed in the Act. Here a distinction must be made between a decision to abort and the performance of the procedure itself. Under the MTP, once an abortion –seeker consents to an abortion, *the decision to abort is made by a medical practitioner and not an abortion-seeker.*

In this utilitarian framework of rights, apart from certain exceptions, the state is not involved in policing abortions. The exceptional cases involve coercion or abortions performed without the consent of an abortion-seeker. Sections 312-316 of the Indian Penal Code, 1860 (Code), criminalises miscarriages without consent; death caused by acts done with intent to cause miscarriage or acts done with intent to prevent children being born alive or to cause death after birth. The MTP requires a medical practitioner to decide whether an abortion-seeker fulfils the conditions laid down in the Act. For instance, after twenty weeks a pregnancy can be terminated only if two registered gynaecologist or obstetricians testify that it is immediately necessary to save the life of the pregnant woman, etc. Once the medical practitioner is satisfied that an abortion-seeker fulfils the conditions set out in the MTP, section 3.4(b) imposes a duty on her to perform an abortion only if she obtains the consent of the abortion-seeker.

The rights, liabilities and powers of both the medical practitioners who perform the operations and abortion-seekers arise in their economic transactions (contracts). The contract frames the correlative legal relationship between the medical practitioner and abortion-seekers. The MTP confers on an abortion-seeker a claim-right to an abortion that reciprocally imposes two duties on the medical practitioner. First, to ascertain whether the abortion-seeker fulfils the conditions set out in the MTP and second to ensure that she then consents to the abortion. The contract between an abortion-seeker and a medical practitioner establishes the claim-rights she has and imposes enforceable duties on the medical practitioners (and not on the state). Thus the contractual framework regulates the actual practice of abortions (and not the state).

The MTP does not define consent. The Act however makes it a prerequisite for legal abortions. For the contracts to engender a set of enforceable, binding obligations, the MTP implicitly relies on 'consent' as defined in section 13 of the Indian Contract Act, 1872. Under contract law, "[t]wo or more person are said to consent when they agree upon the same thing in the same sense". Thus the medical practitioner has to do very little to satisfy the requirement of consent in the MTP as the Act vests the medical practitioner with the power to decide when her duty to ensure consent is fulfilled. The MTP ensures that the abortion-seeker consents to an abortion once a medical practitioner satisfies herself that she fulfils the conditions set out in the Act. Consistently, the MTP also vests the medical practitioner with the discretion to define the terms 'health' 'substantive risk', 'seriously handicapped', 'abortion', 'miscarriage', 'termination of pregnancy' etc.

In its implementation, the MTP ensures that an abortion-seeker is liable to having her legal rights and relationships altered by a medical practitioner subject as she is to the powers guaranteed to the latter under its provisions. In other words, the MTP confers on medical practitioners powers. Hohfeld called 'powers' abilities to alter legal rights and duties or change legal relationships. Powers differ from claim-rights because they are not correlative to a duty in someone else. Hohfeld describes them as being correlative to a 'liability' in the other party, by which he means that the party is liable to have his legal situation altered by an exercise of his power.

It is important to note that the MTP does not confer on abortion-seeker powers to alter the legal relationship between herself and the medical practitioner or the latter's rights, a right to avoid paying for a service she provides, for instance. This is because when it comes to abortions, abortion-seekers are subject to the overriding goal of the state: population control, while medical practitioners as market actors are not. This is a foundational inequality in the MTP and one that reveals its utilitarian premise. This utilitarian premise makes increased and frequent abortions instrumental in achieving the larger welfare aims of the state: population control and simultaneously puts medical practitioners in a position whereby they profit from the practice.

In the period between 1971 and 1991, the population control strategy entrenched in the MTP did not have the desired effect: population continued to grow at a steady rate during the thirty-year period after abortions were legalised.

This framework also reflects a vocal and influential school of thought amongst medical practitioners that justify increasing female sex-selective abortions to stem population growth. At a seminar in 1984, a government official for instance, stated that sex determination tests must be allowed since the population problem called for desperate measures. The Head of Obstetrics and Gynaecology at a government general hospital in Bokaro also echoed this sentiment when he argued that the priority is population control by any means. Further that amniocentesis should be used as a method of family planning and should be made available to everyone at a minimum cost or even free. (Menon 2004, 76). The following section examines the processes by which the regulatory framework established by the MTP linked the profits from the abortion business to population control.

Liberalisation: Linking Profits to Population Control

In 1975, amniocentesis was first used as a means to determine foetal sex and with it the recent trends in frequent and repeated *female* sex-selective abortions (The implications of the widespread availability of sex-determination technology are discussed in the following section). This eventually leads us to the current slowdown in population growth in the inter-census period 1991-2001. The repeated abortions performed in this period reveal that medical practitioners were using the opportunities afforded to them by the MTP albeit with a difference: only aborting female foetuses. The changes in the period leading up to the 2001 census not only indicates that the availability of sex-determination technology increased female sex-selective abortions, but that the medical practitioners were using the technology to fulfil a social demand for sons. The market response to this demand indicates a move away from concerns about population growth that underlies the MTP. With liberalisation in 1991, the existing statutory framework set out in the MTP, unproblematically accommodated the upward trend in female-sex selective abortions and a consequent shift in the framework that regulates abortions during this period. This section maps this shift.

India liberalised its economy in 1991. Vijay Joshi and Little's ebullient assessment of the structural adjustments that liberalisation entails note that the derestriction of domestic production and investment has gone a long way in the ten years since 1991.

"Foreign trade has been extensively decontrolled...Tariffs have been greatly reduced... and foreign direct investment is now more welcome...a good deal has been done to increase the role of the price mechanism, raise efficiency, reduce bureaucratic control, and increase the role of private initiative".

The impact of these macroeconomic changes on the market for reproductive services (the widespread availability of pre-natal sex-determination technology, for instance) has been significant. It is arguably the case that the Indian market for reproductive services is now inextricably linked to the global market. (The evidence that the market for reproductive services has proliferated is examined later.) In any event, liberalisation sets the stage for medical practitioners to exploit the opportunities to profit from the business of abortions: more abortions (male or female) mean more profits.

The implementation of the MTP in India during this transition exposes the foundational inequality between abortion-seekers and medical practitioners on which it is premised in two ways. First, as the medical practitioner has the power to modify her legal relationship with an abortion-seeker, she can do so in a way that furthers her business interest. Secondly, the duty to obtain the consent of an abortion-seeker to perform an abortion merely requires a medical practitioner to satisfy herself that an abortion-seeker fulfils the conditions set out in the MTP.

This low threshold of consent makes it easier for medical practitioners to approve repeated abortions (whatever the cost to maternal health). The MTP ensures that repeated abortions are instrumental in increasing the profits of the medical practitioner. The same framework now unproblematically requires the performance of repeated abortions to increase the profits of medical practitioner when earlier this was required to control population growth. This is one aspect of the shift in the framework that regulates abortions while another is unique to the ongoing project of liberalising the market for reproductive services.

Liberalisation is underpinned by systemic changes that entail shifts in existing regulatory frameworks and thereby introduces distinctive normative frames to state policy. For instance, to improve the quality of services, governments have been urged to be 'cost-effective', and ensure 'cost-recovery', to reintroduce user fees and social marketing schemes; "promote the role of the private sector in service delivery and in the production and distribution ... of high quality reproductive health and family-planning commodities' and 'review legal, regulatory and import policies ...that unnecessarily prevent or restrict the greater involvement of the private sector" (Petchesky 2000, 20).

In addition to removing tariff barriers to increase foreign investment, liberalisation also engenders conditions in which it is possible for markets to achieve some welfare goals more efficiently, cost-effectively etc., than the state. The state pulls back to allow markets to perform certain functions.

The arrow linking repeated abortions to control population growth is broken to represent the withdrawal of the state from achieving one of its welfare aims. The present regulatory framework engenders this shift as the practice of abortions was regulated by the contractual relationship between the medical practitioners and abortion-seekers: a relationship in which the medical practitioner was more powerful than the abortion-seeker. Thus, with liberalisation, the interests of the medical practitioner (profits) predominates those of abortion-seekers. This is the basis on which a welfare aim of the state is being achieved. This section reveals a shift in the framework that regulates abortions after liberalisation.

The following section examines the legal responses to the problem mainly to understand why the law has been ineffective and has in fact bucked the upward trend in female sex-selective abortions.

Illustrating the Effects of an Intervening Illegality

As mentioned earlier, in 1975 the All India Institute of Medical Sciences, a public hospital, conducted trials using amniocentesis to detect foetal abnormalities: sex-determination was now possible in India. During these trials, most of the couples that learnt that the foetus was female went in for abortions. The practice proliferated in public hospitals. To limit this trend, amniocentesis was restricted by the Indian Council for Medical Research, to cases of suspected genetic diseases. Between 1977 and 1985 three circulars to government departments at the centre and the states made the use of pre-natal, sex-determination for the purposes of sex-selective abortions a penal offence (Aravamudan 2007).

The ban on amniocentesis in public hospitals prompted the private provision of the service in clinics all over the country. The widespread use of sex-determination technology to sex-selectively abort female foetuses prompted a civil society campaign against the practice by women's groups and civil liberties and health movements. In 1984, a broad coalition was formed, the Forum against Sex Determination and Sex Pre-selection (FASDSP) whose primary purpose was a sustained campaign to ban sex – determination tests (Menon 2004, 74-81). After ten years of the campaign, the Pre-Natal Diagnostic Techniques (Regulation and Prevention of Misuse) Act, 1994 was framed. Ten years later, liberalisation ensured the proliferation of sex-determination technology: amniocentesis was now only one method by which foetal sex was determined. In response, a campaign against the proliferating practice culminated in a Public Interest Litigation in the Supreme Court calling for the 1994 Act to be extended to other sex-determination technologies. In response to orders from the Supreme Court in the matter, the Indian Parliament amended the 1994 Act in 2001. It is now known as the Pre-Conception and Pre-Natal Diagnostic Techniques Act (PCPNDT).

The PCPNDT extends the 1994 Act to cover pre-conception and pre-natal diagnostic techniques not covered by the 1994 Act. The amended statute brought under its purview some neglected areas like regulating the sale of equipment capable of detecting the sex of the foetus. It also specified under what circumstances diagnostic tests could be conducted on a pregnant woman and laid down certain strict rules regarding advertising of sex-selection techniques as well as services.

Under the Act, it became mandatory for instance, to have a signboard in all ultrasound centres announcing that the detection and disclosure of foetal sex was illegal. The PCPNDT makes it illegal for a medical practitioner (this generic term covers clinicians who have access to sex-determination technology and can legally use the same) to divulge foetal sex or to carry out sex-selective abortions. Any contravention of the Act entails imprisonment and a fine.

In a framework similar to the MTP, the PCPNDT gives abortion-seekers a claim-right to access a pre-natal diagnostic technique say ultrasonography and it imposes two corresponding duties on a person qualified to use the sex-determination technology or perform a sex-selective abortion (medical practitioner) as follows. A duty not to reveal foetal sex and a duty not to perform a sex-selective abortion once the foetal sex is determined.

The PCPNDT is a statute that regulates and controls the use of diagnostic techniques for sex-determination and sex-selective abortions. In the absence of any sex-determination prior to an abortion, the MTP will apply, (which as discussed in the preceding section) to achieve the larger good or welfare of the state namely population control and (after economic liberalisation) the sustenance of the market for reproductive services. In effect, abortion-seekers are still subject to the utilitarian foundations of the MTP. The PCPNDT merely declares the performance of certain acts, such as, revealing the sex of a foetus or the performance of a sex-selective abortion as illegal. Apart from this change, there is no modification in the kind of consent required from an abortion-seeker. There is no change in the power inequality between the medical practitioner and the abortion-seeker: the right to an abortion is still subject to the powers of the former. Thus, for all intents and purposes, repeated abortions are still required to control population growth and sustain the abortion business. This is contrary to the position taken by the women's movement (as part of the FADSP). They claimed it as a victory: one that established a woman's right to an abortion in a way that went beyond the MTP. This view has since been strongly criticised (Menon 2007, 77-80).

The abortion business has now diversified to include sex-determination and has become sex-selective. It is after the promulgation of the PCPNDT that the abortion business becomes the business of sex-selective abortions. In the 13 years since the 1994 Act came into force, there has been one conviction-On March 28, 2006, a court in Haryana convicted a doctor and his assistant to a two-year jail sentence for carrying out sex-selective abortions. Moreover, the abortion business has flourished and population growth has slowed down. This section explores why the PCPNDT has failed to regulate the abortion business. Why have female sex-selective abortions become the business norm (instead of abortions in general)?

By declaring foetal sex-determination as illegal, the PCPNDT allows the state to directly intervene and regulate transactions between abortion-seekers and medical practitioners. The statute is not concerned with other non-sex-selective abortions or the frequency of abortions. This is still regulated by the MTP. The criminalisation of certain aspects of the abortion business could potentially have had a direct financial impact on the business, but it did not. The reasons behind this are explored in the next section.

Mapping the Demand and Supply Continuum

The beginning of the demand and supply continuum that underpins the sex-selective abortion business can be traced back to the period after the technology that made sex-determination possible became available in 1974. In the twenty years leading up to its criminalisation in 1994, medical practitioners publicly defended the practice on the grounds that it was 'the family's right to make this personal decision...the mother will suffer if she has too many daughters and that the daughter will have a difficult life' (Aravamudan 2007, 58). One gynaecologist questioned, "how can you deny [the mother] the right to have a one son instead of a third or fourth daughter?" and commented that:

> *"centuries of thinking [cannot be wished away] by saying that boys and girls are equal...it is better to get rid of an unwanted child that to make it suffer all its life."*

Medical practitioners also pointed out the unreasonableness of making female and not male sex-selective abortions illegal. Furthermore, doctors raised concerns that;

> *"barring of [sex-determination] tests could lead to mushrooming of private clinics headed by quacks where sex-detection tests... abortions will be carried out clandestinely and prove to be extremely hazardous to the mother and the foetus alike."*

The doctors who pioneered the use of amniocentesis in India claimed that;

> *"the destruction of a few female foetuses would not affect the CSR and would actually free women from having to go through multiple unwanted pregnancies."*

Hospitals that specialised in sex-determination services invoked the interests of the nation and claim to be doing the nation a service by 'keeping some check over the accelerating population as well a give relief to the couples requiring a male child'(Aravamudan 2007, 60).

In the years that preceded the PCPNDT, the abortion business embarked on a visible media campaign that both articulated and reinforced social norms such as son preference. There were billboards and posters on train stations advertising sex-determination tests together with an abortion for Rs.70. They stated 'Invest Rs. [rupees] 500 now, save Rs.50, 000 later' (id.) These were designed to encourage prospective parents to sex-selectively abort and thereby save on a future dowry. Clinics advertised their sex-determination services and as the number of clinics grew, competition pushed down the prices of the service, making them more affordable to the lower middle class. From 1982 to 1987, the number of clinics for sex-determination increased from less than 10 to 248 in Mumbai alone. A study of clinics in Mumbai revealed that out of 8000 abortions in six hospitals preceded by amniocentesis, 7,999 were female foetuses. Between 1978, and 1982, according to one study, 78,000 female foetuses were aborted after sex-determination tests in one hospital, while none of the 250 male foetuses were aborted even when there was evidence of a genetic problem (*id.*). Prior to the promulgation of the PCPNDT, information of this kind was relatively easy to find. After the practice was criminalised in 1994, the public campaign stopped, but the sex-determination and sex-selective abortion business (sex-selective abortion business) flourished albeit underground.

In the meantime, liberalisation entailed the removal of tariff barriers between the national and the global market for reproductive services, significantly increasing the sex-selective abortion business. By 2000, ultrasound technology had proliferated and become highly sophisticated. Mobile sonography machines were available widely and they had 'become so sleek and compact that they would now be stowed away in the boot of a car.' Studies conducted revealed that quite a few scanning centres were actually owned and operated by non-trained personnel (Aravamudan 2007, 66). At the beginning of 2004, there were 1621 ultrasound sonography centres in Karnataka for which registration were granted by the state. Over 25 per cent of them had neither an owner nor an operator who was qualified to use the machine, in direct contravention of the PCPNDT (Aravamudan 2007, 68). In Maharasthra, a study conducted established a clear correlation between the number of sonography centres and a decline in CSR. The average number of girls in the CSR for districts with more than 100 sonography centres was 901, and for districts with less than 100 sonography centres, the number of girls was 937 (*id.*). In May 2005, there was evidence that many "doctors in Punjab were keen to make a quick buck ... aborting male foetuses when parents approach them for ante-natal sex determination." Apparently the doctors offered a package deal costing Rs 8000 and Rs 15,000. Before the PCPNDT Act, the test cost Rs.500 (*id.*). By 2005, ultrasound scanning for sex determination had become a Rs.5 billion industry (Aravamudan 2007, 69).

The upward trend in sex-selective abortions and the flourishing abortion business are linked. The regulatory framework established by the MTP underpins this linkage. The evidence that the sex-selective abortion business is flourishing even after the practice has been criminalised indicates two things: there is a demand for sex-selective abortions and the medical practitioners and abortion seekers are strategically avoiding the law to meet this demand. If the latter does not, then section 23 (2) of the PCPNDT will criminalize both her and her family. This mutual, strategic, avoidance is not only necessary to sustain the proliferating business of sex-selective abortions but it reveals a fissure between legal ordering or the formal law (which by all accounts has failed) and the underground system of private orderings (in which the sex-selective abortion business flourishes). Private Orderings is a phrase used to describe empirical instances of community institutions serving economic functions beyond the law. A historical instance of such orderings was first theorised in Grief (1993). The private orderings in this case study relies on Richman, (2005). In this paper, Barak Richman describes the Jewish community institutions that underpin the diamond trade as a private ordering that arose to overcome the limitations of the formal courts. The private orderings that sustain the market for sex-selective abortions are entrenched on account of the intervening illegality imposed by the PCPNDT.

In the case of sex-selective abortions, the private ordering is so entrenched that it has its own language! This is evidenced in sex-determination clinics where medical practitioners have evolved their own specific 'area' code linked to the tradition and jargon of the part of the country in which they are located. In parts of north India, for instance, 'laddu' translates as son and 'barfi or daughter. If a woman was asked to come back on Monday, it meant she was carrying a son. If she was asked to return on Friday, it meant that the foetus was female and he would have to abort it etc. (Aravamudan 2007,74).

The co-operation between the medical practitioner and abortion-seekers and the flourishing sex-selective abortion business reveals how social and market norms such as son–preference, efficiency respectively underpin the market for sex-determination and sex-selective abortions.

Consequently, prenatal sex determination tests and sex-selective abortions may be seen as a more morally acceptable option in the domain of private ordering than the earlier practice of female infanticide, for instance.

Female infanticide required parents to perform elaborate rituals to cleanse themselves of the guilt associated with the practice (Patel 1996). One reason for a marked preference for this technology is that the soul does not enter the foetus until the end of the first trimester. This is one cited reason why sex-selective abortions in the first trimester may be preferred to infanticide after birth (*id.*). The fissure between domains A and B indicates that the PCPNDT notwithstanding, the sex-selective abortion business is unregulated. More significantly however, the fissure indicates that in a post-liberalised economy, the MTP and the PCPNDT have unproblematically made population control, son preference and profit the inseparable goals of the global market for reproductive services.

This case study also requires the recognition that markets are essentially, social practices. Though this recognition may not be as innocuous as it sounds. Unlike other social practices, markets require people to submit their resources and in the case of abortion-seekers their bodies to the simple imperative of demand and supply. This submission is necessary not merely to fulfil a woman's individual interests (as Dr. Malpani in the recent episode of 'We the Nation' would have us believe) but to achieve goals such as profit of powerful market players, population control and wealth maximisation, all more worthy than our own. In other words, as abortion-seekers have no choice but to become market actors their bodies become (unproblematically) instrumental in the achievement of goals larger than their own. Interestingly, the view that a woman's body is normally subject to fulfilling the interests of her family, caste etc is brought home forcefully by Mahasweta Dewi (1997) a popular woman activist and author.

Conclusions

This paper traces the role that the MTP and the PCPNDT play in the market for reproductive services in a transition economy. This analysis of the law moves the public debate in India away from the pro-choice/pro-life frame and rearticulates it as systemic problem that implicates abortion law. This problem does not only raise pro-life/pro-choice concerns as the contemporary debate would have us believe, but does require that the experiences of women who undergo repeated abortions be made a part of the debate. The analysis of abortion law in this paper reveals that since population control is the foundational imperative of the MTP, its implementation requires repeated abortions, to sustain the present slow-down in population growth. It also reveals a foundational inequality in its regulatory framework: abortion-seekers are subject to demands of the larger public good while medical practitioners are not. This inequality entails profits. This may be an incentive for the business of sex-selective abortions but the profits also require an examination of whether exchanges between abortion-seekers are exploitative, thereby denying women the full benefit of accessing the market for reproductive services.

The repeated abortions required to slow-down population growth also obscures concerns about maternal health and an examination of the birth control policies of the state. The upward trend in sex-selective abortions reveals a regulatory gap: the business of sex-selective abortions flourishes and in the process disproportionately affects abortion-seekers and exposes the fallacy of the gender-neutral agenda of economic liberalisation.

Activists like George Sabu and Leela Visaria have highlighted the repercussions of the unregulated business of sex-selective abortions. Activists have re-drawn the battle lines in recognition of the evidence that abortion laws have mediated the impact of liberalisation and that this impact is gendered, affecting women in specific ways. The activist approach developed from the ground up is premised on the recognition that economic globalisation does not merely displace the rights framework but irremediably distorts it. Secondly, these distortions expose regulatory free zones in which markets sustained by oppressive social norms proliferate. The disadvantage that abortion-seekers face can only be understood at the intersection of social, economic and political forces. It is in this vein that Rosalind Petchesky endorses DAWN's (an activist NGO) 'holistic' approach. This approach combines rights and needs to specifically address the impact that privatisation and commodification has on women (Petchesky, 2000).

The analysis of the law in this paper does not provide a template for legal reform and is not a defence of rights. It sets out a conceptual framework to clarify the process by which the demand and supply continuum that underpins the market for reproductive services is sustained by repeated and frequent abortions, with unaccounted and disproportionate costs to maternal health.

Chapter 5

Contraceptive Security

Contraceptive security is a situation in which people are able to reliably choose, obtain, and use quality contraceptives for family planning and sexually transmitted disease (including HIV and AIDS) prevention when they want them.

Organizations, usually government health agencies, work to ensure clients have long-term access to a range of high quality contraceptives and other essential health supplies. Measures taken to provide contraceptive security may include improving contraceptive distribution and availability, promoting product quality, and supporting commodities distribution across. Subsidized products, particularly condoms and oral contraceptives, may be provided to increase accessibility for low-income people. One problem encountered with this subsidization is that individuals who are able to pay regular retail price may chose to buy the discounted items, creating competition with private sector contraceptive distributors.

Decrement Table: Decrement tables, also called life table methods, are used to calculate the probability of certain events.

Birth Control

Life table methods are often used to study birth control effectiveness. In this role, they are an alternative to the Pearl Index.

As used in birth control studies, a decrement table calculates a separate effectiveness rate for each month of the study, as well as for a standard period of time (usually 12 months). Use of life table methods eliminates time-related biases (i.e. the most fertile couples getting pregnant and dropping out of the study early, and couples becoming more skilled at using the method as time goes on), and in this way is superior to the Pearl Index.

Two kinds of decrement tables are used to evaluate birth control methods. Multiple-decrement (or competing) tables report net effectiveness rates.

These are useful for comparing competing reasons for couples dropping out of a study. Single-decrement (or noncompeting) tables report gross effectiveness rates, which can be used to accurately compare one study to another.

Family Planning

Family planning is the planning of when to have children, and the use of birth control and other techniques to implement such plans. Other techniques commonly used include sexuality education, prevention and management of sexually transmitted infections, pre-conception counseling and management, and infertility management.

Family planning is sometimes used as a synonym for the use of birth control, however, it often includes a wide variety of methods, and practices that are not birth control.

It is most usually applied to a female-male couple who wish to limit the number of children they have and/or to control the timing of pregnancy (also known as *spacing children*). Family planning may encompass sterilization, as well as abortion.

Family planning services are defined as "educational, comprehensive medical or social activities which enable individuals, including minors, to determine freely the number and spacing of their children and to select the means by which this may be achieved."

Purposes

Raising a child requires significant amounts of resources: time, social, financial, and environmental. Planning can help assure that resources are available. The purpose of family planning is to make sure that any couple, man or woman who has the desire to have a child has the resources that are needed in order to complete this goal.

With these resources a couple, man or women can explore the options of natural birth, surrogacy, artificial insemination or adoption. In the other case, if the person does not wish to have a child at the specific time, they can investigate the resources that are needed to prevent pregnancy, such as birth control, contraceptives, or physical protection and prevention.

Health

Waiting until the mother is at least 18 years old before trying to have children improves maternal and child health. Also, if additional children are desired after a child is born, it is healthier for the mother and the child to wait at least 2 years after the previous birth before attempting to conceive (but not more than 5 years). After a miscarriage or abortion, it is healthier to wait at least 6 months.

"Family planning benefits the health and well-being of women and families throughout the world. Using contraception can help to avoid unwanted pregnancies and space births; protect against STDs, including HIV/AIDS; and provide other health benefits."

Modern Methods

Some families use modern medical advances in family planning. For example in surrogacy treatments a woman agrees to become pregnant and deliver a child for another couple or person.

In sperm donations, pregnancies are usually achieved using donated sperm by artificial insemination (either by intracervical insemination or intrauterine insemination) and less commonly by invitro fertilization (IVF), usually known in this context as Assisted reproductive technology (ART), but insemination may also be achieved by a donor having sexual intercourse with a woman for the sole purpose of initiating conception. This method is known as natural insemination (NI).

There is generally a demand for sperm donors who have no genetic problems in their family, 20/20 eyesight, with excellent visual acuity, a college degree, and sometimes a value on a certain height and age.

In cases were couples may not want to have children just yet and plan with time family planning programmes help a lot. Federal family planning programmes reduced childbearing among poor women by as much as 29 percent, according to a University of Michigan study.

Finances

Family planning is among the most cost-effective of all health interventions. "The cost savings stem from a reduction in unintended pregnancy, as well as a reduction in transmission of sexually transmitted infections, including HIV."

Childbirth and prenatal health care cost averaged $7,090 for normal delivery in the US in 1996. US Department of Agriculture estimates that for a child born in 2007, a US family will spend an average of $11,000 to $23,000 per year for the first 17 years of child's life. (Total inflation adjusted estimated expenditure: $196,000 to $393,000, depending on household income.)

Birth Control

Birth control is techniques used to prevent unwanted pregnancy. There are a range of contraceptive methods, each with unique advantages and disadvantages. Any of the widely recognized methods of birth control is much more effective than no method. Bahavioural methods that include intercourse, such as withdrawal and calendar based methods have little up front cost and are readily available, but are much less effective in typical use than most other methods. Long-acting reversible contraceptive methods, such as IUD and implant are highly effective and convenient, requiring little user action. When cost of failure is included, IUDs and vasectomy are much less costly than other methods. In addition to providing birth control, male or female condoms protect against sexually transmitted diseases (STD). Condoms may be used alone, or in addition to other methods, as backup or to prevent STD. Surgical methods (tubal ligation, vasectomy) provide long term contraception for those who have completed their families.

Policy

The world's largest international source of funding for population and reproductive health programmes is the United Nations Population Fund (UNFPA). The main goals of the International Conference on Population and Development Programme of Action are:

- Universal access to reproductive health services by 2015
- Universal primary education and closing the gender gap in education by 2015
- Reducing maternal mortality by 75% by 2015
- Reducing infant mortality
- Increasing life expectancy
- Reducing HIV infection rates in persons aged 15–24 years by 25% in the most-affected countries by 2005, and by 25% globally by 2010

The World health organization (WHO) and World Bank estimate that $3.00 per person per year would provide basic family planning, maternal and neonatal health care to women in developing countries.

This would include contraception, prenatal, delivery and post-natal care in addition to postpartum family planning and the promotion of condoms to prevent sexually transmitted infections.

China

China's *one-child policy* forces couples to have no more than one child. Beginning in 1979, the policy was instated to control the rapid population growth that was occurring in the nation at that time. With the rapid change in population, China was facing many impacts of the rapid population growth including poverty and homelessness. As a developing nation, the Chinese government was concerned that a continuation of the rapid population growth that had been occurring would hinder their development as a nation. The process of family planning varied throughout China, as many different people differed in their responsiveness to the one child policy, based on location and socioeconomic status.

For example, many families in the cities accepted this policy more readily based on the lack of space, money, and resources that are often offered in the cities. However, the people in rural areas of China were more hesitant in accepting this policy. Since the policy was put into place in 1979, over 400 million births have been prevented in China. China's population policy has been credited with a very significant slowing of China's population growth which had been higher before the policy was implemented. However, it has come under criticism that the policy has created abuse for women in China. Often times implementation of the policy has involved forcedabortions and forced sterilization. However, while the punishment of "unplanned" pregnancy is a large fine, both forced abortion and forced sterilization can be charged with intentional assault, which is punished with up to 10 years' imprisonment.

Another aspect of family planning in China due to the one-child policy is the differentiation between the desire for male and female children in both urban and rural locations. In the Chinese culture, the desire for a male child is much harder, making the abandonment or abortion of female infants or fetuses common in the rural areas of the nation. Another issue that is raised in the one-child policy in China is the information in regards to naturally giving birth to twins or triplets. If this situation arises, the family is allowed to keep the children because of the natural causes of this impregnation.

Hong Kong

In Hong Kong, the Eugenics League was found in 1936, which became The Family Planning Association of Hong Kong in 1950. The organisation provides family planning advice, sex education, birth control services to the general public of Hong Kong. In the 1970s, due to the rapidly rising population, it launched the "Two is Enough" campaign, which reduced the general birth rate through educational means.

The Family Planning Association of Hong Kong, Hong Kong's national family planning association, founded the International Planned Parenthood Federation with its counterparts in seven other countries.

Ireland

The sale of contraceptives was illegal in Ireland from 1935 until 1980, when it was legalized with strong restrictions, later loosened. It has been argued that the resulting demographic dividend played a role in the economic boom in Ireland in the 1990s (the Celtic tiger) was in part due to the legalization of contraception in 1979 and subsequent decline in the fertility rate. In Ireland the ratio of workers to dependents improved due to lower fertility but was raised further by increased female labour market participation.

Pakistan

In agreement with the 1994 International Conference on Population and Development in Cairo, Pakistan pledged that by 2010 it would provide universal access to family planning. Additionally, Pakistan's Poverty Reduction Strategy Paper has set specific national goals for increases in family planning and contraceptive use.

Russia

According to a 2004 study, current pregnancies were termed "desired and timely" by 58% of respondents, while 23% described them as "desired, but untimely", and 19% said they were "undesired". As of 2004, the share of women of reproductive age using hormonal or intrauterine birth control methods was about 46% (29% intrauterine, 17% hormonal). During the soviet era high quality contraceptives were difficult to obtain, and abortion became the most common way of preventing unwanted births. Since the dissolution of the Soviet Union abortion rates have fallen considerably, but they are still higher than rates in many developed countries.

United Kingdom

Contraception has been available for free under the National Health Service since 1974, and 74% of reproductive age women use some form of contraception. The levonorgestrel intrauterine system has been massively popular. Sterilization is popular in older age groups, among those 45-49, 29% of men and 21% of women have been sterilized.

Female sterilization has been declining since 1996, when the intrauterine system was introduced. Emergency contraception has been available since the 1970s, a product was specifically licensed for emergency contraception in 1984, and emergency contraceptives became available over the counter in 2001. Since becoming available over the counter it has not reduced the use of other forms of contraception, as some moralists feared it might. In any year only 5% of women of childbearing age use emergency hormonal contraception.

Despite widespread availability of contraceptives, almost half of pregnancies were unintended circa 2005. Abortion was legalized in 1967.

United States

Despite the availability of highly effective contraceptives, about half of US pregnancies are unintended. Highly effective contraceptives, such as IUD are underused in the United States. Increasing use of highly effective contraceptives could help meet the goal set forward in Healthy People 2020 to decrease unintended pregnancy by 10%. Cost to the user is one factor preventing many US women from using more effective contraceptives. Making contraceptives available without a copay increases use of highly effective methods, reduces unintended pregnancies, and may be instrumental in achieving the Healthy People 2020 goal. Teenage pregnancies are very involved in today's society and because of this the resources that are around for family planning is vital to the survival of these infants. Federally funded programmes such as Planned Parenthood are very important in the family planning process of adolescents because of the involvement of doctors, gynecologists, or medicine. These family planning practices also help impact the teenager and the infant because of the availability of healthcare and other resources that may otherwise not be offered.

In the United States, contraceptive use saves about $19 billion in direct medical costs each year. Title X of the Public Health Service Act, is a US government programme dedicated to providing family planning services for those in need. But funding for Title X as a percentage of total public funding to family planning client services has steadily declined from 44% of total expenditures in 1980 to 12% in 2006. Medicaid has increased from 20% to 71% in the same time. In 2006, Medicaid contributed $1.3 billion to public family planning. The 1.9 billion spent on publicly funded family planning in 2008 saved an estimated $7 billion in short term Medicaid costs. Such services helped women prevent an estimated 1.94 million unintended pregnancies and 810,000 abortions.

World Contraception Day

The 26th of September is World Contraception Day, devoted to raising awareness of contraception and improving education about sexual and reproductive health, with a vision of *a world where every pregnancy is wanted.* It is supported by a group of international NGOs, including Asian Pacific Council on Contraception, Centro Latinamericano Salud y Mujer, European Society of Contraception and Reproductive Health, German Foundation for World Population, International Federation of Pediatric and Adolescent Gynecology, International Planned Parenthood Federation, Marie Stopes International, Population Services International, The Population Council, The United States Agency for International Development (USAID), Women Deliver.

Red Triangle (Family Planning)

Figure: *The Red Triangle indicates family planning products and services*

An inverted Red Triangle is the symbol for family planning health and contraception services, much as the red cross is a symbol for medical services. It is especially prevalent in many developing nations such as India, Ghana, Gambia, Zimbabwe, Egypt and Thailand, where it can be seen outside shops and clinics that offer family planning products, as well as commercial and government messages that promote reproductive health services and population control. It is also frequently placed on contraceptive products, such as condoms, diaphragms, spermicidal gel and IUDs (for instance, on the government-subsidized Nirodh condoms in India and Sultan condoms in Gambia).

Origins and Variations

The red triangle was invented by Deep Tyagi, a Indian family planning official and activist in the 1960s. Several variations on the basic symbol have since been developed, such as the "Life Choices" and "Family Planning: better life" logos used to promote birth control and reproductive health in Ghana, and the "Naissances Desirables" logo used in Zaire/Congo. The "Men Too" (shortened from "Family Planning is for Everybody ... Men Too") campaign in Australia used a hollow red triangle. The "Stop and think Minyawi : This is a very happy family, a light family" initiative in Egypt used calligraphic Arabic script to create the triangle.

Reproductive Life Plan

A reproductive life plan is a plan for whether, when and how to have children. It includes personal goals, and states how to achieve them. The plan is based on a person's priorities and goals with regards to life and children. The plan may take into account their resources, commitments and values. Reproductive life plan serves as a basis for action to help realize the plan. For instance: it can help in selecting appropriate birth control if have sex before ready to have children; or seeking Pre-conception counseling and care, to improve health of motherand child. Family planning professionals can help in formulating and implementing a reproductive life plan. Unintended pregnancies are associated with an array of negative outcomes for the mother, child and family, formulating a plan can help to make sure that pregnancies are prepared for and intended.

People often delay having children to gathering necessary resources, to gather social support, until career or other goals are met, or to improve health outcomes for mother and child.

Although many people who desire children do so through childbirth, some adopt children, become foster parents, or use other arrangements to achieve their desires (co-parenting, surrogacy).

Many people decide not to have children (childfree).

In 2006 the US Centres for Disease Control (CDC) issued a recommendation, encouraging men and women to formulate a reproductive life plan, to help them in avoiding unintended pregnancies and to improve the health of women and reduce adverse pregnancy outcomes.

Chapter 6

Human Migration

Human migration (derived from Latin: *migratio*) is physical movement by humans from one area to another, sometimes over long distances or in large groups. Historically this movement was nomadic, often causing significant conflict with the indigenous population and their displacement or cultural assimilation. Only a few nomadic people have retained this form of lifestyle in modern times. Migration has continued under the form of both voluntary migration within one's region, country, or beyond and involuntary migration (which includes the slave trade, trafficking in human beings and ethnic cleansing). People who migrate into a territory are called immigrants, while at the departure point they are called emigrants. Small populations migrating to develop a territory considered void of settlement depending on historical setting, circumstances and perspective are referred to as settlers or colonists, while populations displaced by immigration and colonization are called refugees. The rest of this article will cover sense of a "change of residence", rather than the temporary migrations of travel, tourism, pilgrimages, or the commute.

Definition

According to International Organization for Migration, "no universally accepted definition for (migrant) exists. The term migrant was usually understood to cover all cases where the decision to migrate was taken freely by the individual concerned for reasons of "personal convenience" and without intervention of an external compelling factor; it therefore applied to persons, and family members, moving to another country or region to better their material or social conditions and improve the prospect for themselves or their family. The United Nations defines migrant as an individual who has resided in a foreign country for more than one year irrespective of the causes, voluntary or involuntary, and the means, regular or irregular, used to migrate. Under such a definition, those travelling for shorter periods as tourists and business persons would not be considered migrants. However, common usage includes certain kinds of shorter-term migrants, such as seasonal farm-workers who travel for short periods to work planting or harvesting farm products." Also, human migration happened when the Paleo-Indians entered America.

Migration Statistics

According to the International Organization for Migration's World Migration Report 2010, the number of international migrants was estimated at 214 million in 2010. If this number continues to grow at the same pace as during the last 20 years, it could reach 405 million by 2050. While some modern migration is a by product of wars (for example, emigration from Iraq and Bosnia to the US and UK), political conflicts (for example, some emigration from Zimbabwe to the UK), and natural disasters (for example, emigration from Montserrat to the UK following the eruption of the island's volcano), contemporary migration is predominantly economically motivated. In particular, there are wide disparities in the incomes that can be earned for similar work in different countries of the world. There are also, at any given time, some jobs in some high-wage countries for which there is a shortage of appropriately skilled or qualified citizens. Some countries (e.g., UK and Australia) operate points systems that give some lawful immigration visas to some non-citizens who are qualified for such shortage jobs. Non-citizens, therefore, have an economic incentive to obtain the necessary skills and qualifications in their own countries and then apply for, and migrate to take up, these job vacancies. International migration similarly motivated by economic disparities and opportunities occurs within the EU, where legal barriers to migration between member countries have been wholly or partially lifted. Countries with higher prevailing wage levels, such as France, Germany, Italy and the UK are net recipients of immigration from lower-wage member countries such as Greece, Hungary, Lithuania, Poland and Romania.

Some contemporary economic migration occurs even where the migrant becomes illegally resident in their destination country and therefore at major disadvantage in the employment market. Illegal immigrants are, for example, known to cross in significant numbers, typically at night, from Mexico into the US, from Mozambique into

South Africa, from Bulgaria and Turkey into Greece, and from north Africa into Spain and Italy.

The pressures of human migrations, whether as outright conquest or by slow cultural infiltration and resettlement, have affected the grand epochs in history and in land (for example, the decline of the Roman Empire); under the form of colonization, migration has transformed the world (such as the prehistoric and historic settlements of Australia and the Americas). Population genetics studied in traditionally settled modern populations have opened a window into the historical patterns of migrations, a technique pioneered by Luigi Luca Cavalli-Sforza.

Forced migration has been a means of social control under authoritarian regimes, yet free-initiative migration is a powerful factor in social adjustment and the growth of urban populations.

In December 2003, The Global Commission on International Migration (GCIM) was launched with the support of Secretary-General of the United Nations Kofi Annan and several countries, with an independent 19-member commission, a threefold mandate and a finite life span ending December 2005. Its report, based on regional consultation meetings with stakeholders and scientific reports from leading international migration experts, was published and presented to Kofi Annan on 5 October 2005.

International migration challenges at the global level are addressed through the Global Migration Group, established in 2006.

Different Types of Migration Include:

- Seasonal human migration mainly related to agriculture and tourism to urban places
- Rural to urban, more common in developing countries as industrialization takes effect (urbanization)
- Urban to rural, more common in developed countries due to a higher cost of urban living (suburbanization).

Early Human Migrations

Early human migrations began when *Homo erectus* first migrated out of Africa over the Levantine corridor and Horn of Africa to Eurasia about 1.8 million years ago, a migration probably sparked by the development of language (a former rudimentary language as argued by Fischer's hypothesis.) The expansion of *H. erectus* out of Africa was followed by that of *Homo antecessor* into Europe around 800,000 years ago, followed by *Homo heidelbergensis* around 600,000 years ago, where they probably evolved to become the Neanderthals.

Modern humans, *Homo sapiens*, evolved in Africa up to 200,000 years ago and reached the Near East around 125,000 years ago. From the Near East, these populations spread east to South Asia by 50,000 years ago, and on to Australia by 40,000 years ago, when for the first time *H. sapiens* reached territory never reached by *H. erectus*. *H. sapiens* reached Europe around 40,000 years ago, eventually replacing the Neanderthal population. East Asia was reached by 30,000 years ago.

The date of migration to North America is disputed; it may have taken place around 30 millennia ago, or considerably later, around 14 millennia ago. Colonisation of the Pacific islands of Polynesia began around 1300 BC, and was completed by 900 AD. The ancestors of Polynesians left Taiwan around 5200 years ago. The study of early human migrations since the 1980s has developed significantly due to advances in archaeogenetics.

Early Humans (Before Homo Sapiens)

Early members of the *Homo* genus, i.e. *Homo ergaster*, *Homo erectus* and *Homo heidelbergensis*, migrated from Africa during the Early Pleistocene, possibly as a result of the operation of the Saharan pump, around 1.9 million years ago, and dispersed throughout most of the Old World, reaching as far as Southeast Asia. The date of original dispersal beyond Africa virtually coincides with the appearance of *Homo ergaster* in the fossil record, and the associated first emergence of full bipedalism, and about half a million years after the appearance of the *Homo* genus itself and the first stone tools of the Oldowan industry. Key sites for this early migration out of Africa are Riwat in Pakistan (1.9 Mya), Ubeidiya in the Levant (1.5 Mya) and Dmanisi in the Caucasus (1.7 Mya).

China was populated more than a million years ago, as early as 1.66 Mya based on stone artifacts found in the Nihewan Basin. Stone tools found at Xiaochangliang site were dated to 1.36 million years ago. The archaeological site of Xihoudu (n‰¯O!n) in Shanxi Province is the earliest recorded use of fire by Homo erectus, which is dated 1.27 million years ago. Southeast Asia (Java) was reached about 1.7 million years ago (Meganthropus). West Europe was first populated around 1.2 million years ago (Atapuerca).

Bruce Bower has suggested that *Homo erectus* may have built rafts and sailed oceans, a theory that has raised some controversy.

Homo Sapiens Migrations

Homo sapiens is supposed to have appeared in East Africa around 200,000 years ago. The oldest individuals found left their marks by the Omo remains (195,000 years ago) and the *Homo sapiens idaltu* (160,000 years ago), that was found at site Middle Awash in Ethiopia Recent claims of remains of anatomically modern humans with 400.000 years, found at Qesem Cave (Israel), are controversial. Some authors argue that these remains are from Neanderthals or their ancestors. From there they spread around the world. An exodus from Africa over the Arabian Peninsula around 125,000 years ago brought modern humans to Eurasia, with one group rapidly settling coastal areas around the Indian Ocean and one group migrating north to steppes of Central Asia. The migration path is a matter of debate and study. Genetics have shed some light on this matter.

Within Africa

The matrilinear most recent common ancestor shared by all living human beings, dubbed Mitochondrial Eve, probably lived roughly 120-150 millennia ago, the time of *Homo sapiens idaltu*, probably in East Africa. The broad study of African genetic diversity headed by Dr. Sarah Tishkoff found the San people to express the greatest genetic diversity among the 113 distinct populations sampled, making them one of 14 "ancestral population clusters." The research also located the origin of modern human migration in south-western Africa, near the coastal border of Namibia and Angola. Around 100,000-80,000 years ago, three main lines of *Homo sapiens* diverged. Bearers of mitochondrial haplogroup L0 (mtDNA) / A (Y-DNA) colonized Southern Africa (the ancestors of the Khoisan (Capoid) peoples), bearers of haplogroup L1 (mtDNA) / B (Y-DNA) settled Central and West Africa (the ancestors of western pygmies), and bearers of haplogroups L2, L3, and others mtDNA remained in East Africa (the ancestors of Niger–Congo- and Nilo-Saharan-speaking peoples).

Exodus from Africa

There is some evidence for the argument that modern humans left Africa at least 125,000 years before present (BP) using two different routes: the Nile Valley heading to the Middle East, at least into modern Israel (Qafzeh: 120,000–100,000 years BP); and a second one through the present-day Bab-el-Mandeb Strait on the Red Sea (at that time, with a much lower sea level and narrower extension), crossing it into the Arabian Peninsula, settling in places like the present-day United Arab Emirates (125,000 years BP) and Oman (106,000 years BP) and then possibly going into the Indian Subcontinent (Jwalapuram: 75,000 years BP). Despite the fact that no human remains have yet been found in these three places, the apparent similarities between the stone tools found at Jebel Faya, the ones from Jwalapuram and some African ones suggest that their creators were all modern humans. These findings might give some support to the claim that modern humans from Africa arrived at southern China about 100,000 years BP (Zhiren Cave, Zhirendong, Chongzuo City: 100,000 years BP; and the Liujiang hominid: controversially dated at 139,000–111,000 years BP).

Since these previous exits from Africa didn't leave traces in the results of genetic analyses based on the Y chromosome and on MtDNA (which represent only a small part of the human genetic material), it seems that those modern humans didn't survive or survived in small numbers and were assimilated by our major antecessors, responsible for a determinant posterior exit. An explanation for their extinction (or small genetic imprint) may be the Toba catastrophe theory (74,000 years BP). However, some argue that its impact on human population wasn't dramatic.

According to the Recent African Origin hypothesis a small group of the L3 bearers living in East Africa migrated north east, possibly searching for food or escaping adverse conditions, crossing the Red Sea about 70 millennia ago, and in the process going on to populate the rest of the world. According to some authors, based in the fact that only descents of L3 are found outside Africa, only a few people left Africa in a single migration to a settlement in the Arabian peninsula. From that settlement, some others point to the possibility of several waves of expansion close in time. For example, Wells says that the early travelers followed the southern coastline of Asia, crossed about 250 kilometres [155 miles] of sea (probably by simple boats or rafts), and colonized Australia by around 50,000 years ago. The Aborigines of Australia, Wells says, are the descendants of the first wave of migration out of Africa.

Around 50,000 years ago the world was entering the last ice age and water was trapped in the polar ice caps, so sea levels were much lower. Today at the Gate of Grief the Red Sea is about 12 miles (20 kilometres) wide but 50,000 years ago it was much narrower and sea levels were 70 metres lower. Though the straits were never completely closed, there may have been islands in between which could be reached by simple rafts. Shell middens 125,000 years old indicate that the diet of early humans in Eritrea included sea food obtained by beachcombing. This has been seen as evidence that humans may have crossed the Red Sea in search of food sources on new beaches.

South Asia and Australia

Some genetic evidence points to migrations out of Africa along two routes. However, other studies suggest that a single migration occurred, followed by rapid northern migration of a subset of the group.

Once in West Asia, the people who remained south (or took the southern route) spread generation by generation around the coast of Arabia and Persia until they reached India. One of the groups that went north (east Asians were the second group) ventured inland and radiated to Europe, eventually displacing the Neanderthals. They also radiated to India from Central Asia. The former group headed along the southeast coast of Asia, reaching Australia between 55,000 and 30,000 years ago, with most estimates placing it about 46,000 to 41,000 years ago.

During that time, sea level was much lower and most of Maritime Southeast Asia was one land mass known as the lost continent of Sunda. The settlers probably continued on the coastal route southeast until they reached the series of straits between Sunda and Sahul, the continental land mass that was made up of present-day Australia and New Guinea. The widest gaps are on the Weber Line and are at least 90 km wide, indicating that settlers had knowledge of seafaring skills. Archaic humans such as *Homo erectus* never reached Australia, although they crossed the Lombok gap reaching as far as Flores.

If these dates are correct, Australia was populated up to 10,000 years before Europe. This is possible because humans avoided the colder regions of the North favouring the warmer tropical regions to which they were adapted given their African homeland. Another piece of evidence favouring human occupation in Australia is that beginning about 46,000 years ago, all megafauna weighing more than 100 kg became extinct. Tim Flannery and others argue new settlers were likely to be responsible for this extinction. Many of the animals may have been accustomed to living without predators and become docile and vulnerable to attack (as occurred later in the Americas).

While some settlers crossed into Australia, others may have continued eastwards along the coast of Sunda eventually turning northeast to China and finally reaching Japan, leaving a trail of coastal settlements. This coastal migration leaves its trail in the mitochondrial haplogroups descended from haplogroup M, and in Y-chromosome haplogroup C. Thereafter, it may have become necessary to venture inland possibly bringing modern humans into contact with archaic humans such as *H. erectus*. Recent genetic studies suggest that Australia and New Guinea were populated by one single migration from Asia as opposed to several waves. The land bridge connecting New Guinea and Australia became submerged approximately 8,000 years ago, thus isolating the populations of the two land masses.

Europe

Europe is thought to have been colonized by northwest bound migrants from Central Asia and the Middle East. When the first anatomically modern humans entered Europe, Neanderthals were already settled there. Debate exists whether modern human populations interbred with Neanderthal populations, most of the evidence suggesting that it happened to a small degree rather than complete absorption. Populations of modern man and Neanderthal overlapped in various regions such as in Iberian peninsula and in the Middle East and that interbreeding may have contributed Neanderthal genes to palaeolithic and ultimately modern Eurasians and Oceanians.

An important difference between Europe and other parts of the inhabited world was the northern latitude. Archaeological evidence suggests humans, whether Neanderthal or Cro-Magnon, reached sites in Arctic Russia by 40,000 years ago. Around 20,000 BC, 10,000 years after the Neanderthal extinction, the Last Glacial Maximum took place forcing northern hemisphere inhabitants to migrate to several shelters until the end of this period came. The resulting populations, whether interbred with Neanderthals or not, are then presumed to have resided in those hypothetical refuges during the LGM to ultimately reoccupy Europe where archaic historical populations are considered their descendents. An alternate view is that modern European populations have descended from Neolithic populations in the Middle East that have been well documented in this area. The debate surrounding the origin of Europeans has been worded in terms of cultural diffusion versus demic diffusion. Archeological evidence and genetic evidence strongly support demic diffusion, that a population spread from the Middle East over the last 12,000 years. A scientific genetic concept called the Time to Most Recent Common Ancestor or TMRCA has been used to refute the demic diffusion in favour of cultural diffusion.

Migration of the Cro-Magnons into Europe

Cro-Magnon are considered the first anatomically modern humans in Europe. They entered Eurasia by the Arabian Peninsula around 60,000 years ago, with one group rapidly settling coastal areas around the Indian Ocean and one group migrating north to steppes of Central Asia. A mitochondrial DNA sequence of two Cro-Magnons from the Paglicci Cave in Italy, dated to 23,000 and 24,000 years old (Paglicci 52 and 12), identified the mtDNA as Haplogroup N, typical of the latter group. The inland group is the founder of both North- and East Asians (the "Mongol" people), Caucasoids and large sections of the

Middle East population. Migration from the Black Sea area into Europe started some around 45,000 years ago, probably along the Danubian corridor. By 20,000 years ago, the whole of Europe was settled. The first complete human remains that have been preserved is the mummy Ötzi, from 3300 BC, belonging to the K1 MitDNA.

Competition with Neanderthals

The expansion is thought to have begun 45,000 years ago and may have taken up to 15,000 years for Europe to be colonized. During this time the Neanderthals were slowly being displaced. Because it took so long for Europe to be occupied, it appears that humans and Neanderthals may have been constantly competing for territory. The Neanderthals were larger and had a more robust or heavy built frame which may suggest that they were physically stronger than modern *Homo sapiens*. Having lived in Europe for 200,000 years they would have been better adapted to the cold weather. The anatomically modern humans known as the Cro-Magnons, with superior technology and language would eventually completely displace the Neanderthals, whose last refuge was in the Iberian peninsula. After about 30,000 years ago the fossil record of the Neanderthals ends, indicating that they had become extinct. The last known population lived around a cave system on the remote south-facing coast of Gibraltar from 30,000 to 24,000 years ago.

Proponents of the multiregional hypothesis have long believed that Europeans were descended from Neanderthals and not from this homo-sapiens migration. Others believed the Neanderthals had interbred with modern humans.

In 1997 researchers managed to extract mitochondrial DNA from a 40,000 year old specimen of a Neanderthal. On comparison with human DNA, its sequences differed significantly, indicating that based on the mitochondrial DNA, modern Europeans are not descended from the Neanderthals and that no interbreeding took place. Some scientists continue to search autosomal DNA for traces of Neanderthal admixture.

A few alleles of some autosomal genes such as the H2 allele of the MAPT gene have been suggested, since they were only found among Europeans. In the absence of autosomal DNA from a Neanderthal, the scientists conclude that this hypothesis is speculative.

Some archaeologists suspect that Neanderthals and *Homo sapiens* were not interfertile. This is because Neanderthals and Europeans shared the same habitat for up to 20,000 years, yet no undisputed skeletal fossils have been found that show intermediate properties between the two species.

Current (as of 2010) genetic evidence suggests interbreeding took place with Homo sapiens sapiens (anatomically modern humans) between roughly 80,000 to 50,000 years ago in the Middle East, resulting in non-ethnic sub-Saharan Africans having no Neanderthal DNA and Caucasians and Asians having between 1% and 4% Neanderthal DNA.

Central and Northern Asia

Mitochondrial haplogroups A, B and G originated about 50,000 years ago, and bearers subsequently colonized Siberia, Korea and Japan, by about 35,000 years ago. Parts of these populations migrated to North America.

Americas

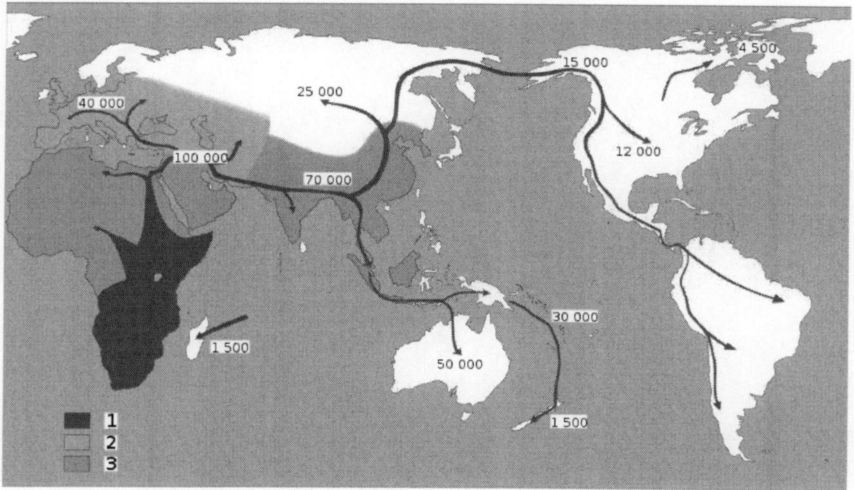

Figure: *A map of early human migrations*

The specifics of Paleo-Indians migration to and throughout the American Continent, including the exact dates and routes traveled, are subject to ongoing research and discussion.

The traditional theory has been that these early migrants moved into the Beringia land bridge between eastern Siberia and present-day Alaska around 40,000 — 17,000 years ago, when sea levels were significantly lowered due to the Quaternary glaciation.

These people are believed to have followed herds of now-extinct pleistocene megafauna along *ice-free corridors* that stretched between the Laurentide and Cordilleran ice sheets.

Another route proposed is that, either on foot or using primitive boats, they migrated down the Pacific North westcoast to South

America as far as Chile. Evidence of the latter would since have been covered by a sea level rise of a hundred metres following the last ice age.

Archaeologists contend that Paleo-Indians migration out of Beringia (eastern Alaska), ranges from 40,000 to around 16,500 years ago. This time range is a hot source of debate and will be for years to come.

The few agreements achieved to date are the origin from Central Asia, with widespread habitation of America during the end of the last glacial period, or more specifically what is known as the late glacial maximum, around 16,000 — 13,000 years before present.

Historical Migration

Pre-historical migration of human populations began with the movement of *Homo erectus* out of Africa across Eurasia about a million years ago. *Homo sapiens* appears to have colonized all of Africa about 150 millennia ago, moved out of Africa some 80 millennia ago, and spread across Eurasia and to Australia before 40 millennia ago. Migration to the Americastook place about 20 to 15 millennia ago, and by 1 millennium ago, all the Pacific Islands were colonized. Later population movements notably include the Neolithic revolution and Indo-European expansion, part of which emerges in the earliest historic records.

Before the modern era, migrations are often confusing in the written record because the history is written by societies on the periphery of the migrating peoples, or by their descendants who have given up the nomadic way of life. This is true of the era that follows the collapse of classical civilization in Europe, including the Early Medieval Great Migrations, and the related Turkic expansion. Much better understood are the Age of Exploration and European Colonialism, which led to an accelerated pace of migration over vast distances as new means of transportation emerged.

Neolithic Revolution

Agriculture is believed to have first been practised some 10,000 years ago in the Fertile Crescent. From there it propagated as a "wave" across Europe, a view supported by Archaeogenetics, reaching northern Europe some 5 millennia ago. VN

Bantu Expansion

The Bantu first originated around the Benue-Cross rivers area in southeastern Nigeria and spread over Africa to the Zambia area. Sometime in the second millennium BC, perhaps triggered by the drying of the Sahara and pressure from the migration of people from the Sahara into the region, they were forced to expand into the rainforests of central Africa (phase I). In the 1st millennium BC, they began a more rapid second phase of expansion beyond the forests into southern and eastern Africa, and again in the 1st millennium AD as new agricultural techniques and plants were developed in Zambia. By about AD 1000 it had reached modern day Zimbabwe and South Africa. In Zimbabwe a major southern hemisphere empire was established, with its capital at Great Zimbabwe. By the 14th or 15th century, the Empire had surpassed its resources and had collapsed.

Pacific

The islands of the Pacific were the last region on Earth to be populated by humans, as recently as twelve to fifteen centuries ago.

With the art of open-sea navigation involving the most confident and courageous use of the available technologies of boat-building, combined with the most sophisticated understanding of currents and prevailing winds, the Polynesians, starting with the Lapita culture, have proven to be the most successful in the art of navigation, if the permanent spread of culture is taken into account, for the Norse adventurers in the North Atlantic and the Arab traders in the Indian Ocean did not create permanent settlements. The Lapita people, who got their name from the archaeological site in Lapita, New Caledonia, where their characteristic pottery was first discovered, came from Austronesia, probably New Guinea. Their navigation skills took them to the Solomon Islands, around 1600 BC, and later to Fiji, Samoa and Tonga. By the beginning of the 1st millennium BC, most of Polynesia was a loose web of thriving cultures who settled on the islands' coasts and lived off the sea. By 500 BC Micronesia was completely colonized; the last region of Polynesia to be reached was New Zealand in around AD 1000. Polynesian migration patterns also have been studied by linguistic analysis, and recently by analyzing characteristic genetic alleles of today's inhabitants. Both methods resulted in supporting the original archaeological findings.

The Americas

The specifics of Paleo-Indians migration to and throughout the Americas, including the exact dates and routes traveled, are subject to ongoing research and discussion. The traditional theory has been that these early migrants moved into the Beringia land bridge between eastern Siberia and present-day Alaska around 40,000–17,000 years ago, when sea levels were significantly lowered due to the Quaternary glaciation.

These people are believed to have followed herds of now-extinct pleistocene megafauna along ice-free corridors that stretched between the Laurentide and Cordilleran ice sheets. Another route proposed is that, either on foot or using primitive boats, they migrated down the Pacific Northwest coast to South America. Evidence of the latter would since have been covered by a sea level rise of hundreds of metres following the last ice age.

Archaeologists contend that Paleo-Indians migration out of Beringia (eastern Alaska), ranges from 40,000 to around 16,500 years ago. This time range is a hot source of debate and will be for years to come. The few agreements achieved to date are the origin from Central Asia, with widespread habitation of the Americas during the end of the last glacial period, or more specifically what is known as the late glacial maximum, around 16,000–13,000 years before present.

Arctic

The Inuit are the descendants of what anthropologists call the Thule culture, which emerged from western Alaska around 1000 CE and spread eastward across the Arctic, displacing the Dorset culture (in Inuktitut, the Tuniit). Inuit historically referred to the Tuniit as “giants”, or “dwarfs”, who were taller and stronger than the Inuit. Researchers hypothesize that the Dorset culture lacked dogs, larger weapons and other technologies used by the expanding Inuit society. By 1300, the Inuit had settled in west Greenland, and finally moved into east Greenland over the following century. The Inuit had trade routes with more southern cultures. Boundary disputes were common and gave rise to aggressive actions. Warfare was common among Inuit groups with sufficient population density. Inuit, such as the Nunatamiut (Uummarmiut) who inhabited the Mackenzie River delta area, often engaged in common warfare. The Central Arctic Inuit lacked the population density to engage in warfare. In the 13th century, the Thule culture began arriving in Greenland from what is now Canada. Norse accounts are scant. Norse-made items from Inuit campsites in Greenland were obtained by either trade or plunder. One account, Ívar Bárðarson, speaks of “small people” with whom the Norsemen fought. 14th-century accounts that a western settlement, one of the two Norse settlements, was taken over by the Skræling.

Eurasian

Indo-Europeans

The Indo-European migration had variously been dated to the end of the Neolithic (Marija Gimbutas: Corded ware, Yamna, Kurgan), the early Neolithic (Colin Renfrew: Starèevo-Körös, Linearbandkeramic) and the late Palaeolithic (Marcel Otte, Paleolithic Continuity Theory).

The speakers of the Proto-Indo-European language are usually believed to have originated to the North of the Black Sea (today Eastern Ukraine and Southern Russia), and from there they gradually migrated into, and spread their language by cultural diffusion to, Anatolia, Europe, and Central Asia Iran and South Asia starting from around the end of the Neolithic period. Other theories, such as that of Colin Renfrew, posit their development much earlier, in Anatolia, and claim that Indo-European languages and culture spread as a result of the agricultural revolution in the early Neolithic.

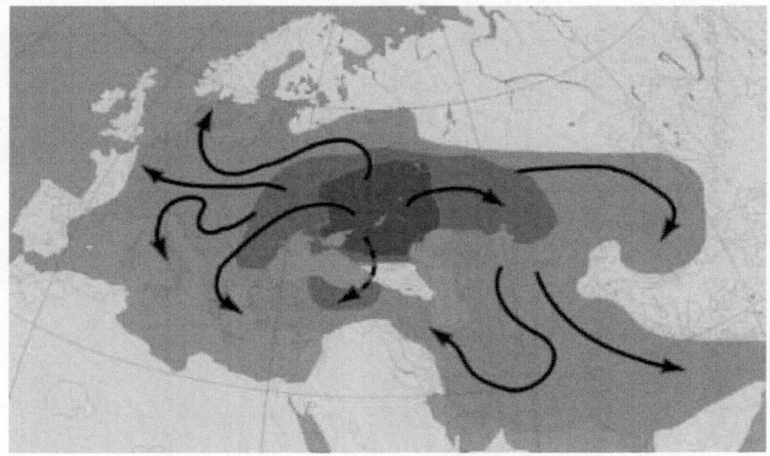

Figure: *Scheme of Indo-European migrations from ca. 4000 to 1000 BC according to the Kurgan hypothesis. The purple area corresponds to the assumed* Urheimat *(Samara culture, Sredny Stog culture). The red area corresponds to the area which may have been settled by Indo-European-speaking peoples up to ca. 2500 BC; the orange area to 1000 BC.*

Relatively little is known about the inhabitants of pre-Indo-European "Old Europe". They are believed to have been garden-plot horticulturalists. The Basque language remains from that era, as do the indigenous languages of the Caucasus. The Sami are genetically distinct among the peoples of Europe, but the Sami languages, as part of the Uralic languages, spread into Europe about the same time as the Indo-European languages. However, since that period speakers of other Uralic languages such as the Finns and the Estonians have had more contact with other Europeans, thus today sharing more genes with them than the Sami.

Bronze Age

The earliest migrations we can reconstruct from historical sources are those of the 2nd millennium BC. The Proto-Indo-Iranians began their expansion from ca. 2000 BC, the Rigveda documenting the presence of early Indo-Aryans in the Punjab from the late 2nd millennium BC, and Iranian tribes being attested in Assyrian sources as in the Iranian plateau from the 9th century BC. In the Late Bronze Age, the Aegean and Anatolia were overrun by moving populations, summarized as the "Sea Peoples", leading to the collapse of the Hittite Empire and ushering in the Iron Age.

Early Iron Age

The Dorian invasion of Greece led to the Greek Dark Ages. Very Little is known about the period of the 12th to 9th centuries BC, but there were significant population movements throughout Anatolia and the Iranian plateau. Iranian peoples invaded the territory of modern Iran in this period, taking over the Elamite Empire. The Urartians were displaced by Armenians, and the Cimmerians and the Mushki migrated from the Caucasus into Anatolia. A Thraco-Cimmerian connection links these movements to the Proto-Celtic world of central Europe, leading to the introduction of Iron to Europe and the Celtic expansion to western Europe and the British Isles around 500 BC.

The Great Migrations

Western historians refer to the period of migrations that separated Antiquity from the Middle Ages in Europe as the *Great Migrations* or as the Migrations Period. This period is further divided into two phases. The first phase, from 300 to 500 AD, saw the movement of Germanic, Sarmatian and Hunnic tribes and ended with the settlement of these peoples in the areas of the former Western Roman Empire, essentially causing its demise.

The second phase, between 500 and 900 AD, saw Slavic, Turkic and other tribes on the move, re-settling in Eastern Europe and gradually making it predominantly Slavic. Moreover, more Germanic tribes migrated within Europe during this period, including the Lombards (to Italy), and the Angles, Saxons, and Jutes (to the British Isles).

German historians of the 19th century referred to these Germanic migrations as the *Völkerwanderung*, the migrations of the peoples. The European migration period is connected with the simultaneous Turkic expansion which at first displaced other peoples towards the west, and by High Medieval times, the Seljuk Turks themselves reached the Mediterranean.

Medieval and Early Modern Europe

The medieval period, although often presented as a time of limited human mobility and slow social change in the history of Europe, in fact saw widespread movement of peoples. The Vikings from Scandinavia raided all over Europe from the 8th century and settled in many places, including Normandy, the north of England, Scotland and Ireland (most of whose urban centres were founded by the Vikings). The Normans later conquered the Saxon Kingdom of England, most of Ireland, southern Italy and Sicily, Iberia was invaded by Muslim Arabs, Berbers and Moors in the 8th century, founding new Kingdoms such as al Andalus and bringing with them a wave of settlers from North Africa. In the other direction, European Christian armies conquered Palestine for a time during the Crusades 11th to 13th centuries, founding three Christian kingdoms and settling them with Christian Knights and their families. This permanent migration was relatively small however and was one of the reasons why the Crusaders eventually lost the their hold on the Holy Lands.

Massive migrations of Germans took place into East Central and Eastern Europe, reaching its peak in the 12th to 14th centuries. These Ostsiedlung settlements in part followed territorial gains of the Holy Roman Empire, but areas beyond were settled, too. At the end of the Middle Ages, the Roma arrived in Europe (to Iberia and the Balkans) from the Middle East, originating from the Indus river.

Internal European migration stepped up in the Early Modern Period. In this period, major migration within Europe included the recruiting by monarchs of landless ers to settle depopulated or uncultivated regions and a series of forced migration caused by religious persecution. Notable examples of this phenomenon include the expulsion of the Jews from Spainin 1492, mass migration of Protestants from the Spanish Netherlands to the Dutch Republic after the 1580s, the expulsion of the Moriscos from Spain in 1609, and the expulsion of the Huguenots from France in the 1680s. Since the 14th century, the Serbs started leaving the areas of their medieval Kingdom and Empire that was overrun by the Ottoman Turks and migrated to the north, to the lands of today's Vojvodina (northern Serbia), which was ruled by the Kingdom of Hungary at that time. The Habsburg monarchs of Austria encouraged them to settle on their frontier with the Turks and provide military service by granting them free land and religious toleration. The two greatest migrations took place in 1690 and 1737. Other instances of labour recruitments include the Plantations of Ireland - the settling of Ireland with Protestant colonists from England, Scotland and Wales in the period 1560-1690 and the recruitment of Germans by Catherine the Great of Russia to settle the Volga region in the 18th century.

European Colonialism from the 16th to the early 20th centuries led to an imposition of a European colonies in many regions of the world, particularly in the Americas, South Asia, Sub-Saharan Africa and Australia, where European languages remain either prevalent or in frequent use as administrative languages. Major human migration before the 18th century was largely state directed. For instance, Spanish emigration to the New World was limited to settlers from Castile who were intended to act as soldiers or administrators. Mass immigration was not encouraged due to a labour shortage in Europe (of which Spain was the worst affected by a depopulation of its core territories in the 17th century).

Europeans also tended to die of tropical diseases in the New World in this period and for this reason England, France and Spain preferred using slaves as free labour in their American possessions. Many historians attribute a change in this pattern in the 18th century to population increases in Europe.

However, in the less tropical regions of North America's east coast, large numbers of religious dissidents, mostly English Puritans, settled during the early 17th century. Spanish restrictions on emigration to Latin America were revoked and the English colonies in North America also saw a major influx of settlers attracted by cheap or free land, economic opportunity and the continued lure of religious toleration.

A period in which various early English colonies had a significant amount of self-rule prevailed from the time of the Plymouth colony's founding in 1620 through 1676, as the mother country was wracked by revolution and general instability. However, King William III decisively intervened in colonial affairs after 1688 and the English colonies gradually came more directly under royal governance, with a marked effect on the type of emigration. During the early 18th century, significant numbers of non-English seekers of greater religious and political freedom were allowed to settle within the British colonies, including Protestant Palatine Germans displaced by French conquest, French Huguenots disenfranchised by an end of religious tolerance, Scotch-Irish Presbyterians, Quakers who were often Welsh, as well as Presbyterian and Catholic Scottish Highlanders seeking a new start after a series of unsuccessful revolts.

The English colonists who came during this period were increasingly moved by economic necessity. Some colonies, including Georgia, were settled heavily by petty criminals and indentured servants who hoped to pay off their debts. By 1800, European emigration had transformed the demographic character of the American continent. This was also due in part to the devastating effect of European diseases and warfare on Native American populations.

The European settlers' influence elsewhere was less pronounced as in South Asia and Africa, European settlement in this period was limited to thin layer of administrators, traders and soldiers.

Landnahme

Landnahme is a German term, literally translating to "land-taking", used for legendary or mythological and historiographical accounts alike concerning how a given people came to inhabit its present territory. Notable *Landnahme* events include:

- The conquest of Canaan in the Hebrew Bible, accounting for the arrival of the Israelites in the Promised Land
- The Indo-Aryan migration and expansion within India alluded to in the Rigveda
- The invasion traditions in the Irish Mythological Cycle, accounting for how the Gaels came to Ireland
- The arrival of the Franks in the territories subsequently known as Francia
- The Anglo-Saxon invasion of Britain
- The arrival of the Slavs in the course of the Slavic migrations
- The settlement of Iceland
- The Seljuk invasion of Anatolia.

Modern Migration

While the pace of migration had accelerated since the 18th century already (including the involuntary slave trade), it would increase further in the 19th century. Manning distinguishes three major types of migration: labour migration, refugee migrations and lastly: urbanization. Millions of agricultural workers left the countryside and moved to the cities causing unprecedented levels of urbanization. This phenomenon began in Britain in the late 18th century and spread around the world and continues to this day in many areas.

Industrialization encouraged migration wherever it appeared. The increasingly global economy globalised the labour market. Atlantic slave trade diminished sharply after 1820, which gave rise to self-bound contract labour migration from Europe and Asia to plantations. Also overpopulation, open agricultural frontiers and rising industrial centres attracted voluntary, encouraged and sometimes coerced migration. Moreover, migration was significantly eased by improved transportation techniques.

During this same period similar large numbers of people migrated over large distances within Asia. Southeastern Asia received 50 million migrants, mainly from India and south China. North Asia, that be Manchuria, Siberia, Central Asia and Japan together, received another 50 million, in a migration that started in the 1890s with migrants from China, Russia and Korea, and was especially large due to coerced migration from the Soviet Union and Japan in the 1930s. Less is known about exact numbers of the migrations from and within Africa in this period, but Africa experienced a small nett immigration between 1850 and 1950, from a variety of origins.

Provisions of the Potsdam Agreement from 1945 signed by victorious Western Allies and the Soviet Union led to one of the largest European migrations, and definitely the largest in the 20th century. It involved the migration and resettlement of close to or over 20 million people. The largest affected group were 16.5 million Germans expelled from Eastern Europe westwards. The second largest group were Poles, expelled westwards from eastern Kresy region and resettled in the so-called Recovered Territories. Hundreds of thousands of Poles, Ukrainians, Lithuanians, Latvians, Estonians and some Belarusians, were in the meantime expelled eastwards from Europe to the Soviet Union. Finally, many of the several hundred thousand Jews remaining in the Eastern Europe after the Holocaust migrated outside Europe to Israel and the USA.

Currently in progress are large migrations to Anglo America from Mexico and Central America, and a slightly smaller migration from the Islamic World into Europe.

Modern Migrations

Industrialization: While the pace of migration had accelerated since the 18th century already (including the involuntary slave trade), it would increase further in the 19th century. Manning distinguishes three major types of migration: labour migration, refugee migrations, and urbanization. Millions of agricultural workers left the countryside and moved to the cities causing unprecedented levels of urbanization. This phenomenon began in Britain in the late 18th century and spread around the world and continues to this day in many areas.

Industrialization encouraged migration wherever it appeared. The increasingly global economy globalized the labour market. The Atlantic slave trade diminished sharply after 1820, which gave rise to self-bound contract labour migration from Europe and Asia to plantations. Overpopulation, open agricultural frontiers, and rising industrial centres attracted voluntary migrants. Moreover, migration was significantly made easier by improved transportation techniques. Transnational labour migration reached a peak of three million migrants per year in the early twentieth century. Italy, Norway, Ireland and the Guangdong region of China were regions with especially high emigration rates during these years. These large migration flows influenced the process of nation state formation in many ways. Immigration restrictions have been developed, as well as diaspora cultures and myths that reflect the importance of migration to the foundation of certain nations, like the American melting pot. The transnational labour migration fell to a lower level from 1930s to the 1960s and then rebounded.

The United States experienced considerable internal migration related to industrialization, including its African American population. From 1910–1970, approximately 7 million African Americans migrated from the rural Southern United States, where blacks faced both poor economic opportunities and considerable political and social prejudice, to the industrial cities of the Northeast, Midwest and West, where relatively well-paid jobs were available. This phenomenon came to be known in the United States as its own Great Migration. With the demise of legalized segregation in the 1960s and greatly improved economic opportunities in the South in the subsequent decades, millions of blacks have returned to the South from other parts of the country since 1980 in what has been called the New Great Migration.

World War I

The twentieth century experienced also an increase in migratory flows caused by war and politics. Muslims moved from the Balkan to Turkey, while Christians moved the other way, during the collapse of the Ottoman Empire. Four hundred thousand Jews moved to Palestine in the early twentieth century. The Russian Civil War caused some three million Russians, Poles and Germans to migrate out of the Soviet Union. World War II and decolonization also caused migrations.

World War II

The Jewish communities across Europe, the Mediterranean and the Middle East were formed from voluntary and involuntary migrants. After the Holocaust (1938 to 1945), there was increased migration to the British Mandate of Palestine, which became the modern state of Israel as a result of the United Nations Partition Plan for Palestine.

Provisions of the Potsdam Agreement from 1945 signed by victorious Western Allies and the Soviet Union led to one of the largest European migrations, and the largest in the 20th century. It involved the migration and resettlement of close to or over 20 million people. The largest affected group were 16.5 million Germans expelled from Eastern Europe westwards. The second largest group were Poles, millions of whom were expelled westwards from eastern Kresy region and resettled in the so-called Recovered Territories. Hundreds of thousands of Poles, Ukrainians (Operation Vistula), Lithuanians, Latvians, Estonians and some Belarusians were expelled eastwards from Europe to the Soviet Union. Finally, many of the several hundred thousand Jews remaining in Eastern Europe after the Holocaust migrated outside Europe to Israel and the United States.

Pakistan-India

In 1947, upon the Partition of India, large populations moved from India to Pakistan and vice versa, depending on their religious beliefs. The partition was promulgated in the Indian Independence Act 1947 as a result of the dissolution of the British Indian Empire. The partition displaced up to 12.5 million people in the former British Indian Empire, with estimates of loss of life varying from several hundred thousand to a million. Muslim residents of the former British India migrated to Pakistan (including East Pakistan which is now Bangladesh), whilst Hinduand Sikh residents of Pakistan and Hindu residents of East Pakistan (now Bangladesh) moved in the opposite direction.

In modern India, estimates based on industry sectors mainly employing migrants suggest that there are around 100 million circular migrants in India. Caste, social networks and historical precedents play a powerful role in shaping patterns of migration. Migration for the poor is mainly circular, as despite moving temporarily to urban areas, they lack the social security which might keep them there more permanently. They are also keen to maintain a foothold in home areas during the agricultural season. Research by the Overseas Development Institute identifies a rapid movement of labour from slower- to faster-growing parts of the economy. Migrants can often find themselves excluded by urban housing policies, and migrant support initiatives are needed to give workers improved access to market information, certification of identity, housing and education. Some people usually move from the Thar Desert, over to Dharavi in Mumbai, whilst shortly living in small towns and cities along the way.

Theories for Migration for Work in the 21st Century

Overview: Migration for work in the 21st century has become a popular way for individuals from impoverished developing countries to obtain sufficient income for survival. This income is sent home to family members in the form of remittances and has become an economic staple in a number of developing countries, namely the Philippines and those in Latin America. There are a number of theories to explain the international flow of capital and people from one country to another.

Neoclassical Economic Theory

This is the newest theory of migration and states that the main reason for labour migration is wage difference between two geographic locations. These wage differences are usually linked to geographic labour demand and supply. It can be said that areas with a shortage of labour but an excess of capital have a high relative wage while areas with a high labour supply and a dearth of capital have a low relative wage. Labour tends to flow from low-wage areas to high-wage areas. Often, with this flow of labour comes changes in the sending as well as the receiving country. Neoclassical economic theory is best used to describe transnational migration, because it is not confined by international immigration laws and similar governmental regulations.

Dual Labour Market Theory

Dual labour market theory states that migration is mainly caused by pull factors in more developed countries. This theory assumes that the labour markets in these developed countries consist of two segments: primary, which requires high-skilled labour, and secondary, which is very labour-intensive but requires low-skilled workers. This theory assumes that migration from less developed countries into more developed countries is a result of a pull created by a need for labour in the developed countries in their secondary market. Migrant workers are needed to fill the lowest rung of the labour market because the native labourers do not want to do these jobs as they present a lack of mobility. This creates a need for migrant workers. Furthermore, the initial dearth in available labour pushes wages up, making migration even more enticing.

The New Economics of Labour Migration

This theory states that migration flows and patterns cannot be explained solely at the level of individual workers and their economic incentives, but that wider social entities must be considered as well. One such social entity is the household. Migration can be viewed as a result of risk aversion on the part of a household that has insufficient income. The household, in this case, is in need of extra capital that can be achieved through remittances sent back by family members who participate in migrant labour abroad. These remittances can also have a broader effect on the economy of the sending country as a whole as they bring in capital.

Relative Deprivation Theory

Relative deprivation theory states that awareness of the income difference between neighbours or other households in the migrant-sending community is an important factor in migration. The incentive to migrate is a lot higher in areas that have a high level of economic inequality. In the short run, remittances may increase inequality, but in the long run, they may actually decrease it. There are two stages of migration for a worker: first, they invest in human capital formation, and then they try to capitalize on their investments. In this way, successful migrants may use their new capital to provide for better schooling for their children and better homes for their families. Successful high-skilled emigrants may serve as an example for neighbours and potential migrants who hope to achieve that level of success.

World Systems Theory

World systems theory looks at migration from a global perspective. It explains that interaction between different societies can be an important factor in social change within societies. Trade with one country, which causes economic decline in another, may create incentive to migrate to a country with a more vibrant economy. It can be argued that even after decolonization, the economic dependence of former colonies still remains on mother countries. This view of international trade is controversial, however, and some argue that free trade can actually reduce migration between developing and developed countries. It can be argued that the developed countries import labour-intensive goods, which causes an increase in employment of unskilled workers in the less developed countries, decreasing the outflow of migrant workers. The export of capital-intensive goods from rich countries to poor countries also equalizes income and employment conditions, thus also slowing migration. In either direction, this theory can be used to explain migration between countries that are geographically far apart.

Historical Theories

Ravenstein: Certain laws of social science have been proposed to describe human migration. The following was a standard list after Ravenstein's proposals during the time frame of 1834 to 1913. The laws are as follows:

- every migration flow generates a return or countermigration.
- the majority of migrants move a short distance.
- migrants who move longer distances tend to choose big-city destinations.

- urban residents are often less migratory than inhabitants of rural areas.
- families are less likely to make international moves than young adults.
- most migrants are adults.
- large towns grow by migration rather than natural increase.
- Migration stage by stage
- Urban Rural difference
- Migration and Technology
- Economic condition.

Lee

Lee's laws divides factors causing migrations into two groups of factors: push and pull factors. Push factors are things that are unfavourable about the area that one lives in, and pull factors are things that attract one to another area.

Push Factors:

- Not enough jobs
- Few opportunities
- Primitive conditions
- Desertification
- Famine or drought
- Political fear or persecution
- Slavery or forced labour
- Poor medical care
- Loss of wealth
- Natural disasters
- Death threats
- Lack of political or religious freedom
- Pollution
- Poor housing
- Landlord/tenant issues
- Bullying
- Discrimination
- Poor chances of marrying
- Condemned housing (radon gas, etc.)
- War.

Pull Factors:

- Job opportunities
- Better living conditions
- Political and/or religious freedom
- Enjoyment
- Education
- Better medical care
- Attractive climates
- Security
- Family links
- Industry
- Better chances of marrying.

See also article by Gürkan Çelik, in Turkish Review: Turkey Pulls, The Netherlands Pushes? An increasing number of Turks, the Netherlands' largest ethnic minority, are beginning to return to Turkey, taking with them the education and skills they have acquired abroad, as the Netherlands faces challenges from economic difficulties, social tension and increasingly powerful far-right parties. At the same time Turkey's political, social and economic conditions have been improving, making returning home all the more appealing for Turks at large. (pp. 94–99)

Climate Cycles

The modern field of climate history suggests that the successive waves of Eurasian nomadic movement throughout history have had their origins in climatic cycles, which have expanded or contracted pastureland in Central Asia, especially Mongolia and the Altai. People were displaced from their home ground by other tribes trying to find land that could be grazed by essential flocks, each group pushing the next further to the south and west, into the highlands of Anatolia, the Pannonian Plain, into Mesopotamia or southwards, into the rich pastures of China.

Other Models

- *Migration occurs because individuals search for food, sex and security outside their usual habitation.* Idyorough is of the view that towns and cities are a creation of the human struggle to obtain food, sex and security. To produce food, security and reproduction, human beings must, out of necessity, move out of their usual habitation and enter into indispensable social relationships that are cooperative or antagonistic. Human beings also develop the tools and equipment to enable them to interact with nature to produce the desired food and security. The improved relationship (cooperative relationships) among human beings and improved technology further conditioned by the push and pull factors all interact together to cause or bring about migration and higher concentration of individuals into towns and cities. The higher the technology of production of food and security and the higher the cooperative relationship among human beings in the production of food and security and in the reproduction of the human species, the higher would be the push and pull factors in the migration and concentration of human beings in towns and cities. Countryside, towns and cities do not just exist but they do so to meet the human basic needs of food, security and the reproduction of the human species. Therefore, migration occurs because individuals search for food, sex and security outside their usual habitation. Social services in the towns and cities are provided to meet these basic needs for human survival and pleasure.

- Zipf's Inverse distance law (1956)
- Gravity model of migration and the friction of distance
- Buffer Theory
- Stouffer's theory of intervening opportunities (1940)
- Zelinsky's mobility transition model (1971)
- Bauder's regulation of labour markets (2006) "suggests that the international migration of workers is necessary for the survival of industrialized economies. [It] turns the conventional view of international migration on its head: it investigates how migration regulates labour markets, rather than labour markets shaping migration flows."

Population Mobility

Population mobility, geographic mobility or more simply mobility is a statistic that measures migration within a population. It is most commonly used in demography and human geography, it may also be used to describe the movement of animals between populations.

Mobility estimates in the Current Population Survey (CPS), produced by the United States Census Bureau, define mobility status on the basis of a comparison between the place of residence of each individual to the time of the March survey and the place of residence 1 year earlier. Non-movers are all people who were living in the same house at the end of the migration period and the beginning of the migration period. Movers are all people who were living in a different house at the end of the period rather than at the beginning. Movers are further classified as to whether they were living in the same or different county, state, region, or were movers from abroad. Movers are also categorized by whether they moved within or between central cities, suburbs, and non-metropolitan areas of the United States.

The CPS also includes information on reasons for a move. These include work-related factors, such as a job transfer, job loss or looking for work, and wanting to be closer to work. Housing factors include wanting to own a home, rather than rent, seeking a better home or better neighbourhood, or wanting cheaper housing. Additional mobility factors include attending college, changes in marital status, retirement, or health-related moves.

Other Measures

Population turnover is a related statistic that measures gross moves in relation to the size of the population, for example movement of residents into and out of a geographic location between census counts. Population mobility has implications ranging from changes in Congressional representation, impact on local economic growth, housing markets, and demand for local services. Mobility may also affect the spread of infectious diseases.

Replacement Migration

In demography, replacement migration is the migration needed for a region to achieve a particular objective (demographic, economic or social). Generally, studies using this concept have as an objective to avoid the decline of total population and the decline of the working-age population. Projections calculating migration replacement are primarily demographics and theoretical exercises and not forecasts or recommendations. The concept of replacement migration may vary according to the study and depending on the context in which it applies. It may be a number of annual immigrants, a net migration, an additional number of immigrants compared to a reference scenario, etc.

Types of Replacement Migration

Replacement migration may take several forms because several scenarios of projections population can achieve the same aim. However, two forms predominate: minimal replacement migration and constant replacement migration.

Constant Replacement Migration

The constant replacement migration does not fluctuate and remains the same throughout the projection. For example, it will be calculated with a projection providing a migration of X throughout the temporal horizon.

Results

The raw results of replacement migration are not necessarily comparable depending on the type of replacement migration used by the author. Nevertheless, major demographics conclusions are recurrent:

- The replacement migration reached impossible levels in practice to avoid aging the population, to maintain dependency ratio or influence significantly the age structure of a region.
- For regions with a relatively high fertility rate, replacement migration avoiding a decline in the total population or the working age is not excessively high. However, for regions with very low fertility rate, migration replacement is very high and unrealistic.
- The level of fertility is a much more important than the Immigration on aging and age structure.
- The principal effect of immigration is on population effective without substantially modifying the structure.

Examples of Results

Replacement migration to prevent the total population decline (annual average):

- *Germany:* 340 000 (net)
- *Canada:* 76 000 (number of immigrants)
- *United States:* 130 000 (net)
- *Europe:* 1 900 000 (net)
- *Japan:* 340 000 (net)
- *Quebec:* 40 000 (number of immigrants)
- Russia 500 000 (net)
- *Slovenia:* 6 000 (additional immigrants relative to the reference) Replacement migration to prevent the decline of population of working age (annual average)
- *Germany:* 490 000 (net)
- *Canada:* 165 000 (number of immigrants)

- *United States:* 360 000 (net)
- *Europe:* 3 230 000 (net)
- Japan 650 000 (net)
- *Quebec:* 70 000 (number of immigrants)
- *Russia:* 715 000 (net)
- *Slovenia:* 240 000 (additional immigrants relative to the reference).

Human Sex Ratio

In anthropology and demography, the human sex ratio is the sex ratio for *Homo sapiens* (i.e., the ratio of males to females in a population). Like most sexual species, the sex ratio is approximately 1:1. In humans the secondary sex ratio (i.e., at birth) is commonly assumed to be 105 boys to 100 girls, an assumption that is a subject of debate in the scientific community. The sex ratio for the entire world population is 101 males to 100 females.

Gender imbalance may arise as a consequence of various factors ranging from natural factors and war casualties to intentional gender control and deliberate gendercide.

More data are available for humans than for any other species, and the human sex ratio is more studied than that of any other species, but interpreting these statistics can be difficult.

Human sex ratios, either at birth or in the population as a whole, might be quoted in any of four ways: the ratio of males to females, the ratio of females to males, the proportion of males, or the proportion of females. If there are 108,000 males and 100,000 females, the ratio would, respectively, be quoted as 1.080, 0.926, 0.519 or 0.481. Sex ratio in scientific literature is often expressed as the proportion of males. In contrast, sex ratio quoted in this article is the ratio of males to females, unless specified otherwise.

Natural Ratio

In a study around 2002, the natural sex ratio at birth was estimated to be close to 1.06 males/female. In most populations, adult males tend to have higher death rates than adult females of the same age (even after allowing for causes specific to females such as breast cancer and death in childbirth), both due to natural causes such as heart attacks and strokes, which account for by far the majority of deaths and also to violent causes, such as homicide and warfare (for example, in the USA as of 2006, an adult non-elderly male is 3 to 6 times more likely to become a victim of a homicide and 2.5 to 3.5 times more likely to die in an accident than a female of the same age), resulting in higher life expectancy of females. Consequently, the sex ratio tends to reduce as age increases, and among the elderly there is usually an excess of females. For example, the male to female ratio falls from 1.05 for the group aged 15 to 65 to 0.70 for the group over 65 in Germany, from 1.00 to 0.72 in the USA, from 1.06 to 0.91 in mainland China and from 1.07 to 1.02 in India, which has a smaller proportion of very old people.

In the United States, the sex ratios at birth over the period 1970–2002 were 1.05 for the white non-Hispanic population, 1.04 for Mexican Americans, 1.03 for African Americans and Indians, and 1.07 for mothers of Chinese or Filipino ethnicity. Among Western European countries ca. 2001, the ratios ranged from 1.04 in Belgium to 1.07 in Switzerland, Italy, Ireland and Portugal. In the aggregated results of 56 Demographic and Health Surveys in African countries, the ratio is 1.03, though there is also considerable country-to-country variation.

Even in the absence of sex selection practices, a range of "normal" sex ratios at birth of between 103 to 108 boys per 100 girls has been observed in different economically developed countries, and among different ethnic and racial groups within a given country.

In an extensive study, carried out around 2005, of sex ratio at birth in the United States from 1940 over 62 years, statistical evidence suggested the following: For mothers having their first baby, the total sex ratio at birth was 1.06 overall, with some years at 1.07. For mothers having babies after the first, this ratio consistently decreased with each additional baby from 1.06 towards 1.03. The age of the mother affected the ratio: the overall ratio was 1.05 for mothers aged 25 to 35 at the time of birth; while mothers who were below the age of 15 or above 40 had babies with a sex ratio ranging between 0.94 to 1.11, and a total sex ratio of 1.04. This United States study also noted that American mothers of Hawaiian, Filipino, Chinese, Cuban and Japanese ethnicity had the highest sex ratio, with years as high as 1.14 and average sex ratio of 1.07 over the 62 year study period.

Factors Affecting Sex Ratio in Humans

Fisher's principle: Fisher's principle is an explanation of why the sex ratio of most species is approximately 1:1. Outlined by Ronald Fisher in his 1930 book, it is an argument in terms of parental expenditure. Essentially he argues that the 1:1 ratio is the evolutionarily stable strategy.

Natural Factors

The natural factors that affect the human sex ratio are an active area of scientific research. Over 1000 articles have been published in various journals. Two of the often cited reviews of scientific studies on human sex ratio are by James. The scientific studies are based on extensive birth and death records in Europe, the Americas, Asia, Australia and Africa. A few of these studies extend to over 100 years of yearly human sex ratio data for some countries. These studies suggest that the human sex ratio, both at birth and as a population matures, can vary significantly according to a large number of factors, such as paternal age, maternal age, plural birth, birth order, gestation weeks, race, parent's health history, parent's psychological stress. Remarkably, the trends in human sex ratio are not consistent across countries at a given time, or over time for a given country. In economically developed countries, as well as developing countries, these scientific studies have found that the human sex ratio at birth has historically varied between 0.94 to 1.15 for natural reasons.

In a Scientific Paper Published in 2008, James States that Conventional Assumptions Have Been:

- there are equal numbers of X and Y chromosomes in mammalian sperms
- X and Y stand equal chance of achieving conception
- therefore equal number of male and female zygotes are formed, and that
- therefore any variation of sex ratio at birth is due to sex selection between conception and birth.

James cautions that available scientific evidence stands against the above assumptions and conclusions. He reports that there is an excess of males at birth in almost all human populations, and the natural sex ratio at birth is usually between 1.02 to 1.08. However the ratio may deviate significantly from this range for natural reasons.

A 1999 scientific paper published by Jacobsen reported the sex ratio for 815,891 children born in Denmark between 1980–1993. They studied the birth records to identify the effects of multiple birth, birth order, age of parents and the sexes of preceding siblings on the proportion of males using contingency tables, χ^2 tests and regression analysis. The secondary sex ratio decreased with increased number of children per plural birth and with paternal age, whereas no significant independent effect was observed for maternal age, birth order, or other natural factors.

A 2009 research paper published by Branum et al. reports the sex ratio derived from data in United States birth records over a 25 year period (1981–2006). This paper reports that the sex ratio at birth for the white ethnic group in the United States was 1.04 when the gestational age was 33–36 weeks, but 1.15 for gestational ages of less than 28 weeks, 28–32 weeks, and 37 or more weeks. This study also found that the sex ratios at birth in the United States, between 1981–2006, were lower in both black and hispanic ethnic groups when compared with white ethnic group.

The relationship between natural factors and human sex ratio at birth, and with aging, remains an active area of scientific research.

Environmental Factors

Effects of Climate Change: Various scientists have examined the question whether human birth sex ratios have historically been affected by environmental stressors such as climate change and global warming. Catalano et al. report that cold weather is an environmental stressor, and women subjected to colder weather abort frail male fetuses in greater proportion thereby lowering birth sex ratios. Cold weather stressors simultaneously extend male longevity thereby raise human sex ratio in its older age bracket. Catalano team finds that a 1°C increase in annual temperature predicts one more male than expected for every 1,000 females born in a year.

Helle et al. have studied 138 years worth of human birth sex ratio data, from 1865 to 2003. They find an increased excess of male births during periods of the exogenous stress (World War II) and during warm years. In the warmest period over the 138 years, the birth sex ratio peaked at about 1.08 in northern Europe.

Effects of Gestation Environment

Causes of stress during gestation, such as maternal malnutrition generally appear to increase fetal deaths particularly among males, resulting in a lower boy to girl ratio at birth. Also, higher incidence of Hepatitis B virus in populations is believed to decrease the male to female sex ratio, while some unexplained environmental health hazards are thought to have the opposite effect. The effects of gestational environment on human sex ratio are complicated and unclear, with numerous conflicting reports. For example, Oster et al. examined a data set of 67,000 births in China, 15 percent of whom were Hepatitis B carriers. They found no effect on birth sex ratio from Hepatitis B presence in either the mothers or fathers. It remains unclear if observations in China can be assumed to be true all over the world.

Effects of Chemical Pollution

A 2007 survey by the Arctic Monitoring and Assessment Programme noted abnormally low sex ratios in Russian Arctic villages and Inuit villages in Greenland and Canada, and attributed this imbalance to high levels of endocrine disruptors in the blood of inhabitants, including PCBs and DDT. These chemicals are believed to have accumulated in the tissues of fish and animals that make up the bulk of these populations' diets. However, as noted in the Social factors section below, it is important to exclude alternative explanations, including social ones, when examining large human populations whose composition by ethnicity and race may be changing.

A 2008 report provides further evidence of effects of feminizing chemicals on male development in each class of vertebrate species as a worldwide phenomenon, possibly leading to a decline in the sex ratio in humans and a possible decline in sperm counts. Out of over 100,000 recently introduced chemicals, 99% are poorly regulated.

Other Factors That Could Possibly Affect the Sex Ratio Include:

- Social status of the mother, known to be a factor in influencing the sex ratio of certain animals such as swine, but apparently not in humans.
- Whether the mother smokes.
- Whether the mother has a partner or other support network, although this correlation is widely considered to be the result of an unknown third factor.
- Latitude, with countries near the equator producing more females than near the poles.

Other scientific studies suggest that environmental effects on human sex ratio at birth are either limited or not properly understood. For example, a research paper published in 1999, by scientists from Finland's National Public Health Institute, reports the effect of environmental chemicals and changes in sex ratio over 250 years in Finland. This scientific team evaluated whether Finnish long-term data are compatible with the hypothesis that the decrease in the ratio of male to female births in industrial countries is caused by environmental factors. They analysed the sex ratio of births from the files of Statistics Finland and all live births in Finland from 1751 to 1997. They found an increase in the proportion of males from 1751 to 1920; this was followed by a decrease and interrupted by peaks in births of males during and after World War I and World War II. None of the natural factors such as paternal age, maternal age, age difference of parents, birth order could explain the time trends. The scientists found that the peak ratio of male proportion precedes the period of industrialization or the introduction of pesticides or hormonal drugs, rendering a causal association between environmental chemicals and human sex ratio at birth unlikely. Moreover, these scientists claim that the trends they found in Finland are similar to those observed in other countries with worse pollution and much greater pesticide use.

Social Factors

Sex-selective abortion and infanticide are thought to significantly skew the naturally occurring ratio in some populations, such as China, where the introduction of ultrasound scans in the late 1980s has led to a birth sex ratio (males to females) of 1.133 (2011 CIA estimate data). The 2011 India census reports India's sex ratio in 0-6 age bracket at 1.094. The 2011 birth sex ratios for China and India are significantly above the mean ratio recorded in the United States from 1940 through 2002 (1.051); however, their birth sex ratios are within the 0.98-1.14 range observed in the United States for significant ethnic groups over the same time period. Along with Asian countries, a number of European, Middle East and Latin American countries have recently reported high birth sex ratios in the 1.06 to 1.14 range. High birth sex ratios, some claim may be caused in part by social factors.

One hypothesis is that these practices are based on a cultural preference for one sex, typically males, over the other. A son is often preferred as an "asset", since he can earn and support the family; a daughter is a "liability" since she will be married off to another family, and so will not contribute financially to her parents. The patriarchal structure of a society is the single most important factor skewing the sex ratio in favour of males, accentuated in some cultures by the burden of raising a dowry for a daughter's marriage. Reported sex ratios at birth, outside the typical range of 1.03 to 1.07, thus call for an explanation of some kind.

Another hypothesis has been inspired by the recent and persistent high birth sex ratios observed in Georgia and Armenia—both predominantly Orthodox Christian societies—and Azerbaijan, a predominantly Muslim society. Since their independence from Soviet Union, the birth sex ratio in these Caucasus countries has risen sharply to between 1.11 and 1.20, some of world's highest. France Mesle et al. consider the hypothesis that the high birth sex ratio may be because of the social trend of more than two children per family, and birth order possibly affects the sex ratio in this region of the world. They also consider the hypothesis that sons are preferred in these countries of the Caucasus, the spread of scans and there being a practice of sex-selective abortion; however, the scientists admit that they do not have definitive proof that sex-selective abortion is actually happening or that there are no natural reasons for the persistently high birth sex ratios.

In all such research, it is important to consider plausible alternative explanations. For example in some populations that have experienced declining sex ratios, researchers have suggested that ecological factors may be at work.

As an example of how the social composition of a human population may produce unusual changes in sex ratios, we can consider a study in several counties of California where declining sex ratios had been observed. Smith and Von Behren observe that: "In the raw data, the male birth proportion is indeed declining. However, during this period, there were also shifts in demographics that influence the sex ratio. Controlling for birth order, parents' age, and race/ethnicity, different trends emerged. White births (which account for over 80%) continued to show a statistically significant decline, while other racial groups showed non-statistically significant declines (Japanese, Native American, other), little or no change (black), or an increase (Chinese). Finally, when the white births were divided into Hispanic and non-Hispanic (possible since 1982), it was found that both white subgroups suggest an increase in male births." They concluded "that the decline in male births in California is largely attributable to changes in demographics."

Early Marriage and Parent's Age

Several studies have examined human birth sex ratio data to determine if there is a natural relationship between the age of mother or father to the birth sex ratio. For example, Ruder has studied 1.67 million births in 33 states in the United States to discern effect of parent's age and birth sex ratios. Similarly, Jacobsen et al. have studied 0.82 million births in Denmark with the same goal. These scientists find that maternal age has no statistically significant role on human birth sex ratio. However, they report a significant effect of paternal age. Significantly more male babies were born per 1000 female babies to younger fathers than to older fathers. These studies suggest that social factors such as early marriage and quickly fertile couples may play a role in raising birth sex ratios in certain societies.

Data Sources and Data Quality Issues

Reported sex ratios at birth for some human populations may be influenced not only by cultural preferences and social practices that favour the birth or survival of one sex over the other (more often favouring males than favouring females) but also by incomplete or inaccurate reporting or recording of the births or the survival of infants. Even what constitutes alive birth or infant death may vary from one population to another. For example, for most of the 20th century in Russia (and the Soviet Union), extremely premature newborns (less than 28 weeks gestational age, or less than 1000 grams in weight, or less than 35 centimetres in length) were not counted as a live birth until they had survived 7 days; and if that infant died in those first 168 hours it would not be counted as an infant death. This led to serious underreporting of the Infant mortality rate (by 22% to 25%) relative to standards recommended by the World Health Organization.

When unusual sex ratios at birth (or any other age) are observed, it is important to consider misreporting, misrecording, or underregistration of births or deaths as possible reasons. Some researchers have in part attributed the high male to female sex ratios reported in mainland China in the last 25 years to the underreporting of the births of female children after the implementation of the one-child policy, though alternative explanations are now generally more widely accepted, including above all the use of ultrasound technology and sex-selective abortion of female fetuses and, probably to a more limited degree, neglect or in some cases infanticide of females. In the case of China, because of deficiencies in the vital statistics registration system, studies of sex ratios at birth have relied either on special fertility surveys, whose accuracy depends on full reporting of births and survival of both male and female infants, or on the national population census from which both birth rates and death rates are calculated from the household's reporting of births and deaths in the 18 months preceding the census. To the extent that this underreporting of births or deaths is sex-selective, both fertility surveys and censuses may inaccurately reflect the actual sex ratios at birth.

Economic Factors

Catalano has examined the hypothesis that population stress induced by a declining economy reduces the human sex ratio. He compared the sex ratio in East and West Germany for the years 1946 to 1999, with genetically similar populations. The population stressors theory predicts that the East German sex ratio should have been lower in 1991, when East Germany's economy collapsed, than expected from its previous years. Furthermore, the theory suggests that East German birth sex ratios should generally be lower than the observed sex ratio in West Germany for the same years, over time. According to Catalano's study, the birth sex ratio data from East Germany and West Germany over 45 years supports the hypothesis. The sex ratio in East Germany was also at its lowest in 1991. According to Catalano study, assuming women in East Germany did not opt to abort male more than female, the best hypothesis is that a collapsing economy lowers the human birth sex ratio, while a booming economy raises the birth sex ratio. Catalano notes that these trends may be related to the observed trend of elevated incidences of very low birth weight from maternal stress, during certain macroeconomic circumstances.

Other Gestational Factors

A research group led by Ein-Mor reported that sex ratio does not seem to change significantly with either maternal or paternal age. Neither gravidity nor parity seem to affect the male-to-female ratio. However, there is a significant association of sex ratio with the length of gestation. These Ein-mor conclusions have been disputed. For example, James suggested that Ein-Mor results are based on some demographic variables and a small data set, a broader study of variables and larger population set suggests human sex ratio shows substantial variation for various reasons and different trend effects of length of gestation than those reported by Ein-Mor. In another study, James has offered the hypothesis that human sex ratios, and mammalian sex ratios in general, are causally related to the hormone levels of both parents at the time of conception. This hypothesis is yet to be tested and proven true or false over large population sets.

Gender Imbalance

Gender imbalance is a disparity between male and females in a population. As stated above, males usually exceed females at birth but subsequently experience different mortality rates due to many possible causes such as differential natural death rates, war casualties, and deliberate gender control.

According to Nicholas Kristof and Sheryl WuDunn, two Pulitzer Prize-winning reporters for the New York Times, violence against women is causing gender imbalances in many developing countries. These authors report that more girls have been killed in the last 50 years, just because they were girls, than the number of males who were killed in all the wars of the 20th century. They detail rampant gendercide in the developing world, particularly in China, India and Pakistan.

Commonly, countries with gender imbalances have three characteristics in common. The first is a rapid decline in fertility, either because of preference for smaller families or to comply with their nation's population control measures. Second, there's pressure for women to give birth to sons, often because of cultural preferences for male heirs. Third, families have widespread access to technology to selectively abort female fetuses.

As a contributing measure to gender imbalance in developing countries, Kristof and WuDunn's best estimate is that a girl in India, from 1 to 5 years of age, dies from discrimination every four minutes (132,000 deaths per year); that 39,000 girls in China die annually, within the first year of life, because parents didn't give girls the same medical care and attention that boys received. The authors describe similar gender discrimination and gendercide in Congo, Kenya, Pakistan, Iraq, Bahrain, Thailand and many other developing countries.

Some of the factors suggested as causes of the gender imbalance are warfare (excess of females, notably in the wake of WWI in western Europe, and WWII, particularly in the Soviet Union); sex-selective abortion and infanticide (excess of males, notably in China as a result of the one-child policy, or in India); and large-scale migration, such as that by male labourers unable to bring their families with them (as in Qatar and other Gulf countries). Gender imbalance may result in the threat of social unrest, especially in the case of an excess of low-status young males unable to find spouses, and being recruited into the service of militaristic political factions. Economic factors such as male-majority industries and activities like the petrochemical, agriculture, engineering, military, and technology also have created a male gender imbalance in some areas dependent on one of these industries. Conversely, the entertainment, banking, tourism, fashion, and service industries may have resulted in a female-majority gender imbalance in some areas dependent on them.

One study found that the male-to-female sex ratio in the German state of Bavaria fell as low as 0.60 after the end of World War II for the most severely affected age cohort (those between 21 and 23 years old in 1946). This same study found that out-of-wedlock births spiked from approximately 10–15% during the inter-war years up to 22% at the end of the war. This increase in out-of-wedlock births was attributed to a change in the marriage market caused by the decline in the sex ratio. The Northern Mariana Islands have the highest female ratio with 0.77 males per female. Qatar has the highest male ratio, with 2.87 males/female. For the group aged below 15, Sierra Leone has the highest female ratio with 0.96 males/female, and the Republic of Georgia and the People's Republic of China are tied for the highest male ratio with 1.13 males/female (according to the 2006 CIA World Factbook).

The value for the entire world population is 1.01 males/female, with 1.07 at birth, 1.06 for those under 15, 1.02 for those between 15 and 64, and 0.78 for those over 65.

The "First World" G7 members all have a gender ratio in the range of 0.95–0.98 for the total population, of 1.05–1.07 at birth, of 1.05–1.06 for the group below 15, of 1.00–1.04 for the group aged 15–64, and of 0.70–0.75 for those over 65.

Countries on the Arabian peninsula tend to have a 'natural' ratio of about 1.05 at birth but a very high ratio of males for those over 65 (Saudi Arabia 1.13, Arab Emirates 2.73, Qatar 2.84), indicating either an above-average mortality rate for females or a below-average mortality for males, or, more likely in this case, a large population of aging male guest workers. Conversely, countries of Eastern Europe (the Baltic states, Belarus, Ukraine, Russia) tend to have a 'normal' ratio at birth but a very low ratio of males among those over 65 (Russia 0.46, Latvia 0.48, Ukraine 0.52); similarly, Armenia has a far above average male ratio at birth (1.17), and a below-average male ratio above 65 (0.67). This effect may be caused by emigration and higher male mortality as result of higher Soviet era deaths; it may also be related to the enormous (by western standards) rate of alcoholism in the former Soviet states. Another possible contributory factor is an aging population, with a higher than normal proportion of relatively elderly people: we recall that due to higher differential mortality rates the ratio of males to females reduces for each year of age.

Buffer Theory

In the late 1950s a number of European countries (most notably West Germany and France) decided on a migration policy known as the Buffer theory. Owing to rapid economic recovery in the post WWII period (aided by the American Marshall plan) there were many more job vacancies than people who were available or becoming available in the workforce to fill them. To resolve this situation they decided to "import" workers from the southern Mediterranean basin (including North Africa) on a temporary capacity to fill this labour shortfall.

These workers were invitees of the governments and came to Europe initially on the understanding that they could at any point in time in the future be repatriated if and when economic circumstances changed. These Gastarbeiter as they became known in Germany were mainly young unskilled males who very often left their families behind in their country of origin and migrated alone as 'Economic Migrant'. They worked predominantly in certain areas of the economy where working conditions were poorer than those of indigenous Germans and where the rates of pay were considerably lower. Ultimately they came to predominate in low paid service rated employment. The situation remained unchanged until the 1970s economic recession.

Jobs were being lost in manufacturing and industry in particular but not necessarily in the occupational types in which the migrants worked. In 1974 the then West German government imposed a ban restricting any future economic migrants and offered the possibility of returning to their country of origin to many others, few migrants took up the offer and stayed at their jobs or began to receive unemployment assistance from the state. This led to increased tensions and feeling of resentment from many German people.

Second Wave of Migration

Throughout the 1970s and into the 1980s family reunification took place between Turkish migrants workers and their families. This reunification however took place in Germany rather than in Turkey.

In a difficult *Economic climate* after the 1973 oil crisis it was generally believed by most Turks already in Germany that their economic circumstances would be measurably better there than back in Turkey at such a difficult time. The welfare state offered considerable financial support to all people within Germany including immigrants communities. The number of foreign residents therefore increased in absolute terms during this time period.

The German government's offer to repatriate people back to their home country was not very successful. Thus, you had a difficult situation for German government becoming increasingly worse as the number of immigrants swelled to their highest levels ever. Any resentment, hostility and bitterness already present between indigenous Germans and the Turkish community became progressively worse.

This often culminated in physical attacks on immigrants, arson and overt racial discrimination. There was a feeling amongst Germans that "they have taken our jobs", but this situation only arose because of Germans themselves losing their jobs in industry and manufacturing in particular in the difficult economic situation post 1973. (N.B. This 'family reunification' corresponds with the second wave on the Everett S. Lee model of migration).

Third Wave of Migration

Dates to the period from 1989 onwards with the collapse of the Iron Curtain and the communist regimes in Eastern Europe. East Germans flooded into West Germany along with many 'ethnic' Germans from central and eastern Europe. Germany accepted them as they were political refugee and very often asylum seekers.

Other Migration Models

- Zipf's Inverse distance law (1946)
- Gravity model and the Friction of distance
- Stouffer's Theory of intervening opportunities (1940)
- Lee's Push-pull theory (1966).

Gravity Model of Migration

The gravity model of migration is a model in urban geography derived from Newton's law of gravity, and used to predict the degree of interaction between two places (Rodrigue et al. 2009, 216). Newton's law states that: "Any two bodies attract one another with a force that is proportional to the product of their masses and inversely proportional to the square of the distance between them."

When used geographically, the words 'bodies' and 'masses' are replaced by 'locations' and 'importance' respectively, where importance can be measured in terms of population numbers, gross domestic product, or other appropriate variables. The gravity model of migration is therefore based upon the idea that as the importance of one or both of the location increases, there will also be an increase in movement between them. The farther apart the two locations are, however, the movement between them will be less. This phenomenon is known asdistance decay.

The gravity model can be used to estimate:

- Traffic flow
- Migration between two areas
- The number of people likely to use one central place.

The gravity model can also be used to determine the sphere of influence of each central place by estimating where the breaking point between the two settlements will be. An example of this is the point at which customers find it preferable, because of distance, time and expense considerations, to travel to one centre rather than the other.

The gravity model was expanded by William J. Reilly in 1931 into Reilly's law of retail gravitation to calculate the breaking point between two places where customers will be drawn to one or another of two competing commercial centres.

Opponents of the gravity model explain that it can not be confirmed scientifically, that it's only based on observation. They also state that the gravity model is an unfair method of predicting movement because its biased towards historic ties and towards the largest population centres. Thus, it can be used to perpetuate the status quo.

Theory of Intervening Opportunities

Theory of intervening opportunities attempts to describe the likelihood of migration. Its hypothesis is that this likelihood is influenced most by the opportunities to settle at the destination, less by distance or population pressure at the starting point.

Stouffer's law of intervening opportunities states, *"The number of persons going a given distance is directly proportional to the number of opportunities at that distance and inversely proportional to the number of intervening opportunities."*

Stouffer theorises that the amount of migration over a given distance is directly proportional to the number of opportunities at the place of destination, and inversely proportional to the number of opportunities between the place of departure and the place of destination. These intervening opportunities may persuade a migrant to settle in a place in the route rather than proceeding to the originally planned destination. Stouffer argued that the volume of migration had less to do with distance and population totals than with the opportunities in each location. This is in contrast to Zipf's *Inverse distance law*. There are links with Ravenstein's laws of migration 2, 3 and 4.

Census

A census is the procedure of systematically acquiring and recording information about the members of a given population. It is a regularly occurring and official count of a particular population. The term is used mostly in connection with national population and housing censuses; other common censuses include agriculture, business, and traffic censuses. In the latter cases the elements of the 'population' are farms, businesses, and so forth, rather than people. The United Nations defines the essential features of population and housing censuses as "individual enumeration, universality within a defined territory, simultaneity and defined periodicity", and recommends that population censuses be taken at least every 10 years. The word is of Latin origin; during the Roman Republic, the census was a list that kept track of all adult males fit for military service.

The census can be contrasted with sampling in which information is obtained only from a subset of a population, sometimes as an intercensal estimate. Census data is commonly used for research, business marketing, and planning, as well as a baseline for sampling surveys. Census counts are necessary to adjust samples to be representative of a population by weighting them as is common in opinion polling. Similarly, stratification requires knowledge of the relative sizes of different population strata which are derived from census enumerations. In some countries, census data are used to apportion electoral representation (sometimes controversially – *e.g.*, *Utah v. Evans*).

Residence Definitions

Individuals are normally counted within households and information is typically collected about the household structure and the housing. For this reason international documents refer to censuses of population and housing. Normally the census response is made by a household, indicating details of individuals resident there.

An important aspect of census enumerations is deciding which individuals to include within a national population. Broadly, three definitions can be used: *de facto* residence; *de jure*residence; and, permanent residence. This is important to consider individuals who have multiple or temporary addresses. Every person should be identified uniquely as resident in one place but where they happen to be on census day, their *de facto* residence, may not be the best place to count them. Where an individual uses services may be more useful and this is at their usual, or *de jure*, residence. An individual may be represented at a permanent address, perhaps a family home for students or long term migrants.

It is necessary to have a precise definition of residence to decide whether visitors to a country should be included in the population count. This is becoming more important as students travel abroad for education for a period of several years. Other groups causing problems of enumeration are new born babies, refugees, people away on holiday, people moving home around census day, and people without a fixed address.

Enumeration Strategies

Historical censuses used crude enumeration assuming absolute accuracy. Modern approaches take into account the problems of overcount and undercount, and the coherence of census enumerations with other official sources of data. This reflects a realist approach to measurement, acknowledging that under any definition of residence there is a true value of the population but this can never be measured with complete accuracy. An important aspect of the census process is to evaluate the quality of the data.

Many countries use a post-enumeration survey to adjust the raw census counts. This works in a similar manner to capture-recapture estimation for animal populations. In census circles this method is called dual system enumeration (DSE). A sample of households are visited by interviewers who record the details of the household as at census day. These data are then matched to census records and the number of people missed can be estimated by considering the number missed in the census or survey but counted in the other. This way counts can be adjusted for non-response varying between different demographic groups. An explanation using a fishing analogy can be found in Trout, Catfish and Roach which won an award from the Royal Statistical Society for excellence in official statistics in 2011.

Triple system enumeration has been proposed as an improvement as it would allow evaluation of the statistical dependence of pairs of sources. However, as the matching process is the most difficult aspect of census estimation this has never been implemented for a national enumeration. It would also be difficult to identify three different sources that were sufficiently different to make the triple system effort worthwhile. The DSE approach has another weakness in that it assumes there is no person counted twice (over count). In *de facto* residence definitions this would not be a problem but in *de jure* definitions individuals risk being recorded on more than one form leading to double counting. A particular problem here are students who often have a term time and family address.

Several countries have used a system which is known as short form/long form. This is a sampling strategy which randomly chooses a proportion of people to send a more detailed questionnaire to (the long form). Everyone receives the short form questions. Thereby more data is collected but not imposing a burden on the whole population. This also reduces the burden on the statistical office. Indeed in the UK all residents were required to fill in the whole form but only a 10% sample were coded and analysed in detail, until 2001. New technology means that all data is now scanned and processed. Recently there has been controversy in Canada about the cessation of the long form with the head, Munir Sheikh Resigning.

The use of alternative enumeration strategies is increasing but these are not so simple as many people assume. The Netherlands has been most advanced in adopting a census using administrative data. This allows a simulated census to be conducted by linking several different administrative databases at an agreed time. Data can be matched and an overall enumeration established accounting for where the different sources are discrepant. A validation survey is still conducted in a similar way to the post enumeration survey employed in a traditional census.

Other countries which have a population register use this as a basis for all the census statistics needed by users. This is most common amongst Nordic countries. A recent innovation is the French instigation of a rolling census programme with different regions enumerated each year such that the whole country is completely enumerated every 5 years.

Technology

Censuses have evolved in their use of technology with the latest censuses, the 2010 round, using many new types of computing. In Brazil, handheld devices were used by enumerators to locate residences on the ground. In many countries, census returns could be made via the Internet as well as in paper form. DSE is facilitated by computer matching techniques which can be automated, such as propensity score matching. In the UK, all census formats are scanned and stored electronically before being destroyed, replacing the need for physical archives. The record linking to perform an administrative census would not be possible without large databases being stored on computer systems.

New technology is not without problems in its introduction. The US census had intended to use the handheld computers but cost escalated and this was abandoned, with the contract being sold to Brazil. Online response is a good idea but one of the functions of census is to make sure everyone is counted accurately. A system which allowed people to enter their address without verification would be open to abuse. Therefore households have to be verified on the ground, typically by an enumerator visit or post out. Paper forms are still necessary for those without access to Internet connections. It is also plausible that the hidden nature of an administrative census means that users are not engaged with the importance of contributing their data to official statistics.

Privacy

Although the census provides a useful way of obtaining statistical information about a population, such information can sometimes lead to abuses, political or otherwise, made possible by the linking of individuals' identities to anonymous census data. This consideration is particularly important when individuals' census responses are made available in microdata form, but even aggregate-level data can result in privacy breaches when dealing with small areas and/or rare subpopulations.

For instance, when reporting data from a large city, it might be appropriate to give the average income for black males aged between 50 and 60. However, doing this for a town that only has two black males in this age group would be a breach of privacy because either of those persons, knowing his own income and the reported average, could determine the other man's income.

Typically, census data are processed to obscure such individual information. Some agencies do this by intentionally introducing small statistical errors to prevent the identification of individuals in marginal populations; others swap variables for similar respondents. Whatever measures have been taken to reduce the privacy risk in census data, new technology in the form of better electronic analysis of data poses increasing challenges to the protection of sensitive individual information. This known as statistical disclosure control. Another possibility is to present survey results by means of statistical models in the form of a multivariate distribution mixture. The statistical information in the form of conditional distributions (histograms) can be derived interactively from the estimated mixture model without any further access to the original database. As the final product does not contain any protected microdata, the model based interactive software can be distributed without any confidentiality concerns.

Another method is simply to release no data at all, except very large scale data directly to the central government. Different release strategies between government have led to an international project (IPUMS) to co-ordinate access to microdata and corresponding metadata. Such projects also promote standardising metadata by projects such as SDMX so that best use can be made of the minimal data available.

Chain Migration

Chain migration has multiple meanings. It refers to the social process by which immigrants from a particular town follow others from that town to a particular city or neighbourhood, whether in an immigrant receiving country or in a new, usually urban, location in the home country. The term also refers to the process of foreign nationals immigrating to a new country under laws permitting their reunification with family members already living in the destination country. This mechanism is also known as serial migration. Chain migration can be defined as a "movement in which prospective migrants learn of opportunities, are provided with transportation, and have initial accommodation and employment arranged by means of primary social relationships with previous migrants."

Chain Migration and the Accumulation of Social Capital

According to James Coleman, "social capital...is created when the relations among persons change in ways that facilitate action." Douglas

Massey, Jorge Durand and Nolan J. Malone apply this theory to chain migration, positing that, "each act of migration creates social capital among people to whom the migrant is related, thereby raising the odds of their migration." In Massey *et al.*'s argument, social capital is the tool by which chain migration occurs. It the context of migration, social capital refers to relationships, forms of knowledge and skills that advance one's potential migration. Massey *et al.* Link their definition to Gunnar Myrdal's theory of cumulative causation of migration, stating that, "each act of migration alters the social context within which subsequent migration decisions are made, thus increasing the likelihood of additional movement. Once the number of network connections in a community reaches a critical threshold, migration becomes self-perpetuating." Therefore, by initiating small social networks of migration, chain migration becomes a larger mass movement in and of itself.

Different Forms of Chain Migration in American History

Different groups of immigrants to the United States throughout its history have employed different strategies to enter, work, and live in America. Some groups, such as Eastern European Jews, emigrated in families en masse from the Russian and Austo-Hungarian Empires of the late nineteenth century. One group of forgotten "immigrants" to America was African slaves brought over forcibly. However, many groups have immigrated to the United States throughout history via chain migration. These social networks for migration are universal and not limited to specific nations, cultures, or crises. Chain migration is an overarching theme of many of the immigration experiences in American history.

Italian immigration in the late nineteenth and early twentieth century relied on a system of both chain and return migration. Chain migration helped Italian men immigrate to the United States for work as migrant labourers. Italians generally left Italy due to dire economic conditions and returned wealthy by Italian standards after working in the United States for a number of years. Italian immigrants were called *ritorni* in Italy and grouped with other Southern and Eastern European migrant labourers under the term "birds of passage" in America. However, after the passage of the Immigration Act of 1924, return migration was limited and led more Italians to become naturalized citizens. The networks that had been built up by information and money due to chain and return migration provided incentives for Italian permanent migration.

Mexican migration to the United States followed some of the same patterns as Italian immigration. The history of Mexican migrant labour in America and return migration to Mexico produced a network that allowed for chain migration once more restrictive legislation was passed hardening the border between the two nations. Chain migration based on the knowledge gained from migrant labour experience and relationships with American residents or citizens again provided some ease of immigration. From 1942 to 1964, the American government sanctioned Bracero Programme allowed hundred of thousands of Mexican migrant workers to "familiarize themselves with U.S. Employment practices, become comfortable with U.S. Job routines, master American ways of life, and learn English," thereby creating social and human capital. After the Hart-Celler Act of 1965 disbanded the Bracero Programme, the incentives and effects of chain migration perpetuated undocumented immigration to the United States. Absent any of the economic incentives, the Mexican American immigration relationship has a longstanding history and the effects of chain migration are pervasive when considering the number of Mexican American citizens, legal residents, and undocumented residents. Social capital provided by chain migration has helped perpetuate Mexican migration, whether it is undocumented or legal.

While immigrants from European nations during the period before the McCarran–Walter Act of 1952 were able to immigrate legally if with relative levels of ease depending on country of origin, the Chinese Exclusion Act of 1882 barred almost all Chinese from immigrating to the United States. Nonetheless, many Chinese immigrants arrived in America by obtaining false documents. The Chinese Exclusion Act allowed the Chinese Americans already settled in America to stay and provided for limited numbers of family members of Chinese Americans to immigrate with the correct paperwork. This loophole and the fateful 1906 earthquake that destroyed San Francisco's public records provided Chinese immigrants, almost entirely men, with the potential to immigrate with false documents stating their familial relationship to a Chinese American. These Chinese immigrants were called "paper sons," because of their false papers. "Paper sons" relied on networks built by chain migration to buy documentation, develop strategies for convincing authorities on Angel Island of their legal status, and for starting a life in America.

Ethnic Enclaves

The information and personal connections that lead to chain migration lead to transplanted communities from one nation to another. Throughout American history, ethnic enclaves have been built and sustained by immigration. Different ethnic groups claimed distinct physical space in city neighbourhoods to provide a reception for chain migration and maintain the community network it created. Examples of this trend include the many neighbourhoods called Kleindeutschland, Little Italy, and Chinatown throughout the United States.

The same was true of rural areas in the eighteenth and early nineteenth century. Some rural towns in the Midwest were founded by immigrants and directly advertised in home countries. This case was especially true for many agricultural German immigrants of the nineteenth century. Certain towns were built on a homogenous group from a particular German principality. Additionally, many of these towns exclusively spoke German until the twentieth century. These enclaves and their contemporaries represent the close relationship between family, community, and immigration.

In the late nineteenth century, distinct Italian provinces and towns immigrated to the United States via chain migration. Regional ties in Italy initially divided Italian ethnic identity in cities like New York, and certain enclaves included only Southern Italians or immigrants from Naples. The community ties remained strong with first generation immigrants concerning social life. These communities were originally composed of only of men who immigrated for work. Once they had made enough money, many Italian men interested in settling began to bring their wives and families to America.

The effects of Chinese Exclusion and discrimination prevented Chinese residents from assimilating into American society in the late nineteenth and early twentieth century. Those factors, as well as social and cultural ties, precipitated the rise of Chinatowns as ethnic enclaves for Chinese Americans. Chain migration and the pseudo-familial nature of "paper sons" produced a relatively cohesive community that maintained ties with China.

Gender Ratios of Immigration

Single, young, male labourers were initially the largest group using chain migration to the United States in the nineteenth and early twentieth centuries. However, each immigrant group maintained a unique composition due to circumstances in home countries, goals of migration, and American immigration laws.

For example, Irish migration after 1880 had a 53.6% female majority, the only migrant group with that distinction. Irish men and women faced economic crisis, overpopulation, and problematic inheritance laws for large families, thereby compelling many of Ireland's daughters to leave with her sons. Italian chain migration was initially wholly male based on intent to return, but became a source of family reunification when wives eventually immigrated.

Chinese chain migration was almost exclusively male until 1946, when the Chinese War Brides Act allowed Chinese wives of American citizens to immigrate without regards to Chinese immigration quotas. Before that time, chain migration was limited to "paper sons" and actual sons from China.

The imbalanced sex ratio of Chinese immigrants was due to Chinese exclusion laws and the inability to bring current wives or to marry and return to the United States, inhibiting the corrective measure of chain migration. When immigrant groups react to economic pull factors in the labour markets, chain migration via family has been used informally to balance out the gender ratio in ethnic immigrant communities.

Remittances

Remittances contribute to chain migration by aiding in both funding and interest in migration. Ralitza Dimova and Francois Charles Wolff argue that besides the recognized benefits remit tances provide to the economies of the home countries of immigrants, money sent home can lead to chain migration. Dimova and Wolff posit that remittances can provide the necessary capital. H. van Dalen et al. "find that recipients of remittances are more likely to consider migrating than non-recipients. This study also references the fact that causes of chain migration through remittances tend to be variable but include such pull factors as family ties and the possibility of success."

Besides the monetary remittances sent to families in the home country, immigrants' letters generally included valuable information about their new life, their work, and information to guide other prospective immigrants in the family or community to ease their journey. Understanding the necessary steps, whether it is what port to leave from or who to seek out to get a job and apartment, was and is vital for successful immigration.

Advertisements

It was common in the nineteenth and early twentieth centuries for companies and even states to advertise to potential European immigrants in their home countries. These advertisements in magazines and pamphlets made information available for immigrants to find travel and decide where to settle once in the United States. Most of the advertising was done in the effort of settling the land in the Midwestern states in the wake of the Homestead Act of 1862.

Consequently, many of the peoples whom this propaganda targeted were already living agricultural lives in Northern and Eastern Europe. Additionally, one the chain of migration had begun from a farm town in Europe, the pamphlets along with letters and remittances sent from America made migration an accessible opportunity for more and more of the people of that community. This chain eventually led to partial community transplantation and development of rural ethnic enclaves in the Midwest.

One example of this phenomenon is the chain migration of Czechs to Nebraska in the late nineteenth century. They were attracted by "glowing reports in Czech-language newspapers and magazines published [in Nebraska] and sent back home. Railroads, like the Burlington & Missouri Railroad, advertised large tracks of Nebraska land for sale in Czech. Many similar advertisements were read in German principalities at the same time, accounting for parallel chain migration to the Great Plains. While the pull factor of these advertisements represent the potential for chain migration, and did in fact produce it, they must be understood within the context of the push factors all potential immigrants weigh when determining to leave their home country. In the case of Czech chain migration to Nebraska and many other similar circumstances in Europe, the various push factors provided the impetus to leave but the pull factors provided by pamphlets and letters provided the chain migration structure to the eventual immigration.

Legislation and Chain Migration

While the networks and effects of chain migration are in effect regardless of laws limiting immigration, the changing goals and provisions of immigration legislation nonetheless effect how the system of chain migration works. Exclusion and quotas have affected who chain migration draws as potential immigrants as well as how immigrants deal with their status once in the new country. However, family reunification policies in immigration law have served to promote chain migration through extended family visas.

The Chinese Exclusion Act of 1882, and its successors creating the Asiatic Barred Zone, and the National Origins quota system built by the Immigration Act of 1924 were effective in limiting chain migration but could not end it entirely. Chinese immigrants took advantage of loopholes and false documents to enter the United States until the McCarran–Walter Act of 1952 gave them a migration quota.

Other migrant groups were limited in number by the National Origins quota system, which designated national quotas based on census ratios from 1890. These ratios heavily favoured Western European nations and older migrant groups, such as the English, Irish, and Germans. The ratios attempted to limit the rising number of Southern and Eastern European immigrants. The National Origins quota system provided limited family reunification as a means for chain migration and placed a preference on naturalization. If an immigrant became a U.S. citizen, he or she had the ability obtain non-quota visas for more family members, but as a resident that number was capped annually. Additionally, the Immigration Act of 1924 formally opened the door to chain migration from the entire western hemisphere, placing that group under non-quota status.

The abolition of the National Origins quota system came with the Hart-Celler Act of 1965. This legislation placed a heavy emphasis on family reunification, designating 74% of visas for that purpose. There was no limit on spouses, unmarried minor children, and parents of U.S. citizens. The percentages for family reunification were as follows: Unmarried adult children of U.S. citizens (20%), spouses and unmarried children of permanent residents aliens (20%), married children of U.S. citizens (10%), brothers and sisters of U.S. citizens over age 21 (24%). These new visa preferences created a swell of new chain migration and immigration in general. The Third World began to outpace European immigration to America for the first time in history, surpassing it by the end of the 1960s and doubling the numbers of European migration by the end of the 1970s. In reaction to the flood of new immigrants brought by the Hart-Celler Act, and increasing numbers of undocumented immigrants from Mexico and Latin America, Congress attempted to reverse the consequences of the 1965 legislation by enforcing border patrol, using amnesty for undocumented immigrants in the Immigration Reform and Control Act of 1986, and proposing limits to family reunification policies. The effects of the ending the Bracero Programme were increased undocumented Mexican migration because of the social capital gained during that period. Chain migration had provided relatively easy access to migration for Mexicans that the immigration legislation of the 1980s to the present has attempted to deal with.

The Current Effects of Chain Migration in the United States

In the United States, the term 'chain migration' is used to partially explain why legal immigration has quadrupled from levels during the 1960s. As such, 'chain migration' is held up as one of the causes of the United States' current immigrant population boom. Family reunification allows U.S. citizens and immigrants (Lawful Permanent

Resident or "Green card" holders) to petition for visas for their immediate relatives. Until the late 1950s, America's family reunification policies included only spouses and minor children of immigrants. However, since that time, family reunification policies of the United States have included the ability of immigrants to sponsor not only their minor children and spouses, but also their parents, siblings, and adult children.

According to the theory of 'chain migration' as applied to immigrants to the United States, subsequent immigrant Lawful Permanent Resident parents and adult children can, in turn, sponsor their other children, parents, etc., thus representing a chain of immigrants following the first family member into the country. In practice, however, the wait times from when the petition is filled until the adult relative is able to enter the U.S. can be as long as 15–20 years (as of 2006). This is a result of backlogs in obtaining a visa number and visa number quotas that only allow 226,000 family-based visas to be issued annually. There are four family-based preference levels:

First: Unmarried Sons and Daughters of Citizens: 23,400 plus any numbers not required for fourth preference.

Second: Spouses and Children, and Unmarried Sons and Daughters of Permanent Residents: 114,200, plus the number (if any) by which the worldwide family preference level exceeds 226,000, and any unused first preference numbers:

A. Spouses and Children: 77% of the overall second preference limitation, of which 75% are exempt from the per-country limit;

B. Unmarried Sons and Daughters (21 Years of Age or Older): 23% of the overall second preference limitation.

Third: Married Sons and Daughters of Citizens: 23,400, plus any numbers not required by first and second preferences.

Fourth: Brothers and Sisters of Adult Citizens: 65,000, plus any numbers not required by first three preferences.

Backlogs in obtaining visa numbers range from four-and-a-half years (for preference level 2A) to 23-years (for preference level 4 immigrants from the Philippines).

While some backlogs have remained relatively steady for some time, since 1995, backlogs for other family-sponsored preferences have steadily increased. For first preference, adult children of U.S. citizens, for instance, the backlog for a visa number has increased from zero in 1995 to over 6½ years today.

Problems Associated with Chain Migration

Currently there is a movement against chain migration and its effects. Specifically, the family reunification emphasis of the Hart-Celler Act had the unintended consequence of dramatically increasing levels of migration in general and chain migration in particular.

FAIR, the Federation for American Immigration Reform, a conservative think tank, promotes the idea that, "chain migration-and the expectations and long lines it produces-increases illegal immigration.

Additionally FAIR argues that, "illegal aliens given amnesty by Congress in 1986 are now fueling naturalization in record numbers. As these former illegal aliens become citizens, all of their immediate relatives qualify to come immediately to the United States, and start new migration chains of their own."

Numbers USA, a group that lobbies Congress for lower levels of immigration, states that, "one of the chief culprits in America's current record-breaking population boom and all the attendant sprawl, congestion, school overcrowding, and other impacts that reduce American's quality of life."

Numbers USA cites the tradition of chain migration to America as a main cause for creating incentives for undocumented immigration.

Numbers USA, FAIR, and other groups are working to change immigration law to limit chain migration favour. Numbers USA cites a specific bill it supports. "On Feb. 4, 2009, Rep. Phil Gingrey (R-GA) introduced the Nuclear Family Priority Act (H.R. 878). The bill would eliminate the extended family visa categories (e.g., married sons and daughters of citizens, etc.), thus ending "chain migration" as recommended by the bi-partisan Barbara Jordan Commission in 1997."

Some academics agree. Massey *et al.* Argue that while immediate family immigration provisions were created to promote and stabilize the family unit in American immigration and society, family reunification visas for extended family, such as adult siblings, are unnecessary when faced with rising immigration numbers. Massey *et al.* Support eliminating those quotas.

Chapter 7

Population and Poverty: The Policy Issues

This discussion paper aims at a policy-relevant understanding of the population-poverty relationship. It has six sections:

(1) A brief discussion of the relationship (or apparent absence of relationship) at the aggregate level;

(2) An analysis of the ways in which population growth can influence poverty, working through a society's institutional and cultural make-up, its resource endowments, and its natural and built environments;

(3) A partial typology of situations in which poverty is sustained through localized actions that are rational within their immediate context but harm others in the society;

(4) A discussion of policy options and issues, that arise from (2) and (3);

(5) A note on some political dimensions of the subject; and

(6) Where not further qualified, "poverty" here will be taken to refer to "absolute poverty" or "income poverty"-a condition of per capita income below a fixed "poverty line" that is typically set at a purchasing power equivalent of US$1 per day at 1985 prices.

Aggregate Links: a Confused Picture

Surprisingly to those who have only casual knowledge of research in the area, the relationship between population growth and poverty is neither obvious nor well established. Simple economic arguments would suggest that rapid population growth aggravates poverty.

Population growth holds down returns to labour relative to capital and other factors of production, depressing wages and worsening the income distribution.

Or, if we picture development in terms of an initially small but expanding modern sector within a larger, backward economy, population growth swells the traditional and informal labour force, and delays the time at which modern-sector capital accumulation exhausts the supply of subsistence-level workers. Yet such pieces of theory do not suffice to demonstrate a negative effect. In more elaborate models and in the real world things are more complicated. Time lags, feedbacks, non-linearities, and reverse causation enter the picture, as do the institutional practices through which societies mediate among competing claims on the social product.

For example, rapid population growth may be a consequence of advances in health, signaling broad-based welfare improvement; economies may expand rapidly with scant regard for equity, but nevertheless show plummeting fertility levels; or societies may be in such economic disorder that continued impoverishment coexists with virtually zero population growth.

These complications explain the hesitant way in which the link between population growth and poverty has been summarized in the recent research literature. The dominant tone is caution and uncertainty in the face of a complex relationship. There is little in this literature to support a strong poverty-based rationale for reducing fertility. The most that the 1992 UNFPA Consultative Meeting of Economists could conclude on the matter was that "The causal links between population growth and absolute deprivation are not well understood.... Research has not established a strong causal link running from high fertility to poverty" (United Nations Population Fund 1993:50-51). World Bank economist Lant Pritchett (1997:51) is brusquer: solid evidence that population growth is "a cause or even an exacerbating condition of poverty" cannot be given "because there is none".

Nevertheless, while acknowledging the complexity, it is likely that most social scientists would accept that there is a connection between population growth and poverty.

In particular, achieving lower fertility, at least in some circumstances (probably including those of most of the world's poorest countries), is likely to help alleviate poverty. The reverse relationship-of poverty alleviation on fertility reduction-is also widely accepted. Hence, for instance, the Programme of Action of the 1994 International Conference on Population and Development in its section entitled

"Population, sustained economic growth and poverty" (3.10-3.22) asserts that efforts to slow population growth and to reduce poverty are mutually reinforcing.

We therefore have a case in which common sense views about a particular consequence of demographic change rest on an inconclusive body of research. This is unfortunately a familiar situation. It underlies the so-called revisionist arguments that hold population growth to be a comparatively marginal factor in the development process. The 1986 report on population and economic growth of the U.S. National Research Council was summarized by its co-chair as "support [ing] the conclusion that population growth has little or no negative effect on economic development" (Johnson 1994: 524). An intriguing development in the 1990s has been the second thoughts about the effects of population growth that have emerged from a close look at the strong economic performance of East Asia in the 1970s and 1980s.

The early fertility decline and consequent fall in youth dependency in most of these countries is now seen by some economists, echoing the classic Coale-Hoover result, as contributing to their surge in investment. Significantly, East Asian poverty rates also fell sharply over this period. However, the case is still circumstantial: there are various competing accounts of the "East Asian miracle"-indeed, since the "meltdown" of some of these same economies in 1997, pushing large numbers of people back into poverty, many would deny that there even was a miracle. The prima facie empirical case for the unimportance of population to economic change has come from cross-country analysis.

Scatter plots of countries on axes representing population growth rates versus per capita GNP or more refined indexes of income poverty are famously unpersuasive. a typical example: high-population-growth countries are nearly all poor, but the association is anything but tight. (It is certainly negative, but that is hardly surprising given the overall demographic contrast between rich and poor countries.) The same opaque relationships can be reproduced using numerous pairs of demographic and economic variables.

Multivariate analysis does little to clarify the matter. Theoretical support can be found for various causal paths between population and poverty, in both directions. Moreover, the underlying models must assume cross-country regularities in development patterns that are belied by the actual diversity among countries. Unsurprisingly, no sharp picture emerges. The careful aggregative modelling by Rodgers (1984) concludes on the overall slightness of the adverse population growth effect. In a later piece he writes: "there is little empirical evidence to support the proposition that population growth is a major constraint on the alleviation of poverty... Population growth is both a cause and a consequence of poverty, and unraveling the pattern of causation may be an almost hopeless task" (Rodgers 1989: 9). Ahlburg (1996) finds no association of population growth with changes in poverty. Virtually the only exception in this literature is a study by Michael Lipton (1997), which reports a "large" positive effect of fertility on subsequent poverty in a 28-country analysis. Timmer (1994: 262) comments on population-poverty research that "because of path-dependency and important dynamic feedback effects, cross-sectional evidence can offer only limited insights." Is aggregative analysis then of no help in illuminating the population-poverty relationship? That would be an overstatement, on two grounds. First, an explanatory calculus that finds little to be explained may simply be unsuited to the analytical task. Second, a murky cross-sectional picture does not prove the absence of a relationship.

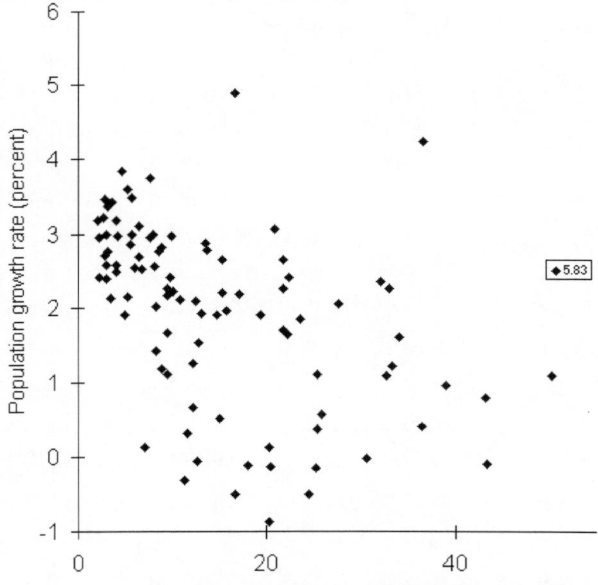

***Figure:** Both mortality and fertility contribute to the confused picture (migration does too, in the case of some outliers). There are steep income effects on mortality at low incomes-see Preston (1980)-and few exceptions to low fertility at high incomes, but wide variations in each over a broad middle income range. Poverty measures with substantial demographic content, like the Human Poverty Index, are by definition linked to mortality. Considerable noise is added to this and other similar bivariate relationships by the variation among countries in political and economic systems and social institutions-which together affect both economic performance and capacities to influence demographic outcomes.*

We may never obtain simple conclusions on population and poverty, but it does not follow that the relationship is unimportant. Complexity does not imply inconsequence. If cross-country studies tell us little, we are thrown back on single country analysis or on cautious and selective use of country comparisons. The difficulties of dealing with counterfactuals-investigating what would have happened had conditions been different in specified ways-then have to be faced, but that task is familiar to historians and differs mainly in degree from the one routinely encountered in doing sensitivity analysis.

Social and Environmental Settings of Population-poverty Relationships

A simple framework for organizing this discussion would identify three routes through which population change may affect poverty. First is the "direct" route linking population and economy. The economy, broadly interpreted, incorporates market-based and other institutional means of income distribution. Included in those "other" means are contributions to the social wage through the public-sector provision of health, educational, and other services. Poverty outcomes are one part of this overall distributional function. In addition, population change itself, to the extent that it brings about or entails an altered demographic structure of households, may have a simple arithmetic effect on consumption.

The second and third routes take account of possible changes in the environmental and social setting. Many population-related environmental changes have effects on poverty. We can write:

Δ Population —> Δ Environment —> Δ Poverty

(where Δ signifies "change in"). A somewhat distinct triplet would link population and poverty through effects on social organization, though this one as yet has been far less researched than the other:

Δ Population —> Δ Social organization —> Δ Poverty.

Poverty, in turn, would often have consequences for both environment and the social order, and environmental change and social (in)stability are themselves sometimes connected. These additional relationships rapidly complicate the picture. Moreover, the D notation leaves ambiguous the matter of contingency: it does not specify what else is being held constant. Thus, to identify any relationship working through environmental change involves making assumptions about social organization-at a minimum, a ceteris paribus stipulation. Analogous assumptions on the environment are required in tracing causal paths through social arrangements. Poverty links to environmental change and to social instability are discussed separately below.

Poverty and the Environment

Take first the rural sector. A necessary by product of rapid urbanization and declining fertility is a fall in rural population growth. In much of the developing world, rural populations will cease expanding within a decade or two; in places, they have already started to contract. Population growth effects, whatever they may have been, will diminish. Sub-Saharan Africa is the main exception, with population growth remaining a rural as well as urban reality.

There is of course no simple connection between rural poverty and population growth. There are often conflicting Malthusian and Boserupian interpretations of past trends, and possibilities for "tragedies of the commons". Moreover, it is not just population numbers that potentially matter: poverty outcomes may be influenced, for example, by disproportionate out-migration from the most economically active age groups. Consider the range of responses to population growth in a subsistence agrarian economy. They might be categorized as follows:

- extension of cultivated area through conversion of pastoral or forested land or cultivation of steeper slopes and other marginal land;
- intensification of production through improved varieties and inputs, multiple cropping, etc.;
- population limitation through (voluntary) out-migration or birth control;
- forcible exclusion of part of population from access to the social product;
- diminished welfare for some or all of the population or increased dependency on outside subventions.

The list is not exhaustive but covers the principal possibilities. It mixes "effective" responses, in which agriculture proves a dynamic growth sector and a potential source of investment for the rest of the economy, and "ineffective" responses that yield poverty, social disorder, and environmental degradation. Commonly, responses would encompass elements of several of these categories, the balance varying over different social groups. The actual outcome in a particular case depends on resource endowments, inherited institutional and cultural practices, the course of political development, competency in public administration and development planning, and some measure of chance. There would be usually be winners and losers but a rough consensus could probably be reached on whether rural poverty had risen or fallen. Where there is a net income gain, it is at least theoretically possible for the losers to be compensated so that no one is worse off, or for the same to happen through trickle-down effects.

Consider some instances on the ineffective side. Population growth in 19th century Ireland played an underlying role in creating that region's extreme vulnerability to crop failure, with its outcome at mid-century of starvation and mass emigration. Nepal and the Philippines in recent decades offer pictures of population pressures leading to ecologically unsound spread of upland cultivation, producing severe environmental degradation and out-migration-to the Terai and to Mindanao, respectively. In the lowland tropics, even where erosion is not a problem, the soil quality of much newly-deforested land falls off sharply after a few seasons, offering little prospect for subsequent intensification-indeed, often ending in abandonment. The case of Brazil is most familiar, with rapid population growth in Amazonia (the migrants coming from elsewhere in the rural sector) producing these outcomes. Bangladesh has witnessed a long process of impoverishment through plot subdivision and extension of cultivation on to hazardous delta islands, as rural population densities have risen to extreme levels. Sub-Saharan Africa presents notable instances of the breakdown of rural agricultural systems and subsequent impoverishment, but for the most part these do not belong in this category: the environmental outcomes have been by products of destruction of social infrastructure, leading to endemic insecurity, population displacement, and heightened mortality.

It is important to recognize that environmental destruction also occurs for reasons that have little or nothing to do with population. For example, ecological degradation in Nepal and elsewhere in the Himalayas can be explained in some part without invoking human agency. The deep lowland soils of the northern subcontinent come from eons of heavy but "natural" erosion, leading some alpine ecologists to dismiss "ecocatastrophe" accounts such as Eckholm's. The apparently irreversible environmental degradation of the agricultural region surrounding the Aral Sea-and the shrinkage of the sea itself-while it has clearly led to widespread rural impoverishment, is almost entirely attributable to drastically ill-conceived planning decisions (Kasperson et al. 1995). Again, natural increase of population had little to do with the Brazilian experience of falling incomes of small farmers as landholdings were consolidated and operations commercialized in the 1970s. Both the frontier migration and the expulsion of labour out of the agricultural sector altogether were consequences of this severe contraction in labour demand.

Deterioration of the natural systems on which agriculture depends, such as watersheds and aquifers, can be potent causes of increased poverty in expanding rural populations. Even if these factors are comparatively stable, however, behavioural responses to rising densities may impede economic progress. Unquestionably the rural populations of, say, Bangladesh or India would be much better off today if they had not more than doubled their numbers over the last few decades. There must be structural reasons why the society allowed itself to expand rather than following the path of macro-level rationality. The exploration of such reasons, however, calls for research at a less aggregative level.

A discussion of poverty and the environment should also take account of the urban sector-where half of the world's population live and nearly all of current population growth in the world is taking place. If industrial employment generation fails to keep up with growth in the labour supply, the urban working age population backs up in low-productivity activities and all-but-open unemployment-that is, in the usual understanding of the term, in the informal sector. This sector is seen as a kind of labour sump, "a refuge for those unable to find jobs in the modern sector" (Portes 1997: 249).

There is an alternative, far less pessimistic, view of the urban informal sector. Sachs (1990: 99), writing of Brazil, notes the intricate organizational structures that develop and the social capital that can be mobilized. The result is "a maze of interconnected labour, service, and goods markets, ranging from organized business to organized crime, a non-market household sector, as well as an incipient non-market social sector based on mutual help." Indeed, the informal sector can be seen less as a labour sump than as a dynamic source of microscale entrepreneurship for the economy. This view first came to prominence in the work of Hernando De Soto (1989), to whom informal economic activity appears as a dynamic response to the institutional rigidities of over-regulated or statalist economies. Unregulated enterprise, far from being the survival behaviour of a near-destitute labour reservoir, becomes the entrepreneurial feedstock of development. The poverty issue does not wholly vanish but is relegated to the status of a comparatively fringe concern. In Portes and Schauffler's (1994: 55) paraphrase of De Soto, "the informal sector is not part of the problem of underdevelopment, but part of its solution."

In any particular case, these contrasting pictures must somehow be reconciled with the single empirical reality. Part of that reality is a physical environment that for many cities is dominated by shantytowns, bidonvilles, and favelas. Many cities in the developing countries have been growing at double the rate of natural increase of population: rates of 5 percent per year are common, a doubling time of 14 years. Under those conditions the quality of the built environment is bound to decline; public health is likely to suffer along with it. Using DHS data, Brockerhoff and Brennan (1998) show the adverse effects of rapid population growth on infant mortality in cities, a link found to be especially pronounced in Latin America.

Plausibly, the two pictures are only superficially inconsistent. Portes and Schauffler (1994) propose a compromise. Their interpretation calls for a typology of informal activities, recognizing both the dynamism of many microenterprises and the precarious lives of many people in the sector. Some amount of dynamism and off-the-books organization in economic activity and elaborate networks of mutual assistance can coexist with a broad degree of material poverty. How much is hard to gauge: by their nature, estimates of the size of the informal economy, and thus of the incomes of its participants, are error-prone. (Mortality rates, or more general measures of "human poverty", escape this problem for population groups.) The static aggregate situation, however, would be of less interest than the detailed directions of change: whether poverty was a diminishing phenomenon along the life cycle of most individuals or whether it permanently identified a substantial subgroup.

Population Growth and the Social Order

A potentially powerful macro-level argument linking population growth and poverty derives from the assertion that demographic forces can undermine the social order-and in the limiting case, lead to outright state failure. Political disorder and consequent erosion of social capital can drastically impede routine economic activity. If it persists, it may destroy the institutional-and material-base of production and distribution, generating widespread poverty. Can such a link be empirically sustained?

Recent writings making a population-growth/conflict case include those of Homer-Dixon (1991, 1994), Goldstone (1991, 1997), and, in more popular vein, R. Kaplan (1996). Numerous country studies have been undertaken in recent years investigating the likely political consequences of upcoming scarcities in renewable resources. Population growth is one of the causes of scarcity, out-migration is often one of the effects. Goldstone investigates the tensions generated by population expansion under inflexible or maladapting institutions in a series of historical and contemporary contexts.

Environmental scarcity, in Homer-Dixon's usage, can result from change in access to resources or a change in distributive systems as well as from resource depletion or degradation, so that demographic causes would rarely stand alone. In turn, scarcity raises the financial and political demands on governments and reduces their revenues. "A widening gap between state capacity and demands on the state, along with the misguided economic interventions such a gap often provokes, aggravates popular and elite grievances, increases rivalry between elite factions, and erodes the state's legitimacy" (Homer-Dixon 1994: 25).

Drawn-out civil conflict and resulting decay of state legitimacy and capacity would nearly always be accompanied by drastic economic deterioration. The African examples of Somalia, Liberia, and Sierra Leone are cases in point. (The converse argument, that impoverishment will generate civil unrest, finds relatively little support.) However, conflict does not necessarily lead to impoverishment. For example, the economic impact of a violent change of regime would usually be severe but may be fairly transitory and affect mainly the more capitalized sectors.

Local Scenarios of Impoverishment

The discussion in the preceding section points strongly to population growth contributing to poverty in many situations, either through direct distributional changes in the economy or through routes that involve changes in environmental conditions and social institutions. In each case, no blanket conclusions can be drawn, since outcomes depend on the detailed specification of the setting. There are no automatic linkages, only contingent ones. However, we can appreciably buttress the overall argument by examining the sorts of circumstances that generate population-poverty relationships at the local level.

Economic demographers have spent much time modelling the demographic calculations of individuals and families. But understanding the family economy and its demographic responses to changed circumstances and opportunities does not in itself shed much light on population-poverty relationships. The prices and other incentives that determine the costs and benefits of demographic behaviour are set by economic forces, social organization, and cultural patterns that an individual family neither controls nor much influences. We thus need to set the family within its material and social environment, and explore the dynamics of this somewhat larger system. The aim is to identify the kinds of organizational patterns that tend to connect population growth and poverty.

Intra-family Transmission of Poverty

A familiar explanation for continued high fertility early in the development process is that parents expect to benefit from having many children. Children may contribute to family income and to the care of younger siblings from a relatively early age, perhaps at some cost to their own economic prospects; and they may have an asset- and insurance-role for the family-bringing in dowry or bridewealth, establishing kinship links through marriage, and providing support and protection to the parents in old age. In the terms used by Caldwell (1978), the net "wealth-flows" in the family go from children to parents. This intuitively plausible argument would suggest that at the family level, in poor countries, high fertility need not be associated with poverty. However, empirical support for the proposition is inconclusive. There are also theoretical counter arguments: H. Kaplan (1994) applies evolutionary theory to call into question the hypothesis itself.

As development proceeds, the economic disadvantage of high fertility to parents should become ever more apparent. Notably, parents come to recognize the increasing need to invest in education-in the "quality" of children rather than the quantity. Yet here also the family-level evidence is weak. Lloyd (1994) finds only a small negative effect on children of large family size-though the average disguises substantial selective disadvantage to some siblings, particularly females. Kelley (1994: 57) concludes from an exhaustive review of quantitative studies that "evidence on the impact of family size on educational outcomes is mixed, showing no convincingly consistent and strong impact, one way or the other."

Notwithstanding this ambiguity, there are particular circumstances in which the costs of a family's high fertility clearly fall on the children. This is the case where high fertility is associated with an early start to childbearing and close birth spacing, or with "unwanted" births. Poor families are likely to be especially susceptible in these respects, through initially lower education, less access to health care, and often less effective birth control. Children's health as well as their education may suffer: for example, parental malnutrition can lead to low birth weight children and greater risk of stunted development. The likely outcome is to reproduce poverty in the next generation.

Oberai (1993: ch. 6) cites various studies that find high fertility in poor urban families-two or more sons-to be in part a strategy aimed at combating poverty by enhancing economic security, leading to a vicious circle: "low incomes ensure poor education, nutrition and health, which in turn lead to low productivity and low incomes" (p. 191). Efforts to achieve low fertility as a path to economic mobility-as argued, for example, by those who perceive "poverty-induced" fertility declines - are consistent with this story.

At least as important as formal education in the intergenerational transmission of poverty are the intangible qualities of child rearing.

Low human capital may be perpetuated within a family or social group through poor parenting, economic insecurity, and cultural impoverishment. Thomas Sowell (1983: 255) has stressed the effect of disadvantage here, in contrast to family surroundings "where the values and patterns of life were a human capital that made economic success more readily attainable." As fertility comes to acquire an inverse gradient by income, the proportion of children raised in conditions of disadvantage rises substantially.

"Tragedy of the Commons"

Garrett Hardin's famous article (1968) gives a stylized picture of population-induced impoverishment through over exploitation of common-property resources. His reference is to pre-enclosure rural Britain, describing a situation in which each new person in a rural community supposedly added a further claim to use of common grazing lands. Beyond some limit in livestock numbers the productivity of the commons would decline, perhaps drastically. Implicitly, the community is taken as composed of members with more or less uniform power, unable or unwilling to act concertedly to impose a management regime to resolve the predicament or to countenance its imposition by unilateral action. The situation is modelled by a n-person Prisoner's Dilemma, in which each player has an immediate incentive to pursue autonomously self-interested behaviour unless a binding agreement to act in the common interest can be reached. Of course if such an agreement can be reached, the outcome is superior for all. Dasgupta and Mäler (1994: 23-4) note that there is no necessity that agreement has to entail centralized intervention: decentralized participatory arrangements can be found and would often be preferred.

Hardin's aim, like many subsequent writers on the case, is to illuminate processes of ecological degradation in rural poor country situations. The common property resources in question are usually assumed to be open-access forests (as sources of fuelwood and leaf fodder) and local aquifers (for well water). For the dry regions of India, Jodha (1985, 1990) lists community pastures, community forests, waste lands, common dumping and threshing grounds, watershed drainage, village ponds, and rivers. With overuse, the productivity of these resources declines, with immediate and disproportionate impact on the poor. The population connection is evident.

From an early age children can undertake such essential family tasks as gathering fuel, carrying water, or caring for livestock. But the population growth thereby sustained further worsens the environment's capacity to supply fuel, water, and pasture-thus maintaining or even raising the value of children to parents. Dasgupta's (1993) treatise, An Inquiry into Well-Being and Destitution, discusses the situation in detail, and formalizes the underlying theory.

An urban parallel can be drawn to the Hardin case, identifying a similar kind of prisoner's dilemma. The urban analogue to common property resources in rural communities is the condition of physical security and comparative social stability that provides the setting for the informal labour market and allows predictability in patterns of social relations. These background conditions in poor urban areas are as potentially subject to "degradation" as the rural environment.

The circumstances in which population growth does actually lead to impoverishment through these kind of mechanisms are those where cultural or institutional factors impede collective or unilateral action at the local level to limit degradation. Privatization of the resource (alienation or enclosure) or cooperative or state management of it are among the options that can halt the decline, an outcome produced by proper alignment of the various economic and political interests in play. Unfortunately, one route for preventing over exploitation is through simple exclusion of some category of claimants. Poverty for all, Hardin-style, may then be avoided but not for the excluded group. Clearly critical for a poverty-alleviating outcome is a remedy that also protects against adverse distributional effects. Finally, for longer-run viability, the incentives that are set up should be such as to maintain or increase per capita returns-by raising production or limiting further population growth.

Low-level Social Equilibria

The preceding case falls squarely within a rational microeconomic calculus. Theorists within this tradition tend to dismiss the notion that apparently improvident or dysfunctional behaviour might be explicable in terms of "tradition" or "culture." But as the understanding of how institutions emerge has grown, so has a new appreciation of customary behaviour.

Dasgupta (1993: 351) describes how enmeshed custom can create a social equilibrium that gives rise to significant externalities:

In many societies, there are practices encouraging high fertility rates that no household desires unilaterally to break.... [S]o long as all others follow the practice and aim at large family sizes, no household on its own will wish to deviate from the practice; however, if all other households were to restrict their fertility rates, each would desire to restrict its own fertility rate as well. Thus, there can be multiple social equilibria, each sustained by its own bootstraps, so to speak, and a society can get stuck in one which, while it may have had a collective rationale in the past, does not have one any more. This picture, novel as it may be to modern economists, is close to the perception of classical theorists like Malthus and J. Stuart Mill who saw education as the input that could shake a society out of a poverty equilibrium. It recognizes that values and preference sets are not fixed as assumed in most welfare theory but are determined in the course of socialization and acculturation and are modified by experience and opportunity, all processes that are not independent of societal design.

A different kind of poverty equilibrium is vividly portrayed in the analysis of social development by Robert D. Putnam (1993). Putnam describes an n-person prisoner's dilemma over whether or not individuals and families should put trust in civic institutions. Expectations of economic progress take for granted a social infrastructure based on some measure of trust-for instance, belief in security of contract and in a degree of legal and administrative impartiality. This amounts to a cooperative solution to the dilemma under which both the economy and social capital can grow. But there is also a stable equilibrium of shared distrust, with minimal social capital beyond the family and kin-group and a self-reinforcing pattern of exploitative behaviour that produces a meager economic performance.

A social equilibrium would seem to bear some resemblance to the problematic idea of a class culture, and a low-level social equilibrium to that of a "culture of poverty." These concepts have fallen into disuse in research, though they clearly persist in popular understanding of, for example, the urban underclass. Traits making up a culture of poverty included authoritarianism, present-time orientation, and fatalism (O. Lewis 1961), with the all-too-easy implication that they formed a coherent belief system resistant to change. Critics of the concept preferred to see the behaviour of low-income people as a pragmatic response to deprivation and stress-as "responsive to the conditions of life rather than to cultural guidelines" (Rodman 1968: 335). Policy is thereby given something tangible to work with. "Traps" and similar equilibrium concepts are always contingent on a modelling structure that, even if initially valid, trends in the real world may be rendering obsolete.

Unilateral Transfers: Offloading Costs on to the Weak

The two preceding scenarios have dealt with poverty arising from or maintained by the presence of reciprocal negative externalities-situations in which each family transfers some of its fertility costs on to the rest of society and reciprocally bears part of others' costs itself, with the resulting diffusion of costs making remedial action difficult.

Transfers of costs need not of course be reciprocal. In the intra-family case with which we started, children could be disadvantaged by having many siblings: that is, there could be unilateral transfers on to children within a household. There are other kinds of unilateral transfers, however, some of which are probably more important in influencing poverty outcomes.

Members of one community can worsen conditions in another through environmental spillovers-for instance, through poor agricultural practices whose local effects can be avoided but that are felt elsewhere through, say, pollution or flooding. They can also do so by exertion of political power or direct force to gain an economic advantage, for example through alienation of what previously had been common-property resources. In a weaker sense, labour migration also represents a transfer of costs of population growth, in this case on to participants in the recipient area's labour market. (Employers in the recipient area may of course stand to benefit from greater labour market competition, complicating the cost calculation.) Rural-urban migration can sometimes be viewed in this way, as in the Brazilian case noted earlier. "Communities" here would usually refer to territorially defined entities like villages or regions; quite analogous arguments, although for a possibly different range of transfers, can apply to groups defined by economic status, such as class or caste groups. Indigenous minorities are often the involuntary recipients of offloaded costs associated with population growth elsewhere. In some circumstances, women may be too.

Unilateral transfers with implications for poverty outcomes can also be intertemporal. The next generation in a society "inherits" from the present generation its physical and human capital, natural resources, and environmental amenity. Under rapid population growth, population numbers would often double in a generation, imposing a major dilution effect on this inheritance. It is the case of intra-family transfers writ large. (There are many conceptual and even ethical problems in delineating this case. Dasgupta [1993: ch.13] gives a brief treatment of them.)

The common feature of unilateral transfers is the inability of those on to whom the costs are imposed to organize effectively to protect their interests. This may reflect the structural weakness of their position in the larger society, geographical remoteness, or, in the intertemporal case, inherent obstacles to intergenerational contracting.

Poverty and the "Threat Economy"

The "threat economy" is a term of Kenneth Boulding's, applied to the economy of arms races. At the micro level, however, resources similarly have to be allocated to protection-against social predation. As the earlier discussion of political stability suggested, demographic pressures are one among various factors that might be expected to harm the social fabric. R. Kaplan (1996) gives an anecdotal account of such harm in various countries of West Africa and West and Central Asia, arguing for at least partial demographic causation. The erosion of social capital is not easily reversed: indeed, it is likely to result in forms of social organization that are antithetical to economic and political development. Such forms-warlordism, for instance-might offer protection for some but at the expense of predation on others; plausibly they would entrench both pre-transition demographic outcomes and widespread poverty.

Population Policy and Poverty Alleviation Policy: Finding the Intersections

Poverty and fertility are not in themselves policy instruments, in the sense of one of them being able to be modified so as to affect the other. We cannot expect that remedying inequality will necessarily bring down high fertility. Nor can we expect that a fertility decline will itself necessarily help to alleviate poverty. But dismissing policy prospects at that broad level does not dispose of the matter. The policy domains within which population and poverty are open to intentional influence intersect, allowing for measures that impinge on both areas. Because population-poverty relationships are institutionally contingent, such measures have to be tailored to the specific situation. However, a few more general observations can be made.

Programmatic Policies: Education, Health, Family Planning

Both poverty and the components of population growth (fertility especially) are what might be described as devolved phenomena. They refer to individual- or family-level characteristics and behaviours. They are reachable by government only through broad scale extension services or by policies that yield welfare gains across the income distribution and across gender lines-or, we need to add, by the elaborate measures of administrative control entailed in detailed "targeting" of policy. This devolution makes for a degree of consonance in policies directed at limiting population growth and those concerned with poverty alleviation.

Improvements in education and health are closely linked to demographic modernization. Caldwell's (1986) analysis of low-mortality "outliers" among poor countries argues the mortality case; the fertility relationship is attested by numerous quantitative studies. Significantly, education and health are precisely the sectors where government action, properly designed, can also most readily serve redistributive ends. Sectoral budgets themselves may not mean much: universities and high-technology hospitals can consume large amounts of resources but reach few in the population and raise rather than reduce economic inequality. Primary and secondary schooling and primary health care are the relevant extension services, contributing directly to well being as well as to earning capacity. Achievement of high primary- and secondary school enrolment rates necessitates near universality of service provision; and to be effective, primary health care must similarly be widely available at the local level and acceptable in quality.

The administrative and financial structures of these sectors are also relevant to their impact. Accountability to clients may be a surer means of achieving service quality than bureaucratic supervision. Such accountability is more likely to be found where the financing of services includes a significant locally raised component-through local taxes and perhaps user fees (provided access is not thereby skewed). De facto, such devolved financing is often the case, but without insistence on accountability.

There is some evidence at the macro level that rapid population growth is associated with poorer budgetary provision for education and health. This is a disputed area, however. Budgets reflect government priorities, and social services often do not rank very high. Conditionality stipulations-particularly those associated with structural adjustment programmes-are sometimes blamed for this ranking, but the case tends to be weak. Conditionality may even work in the opposite direction: the 1990 World Development Report argued that aid allocations "should be based on a demonstrated commitment to the goal of reducing poverty."

Family planning programmes, at least in their pre-Cairo formulation, are in essence just another kind of extension service. The client-demand may be softer than in the case of health and education, but the administrative requirements qua programme are not radically different. Their welfare effect on the poor is less easily identified, however. Most of this review has assumed that fertility outcomes reflect the interests of parents or families; but some part of fertility reflects ineffectiveness of available birth control methods. Access to safe and effective birth control is likely to be strongly associated with parents' socioeconomic status, in particular with education and income. Thus "unwanted" fertility is disproportionately found among the poor. Family planning programmes, aimed principally at those who lack access to private sources of modern contraception, thus have an important distributional dimension: the services they provide, in addition to any social gain that may come from reduced fertility, offer a private gain mostly to the poor. (This, of course, assumes that the services are fully voluntary; if they are not, the social gain would be set against a private cost.)

Family planning post-Cairo, with its aim of cutting back any explicit demographic intentions and focusing instead on improving the reproductive health of women and their access to high-quality services, is still closer to an extension service-conceptually not distinct from other more or less specialized components of the health programme. The changed orientation may attenuate the programme's redistributive effect: as service quality is raised, the programme may well find itself catering to a more middle-class clientele than before.

Programmatic Policies: Target Groups for Poverty Alleviation

If women are over-represented among the poor, measures to lessen poverty are reasonably directed disproportionately towards women. Analogous propositions would apply to the various other population categories where poverty rates may be high: children, the elderly, ethnic minorities, inhabitants of particular backward regions, refugees, and so on-depending on the specific circumstances in the society. The potential target groups that also have particular demographic significance, because of their size, are women, children, and the elderly.

Women

Women are more often in poverty than men. Detailed statistical materials, for example from the 1995 Human Development Report, support the proposition. A.M. Basu (1994: 18) finds conclusive evidence of "a widespread disproportionate impact of poverty on women". Kabeer (1996: 19) remarks that women "are less able than men to translate labour into income, income into choice and choice into personal well-being."

Two fairly distinct phenomena are implicated. One relates to the status of women who are widowed, divorced, or separated, and to the level of autonomy and economic opportunity open to single women; the other, to the position of women within marriage and within the household. The first of these combines effects of gender with those of social isolation and old-age dependency (sex differences in average age at marriage and in adult mortality mean that the single elderly are predominantly women). Poverty can be linked to gender-differentiated aspects of law and social practice in areas of property, inheritance, and occupational choice, and to the (precarious) economics of single-person or single-parent households. Children, and sons especially, may be an important economic resource for widows-as stressed, for instance, by Cain (1978)-but this fertility connection would plausibly diminish as alternative sources of security emerge in the course of economic development.

The second phenomenon is more complex. Its documentation hinges on fairly intricate research on intra-household allocation and on assumptions about nutritional needs, culture, and equity. South Asia has been the locus of much of this research. Harriss (1990) presents a lengthy and thorough survey of the evidence and explanations for intra-household food allocation in that region. External conditions may give rise to a material rationale for discrimination against women and girls under conditions of scarcity, in terms of a household's survival strategy in confronting a labour market structured in favour of males and in terms of differences in expected future costs and returns to child rearing between girls and boys. There is also a cultural level of explanation, involving "observance of the moral order governing distribution" of food (p. 409)-an order that seemingly is poorly informed of nutritional basics. Allocative outcomes are conditioned by patriarchal beliefs and social relations - ones that exist as much outside the household as within it. Harriss lists the various elaborate proposals for "more or less highly targeted therapeutic interventions to remedy nutritional discrimination" (p.411) but is quite skeptical of their worth.

Consider policies that might lessen female poverty. The structural causes of poverty, such as women's second-class status in inheritance and property rights in some societies, may be resistant to change except over the long run; indirect means of enhancing female earning power and autonomy may have more prospects of near-term effect. Ensuring equal access to education is clearly important, as is ensuring that health and family planning programmes meet women's needs. To the extent that net fertility and child rearing costs fall more heavily on women than men, the economic benefit of these programmes also goes disproportionately to women. Design changes in certain other government extension activities can make them more oriented to women-for example, in credit systems or in the targeting of agricultural extension services in situations where food crops are predominantly cultivated by women.

What of the demographic effect of these measures? There is a general belief that policies to improve women's autonomy-particularly in their access to education and health services-are effective in reducing both fertility and mortality (A.M. Basu 1992: 241). Evidence on the mortality side seems incontestable; on fertility, the case is somewhat blurred by the prominent instances of fertility decline under much less than autonomous circumstances.

Attention to gender equity resounds in international declarations and covenants; it has become one of the routine emphases of the policy recommendations of international agencies. Increasingly, it is translated into practice by national governments. For example, Knodel and Jones (1996) find that gender inequality in access to secondary education is fast diminishing in much of the developing world. However, these authors caution that poverty considerations may get neglected along the way: "in most developing countries a specific gender focus [in education] is misplaced, or should be given only secondary priority relative to reducing socioeconomic inequality for both sexes" (p.698).

Children

The link between poverty and high child dependency can involve both directions of causation as well as the joint effects of other factors. The income-diluting effect of a larger number of dependent consumers in the family would presumably diminish as the children become economically active, but it is not less real for being transitory. It may also have long run consequential effects by curtailing the children's education in the interests of raising family income.

To the extent that poorer families have more children, the proportion of children in poverty will be higher than the proportion of families or of adults in poverty. The usual pattern of fertility decline can exacerbate this effect. Jones and Potter (1978: 22) cited the case of Colombia over a period during which the annual growth rate decreased from 3.1 per cent to 2.2 per cent: "when the birth rate was above 45 in 1964 about half of each cohort was born into the poorest 50 percent of all households. In 1973, when the birth rate had declined to the low thirties, the share of children born into these households increased to about two-thirds."

In democratic welfare states, fertility decline can also worsen child poverty through the political arena. The proportionately more numerous elderly brought about by population aging acquire greater influence over social policy, particularly as it affects the direction and scale of transfer payments. Payments that benefit the older age groups may become politically unassailable, so that any constraints on the overall scale of budgetary transfers are disproportionately felt by other potential claimants-notably, poor families with dependent children. This is the generational politics argument developed in Preston (1984).

The Elderly

In most developing societies welfare-state institutions are in their infancy. In particular, broad-based provisions for old-age security have yet to emerge. Only a minority of employees, chiefly in the public sector, is covered by pension schemes. Instead, the state takes it for granted that old-age security should be the responsibility of families. It may even enshrine this obligation in law, as in the 1980 marriage law of China, seeking to insist on familial responsibility against the forces tending to erode it. But such efforts, whether hortatory or regulatory, seem bound to fail-if only because, with declining fertility, networks of kin become thinner and the burden of upward transfers per working member of the family increases. Moreover, there would remain a need to provide for the childless elderly and for those whose families for whatever reason default on this obligation.

Many elderly would of course expect to support themselves from accumulated assets. Some part of a family's support of its aged members is in fact a graduated process of asset transfer. Poverty among the old is concentrated among those with few or no assets: to a first approximation, it is a continuation of poverty among the population in general. The additional components are contributed by ill health and disability, by increased vulnerability to predation, and by whatever structural disadvantage there may be in the society's treatment of widowhood. To the extent that low fertility and consequent population aging are occurring in contemporary societies at lower economic levels than experienced historically, problems of old-age support and of old-age poverty are the greater.

Ill health and disability are causes of poverty that are not only felt in old age. Disability in the sense of productivity impairment is not a well-defined concept: the degree of impairment may depend on numerous technological, societal and policy factors and be specific to occupation. Certain disease regimes, however, almost guarantee poverty-e.g. river blindness.

Problems with Targeting

If the numbers in such categories start adding up to appreciable fractions of the whole population, any programme benefits proffered would potentially include a large consumer surplus and become unaffordable. If the poor within each target group can be identified, of course, the group designation becomes redundant. Programmatic efforts and the targeting that typically accompanies them entail close government involvement. Less statalist development strategies would rely primarily on the aggregate growth in the economy to raise base-level wages and absorb unskilled labour, and to effect changes in demand (particularly for education and for health and family planning services) that in turn elicit private-sector responses.

The now-universal early development strategy of encouragement of labour-intensive manufactured exports is directed at overall economic growth rather than specifically at poverty reduction, but it was the underpinning of the strong "growth with equity" performance of the East Asian economies-and promises significant poverty alleviation elsewhere.

The large ideological gap between the programmatic and growth-promotion approaches is narrowed in practice by the common fact of governments falling well short of declared programme intent, together with de facto part-privatization of their operations.

Institutional Renovation

Poverty traps of the kind discussed earlier in this review are cases where the patterns of economic, social, or political organization create the wrong incentives for individuals or groups, resulting in economic decline, environmental degradation, or decay of social capital. Provision of programme services often would not affect those incentives, even though such services may still deliver significant welfare benefits. What would be needed to alter the incentive structure is intervention at the institutional level-through changes that realign the expectations, opportunities, and constraints facing individuals and families. That is not necessarily any more difficult a task for policy implementation than effective service delivery: many kinds of government intervention generate institutional change, both intended and unintended. It does, however, make greater demands on policy design.

The earlier discussion of local poverty scenarios indicated some of the policy directions that might resolve each of the various types of predicament. Unfortunately, there are no general rules to apply in these cases: even the economist's dictum of internalizing the externalities is not always appropriate. Each case requires separate analysis. One kind of policy intervention is aimed at dealing with the environment of risk faced by the poor. Mink (1993) emphasizes security of tenure for farmers and urban squatters and collective rights in the case of common property resources. This helps to lengthen time horizons and lessen the "mining" of resources.

Institutional programmes to cope with crisis events such as crop failure, to prevent distress sale of land, are also called for-such as formal or informal crop insurance, or supplementary public works schemes like that of Maharashtra (Cain 1981). For those suffering from unilateral cost transfers and not able to organize to protect their interests, the options are few. Government may be persuaded to exercise a supervening authority in halting the transfers or granting some compensation; more often, little is done and perhaps little can be done. If overall poverty is diminishing, there is rarely any insistence on ensuring that the growth path obeys strict principles of Pareto improvement.

The most intractable setting for policy is that of the failed state, where much of the physical infrastructure has been damaged or destroyed and minimal social capital remains. While there is ample reason for pessimism that any development progress is possible in the worst cases, there are instances of countries that have undergone a prolonged deterioration in civil order but are again moving up. Ghana and Uganda are cases in point. People retain institutional memories, of course, but the scope for institutional renovation or redesign is potentially large.

Policy Contexts: Authoritarianism and Democracy

A recurrent and contentious debate in development studies has concerned the relationship between development performance and political circumstances-whether, to put the issue bluntly, an authoritarian regime was better able to foster economic and social change than a democratic regime. A discussion of policy in the fields of population and poverty cannot avoid touching on this issue. For several decades up to the 1997 financial crisis, a number of East and Southeast Asian countries experienced both a remarkable performance in economic growth and at the same time major reductions in both poverty and fertility. The achievement was nearly uniformly applauded, but is variously interpreted. Good policy design is no doubt a major part of the explanation, but some analysts, both within and outside the region, also pointed to the restrictions imposed on populist political opposition.

Birdsall et al. (1995) stress the former explanation, emphasizing measures that raised productivity of the poor: promotion of a dynamic agricultural sector and labour-demanding, export-oriented manufacturing; and rapid expansion of basic education.

One of the "virtuous circles" they identify has the growing numbers of educated workers eroding the scarcity rents of the more educated, reinforcing low inequality and further increasing the labour demand. Equally virtuous is the economic gain from the reduction in child dependency following from the fertility decline that the economic expansion promoted. Job creation, higher agricultural productivity, and improved health and education enhanced earnings power at the grass-roots level.

These same trends, together with changed expectations about the economic future and recognition of the need for (and costs of) education, lowered family size goals. An effective distribution system for modern contraceptives met the consequent demand for birth control.

Reduction in fertility among the poor has helped their economic circumstances under the new conditions in which "quality" rather than "quantity" of children matters.

Both in the implementation of programmatic measures and in the overall system of local administration most of the East and Southeast Asian states relied on strong government authority. Both in programmes and administration, these pressures and mechanisms of control plausibly contributed to the resulting performance. In strictly economic terms, the major offsetting consideration is that the absence of political opposition may also have encouraged the so-called cronyism that led to poor investment policies in the modern sector and the dramatic economic reversals seen in the last year. In more general welfare terms, the offsetting consideration is the curtailment of individual liberty. Economic and social policies necessarily have a political dimension, and one where rhetoric and practice may diverge. Thus, in the rhetoric of family planning policy a fully voluntaristic model prevails; in practice it may not. Birth control programmes, like many other government activities, draw on the administrative power of the state.

An authoritarian state tends to run authoritarian programmes, whether in fertility or in the kinds of extension services that have contributed to a reduction in (narrowly construed) poverty. At least early in the course of development, programme effectiveness, it seems, does not imply or require democracy. Once the development process has lifted a society significantly above subsistence levels, however, the case for taking seriously this further dimension of well being, and the voice for service quality that it makes room for, rapidly gains strength. The rhetoric of the Cairo Programme of Action, of course, sees individual rights as paramount throughout the course of development.

Conclusion

In most of this discussion I have used an organizing framework that distinguished "direct" influences of population growth on economic distribution (and hence on poverty outcomes) from influences working through environmental change and change in the social order and governance. In turn, poverty outcomes could be analyzed in terms of the economic transfers generating them-transfers that show some degree of stability, with the winners able to sustain the arrangement or the losers unable to disrupt it.

It is this stability-the equilibrium trap situation-that policy measures have to deal with. Equilibrium traps can, of course, be escaped from by simple geographic mobility: the option of "exit." That may be effective for those who move, but is would rarely be an adequate policy response. The two main policy-driven ways of escape considered above were programmatic interventions and institutional interventions.

When tailored to the particular circumstances and existing organizational and administrative capabilities, either of these kinds of intervention can transform local perceptions and realities in ways that create new avenues of economic mobility and associated demographic behaviour. Needless to say, in neither case is success assured.

Objections to these policy directions have come from the left and the right of the political spectrum. On one side are those who oppose any linking of demographic concerns to poverty alleviation. They would see that linkage as in effect blaming the poor for their fertility as well as their poverty. On the other side are those who hold that these intervention efforts are mere sideline activities unconnected to the main task of creating a modern economy and the prosperity it affords-byproducts of which are assumed to be a modern demographic regime, disappearance of poverty, improved environmental quality, and democracy. That assumption, however, needs continual testing. Part of the problem of policy design in this area is to ensure that any such "sideline activities" clearly contribute to favourable economic, demographic, and environmental outcomes.

Population and Environmental Change: From Linkages to Policy Issues

Population dynamics, poverty and environmental change are linked in many ways and through multiple social and economic mechanisms, at various geographic levels. But not all those linkages have relevance for policy formulation in one of the three domains thus interconnected. This paper tries to identify policy issues among the array of conceivable linkages, placing emphasis on environmental policy. It considers both the environmental issues regarding the management of natural resources and those regarding the pollution of humankind's living quarters. These groups, which broadly correspond to the respective concerns of the rural and the urban environment - the "green" and "brown" agendas - differ in nature, and population dynamics plays different roles in them.

Like in all sectors, the search for policies that address population-poverty-environment linkages must be based on some representation of the nature of those linkages. But - like with population and development - there exist various, conflicting representations. I first quickly review the main perspectives and their general policy implications. Then I offer some leads for a discussion on how population programmes and professionals can concretely operate within the context thus sketched.

Alternative Views on Population-environment Linkages

Most theories of population and environment are expounded primarily in relation to agricultural resource usage, but they can be applied *mutandis mutatis* to all types of natural resources.

For the *natural science* perspective humankind is one of the many species competing for the resources of the biosphere. As the resources of any ecosystem are finite, so is the latter's carrying capacity; hence, beyond a point, each additional inhabitant has a negative impact on the productivity of resources; this in turn depresses labour productivity and incomes. Policy-wise, this perspective leads to advocate population stabilization. At first sight, it thus seems redundant with policy prescriptions that emphasize the need to slow down population growth for the sake of enabling more productive investment and a higher rate of economic growth.

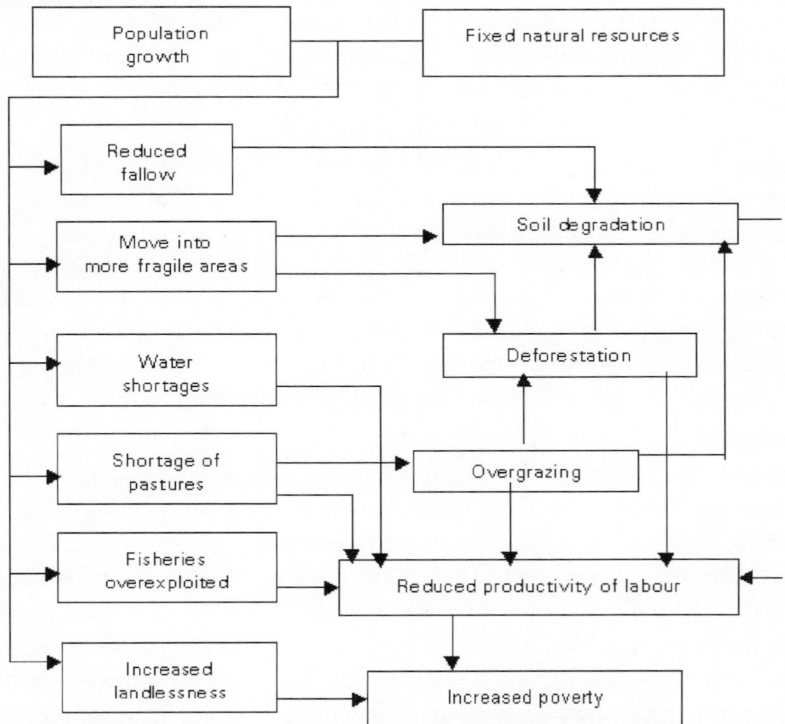

Figure: *Population growth and natural resources: Poverty trap*

That, however, is not exactly the case. This perspective proposes that population growth must be stopped as soon as possible: this drastic goal is a logical consequence of explicitly raising the issue of the scale of human interaction with the environment (and therefore of limits to economic growth). Such a goal is not much on national agendas yet. The largely accepted policy merely seeks a slowdown; in fact, many of its proponents concede that slow population growth helps stimulate the economy, and they avoid to address the long-term view and the difficult question of an eventual upper limit to population size. The fate of natural resources and the environment is absent from this perspective, but the concept of sustainable development now imposes a re-examination of the problem.

In fact, the two ideas (stabilizing population to protect the environment versus slowing population growth to foster more rapid economic growth) are at sharp variance. The problem is that economic growth, even coupled with slower population growth or even population stabilization, other things being equal, brings about greater environmental damage. The ICPD Programme of Action (henceforth PoA) does evoke repeatedly "sustained economic growth in the context of sustainable development", but the two concepts are mutually contradictory. In conclusion, this perspective does add a dimension to the "population slowdown" doctrine, but it is a thorny dimension that does not necessarily facilitate advocacy work.

This view also recommends a balanced population distribution, i.e. a more even pressure on natural resources. It is difficult to make much of that policy-wise. First of all, the population of a given territory can exert very different degrees of pressure on land, water, biomass, and other resources, because those may be present in different quantities and qualities. Some concepts may be of help here, for instance the "potential population-supporting capacity" (PPSC). But human pressure also depends on resource-specific patterns of use, which also vary across space, cultures etc.

Equalizing degrees of resources exploitation depends on much more than population distribution, because non-resident populations participate in that exploitation (e.g. urban dwellers require agricultural products or water - in greater quantities than rural people - so they too exert a pressure on rural resources). In sum, this policy recommendation is potentially very relevant, but it requires conceptual deepening and the development of appropriate methods of analysis. A major source of criticism to the natural science view is based on neo-classical economics and market-based adjustment mechanisms.

In this framework natural resources degradation is not necessarily a problem, since resources can be depleted at an acceptable rate, i.e. one that allows the market to replace those resources by alternative ones for the future ("efficient depletion"). Excessive degradation also may happen, either as a temporary consequence of population growth while adaptations take place, or as a structural problem where markets do not work efficiently (because some resources are not privately held and because prices do not reflect the scarcities and "sustainable values").

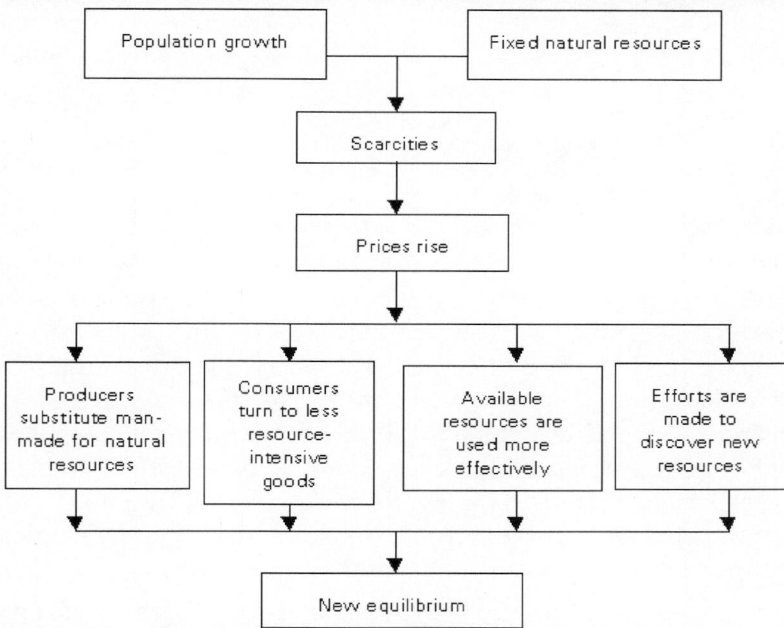

Figure: *Population growth and natural resources: Market-based harmony*

The policy prescription deriving from the neo-classical perspective is to give full efficiency to the market, meaning: define and price the use of common property resources; do not subsidize the exploitation of natural resources; and let the market, not the government, allocate resources. In this view population policy may "buy time", but it is not a "proper solution". This perspective leaves no role for population policies and programmes (else, of course, than their health value).

A third perspective (sometimes labelled *political ecology)* argues that environmental degradation and rapid population growth are both consequences of poverty. In this framework, resource degradation is the result of poor farmers eking out a living in marginal areas, with few resources and an inappropriate technology. Distortions in social structures, particularly unequal land distribution, inequitable relationships between landowner and tenants, limited access to credit, and biases in technology against small peasants, are designated as culprits.

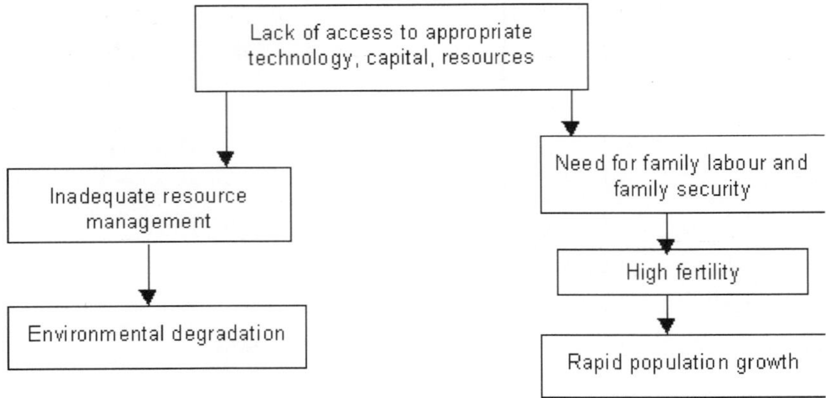

Figure: *Population growth and natural resources: Dual effect of poverty*

Policy-wise, this line of thought sees usefulness neither in population policy nor in mere technical interventions (such as terracing to fight land degradation), that it regards as inefficient as long as the "real" factors of degradation are not addressed. Therefore, it advocates poverty alleviation, through a more equitable distribution of resources and the redressing of distorted relations both within developing societies and between countries. This policy conclusion is entirely redundant, since the objective of poverty alleviation imposes itself on mere grounds of human rights, without any need to assume that it is the single most effective manner of tackling environmental problems.

Unlike natural resource degradation issues, there has been little analysis of the role of population dynamics in pollution. Soil, air and water pollution is mostly urbanization- and industry-related: rural pollution by agricultural chemicals (or local mining or industrial activities) is limited if compared to industrial wastes from urban areas; domestic wastes are a much more serious problem in urban areas than in rural ones because they are emitted in much higher quantities on a per caput basis; and population concentration plays a specific role in that it physically makes the dispersion of pollutants in the air or water much more difficult.

These problems cannot be much alleviated by population policies. They have to do mostly with [a] economic and technological models that favour mass production and place paramount value on GDP and income considerations, downplaying quality of life (including health) and the importance of a clean and pleasant environment; and [b] careless individual and household behaviour. Population composition has been shown to play a small part, in that household structure affects greenhouse gas emissions, but it is not likely to be a policy variable for emission reduction policies. As for population concentration, it is the very substance of urbanization; of course, one may seek to keep population and housing densities within ecologically (and socially) acceptable limits.

Some policies have attempted to reduce the rate of growth of urban agglomerations, but clearly the margins for intervention are limited in this domain. It is sensible to aim to harmonize urban population growth rates with the rates of growth of productive employment in cities, just like national policies aim to moderate overall population growth in order to enable tackling investment and equipment needs in a more progressive and orderly way. But this should be done by reducing the "push" factors in rural areas, especially when this leads to redressing unjustifiable inequities.

Finally, population has been viewed as an *intermediate variable:* technical, economic or social variables (e.g. poverty, defective markets, polluting technologies, distortionary policies etc.) would work "through" population growth, which merely "exacerbates" the effects of these processes. Of course the broad policy conclusion then is that measures are needed to attack the "root causes". However, population policy in this framework is accepted, as it "buys time". Further, the population variable is viewed by some as more tractable than some other factors, especially those more politically charged such as the urban bias, land mismanagement or distortionary fiscal and price policies. Accordingly, it has been for instance recommended to focus population policies on the more ecologically problematic areas, or to focus family planning efforts on landless families (thus also contributing to improve human capital).

The above review seems to tell us that single-minded perspectives do not help very much in understanding the issues - nor in designing appropriate policies in response. I shall propose some ideas for going further in policy analysis. Beforehand, however, I wish to take for a brief moment the advocacy viewpoint and offer a general defence of the relevance of the population variable.

Environmental Issues: Relevance of Population Dynamics

How do we enter the debate between the conflicting theoretical and policy perspectives when it comes to providing advice on their application at the country level? I think we have a duty to say that population dynamics do matter, and to show why and how.

- Opponents of the natural science perspective stress the static character of the model. In reality, this perspective does not ignore the role of technological change in enabling adaptations, and therefore in accommodating more population. But in this view technology merely "buys time": it is a temporary remedy, with increasing costs, and an ultimately limited capacity to solve problems. Critics reply that this underrates the adaptive capacities of humankind, and point for instance to the record of technological successes of the last century. But, in turn, the natural science perspective asks: must we mobilize ever more technological ingenuity and resources simply to crowd up the ecosystem with human beings?

- The neo-classical perspective underrates the importance of population growth, whose place in the theory is flawed in two manners: (a) population growth is not a one-time event, but a continuous process: therefore, the necessary adaptations must be continuous also and their failures cannot be regarded as a temporary inconvenience; and (b) "true prices" reflecting expected future values would be affected by the rate of population growth, as the latter increases competition for resources - hence discount rates - and raises amortization costs. Conversely, this perspective overrates the capacity of markets to generate a sustainable use of resources. If anything, markets have been shown not to adequately take into account the long-term view. Intergenerational equity can only be entrusted to a collective entity, also because decisions based on private utility functions usually ignore the ecological and social functions of the environment (e.g. aquifer recharge, flood control, health protection). Indeed, private property does not guarantee that resources will be managed with a concern for long-term sustainability.
- The "political ecology" analysis does provide an explanation for situations in which the outcome contradicts expectations based on the mere population-resources ratio, but it also has limitations. One of those is the rejection of a territory's carrying capacity as a significant factor in ecological outcomes - a view contradicted by empirical data, since population/PPSC ratios are rather well correlated with the incidence of land degradation. Another is the simplification of the poverty-fertility linkage (there is high fertility in a number of high-income populations, while in certain institutional and cultural contexts poverty may trigger a fertility transition). Yet another is the neglect of the influence of population dynamics on poverty. Access to natural resources is affected, among others, by

population density: population pressure "is an important and reinforcing link in reducing that access to sectors of an agrarian population" so that, while not causing inevitably land degradation, it "may almost inevitably lead to extreme poverty when it occurs in underdeveloped, mainly rural, countries". And inequality reduction is insufficient as a remedy when that pressure is strong.

Besides, the idea of a causal linkage between poverty and environmental degradation is questionable. Poverty has been seen as contributing much to resource overuse in developing countries: "[p]oor households are often virtually forced to overuse natural resources for daily subsistence. Thus, landless farmers colonize tropical forests, or [cultivate] highly erodible hillsides. Rural households in fuelwood-deficit countries strip foliage and burn crop and animal residues for fuel rather than using them for fertilizer and this contributes to desertification. Underemployed men in coastal villages overexploit already depleted inshore fisheries". But this view seems to be an illusion caused by the fact that the damage caused by the poor - unlike that caused by the affluent - is immediately visible at their doorsteps. The poor "possess neither fields nor livestock. Since they have no access to land, they cannot degrade it"; overall, "consumption and waste per person is also lowest among the poorest ... all in all, the poor probably tread lightest of all upon the earth, and do less damage to the environment than any other group. They are victims, not perpetrators".

- The view of population as an intermediate variable recognizes the value of policies that slow down population growth. On the other hand it is conceptually poor - it contains no useful economic or social analysis and offers no guidance on key possible policy variables and linkages between those.

The pressure of human activities on natural resources can arise from a host of factors: a large or growing population; outside market demands; the nature of agricultural activities; or institutional, social and economic conditions which lead to the extraction of surpluses from the land managers, forcing them in turn to extract from the resources more than is sustainable. Such conditions may be: heavy tax or tribute; very low wages; denial of access to CPRs; low commodity prices due to state intervention or market distortions; indebtedness; and so on.

In this context, population factors appear both as part of the basic conditions within which the socio-economic system operates (population density with regard to resources) and of the forces that affect its patterns of change (population growth, urbanization, migration).

Density is relevant to the level of direct pressure on resources; population growth and urbanization affect the volume of market demands; urbanization absorbs land, and is conducive to biased pricing policies; a large and growing rural labour force contributes to low wages; excess demand for access to CPRs may shut out part of the population.

Population dynamics must be taken into account, and it must be regarded as more than an exogenous variable: two-way linkages between population change and other elements of the system must be recognized. A systemic view of the "linkages" is therefore needed. This being said, what specific, self-standing policy recommendations can we reasonably sustain?

A Policy Analysis Perspective

How should policy analysis orient itself in the "population-poverty-environment nexus"? The negative view of a nexus is that the elements are linked in a vicious circle, so that people are caught in a deadlock if not in a downward spiral. a simplified image of one such nexus.

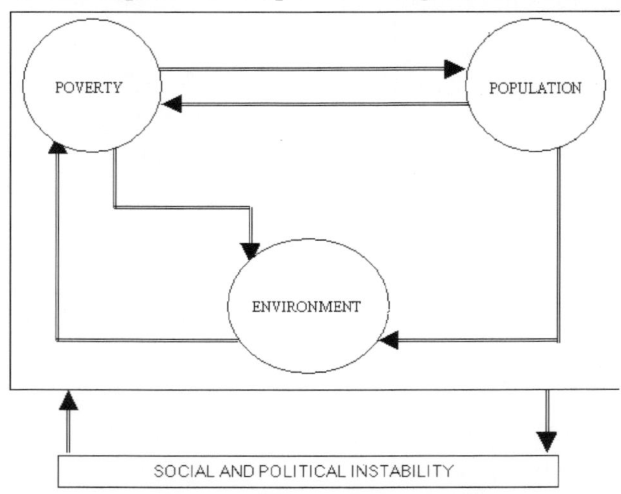

Figure: *"The P-P-E spiral"*

The detailed linkages are as follows:

- "Poverty" affects "population" through:
    - High child death rates lead parents to compensate or insure by having more children.
    - Lack of water supply, fuel and labour-saving devices increases the need for children to help in fields and homes.
    - Lack of security in illness and old age increases the need for many children.

- o Lack of education means less awareness of family planning methods and benefits, less use of clinics.
- o Lack of confidence in future and control over circumstances does not encourage planning - including family planning.
- o Low status of women, often associated with poverty, means women often uneducated, without power to control fertility.

- "Population" affects "poverty" through:
  - o Unemployment, low wages for those in work, dilution of economic gain.
  - o Increasing landlessness - inherited plots divided and subdivided among many children.
  - o Overstretching of social services, schools, health centres, family planning clinics, water and sanitation services.
- "Poverty" affects "environment" through:
  - o Difficulty in meeting today's needs means that short-term exploitation of the environment must take priority over long-term protection.
  - o Lack of knowledge about environmental issues and long-term consequences of today's actions.
- "Environment" affects "poverty" through:
  - o Soil erosion, salination, and flooding cause declining yields, declining employment and incomes, loss of fish catches.
  - o Poor housing, poor services and overcrowding exacerbate disease problems and lower productivity.
- "Population" affects "environment" through:
  - o Increasing pressure on marginal lands, over-exploitation of soils, overgrazing, overcutting of wood.
  - o Soil erosion, silting, flooding.
  - o Increased use of pesticides, fertilizer, water for irrigation-increased salination, pollution of fisheries.
  - o Migration to overcrowded slums, problems of water supply and sanitation, industrial waste dangers, indoor air pollution, mud slides.

The positive view of a nexus is that progress in one of the interlinked sectors is likely to generate positive effects on the others. For instance: "[e]fforts to slow down population growth, to reduce poverty, to achieve economic progress, to improve environmental protection, and to reduce unsustainable consumption patterns are mutually reinforcing" (ICPD PoA). But, since efforts in one sector will meet constraints rooted in the other sectors, the question arises: if there are vicious circles of population-poverty-environmental change, how much do conventional policy formulations help? For instance, the ICPD PoA states that "[e]radication of poverty will contribute to slowing population growth and to achieving early population stabilization". But it also adheres to the common wisdom that sustained economic growth "is essential to eradicate poverty". On the other hand, rapid population growth is an obstacle to sustained economic growth.

Ostensibly ignoring this vicious circle implies a belief that it can be broken simply by cumulating classical sectoral policies. Thus the ICPD's "comprehensive" view of population, development, poverty and environment did not produce any new policy perspective - because it contained no paradigm of the nature of the articulations between key phenomena. But in policy analysis work we cannot content ourselves with assuming general synergies: we must seek specific sectoral approaches that strengthen, and benefit from, those adopted in the connected sectors. In order to do that, we need to identify and address key articulation points of the single issues.

Taking as a starting point the need for improving environmental policy, here follow a few ideas derived from the preceding considerations.

- A basic step is the identification of the country's or region's *priority environmental issues.* One sensible approach to that identification, from our viewpoint, would be to quantitatively assess and compare the impacts of the various issues on human populations. The task of assessing, comparing and classifying those impacts is complex, but probably no more than other valuation and decision problems that are tackled in various fields of human activity through multicriteria analysis techniques. The criteria should not be only economic, but include for instance labour use and health indicators, with a gender dimension. The size of populations affected would be an important consideration in assessing priorities. This would go some way towards implementing Agenda 21 recommendation to "assess human vulnerability in ecologically sensitive areas and centres of population to determine the priorities for action at all levels, taking full account of community-defined needs".
- When the possibilities for designing broad strategies from scratch are limited - because there exist on-going sectoral strategies and programmes with their institutional stakes - the problem is to provide advice as to how to redirect existing policies to seek [a] greater *internal efficiency* and [b] greater *synergies.*

- The efficiency concern points to the need to address the *processes* that underlie specific demographic, poverty and environmental outcomes (creating an overall favourable context through legislation, IEC and macro-economic measures is not enough). For example, abating high rural fertility entails an understanding of the economic and social functions of large family sizes in rural societies. It also entails synergetic economic and social policies that modify those functions. Likewise, improving environmental outcomes requires addressing the various actors in those outcomes and their rationales.
- On this latter point, when looking for policy variables, it may be useful to think in terms of *chains of explanation:* with the land degradation issue, for instance, the chain "starts with the land managers and their direct relations with the land ... [The] next link concerns their relations with each other, other land users, and groups in the wider society who affect them in any way ... The state and the world economy constitute the last links in the chain".
- The operationally important processes will often be *location- or group-specific:* their causes (and consequences) differ from one ecological, economic and socio-cultural context to another. Environmental problems are known to be highly location-specific. Demographic dynamics and patterns can vary significantly among groups of population defined e.g. along socio-economic or cultural lines. Likewise, constraints differ among categories of poor (urban/rural, with/without access to land, early/late in the family life cycle, etc.). Across-the-board policies in these conditions are far less than optimal instruments, and disaggregated scales of analysis (in the geographic sense but also in the social sense) are useful.
- The concern for synergies points to the need for identifying sectoral policies that are most likely to have a positive effect on a connected sector (and possibly positive feedbacks on the sector directly concerned). This requires a sensible representation of the key linkages in the context at hand (territory and population). In forming such a representation, the theoretical perspectives reviewed above can be useful, but probably no more than as hypotheses, because the respective relevance of population pressure, market failures, will vary from one place to another.
- Policies should be built upon an understanding of the rationality of *households* - where migration, labour use, mixes of economic

activities, production techniques etc. are decided. The household is the right locus to seek policy measures that facilitate population-poverty-environment adaptations.

- A central concern should be the *productivity of labour*. Women's labour is of special relevance, not only on equity and health grounds, but also because children's labour often is a complement or substitute for it. In such situations, low female productivity has been shown to be an incentive to high "demand" for children. Progress in this respect reduces the need for large families, improves health conditions, alleviates poverty and, if it increases flexibility of time use, enables better management of the local resources and environment. But from the viewpoint of sustainability it is important that this does not bring about a higher rate of exploitation of the resources. Hence, the priority should be on implementing productivity-raising measures in areas least at risk of resource degradation.

Conclusion (Provisional)

By way of closing remarks I wish to address the research issue. The existing corpus of research on P-P-E linkages is disappointing. Methods often are questionable - like with much research on population and development in general - and "findings" often are contentious. It is fair to note that population specialists have not participated much in these efforts so far. Yet, they can contribute significantly to the advancement not of an abstract "knowledge" of the linkages, but of policy making. For that, efforts should be targeted to shed light on specific decision problems. Initiatives could be taken in the context of population and development strategy support programmes, to illustrate to policy makers the potential practical value of the oft-repeated proposition about integrating demographic factors in the study of environment and formulation of related policies.

Examples of this would be:

- Study current or contemplated environmental, economic and anti-poverty policies with a view to assess their possible effects on demographic dynamics.
- Detect possible environmental crises. This has much to do with the *Agenda 21* idea of identifying areas at risk and populations at risk, and the articulation of these two types of study has very interesting aspects.
- *Study the possible consequences of specific courses of action:* e.g. [a] identify populations at risk given the trends in resources

exploitation (including risks of population displacement), or [b] identify potential migration flows linked to the development of new areas. This kind of work may improve resource management, or help trigger and orient government intervention where the latter has not been completely banned.

- Assess the current distribution of population by agro-ecological zone. Calculate population/PPSC ratios. Interpret migration flows in that context. Draw scenarios of territory use and migration for the medium-term future.
- Do scenario analyses on a "desirable" national population distribution, e.g. to define an economically efficient distribution, or to assess the economic implications of achieving a desirable distribution according to non-economic criteria (social, strategic etc.).
- Assess the environmental implications of the current population distribution.
- Study the dynamics of migrant and resettled populations.

In all cases, a necessary ingredient of this type of efforts would be experimentation on a variety of assessment and scenario analysis methods applicable to the substantive questions discussed here.

Population Ageing

Population ageing occurs when the median age of a country or region rises. This happens because of rising life expectancy or declining birth rates. Excepting 18 countries termed 'demographic outliers' by the UN) this process is taking place in every country and region across the globe. In the entirety of recorded human history, the world has never seen as aged a population as currently exists globally. The UN predicts the rate of population ageing in the 21st century will exceed that in the 20th. Countries vary significantly in terms of the degree, and the pace, of these changes, and the UN expects populations that began ageing later to have less time to adapt to the many implications of these changes.

Overview

Population ageing is a shift in the distribution of a country's population towards older ages. This is usually reflected in an increase in the population's mean and median ages, a decline in the proportion of the population composed of children, and a rise in the proportion of the population that is elderly. Population ageing is widespread across the world. It is most advanced in the most highly developed countries. However the Oxford Institute of Population Ageing, one of the top institutions looking at global population ageing, has concluded that population ageing has slowed considerably in Europe and will have the greatest future impact in Asia, especially as Asia is in stage five of the demographic transition model.

Among the countries currently classified by the United Nations as more developed (with a total population of 1.2 billion in 2005), the overall median age rose from 29.0 in 1950 to 37.3 in 2000, and is forecast to rise to 45.5 by 2050. The corresponding figures for the world as a whole are 23.9 in 1950, 26.8 in 2000, and 37.8 in 2050. In Japan, one of the fastest ageing countries in the world, in 1950 there were 9.3 people under 20 for every person over 65. By 2025 this ratio is forecast to be 0.59 people under 20 for every person older than 65.

Population ageing arises from two (possibly related) demographic effects: increasing longevity and declining fertility. An increase in longevity raises the average age of the population by increasing the numbers of surviving older people. A decline in fertility reduces the number of babies, and as the effect continues, the numbers of younger people in general also reduce. A possible third factor is migration.

Of these two forces, it is declining fertility that is the largest contributor to population ageing in the world today. More specifically, it is the large decline in the overall fertility rate over the last half century that is primarily responsible for the population ageing in the world's most developed countries. Because many developing countries are going through faster fertility transitions, they will experience even faster population ageing than the currently developed countries in the future.

The speed of population ageing is likely to increase over the next 3 decades, yet few countries have the evidence to determine if their growing older populations are living the extra years of life in good or poor health. A "compression of morbidity" would imply reducing reduced disability in old age, whereas an expansion would see an increase in poor health with increased longevity. Another option has been posed for a situation of "dynamic equilibrium" (Manton, 1982). This is crucial information for governments if the limits of lifespan continue to increase indefinitely, as some researchers believe it will. The World Health Organization's suite of household health studies is working to provide the needed health and well-being evidence, including, for example the World Health Survey, and the Study on Global Ageing and Adult Health (SAGE)). These surveys cover 308,000 respondents aged 18+ years and 81,000 aged 50+ years from 70 countries. The Global Ageing Survey, exploring attitudes, expectations and behaviours towards later life and retirement, directed by George Leeson, and covering 44,000 people aged 40–80 in 24 countries from across the globe has revealed that many people are now fully aware of the ageing of the world's population and the implications which this will have for their lives and the lives of their children and grandchildren.

Canada has the highest per capita immigration rate in the world, partly to counter population ageing. The C. D. Howe Institute, a conservative think tank, has suggested that immigration cannot be used as a viable mean for countering population ageing. This conclusion is also seen in the work of other scholars. Demographers Peter McDonald and Rebecca Kippencomment, "[a]s fertility sinks further below replacement level, increasingly higher levels of annual net migration will be required to maintain a target of even zero population growth."

Ageing Around the World

Asia and Europe are the two regions where a significant number of countries face severe population ageing in the near future. In these regions within twenty years many countries will face a situation where the largest population cohort will be those over 65 and average age will be approaching 50. The Oxford Institute of Ageing [2] is an institution looking at global population ageing. Its research reveals that many of the views of global ageing are based on myths and that there will be considerable opportunities for the world as its population matures. The Institute's Director, Professor Sarah Harper [3] highlights in her book Ageing Societies the implications for work, families, health, education and technology of the ageing of the world's population.

Most of the developed world (with the notable exception of the United States) now has sub-replacement fertility levels, and population growth now depends largely on immigration together with population momentum which arises from previous large generations now enjoying longer life expectancy.

Ageing, Well-being and Social Policy

The economic effects of an ageing population are considerable. Older people have higher accumulated savings per head than younger people, but may be spending less on consumer goods. Depending on the age ranges at which the changes occur, an ageing population may thus result in lower interest rates and the economic benefits of lower inflation. Some economists (Japan) see advantages in such changes, notably the opportunity to progress automation and technological development without causing unemployment. They emphasize a shift from GDP to personal well-being.

However population ageing also increases some categories of expenditure, including some met from public finances. The largest area of expenditure in many countries is now health care, whose cost is likely to increase dramatically as the population ages. This would present governments with hard choices between higher taxes, including a possible reweighing of tax from earnings to consumption, and a reduced government role in providing health care. The second largest expenditure of most governments is education and these expenses will tend to fall with an ageing population, especially as fewer young people would probably continue into tertiary education as they would be in demand as part of the work force.

Social security systems have also begun to experience problems. Earlier defined benefit pension systems are experiencing sustainability problems due to the increased longevity. The extension of the pension period was not paired with an extension of the active labour period or a rise in pension contributions, resulting in a decline of replacement ratios. In recent years, many countries have adopted policies to strengthen the financial sustainability of pension systems, although the challenges regarding pension adequacy remain.

Population Biology

Population biology is a study of populations of organisms, especially the regulation of population size, life history traits such as clutch size, and extinction. The term *population biology*is often used interchangeably with population ecology, although 'population biology' is more frequently used when studying diseases, viruses, and microbes, and 'population ecology' is used more frequently when studying plants and animals. Although Reverend Malthus's book, *An Essay on the Principle of Population*, dealt only with the economy of human population fluctuations, which he theorized as being related to finite food resources, abundance and decadence, it gave inspiration to Charles Darwin for the theoretical basis of his seminal work, *The Origin of Species.*

In October 1838, that is, fifteen months after I had begun my systematic inquiry, I happened to read for amusement Malthus *on Population*, and being well prepared to appreciate the struggle for existence which everywhere goes on from long- continued observation of the habits of animals and plants, it at once struck me that under these circumstances favourable variations would tend to be preserved, and unfavourable ones to be destroyed. The results of this would be the formation of a new species. Here, then I had at last got a theory by which to work; but I was so anxious to avoid prejudice, that I determined not for some time to write even the briefest sketch of it. In June 1842 I first allowed myself the satisfaction of writing a very brief abstract of my theory in pencil in 35 pages; and this was enlarged during the summer of 1844 into one of 230 pages, which I had fairly copied out and still possess.

Chapter 8

Floating Population

Floating population is a terminology used to describe a group of people who reside in a given population for a certain amount of time and for various reasons, but are not generally considered part of the official census count. A population is usually broken down into two categories—the residents, who permanently stay in an area for a considerable amount of time and are part of the official population count, and the floating types, who are in the area but do not live there permanently and are not considered part of the official census count.

The residing population of a city can be sub-classified into two groups, one who permanently resides in a city for a considerably long duration of time like ten to fifteen years, and the others are those, like hostel students and transferable government servants, who might live for two to three years in a given area, as per their requirements, but are replaced by an equal number of new population for the same purpose after their departure. Thus, at any given time the number of people under this category remains more or less the same. The floating population, on the other hand, of a city constitutes of two types. The first category is those who visit a place regularly but do not stay in that area permanently or long enough to be considered official, like any person working in a city for a short time job. The second type constitutes visitors or guests who might live for a small span of time, but their time of stay and their next visit are not predictable, like tourists and seasonal visitors.

Geodemographic Segmentation

In marketing, Geodemographic segmentation is a multivariate statistical classification technique for discovering whether the individuals of a population fall into different groups by making quantitative comparisons of multiple characteristics with the assumption that the differences within any group should be less than the differences between groups.

Technologies Employed

The information technologies employed in geodemographic segmentation include geographic information system and database management software.

- *Geographic information system:* a business tool for interpreting data that consists of a demographic database, digitized maps, a computer and software.
- *Database management software:* a computer programme in which data are captured on the computer, updated, maintained and organized for effective use and manipulation of data.

Principles

Geodemographic segmentation is based on two simple principles:

- People who live in the same neighbourhoods are more likely to have similar characteristics than are two people chosen at random.
- Neighbourhoods can be categorized in terms of the characteristics of the population which they contain. Any two neighbourhoods can be placed in the same category, i.e., they contain similar types of people, even though they are widely separated.

Clustering Algorithms in Geodemographic Segmentation

The use of different algorithms leads to different results, but there is no single best approach for selecting the best algorithm, just as no algorithm offers any theoretical proof of its certainty (Grekousis and Hatzichristos 2012). One of the most frequently used techniques in geodemographic segmentation is the widely known k-means clustering algorithm. In fact most of the current commercial geodemographic systems are based on a k-means algorithm. Still, clustering techniques coming from artificial neural networks, genetic algorithms, or fuzzy logic are more efficient within large, multidimensional databases (Brimicombe 2007). Neural networks can handle non-linear relationships, are robust to noise and exhibit a high degree of automation. They do not assume any hypotheses regarding the nature or distribution of the data and they provide valuable assistance in handling problems of a geographical nature that, to date, have been impossible to solve. One of the best known and most efficient neural network methods for achieving unsupervised clustering is the Self-Organizing Map (SOM). SOM has been proposed as an improvement over the k-means method, for it provides a more flexible approach to census data clustering The SOM method has been recently used by Spielman and Thill (2008) to develop geodemographic clustering of a census dataset concerning New York City.

Another way of characterizing an individual polygon's similarity to all the regions is based on fuzzy logic. The basic concept of fuzzy clustering is that an object may belong to more than one clusters. In binary logic, the set is limited by the binary yes - no definition, meaning that an object either belongs or not to a cluster. Fuzzy clustering allows a spatial unit to belong to more than one clusters with varying membership values. Most studies concerning geodemographic analysis and fuzzy logic employ the Fuzzy C-Means algorithm and the Gustafson-Kessel algorithm (Grekousis and Hatzichristos 2012, Feng and Flowerdew 1999).

Geodemographic Segmentation Systems

Famous geodemographic segmentation systems are Prizm (US), Tapestry (US), CAMEO (UK), ACORN (UK) and MOSAIC (UK) system. New systems targeting subgroups of the population are also emerging. For example, Segmentos examines the geodemographic lifestyles of Hispanics in the United States.

CAMEO System

The CAMEO Classifications is a set of consumer classifications that are used internationally by organisations as part of their sales, marketing and network planning strategies. CAMEO UK has been built at postcode level and classifies over 42 million British consumers. It has been built to accurately segment the British market into 57 distinct neighbourhood types and 10 key marketing segments. CAMEO was developed and is maintained by Callcredit Marketing Solutions.

ACORN System

A Classification Of Residential Neighbourhoods (ACORN) system is conducted by Consolidated Analysis Centres Incorporated (CACI). It is the first and leading geodemographic tool to identify and understand the UK population and the demand for products and services. ACORN categorizes all 1.9 million UK postcodes using over 125 demographic statistics within England, Scotland, Wales and Northern Ireland and employing 287 lifestyle variables. The classification system of ACORN contains 56 types of household under the 14 groups in 5 categories.

MOSAIC System

Mosaic UK is Experian's people classification system. Originally created by Prof Richard Webber (visiting Professor of Geography at Kings College University, London) in association with Experian. The latest version of Mosaic was released in 2009. It classifies the UK population into 15 main socio-economic groups and, within this, 67 different types.

Mosaic UK is part of a family of Mosaic classifications that covers 29 countries including most of Western Europe, the United States, Australia and the Far East.

Mosaic Global is Experian's global consumer classification tool. It is based on the simple proposition that the world's cities share common patterns of residential segregation. Mosaic Global is a consistent segmentation system that covers over 400 million of the world's households using local data from 29 countries. It has identified 10 types of residential neighbourhood that can be found in each of the countries.

These systems are consisted of the different types of businesses

Geo Smart System

In Australia, geoSmart is a geodemographic segmentation system based on the principle that people with similar demographic profiles and lifestyles tend to live near each other. It is developed by an Australian supplier of geodemographic solutions, RDA Research.

geoSmart geodemographic segments are produced from the Australian Census (Australian Bureau of Statistics) demographic measures and modelled characteristics, and the system is updated for recent household growth. The clustering creates a single segment code that is represented by a descriptive statement or a thumbnail sketch.

In Australia, geoSmart is mainly used for database segmentation, customer acquisition, trade area profiling and letter box targeting, although it can be used in a broad range of other applications.

The Output Area Classification

The Output Area Classification (OAC) is the UK Office for National Statistics' (ONS) free and open geodemographic segmentation based upon the UK Census of Population 2001. It classifies 41 census variables into a 3 tier classification of 7, 21 and 52 groups. It is expected that a revised and enhanced version of OAC will becoming available with the release of the UK 2011 Census data in roughly 2013.

The perceived advantages of OAC over other commercial classifications stem from the fact that the methodology is open and documented, and the data is open and freely available. This means that OAC is not a black box, nor is it expensive to use, in fact it is free.

OAC has a wide variety of potential applications, from locational analysis to social marketing and consumer profiling. The UK public sector are increasingly taking up OAC as it represents a real cost saving during a time of recession.

Geodemography

Geodemography includes the application of geodemographic classifications for business, social research and public policy but has a parallel history in academic research seeking to understand the processes by which settlements (notably, cities) evolve and neighbourhoods are formed. It links the sciences of demography, the study of human population dynamics, geography, the study of the locational and spatial variation of both physical and human phenomena on Earth, and also sociology. In short, geodemography is the art and science of profiling people based on where they live. Geodemographic systems estimate the most probable characteristics of people based on the pooled profile of all people living in a small area near a particular address.

Origins of Geodemography

The origins of geodemographics are often identified as Charles Booth and his studies of deprivation and poverty in early twentieth century London, and the Chicago School of sociology. Booth developed the idea of 'classifying neighbourhoods', exemplified by his multivariate classification of the 1891 UK Census data to create a generalized social index of London's (then) registration districts. Research at the Chicago

School - though generally qualitative in nature - strengthened the idea that such classifications could be meaningful by developing the idea of 'natural areas' within cities: conceived as geographical units with populations of broadly homogenous social-economic and cultural characteristics.

The idea that census outputs could serve to identify and to characterize the geographies of cities gathered momentum with the increased availability of national census data and the computational ability to look for patterns in such data. Of particular importance to the emerging geodemographic industry was the development of clustering techniques to group statistically similar neighbourhoods into classes on a 'like with like' basis. More recently, data have become available at finer geographical resolutions (such as postal units), often originating from private commercial (i.e. non-governmental) sources.

Commercial geodemographics emerged from the late 1970s with the launch of PRIZM by Claritas in the US and ACORN by CACI in the UK. Geodemography has been used to target consumer services to 'ideal' populations based on their lifestyle and location. These parameters have been taken from geographical databases as well as from electoral lists and credit agencies. Combining these builds a picture of the population characteristics in different locations. The *geodemographic* data that this provides can then be used by marketers to target information towards those that they want to influence. This can be in the form of sales, services or even political information. At heart, geodemographics is just a structured method of making sense of complex socio-economic datasets.

Geodemography in the UK

In 2005 the Office for National Statistics (ONS) in collaboration with Dan Vickers and Phil Rees of the University of Leeds, released a free small scale social area classification of the UK based on 2001 UK small area census data. Similar classifications had been developed for earlier censuses, notably by Stan Openshaw and colleagues at Newcastle and Leeds Universities, but access to these generally was restricted to the academic communities.

The 2005 Output Area Classification (OAC) of the UK is a move to 'open geodemographics' and reflects a concern that applications of commercial geodemographics in policy and social research can otherwise be 'black box': it is not always clear exactly what variables were used to classify small areas and to define their neighbourhood type, how those variables were weighted, or how similar (or otherwise) each of the neighbourhoods within a class type actually are. Open geodemographics provides such information (because it is not constrained by commercial interests) and is an important development for applied social research that also seeks to understand and to explain the roots causes or processes that generate aggregate spatial patterns of social behaviour and attitudes. The Output Area Classification is now supported by a user group here. Geodemographic profiles have widened their application in the UK, with many life insurance companies and pension funds using them to assess longevity for pricing and reserving.

Geodemography in Australia

In Australia, general purpose geodemographic systems summarises a broad range of profiling data, largely derived from the Australian Census to create a thumbnail sketch of the type of people living in a particular small area. These small areas are either CCD (Census Collection District) or a sub-CD area, like a Meshblock. The types of characteristics mainly taken into account in geodemographic system construction are:

- Age distribution;
- Socioeconomic status indicators like income, education, and occupational status;
- Household and family composition;
- Cultural factors, such as ethnicity, language spoken, country of birth, and (but not limited to) religion;
- Employment factors, such as type of job, type of industry, and hours of work;
- Household economic factors, like indebtedness, investments, and poverty;
- Regional factors (e.g. whether the resided area is classified as metropolitan, provincial, or sparsely settled), and;
- Residential stability.

In 1987, geodemographic systems were first introduced as social analysis tools with CCN's (later Experian) introduction of the MOSAIC system. In 1990, RDA Research built their first system, geoSmart.

Criticisms

Geodemographics has drawn critical attention. Some focus on the possible discriminatory and intrusive effects of geodemographic practices. Others wonder whether members of geodemographic groups really are sufficiently alike to be analysed together. The generally unknown variance within geodemographic groupings makes it difficult to assess the significance of trends found in data. This may not matter for commercial and service planning applications but is of some concern for public sector and social research. A way forward is to integrate geodemographics with more statistical frameworks of analysis, using multilevel methods for example.

Commercial Demography Systems

- CAMEO by Eurodirect
- OAC by ONS/University of Leeds
- ACORN by CACI
- CLOUD CLIENT by Cloud Client Ltd
- C-Australia by Pathfinder Solutions
- C-New Zealand by Pathfinder Solutions
- C-Japan by Pathfinder Solutions
- Mosaic by Experian
- MicroVision by NDS/Equifax
- Crucible by Tesco
- geoSmart by RDA Research
- HomeTypes and ZoneTypes by Arvato Services (Bertlsmann)

NuMaps DemographicDrapes

Gompertz–Makeham Law of Mortality

	Gompertz Makeham
Parameters	$\alpha > 0$ (real) $\beta > 0$ (real) $\lambda > 0$ (real)
Support	$x \in \mathbb{R}^+$
PDF	$(\alpha e^{\beta x} + \lambda) \cdot \exp(-\lambda x - \frac{\alpha}{\beta}(e^{\beta x} - 1))$
CDF	$1 - \exp(-\lambda x - \frac{\alpha}{\beta}(e^{\beta x} - 1))$

The Gompertz–Makeham law states that the death rate is the sum of an age-independent component (the Makeham term, named after William Makeham) and an age-dependent component (the Gompertz function, named after Benjamin Gompertz), which increases exponentially with age. In a protected environment where external causes of death are rare (laboratory conditions, low mortality countries, etc.), the age-independent mortality component is often negligible. In this case the formula simplifies to a Gompertz law of mortality. In 1825, Benjamin Gompertz proposed an exponential increase in death rates with age.

The Gompertz–Makeham law of mortality describes the age dynamics of human mortality rather accurately in the age window from about 30 to 80 years of age. At more advanced ages, death rates do not increase as fast as predicted by this mortality law—a phenomenon known as the late-life mortality deceleration. The decline in the human mortality rate before the 1950s was mostly due to a decrease in the age-independent (Makeham) mortality component, while the age-dependent (Gompertz) mortality component was surprisingly stable. Since the 1950s, a new mortality trend has started in the form of an unexpected decline in mortality rates at advanced ages and "de-rectangularization" of the survival curve.

The hazard function which the Gompert-Makeham distribution is most often through characterised is

$$h(x) = \alpha e^{\beta x} + \lambda$$

The quantile function can be expressed in a closed-form expressions using the Lambert W function:

$$Q(u) = \frac{\alpha}{\beta\lambda} - \frac{1}{\lambda}\ln(1-u) - \frac{1}{\beta}W_0\left(\frac{\alpha e^{\alpha/\lambda}(1-u)^{-(\beta/\lambda)}}{\lambda}\right)$$

The Gompertz law is the same as a Fisher–Tippett distribution for the negative of age, restricted to negative values for the random variable (positive values for age).

Lee-Carter Model

The Lee-Carter model is a numerical algorithm used in mortality forecasting and life expectancy forecasting . The input to the model is a matrix of age specific mortality rates ordered monotonically by time, usually with ages in columns and years in rows. The output is another forecasted matrix of mortality rates.

The model uses the Singular Value Decomposition (SVD) to find a univariate time series vector "k_t" that captures 80-90% of the mortality trend (here the subscript "t" refers to time), a vector "b_x" that describes the amount of mortality change at a give age for a unit of yearly total mortality change (here the subscript "x" refers to age), and a scaling constant (referred to here as s_1 but unnamed in the literature). Surprisingly, k_t is usually linear, implying that gains to life expectancy are fairly constant year after year in most populations. Before being input to the SVD, age specific mortality rates are transformed into "$a_{x,t}$", by taking their logarithms, and then centreing them by subtracting their age-specific means (calculated over time). (The subscript "x,t" refers to the fact that $a_{x,t}$ spans both age and time.) Many researchers adjust the k_t vector by fitting it to empirical life expectancies for each year, using the a_x and b_x just generated with the SVD; when adjusted using this approach, changes to k_t are usually small.

To forecast mortality, the above k_t (either adjusted or not) is projected into the future using time series methods, the corresponding future $a_{x, t+n}$ is recovered by multiplying k_{t+n} by b_x and the appropriate diagonal element of S (when [U S V] = svd (mort)), and the actual mortality rates are recovered by taking exponentials of this vector. Because of the linearity of k_t, it is generally modelled as a random walk with trend. Life expectancy and other life table measures can be calculated from this forecasted matrix after adding back the means and taking exponentials to yield regular mortality rates. In most implementations, confidence intervals for the forecasts are generated by simulating multiple mortality forecasts using Monte-Carlo methods; a band of mortality between 5% and 95% percentiles of the simulated results is considered to be a valid forecast. These simulations are done by extending k_t into the future using randomization based on the standard error of k_t derived from the input data.

In outline and Matlab-style pseudocode, the algorithm is as follows:

1. Create a_x by taking logarithms of the mortality rates and centreing the results with the average log mortality at a given age.
2. Derive k_t, a scaling eigenvalue, and b_x from U(:,1), S(1,1), V(1,:), where [U S V] = svd (mort).
3. Forecast k_t with standard univariate ARIMA methods.
4. Use the forecast k_t with the original b_x and a_x to calculate logged mortality rates for each forecast year.
5. Recover regular mortality rates by calculating the exponential of the forecasted log mortality rates.

Without applying SVD or some other method of dimension reduction the table of mortality data is a highly correlated multivariate data series; the complexity of these multidimensional time series makes such them almost impossible to forecast. SVD has become widely used as a method of dimension reduction in many disparate fields, including by Google in their Page Rank algorithm. The Lee-Carter Model was introduced by Ronald D. Lee and Lawrence Carter in 1992 with the article "Modelling and Forecasting the Time Series of U.S. Mortality," (Journal of the American Statistical Association 87 (September): 659-671). The model grew out of their work in the late 1980s and early 1990s attempting to use inverse projection to infer rates in historical demography. The model has been used by the United States Social Security Administration, the US Census Bureau, and the United Nations. It has become the most widely used mortality forecasting technique in the world today.

There have been extensions to the Lee-Carter, most notably to account for missing years, correlated male and female populations, and large scale coherency in populations that share a mortality regime (Western Europe, for example). Many related papers can be found on Professor Ronald Lee's website. There are surprisingly few software packages for forecasting with the Lee-Carter Model. LCFIT is a web-based package with interactive forms. Professor Rob J. Hyndman provides an R package for demography that includes routines for creating and forecasting a Lee-Carter Model. Professor German Rodriguez provides code for the Lee-Carter Model using Stata.

Leslie Matrix

In applied mathematics, the Leslie matrix is a discrete, age-structured model of population growth that is very popular in population ecology. It was invented by and named after Patrick H. Leslie. The Leslie matrix (also called the Leslie Model) is one of the best known ways to describe the growth of populations (and their projected age distribution), in which a population is closed to migration and where only one sex, usually the female, is considered.

The Leslie Matrix is used in ecology to model the changes in a population of organisms over a period of time. In a Leslie Model, the population is divided into groups based on age classes. A similar model which replaces age classes with life stage is called a Lefkovitch matrix, whereby individuals can both remain in the same stage class or move on to the next one. At each time step the population is represented by a vector with an element for each age classes where each element indicates the number of individuals currently in that class. The Leslie

Matrix is a square matrix with the same number of rows and columns as the population vector has elements. The (i, j)th cell in the matrix indicates how many individuals will be in the age class i at the next time step for each individual in stage j. At each time step, the population vector is multiplied by the Leslie Matrix to generate the population vector for the following time step.

To build a matrix, some information must be known from the population:

- n_x, the number of individual (n) of each age class x
- s_x, the fraction of individuals that survives from age class x to age class *x+1*,
- f_x, fecundity, the per capita average number of female offspring reaching n_0 born from mother of the age class x More precisely it can be viewed as the number of offspring produced at the next age class b_{x+1} weighted by the probability of reaching the next age class. Therefore $f_x = s_x b_{x+1}$

The observations that n_0 at time *t+1* is simply the sum of all offspring born from the previous time step and that the organisms surviving to time *t+1* are the organisms at time *t* surviving at probability s_x we get $n_{x+1} = s_x n_x$ This then motivates the following matrix representation:

$$\begin{bmatrix} n_0 \\ n_1 \\ \vdots \\ n_{\omega-1} \end{bmatrix}_{t+1} = \begin{bmatrix} f_0 & f_1 & f_2 & f_3 & \cdots & f_{\omega-1} \\ s_0 & 0 & 0 & 0 & \cdots & 0 \\ 0 & s_1 & 0 & 0 & \cdots & 0 \\ 0 & 0 & s_2 & 0 & \cdots & 0 \\ 0 & 0 & 0 & \ddots & \cdots & 0 \\ 0 & 0 & 0 & \cdots & s_{\omega-2} & 0 \end{bmatrix} \begin{bmatrix} n_0 \\ n_1 \\ \vdots \\ n_{\omega-1} \end{bmatrix}_t$$

Where ω is the maximum age attainable in our population.

This can be written as;

$$\mathbf{n}_{t+1} = \mathbf{L}\mathbf{n}_t$$

or;

$$\mathbf{n}_t = \mathbf{L}^t\mathbf{n}_0$$

Where $\mathbf{n}_t$ is the population vector at time t and L is the Leslie matrix. The dominant eigenvalue of L, denoted λ, gives the populations asymptotic growth rate (growth rate at the stable age distribution). The corresponding eigenvector provides the stable age distribution, the proportion of individuals of each age within the population. Once the stable age distribution has been reached, a population undergoes exponential growth at rate λ.

The characteristic polynomial of the matrix is given by the Euler–Lotka equation.

The Leslie model is very similar to a discrete-time Markov chain. The main difference is that in a Markov model, one would have $f_x + s_x = 1$ for each *x*, while the Leslie model may have these sums greater or less than 1.

Stable Age Structure

This age-structured growth model suggests a steady-state, or stable, age-structure and growth rate. Regardless of the initial population size, N_0, or age distribution, the population tends asymptotically to this age-structure and growth rate. It also returns to this state following perturbation. The Euler–Lotka equation provides a means of identifying the intrinsic growth rate. The stable age-structure is determined both by the growth rate and the survival function (i.e. the Leslie matrix). For example, a population with a large intrinsic growth rate will have a disproportionately "young" age-structure. A population with high mortality rates at all ages (i.e. low survival) will have a similar age-structure. Charlesworth (1980) provides further details on the rate and form of convergence to the stable age-structure.

Lexis Diagram

In demography (the branch of statistics that deals with the study of populations) a Lexis diagram (named after economist and social scientist Wilhelm Lexis) is a two dimensional diagram that is used to represent events (such as births or deaths) that occur to individuals belonging to different cohorts. Calendar time is usually represented on the horizontal axis, while age is represented on the vertical axis. In some textbooks the y-axis is plotted backwards, with age 0 at the top of the page and increasing downwards.

However, other arrangements of the axes are also seen. As an example the death of an individual in 2009 at age 80 is represented by the point (2009,80); the cohort of all persons born in 1929 is represented by a diagonal line starting at (1929,0) and continuing through (1930,1) and so on.

Chapter 9

Population, Environment and Consumption

Population, consumption, and the environment—what a formidable and frightful combination! Yet the systemic linkages among these and other concerns are so abundant, intricate and dynamic that they are impossible to interpret or resolve in isolation. The contemporary context forces relational thought and action. The problems of population, consumption, and the environment are inseparable, and also of comparable moral significance. On the one hand, problems of consumption, understood as both underconsumption and overconsumption, are major contributing factors in the excessive exploitation and toxication of the rest of nature. On the other hand, overpopulation, which I will interpret as excessive consumption in relation to environmental capacity, jeopardizes both ecological integrity and the prospects of sufficient consumption for human development.

In reality, "consumption" is a distorted designation of the material excesses associated with affluence. These excesses are more a consequence of the needs of profitable production than the inherent wants of consumers. The production dynamic arouses our wants by marketeering in order to realize profits by supplying goods and services to satisfy demands it has created. To confront the inequities and prodigalities inherent in excessive consumption, we must first grasp that the problem is not only consumerism but productionism.

My purposes in this essay are first, to interpret the connections between ecological degradation and the problems of population and consumption, both overconsumption and underconsumption, and second, to identify some of the ethical issues that nations must face. I intend to highlight some of the virtues or moral norms that we need to cultivate as part of a global ethic in facing the demographic-ecological crisis.

From the perspective of ecological studies, population and consumption (which includes pollution as a resource use) are the two interactive sides of a species' impact on its environment. Overpopulation is not determined by numbers alone, but rather by numbers times the per capita consumption of natural resources. Thus a numerically large human population might be sustainable with modest or light consumption of environmental resources. But the tragedy of our emerging situation is our potential for reaching a saturation point in numbers when even light consumption, justly distributed, will be in excess of available resources, so that human development for all will be biophysically impossible. Conversely, a numerically smaller population of high producers/consumers is overpopulated when it exceeds key limits of its environment. Ecologically, consumption rates are as relevant as fertility rates. The reason is that the average additional person in affluent nations consumes far more and places far greater stress on the biosphere than the average person in poor nations. Interpreted this way, the reduction of population growth is an urgent moral demand on all nations, and it is accompanied by an equally urgent moral demand on affluent nations for reduced production/consumption and equitable distribution. The concept of carrying capacity is simply a reminder that the planet is finite. Look first at nonrenewable resources, which include fossil fuels and minerals, now being used in massive amounts under the prods of population and consumption growth. By definition, nonrenewables will run out. The implicit question in much of the public debate has been whether practical exhaustion will be in the short or long run. But does that question make an ethical difference if we have long-term responsibilities to future generations? On nonrenewable resources, there really is no moral substitute for careful conservation, comprehensive recycling, ultra-efficiency, constrained consumption, and product durability and reparability.

So-called renewable resources—like fisheries, forests, and soils—are periodically regenerated through natural cycles. But they can become functionally nonrenewable when used excessively or abusively. Some signs appear ominous. Croplands in many places are declining or disappearing; desertification is proceeding dangerously. These losses represent millions of tons of foodstuffs not being available to feed hungry people. Potable water—the indispensable resource—is becoming scarce in many places. Water insufficiencies will not only constrain agricultural productivity and economic development but also create political and economic tensions. Fisheries, a prime source of animal protein in many developing countries, show danger signals of unsustainable and unjust use. All the world's major fishing areas apparently have reached or exceeded the limits of sustainability.

A major concern is: will food supplies—the very foundation of health, education, and vocation—be adequate for the impending future, or will they be overwhelmed by human numbers? To meet anticipated demands from population growth, the nations will need at least a doubling of food production by the middle of the next century. One must ask: Is this doubling of food production biophysically possible? If so, will it entail the massive destruction of natural ecosystems? What changes in this scenario can be created through reductions in fertility and consumption rates?

Though pollution is not a peculiar effect of overpopulation and overproduction, these greatly aggravate pollution. Pesticides and fertilizers used abundantly and indiscriminately in agriculture, human-induced climate change resulting from the production of carbon dioxide and other "greenhouse gases," diverse industrial emissions, nuclear wastes, municipal wastes, the overburden from mining, oil spills—all these problems are intensified by increases in reproduction and production. They reduce the planetary carrying capacity.

These factors also threaten major reductions in the Earth's rich biodiversity. By the end of the next century, with the continuation of rapid destruction of diverse habitats, 20% to 50% of current species could be extinguished, some biologists estimate. These losses are morally serious, not only because of the instrumental values that other species are for human needs, but also because they are intrinsic values for themselves, which humans ought to honor.

No doubt, some biophysical limits can be extended through human ingenuity, but there are limits even on technological powers to transcend biophysical limits. Technology is not alchemy. The context of human existence is not the inexhaustibility of the products and capacities of nature, but ecological scarcity. This is the context in which the human community must decide questions of population and consumption.

The depth and breadth of global underconsumption are startling. Radical disparities in economic capacities within and among nations are a prominent feature of the modern world. Less than a fifth of the world's human population, concentrated in the "industrialized" nations including the U.S., live in relative comfort or luxury, some in gluttony. These nations receive more than 80% of global income. More than another fifth of humanity, however, lives in desperate poverty— on an average equivalent income of $1 or less per day per person. Their numbers are generally estimated at 1.1 billion people; in fact however, the numbers of serious underconsumers are considerably higher, given that the statistical line for measuring global poverty is set ridiculously low. And income disparities are growing: the ratio of the richest fifth's share to the poorest grew from 30 to 1 in 1969 to 59 to 1 in 1989. The Human Development Report 1993, moreover, says that the ratio now is really 150 to l.

Chronic poverty—underconsumption—has not only severe social effects but also comparable ecological effects. Indeed, the problem infects every dimension of the ecological crisis. In the absence of economic sufficiency, poor people and nations are often forced to exploit their natural resources—croplands, grasslands, forests, fisheries, etc.—beyond the thresholds of sustainability simply to survive in the present. The process is accentuated by the continuation of population growth (bred partly by underconsumption) which contributed to the pressures of overexploitation in the first place. Thus, underconsumption spurred by overpopulation is a driving force behind ecological deterioration. Then, in a vicious cycle, this deterioration further reduces the availability of resources and further propels poverty. In an interdependent global market, the economic activities of the overdeveloped nations of the North often seem to be significant factors in depriving some poor nations of the South of sufficient resources for their essential needs. Transnational corporations have contributed to this process by unsustainably destroying tropical forests to provide exotic woods for the affluent, severely polluting rivers and lands, withdrawing minerals with excessive destruction, uprooting indigenous peoples, exploiting lax labor and environmental laws, promoting cash crops for export and reducing thereby the availability of food for domestic consumption, and using poor nations as sites of hazardous industries and technologies. On the moral assumption that we are an interdependent community of moral equals sharing responsibility for one another's welfare, the deprivation of necessities for any is an issue of justice and a demand for frugality by the prosperous, whether or not a causal connection exists between poverty and prosperity. In all cases, the wealthy must reduce their consumption in order to share essentials with the poor.

Yet, despite the fact that the nations even now seem to be approaching or surpassing some ecological limits in using the rest of nature as source and sink, the dominant response in international circles to the dynamic of over- and underconsumption is not an emphasis on frugality and sharing but rather the advocacy of intensive economic growth enhanced by technical efficiency. The World Commission on Environment and Development, for example, argues that the "quality" or "content" of growth must be changed, to be "less material- and energy-intensive and more equitable in its impact." Nevertheless, it insists that a five- to tenfold increase in manufacturing output will be necessary, given the current rates of population growth, to raise the "developing" world's production and consumption to the level of the industrialized world in the next century.

But is this economic vision ecologically possible? Even if it is, is it ecologically desirable or morally responsible? Should our global economic goal simply be to elevate all peoples to "the American way of life?" Or is there an alternative that lifts the poor and preserves the biosphere? This economic growth model seems to be a utopian illusion. It optimistically circumvents the problem of limits, and it operates on the assumption that the rest of nature is nothing more than instrumental values for human wealth and welfare. In reality, the globalization of North American standards of living probably would be ecologically disastrous—and also therefore, economically ruinous. Yet it would be seriously discriminatory to advocate a double track in which the nations of the South restrict their production while the nations of the North continue their wanton ways. Justice in traditional Jewish and Christian understandings would seem to require not only floors but ceilings on economic production and consumption. The process of redistribution contributes indirectly to both ecological integrity and population stability, since these goals depend in part on distributive justice. Assessments of overpopulation and overconsumption are not simply empirical calculations, but also moral judgments. They involve questions of morally desirable ends or living conditions, just distribution, and benevolent sharing. Ethically, the essential questions are: What is a good quality of life for humans, and what material and demographic conditions are necessary to ensure that good quality for all on a finite planet? What are our moral responsibilities to the rest of humanity, other species, and future generations? What is the appropriate size of the human population and the amount of material consumption to enable us to fulfill these responsibilities? What are the moral limits to human production and reproduction? The final question for this essay is then: What are the moral norms that we ought to be cultivating and promoting as responses to the ecological degradation resulting from productionism and reproductionism? These norm might be called ecological/demographic virtues or productive/reproductive virtues, so long as it is understood that they apply to both individuals and societies, as moral standards for both character formation and social transformation. They are critically important to policy-making because they are the moral guidelines for policy. They are also the conditions for a hopeful future. These six seem especially relevant to our focus here:

Equity is here simply a synonym for justice in the distribution of the world's goods and services, so that all humans have the essential material conditions for human dignity and social participation. This concern is a fundamental theme in Jewish and Christian concepts of covenant fidelity to God, the "Lover of Justice" (Psalm 99.4). Since economic deprivation is a major cause and effect of ecological degradation in a vicious cycle, economic justice is not only an essential good in itself but also a necessary condition of ecological integrity. Thus, economic equity is a matter of both social and ecological ethics. Similarly, population stabilization is a matter of both social and ecological justice. Indeed, population stabilization needs to be part of strategies for socioeconomic justice, since socioeconomic conditions seem to be prime factors affecting fertility rates, with improvements in the quality of life associated with reductions in the rates and numbers of births.

Sustainability is living within the bounds of the regenerative, assimilative, and carrying capacities of the planet indefinitely, as an expression of a covenant of solidarity with future generations. The present pattern of using the planet's resources is characterized by un sustainability. Future generations will be major victims of our generation's excessive production, consumption, toxication, and reproduction. Sustainability forces us to think of our moral responsibilities in terms of the truly long run—even millennia when relevant— rather than the decades characteristic of most advocacy of sustainable development. It is particularly important that we highlight the generally neglected principles of sustainability for production and reproduction. Thus sustainability depletes renewable resources no more, and preferably far less, than their rate of regeneration. Sustainability pollutes no more, and preferably far less, than can be naturally assimilated and justified as necessary for compelling purposes. Sustainability depletes nonrenewable resources only conservatively, efficiently, frugally, and only to the extent that it can clearly provide substitutions, preferably better and renewable ones, like solar energy for the overuse of fossil fuels, as reparations to future generations. Sustainability reproduces progeny no more, and preferably far less, than is compatible with preserving the ecological conditions necessary for the continuous thriving of humans and other species in our connectional system. Sustainability reminds us that our moral responsibilities extend into the future as far as our influences are relevant and plausibly foreseeable. Bioresponsibility. Against the dominant economic reductionism which treats nonhuman life as utility values for human wealth and welfare, bioresponsibility is an effort to redefine responsible human relationships with the rest of the planet's biota and to ground these responsible relationships not only (weakly) in utility or even generosity, but also (strongly) in the just dues and demands imposed on us by the vital interests of otherkind. Whatever instrumental values other species have for humans, they are also intrinsically valuable for themselves. These intrinsic values are a sufficient condition for our moral respect.

The moral issues surrounding this extension of justice to the rest of the biota are mind-numbing in their novelty and complexity. Nevertheless, one conclusion seems clear: biotic justice imposes obligations on the human community to limit our economic production and our sexual reproduction to prevent the excessive destruction of wildlife and wildlands. If other species are ends or goods for themselves, then our economic and population policies need to pursue what Herman Daly calls the "biocentric optimum," in contrast to the "anthropocentric optimum" which presently prevails as the norm. Both humans and nonhumans are wronged when human problems of excessive population and production are "resolved" by the further sacrifice of nonhuman species and their habitats. We humans have already used far more than any reasonably defined fair share of this world's goods. These human dilemmas are best resolved not by the tacky tactic of pitting the poor against endangered species and habitats, but rather by confronting directly the prime sources of both poverty and ecological degradation: overconsumption by an economic elect, human overpopulation, and economic maldistribution. Frugality is the most neglected norm in modern morality. Yet, solutions to social and ecological problems depend on the revival of this norm and its reformation from a strictly personal virtue to a social norm. It is a revolt against the ethos of the Sumptuous Society. As a norm for the economic activity of individuals and societies, denoting moderation and material sufficiency, frugality entails morally disciplined production and consumption for higher ends, especially the social and ecological common good. Thus, appropriate production and consumption should be measured not merely individualistically, in reference to our personal, spiritual, and moral well-being, but relationally, because we exist as relational beings—social, political, and ecological animals—and our well-being depends on sharing.

Frugality is an earth-affirming and enriching norm that delights in the less consumptive joys of the mind and flesh. It is "sparing" in production and consumption, literally sparing of the scarce resources for human communities and sparing of the members of other species. It minimizes harm and thereby enables a greater thriving of all life. Frugality is a necessary condition of justice (including biotic justice) and sustainability in situations of relative scarcity, where "enough" can be available for all—human and nonhumankind, present and future—only if essential resources are shared justly and generously.

A moral affirmation of frugality tends to induce guilt in some of the economically privileged, according to more than one indignant critic of the concept. If so, fine; that is a good guilt, from which we ought not to seek any therapeutic relief in denial or rationalization of our complicity in unjust consumption. That guilt is a moral elixir, stimulating a conversion that integrates our norms and our practices, prompting us to seek justice and sustainability by living frugally.

Reproductive Responsibility. It is essential that we defend a variety of reproductive rights—such as universal accessibility to diverse, safe, effective, simple, and reversible contraception for both women and men; equality for women in all dimensions of life, from economic and political participation to adequate nutrition; and a full range of reproductive health services. Indeed, I want to defend a universal right not to procreate, which includes a woman's right to choose abortion. Moreover, it seems indefensible to claim that anyone has an unrestricted right to procreate under current and emerging circumstances. Along with reproductive rights, it is important for our integrity and credibility to emphasize responsibilities. This includes the moral presumption that no one should reproduce beyond the replacement rate, unless one can provide a compelling moral justification to the contrary. The moral mandate for reproductive responsibility applies to both rich and poor families, Southern and Northern nations, men and women. Procreative decisions cannot be made simply on the basis of what is desired by individuals (perhaps to display their virility or satisfy customary expectations) or what is geopolitically or economically desirable for a nation or ethnic group. In light of the dangers of overpopulation, these decisions also must be made on the basis of what is good for the human community and the biosphere as wholes—and that includes no more (indeed, less if population reduction is a necessary goal) than procreative replacement, assuming that we are an international community of moral equals, functioning fairly in the distribution of procreation. Clearly, this emphasis on reproductive responsibilities demands certain rights—for example, accessible contraception, reproductive health care, gender equality, and adequate education—as means to the exercise of these responsibilities. The realization of these reproductive responsibilities and rights, moreover, will not happen spontaneously; it will entail national or even regional population planning and policies, coordinated internationally for the sake of effectiveness and fairness.

Magnanimity is a willing responsiveness to our duties in justice and/or benevolence that is characterized by generous sharing. Magnanimity is an essential virtue to cultivate in our citizenry because we are becoming seriously deficient in its practice. Shamefully, as a corporate entity, the United States is becoming a nation of skinflints—a nation of vast but vastly maldistributed wealth in which the wealthiest are constantly complaining that they are overtaxed and can no longer afford a variety of public services. The most furiously bashed services are welfare, immigrant services, and, of course, foreign aid. The U.S. gave an average of $10.1 billion in overseas development assistance (ODA) in 1989-91. This amount is significant, of course, but it was 0.2% of gross national product (GNP)—less than given by all other industrialized nations. In fact, much of that aid was determined by U.S. military, geopolitical, and commercial interests, rather than by authentic development needs like reproductive services and the eradication of hunger. Yet, while global poverty is expanding, population growing, and environmental problems increasing, even this insufficient economic aid is now seriously shrinking as an ideology of self-indulgent greed and gluttony infects our nation's economic and political life.

Never has there been a greater need for magnanimity by the American people! We can begin—but not end—by increasing U.S. foreign assistance to the modest UN target of 0.7% of GDP.

Despite the diatribes against foreign aid, as well as its deficiencies which demand correction, the fact remains that aid has contributed significantly to reducing infant and maternal mortality, improving public sanitation, increasing food production, increasing literacy and various skills, promoting primary health care, expanding employment, etc. More and better aid can greatly enhance human well-being in the future. The advancement of full human development and ecological integrity is unrealistic—nay, illusory—apart from the prevention of overpopulation and the conclusion of both under- and overconsumption. Equally, overcoming these problems is unrealistic—nay, a fantasy of the privileged—apart from the embodiment of the above moral norms in our personal lives and public policies. Contrary to the prayers and pretenses of too many of the prosperous, there is no cheap and easy way to global social and ecological well-being. Real sacrifices will be required of the haves, and the typical arguments from enlightened self-interest will not make these sacrifices appear psychologically or politically palatable. Yet, people can find real satisfactions in seeing the enhanced lives in human and biotic communities that only constrained production and reproduction on a finite planet can make possible. If privileged people must have some self-benefiting reason for moral conversion, then maybe the major motivation that advocates ought to cultivate in themselves and their societies is one that is deeply rooted in our moral traditions: Genuine joy is gained by being just and generous.

The Challenge to Balance Population Increase and Food Supply

- If the world is to avoid increasing hardship as a result of the population explosion and excessive consumption, a significant change in attitude is needed by the leadership of both developed and developing countries. The high-level expert group emphasizes that continuous global expansion of population and wasteful consumption are inevitably going to increase pressure on future food supplies. While some official global projections may not in themselves be alarming, once the position of the individual countries or regions are examined, it is clear that pressures on a regional and a country basis will be great. Over the next 30 years, they will also be great at the global level.
- Official estimates of population and food production should not lead to any complacency. The most vigorous efforts will be required from third world countries and from donor countries to avoid an increasingly serious and unsustainable situation.
- On the one hand, low-income developing countries, where the greatest pressures already exist, must redouble their efforts to introduce effective and wide-ranging population policies. These polices must fully recognize the status of women. Redoubled efforts are needed to reduce the dramatically high birth rate, which in a number of developing countries, has led to reduced per capita food production over the last 25 years.
- On the other hand, many donor countries must target their aid more effectively. This is important because most, but not all donor countries, contrary to their own and the world's interest, have been reducing Official Development Assistance (ODA). This makes it all the more essential to target assistance to the poorest countries to reinforce the efforts of those developing countries that are themselves doing what they can to overcome their problems.
- Such assistance needs to pay particular attention to supporting agriculture and family planning in its broadest concept. Even the most optimistic forecasts suggest that some 700 million

people, 200 million of whom are children, are likely to remain malnourished by the year 2020. This must be regarded as totally unacceptable in a civilized and humane society. The report also provides some details assessing the efforts required.

- Consumption patterns in the wealthiest nations are depleting world resources in ways that jeopardize the future of world development. It cannot be right or sensible that the wealthy 23 percent consume 83 percent of the resources. Moderation and a sense of sharing our common world are required.
- The global challenge of population growth and food security is not insurmountable. It requires large-scale efforts from both North and South, starting now. Such efforts should address four interrelated questions:
  — redoubling efforts to reduce fertility and stabilize the global population at the lowest possible level;
  — increasing food production by modernizing and intensifying agriculture in an environmentally sustainable fashion;
  — ensuring long-term sustainability through more efficient use of resources, especially water, developing cleaner forms of energy, and undertaking appropriate environmental actions; and
  — reaching out to the poorest, the hungry and the malnourished by addressing head on the problem of extreme poverty and access to available food.
- These actions will require appropriate policies, in both North and South, and substantial investments from domestic resources from foreign investment and from aid.
- The high-level group has detailed a number of recommendations which place obligations on developing countries, on OECD donor countries, and on the international community.

Recommendations

Developing Countries

- In order to ensure the world's capacity to feed 8.3 billion people in 2025, the U.N. median likely projection, major efforts must be deployed now to improve efficiency in use of resources and to strengthen research focused on sustainable agriculture.
- Greater attention to social policy, including health care, family planning and greatly increased investment in education, is required.

- Special attention is required to the status of women to ensure that in all respect they enjoy the same quality of rights and opportunities. This will lead to better informed women and voluntary choice in bearing children.
- Governments must take daring measures to bring about major changes in the status of women which will ensure greater access to property, equality before the law, and access to credit and extension services that increase agricultural productivity.
- Distorted policies of governments have too often adversely affected the performance of agriculture. Government policies must encourage investment and clarify the roles of public and private investment, in agriculture and in infrastructure in poorer countries.
- In Africa, where major problems continue, particular action is required by national governments and the international community to ensure a sustained reduction in malnutrition.

International Community

- ODA should be increased substantially, especially by those countries which have reduced aid over the last 10 years. Flows of aid should be depoliticized and targeted towards the neediest countries and so to lay the foundation for dealing with long-term problems of population growth, environmental degradation, food security and extreme poverty.
- OECD countries should target some of their assistance to breaking bottlenecks and barriers to trade, in parallel with opening their markets to poor country exports.
- Farm subsidies in the North should be gradually reduced to create more opportunities for enhanced production and marketing of farm products produced by the South.
- Lesser developed countries need special assistance in their efforts to establish greater self-reliance in assuring food security.
- Countries lacking human resources for receiving agricultural technology transfer to locate a national agricultural research system should be assisted. Training opportunities should also be provided for planning and management of agricultural policies.
- The goals of social policy should be the promotion of social cohesion, equity and mobility, and accordingly policies must address the cultural and institutional dimensions of development.
- In view of the huge burden of debts, especially in poor countries, multilateral nonconcessional debt should be retired and/or

concessionalized. Debt reduction must be carefully managed so as not to impede the possible access of the poor countries to credit markets, especially for trade finance.

- The creative use of guarantees or other mechanisms should be explored to draw private capital into making long-term investments in developing countries.
- Broader partnership with NGOs should be sought to encourage more efficient ways to meet the needs of the poorest people and ensure more equitable sharing of development benefits so as not to exacerbate the already critical situation.
- The capacity to monitor the impact of environment degradation by agricultural and industrial intensification should be strengthened, and research on environmentally sound farming systems should be increased.
- In countries badly damaged by civil strife, special programs should be established for getting rid of the mines that render large parts of the arable land inaccessible, and such programs should be funded by donors.
- The affluent industrialized countries should instill consciousness among their own people that their excessive consumption is an integral part of the problem. It is not permissible for the North unilaterally to ask developing countries to curtail population growth, while they themselves continue to aggravate the ecosystem with their excessive life style.
- Global efforts on reforestation should be promoted by such campaigns as each inhabitant on earth planting one tree a year.

Introduction: Global and Regional Conditions

The Present

The population-food balance of the world today presents major challenges, but there are reasons for cautious optimism. There are two major caveats, however. First, the optimism comes at the global level, while many serious problems remain at the regional and country levels. There is also the persistent and near universal problem of the very poor. Second, realizing any progress will require much hard work and improved national and international policies.

The global population is today 5.7 billion, growing at about 1.57 percent per year according to the 1994 U.N. World Population Prospects. This represents some progress in that the growth rate has declined from its peak of 2 percent 30 years ago, but the absolute growth will still add 900 million people in this decade. On the positive side, although population growth represents a challenge, it also reflects declining mortality and increasing life expectancy, indicating a general increase in the quality of human life. The global agricultural situation has shown impressive progress. For the past half a century, total agricultural output has kept ahead of population growth. Supply has kept ahead of demand, and there has been a general decline in world food prices. However, there is less certainty that this trend will continue. The hopeful global situation hides serious regional and national imbalances. Though population growth rates have declined in most of the less developed world, they have not yet declined significantly in Africa, and parts of South and West Asia. These areas show the lowest gains in life expectancy and the quality of life. Progress has yet to be seen in solving entrenched environmental problems, both at global and regional levels. Global atmospheric emissions and regional problems of environmental degradation, pollution, water shortage, desertification and deforestation, soil erosion and salinization have reached proportions that are clearly unsustainable. Annually, 16 million hectares of forests are cleared, resulting in a net reduction in the world's forests of 10 million hectares.

Although global agricultural output has increased, per capita output has been declining in Africa for the past 20 years. Moreover, even where regional per capita output has increased, there remain large numbers of malnourished people, possibly numbering 800 million, of whom perhaps 200 million are children. The problem is not inadequacy of overall supply, but the inability of the poor to obtain access to the available food. It is particularly worrying that 200 million children remain malnourished since this is likely to restrict their learning ability and handicap them throughout their lives. It must be recognized that poverty and malnourishment are prevalent in many countries, both rich and poor. The need to attack poverty is a near universal one.

The Future

The great uncertainty about the future has led to conflicting statements of both extreme pessimism and optimism. Pessimists contend that global famine lies near at hand, while optimists are confident that there is no limit to what the earth and its people can produce in a sustainable manner.

We believe that neither of these extreme positions is warranted. The grounds for optimism lie at the global level, where we foresee world agricultural output remaining ahead of world population growth. At the regional level, however, we fear increasing imbalances leading to rapidly rising food imports. In a number of countries, the number of malnourished people will continue to grow. One vital question is for how long food output can outpace population growth. Another worry is that, serious output constraints or reverses (e.g. a protracted drought) in major food exporting country like the United States, or in producing countries might produce challenges that the world is poorly organized to meet. Finally, even in the best scenarios, we see little likelihood that present programs will lead to a significant decrease in the incidence of malnourished people, especially malnourished children. On present trends, it is likely that world population will reach 8.3 billion by about 2025, and possibly 10 billion before leveling off. However, if appropriate measures are taken, it would be possible to stabilize at the U.N. low variant of around 7.5 billion. Urgent efforts must be taken now to move in that direction. On the agricultural side, it is reasonable to expect that the world could feed 8 billion people in 2025, if research and technology investment are sustained and increased. This will require, however, that major efforts are made now to use resources more efficiently and to strengthen agricultural research especially focussing on sustainable agriculture for food security in the developing countries.

Both hopeful global scenarios still reflect serious regional and national imbalances. Sub-Saharan Africa, where the number of malnourished people continues to grow, will remain a major regional problem for years to come. If Sub-Saharan Africa doubles its population in the next 30 years to 1.6 billion as projected, and does not experience per capita gains in agricultural output, we do not see how Africa would be able to pay for the needed high food imports. Prospects for reducing the number of malnourished are better in Asia, Latin America, the Near East and North Africa, but even in those areas there is much inefficiency both in population programs and agricultural production. These inefficiencies must be overcome if the more hopeful scenarios are to be realized, and particularly if the problems of the poor and the disadvantaged are to be solved.

In East and Southeast Asia, which have demonstrated remarkable economic growth, this has led to important changes in diet. Many people becoming more prosperous, are dramatically increasing indirect consumption of grain by eating more meat. This development could put pressure on the world's grain supply in times of poor harvests. On top of this, increases in food production are unlikely to meet the growing demand in East Asia.

Promoting Human Efficiency

In both population programs and agriculture, there remain major challenges throughout the world, and especially in developing countries. Looking on the bright side, the world also has the technology and the organizational capacity to address these problems more effectively. One important but simple way of boosting the efficiency of production is by teaching the known modem technology for agricultural output to more farmers. In this way, yields of the owest producers can be raised to those of the average, those of the average can be raised to those of higher producers. Improvements can be made in agronomic practices, water management, and in adapting research to local conditions. In particular, given the fact that improved irrigation has increased yields per hectare, greater attention should be paid to improving water management. This does not deny the importance of continuing and increasing basic agricultural research to improve biological yields and to make sure that new technologies reach the next generation of farmers. For every 0.1 percent increase in yields, the world gains the equivalent of 25 million hectares of rain-fed cropland. Thus both research and gains from more efficient farming practices are needed. Substantial immediate gains can be made through putting into fuller practice technologies that are now already available.

One of the greatest problems in developing countries is the shortage of institutions and human resources that can assist in accepting and adapting transfer of technology from industrialized countries. It is necessary to help establish and manage national agricultural research systems in less developed countries. Moreover, training opportunities should be provided for planning and implementation of agricultural policy and family planning. Greater use should be made of the Consultative Group on International Agricultural Research for that.

The Role of Developing Countries

Population

The population of the developing countries reached 4.0 billion in 1990, and is projected to rise to 5.7 billion by 2010 and nearly 7 billion by 2025. More than 90 percent of the increase in the world's population will take place in developing countries. The absolute increase in developing country population is projected to be nearly 800 million persons for this decade and to remain close to an all time high. Though numbers will decline slightly, they imply a world which will have twice the current population and possibly even more in the next century. Among developing countries, the rate of population growth is highest in Sub-Saharan Africa, followed by the Near East and North Africa, South Asia, Latin America and the Caribbean, while East Asia has the lowest rate of growth. Many developing countries are endeavoring to slow down their relatively rapid population growth by devising a population policy suitable to their countries. As recognized at the

International Conference on Population and Development, the solution to the population problem requires social and economic development as well as improved family planning services, especially to the rural and urban poor. These services will need paying for, which means more money, though the amounts are modest in comparison with the benefits to be gained. Total annual expenditures must rise from approximately $4 billion to roughly $11 to 12 billion by the end of the century, according to UNFPA estimates. Of the extra amount, some $4 billion must come from the donor community. Among those actions endorsed at the High-Level Expert Group Meeting are: ensuring a rise in the literacy rate, vital in promoting a well-informed voluntary choice of the number of children, and improving reproductive health and family planning services, public sanitation and safe potable water.

Food Production

Although there is a widespread agreement among economic and social forecaster that the continued slow gains in the availability of food on a per capita basis are likely to continue into the 21st century, developing countries as a whole are expected to increase their net cereal imports. The pressure to increase food production is particularly intense in countries with high population growth and a high incidence of chronic malnutrition. Natural resources are under intense pressure in many countries and yields are far below their potential.

Greater food production will require investment and development of research and technology. This means encouraging research and dissemination, including through demonstration, of sustainable agricultural technology, environmentally-friendly integrated pest management and plant nutrient systems. As time goes on, the control of water for food and agricultural uses will become a more pressing issue. In addition to better maintenance of existing systems and implementing more efficient pricing policies for water, priority should be given to small-scale water bar-vesting and control techniques. With growing urban populations (and urban growth in Asian developing countries over the next 30 years will equal the current population of the continent), it is necessary to consider where food is produced. Food transport and energy costs are part of the sustainability equation. In view of the rapid urbanization in prospect, and the widespread reliance on private agents and markets, it is essential that input supply, marketing and processing assistance be available to producers.

Government Policy

Poverty alleviation, improved nutrition and food security should be principal objectives of government policy. Such priorities should be reflected in official investment programs. In the least developed countries, agriculture is the dominant sector of the national economy and, unless it can be stimulated, neither incomes nor food availability will improve appreciably.

Distorted government policies have too often damaged the performance of agriculture. Government policies must provide the incentives to invest and sustain production of foods in which the country has a comparative advantage. In pursuing national nutrition and food security goals, each region within a country should also be encouraged to concentrate on its comparative advantage, and adopt a more socially equitable and environmentally friendly technology for food production.

Governments, directing the roles of public and private sector funds, must also invest or encourage the investment in roads and infrastructure to facilitate internal and external trade in food and agricultural products. Trade policies must ensure that foods subsidized by some developed countries do not create a disincentive to internal production. This can be done through the use of tariffs if necessary.

Social Policy

Much of the current misery in developing countries stems from failures of social policy. Civil strife is frequently caused by hunger and starvation. Very often, the legacy of civil strife lives on even when the conflict has ended.- For example, mines left over from wars may render large parts of the arable land inaccessible. This is true in Cambodia, Afghanistan, Mozambique and Angola, where about one third of the arable land is mined, and unusable. To solve such problems, special programs for demining are needed and should be funded by donors. The lack of adequate progress in increasing food production and social welfare is a factor fomenting widespread civil unrest. Moreover, such unrest is in danger of spreading geographically, as food shortages and widening income gaps encourage massive migrations from North Africa and Eastern Europe to Western Europe and from the Caribbean and Latin America to the United States. The goals of social policy, therefore, should promote social cohesion, equity and mobility, with a special focus on the needs of vulnerable groups. They should address the cultural and institutional dimensions of development.

Policies in Relation to Women

- A more pernicious problem discouraging development is the unequal social status of women, many of whom are locked in extreme poverty. It is clear that economic progress has not been shared equally by both men and women. The needs of women present major challenges for the present and future.

- Effective progress will require major changes in the status of women. Traditional biases against women and girls must be reversed. To help accelerate the reduction of population increase, it is especially essential to raise the status and decision-making of women.
- Family planning programs are an essential complement to help accelerate the reduction of fertility. Such family planning programs should be as broadly based as possible and include primary health care, safe potable water, education of girls and the empowerment of women generally, as well as the distribution of contraceptives and clinical advice.
- Education is particularly critical, since a rise in female literacy rate is vital in allowing women a well-informed voluntary choice of the number of children they bear.
- Together these can speed the decline of fertility at the same time as they increase the quality of life. Success in increasing the speed of bringing women into the economy will be especially important for the poor.
- In addition, women in the poorest countries are the backbone of the farm labor force. Greater access to property, equality before the law, and access to services such as credit and agricultural extension services that increase their productivity are all key ingredients.

Africa

- Every indicator and all assessments of prospects for future food security identify Sub Saharan Africa as the region for priority action. Its rate of population growth is the highest, and its decline in per capita food production over the last three decades is unique. The incidence of chronic malnutrition increased over the decade of the 1980s and is most likely to remain unacceptably high, well into the 21st century, unless extraordinary measures are taken not just by the governments involved but by the entire international community.
- The potential for increases in agricultural productivity as well as food production is impressive. At present, only 2-3 percent of the land used to produce food is irrigated, fertilizer is seldom used except for cash crops for export and proven technology is frequently ignored. Farmers often have difficulty in obtaining inputs for production in a good time. In addition, too often the marketing system means that prices plummet when producers harvest good crops.. The inability to control water makes the

region extremely vulnerable to year-on-year variability in production and thus in emergency food needs.

- Priority attention should be given to setting up small pilot demonstration projects that can show actual farmers how they can increase productivity through the control of water and the use of appropriate technology.

The Role of Donor Countries

Consumption in the North is an integral part of the problem. If all people in the world consumed the same amount of meat as the North Americans do, the entire world's grain supply and more would be needed just to feed the livestock. And if the world consumed fish like the Japanese, world fish stocks would soon be fully depleted. The affluent industrialized countries should awaken the consciousness of the people about their wasteful consumption. It is not acceptable for the North unilaterally to ask developing countries to curtail their population increase, while they themselves continue to aggravate the eco-system with their excessive life styles. The level of Official Development Assistance (ODA), from the OECD countries declined to 0.3 percent of GNP in 1993. This figure masks wide disparities, with the United States, providing only 0.15 percent, much of it earmarked for assistance to the Middle East, and a large part of that given for non-development purposes.

There is no question that although the bulk of the resources required for the development of the LDCs will have to come from their own resources, well-targeted and timely ODA support, especially for the poorest countries and developing country governments with good governance, can be very beneficial in helping them achieve their development objectives.

The developed countries today represent over 83 percent of the world income but less than 23 percent of the world population. On the other hand, 80 percent of the world population receives less than 17 percent of the income. The poorest 20 percent barely survive on 1.4 percent of the world income. This inequality is both unstable and unsustainable. Further efforts must be made to increase ODA substantially, especially by the United States.

However, these flows of aid should be depoliticized and targeted towards the neediest countries with a dual perspective: first, to assist in overcoming current hurdles such as balance of payments problems and' severe investment shortfalls; and second, to lay the foundations for dealing with long-term problems of population growth, environmental degradation, food security and extreme poverty.

This will require a more farsighted view of development assistance. It should be linked to the objectives of development in the recipient countries, not to the political or economic interests of the donor countries. Transparency and adequate frameworks for aid coordination would assist in this direction. Given the severe budget stringencies in all the donor countries, it is necessary to consider shifting support so as to maximize the impact of the flows available from any individual donor. Donor countries could usefully reexamine levels of spending on the military since a broad minded view of the security of these countries would include support for the development efforts of the poor.

Broader partnership with NGOs should be sought to encourage better ways to service the needs of the poorest people of the world to ensure more equitable sharing of development benefits and not to exacerbate the already critical situation. In the absence of major increases of ODA flows from the OECD countries, we should consider a stronger targeting on sustainable food production and agricultural research, and population programs. These collectively would form the core of the attack on the nexus of problems that tie together environmental degradation, population pressure, food security and poverty reduction. In this context, it is important to recall that agriculture is the primary interface between human economic activity and the environment.

Agriculture accounts for over 70 percent of the world's fresh water use and 70 percent of the land use. Current problems of agriculture are already putting tremendous pressure on fragile ecosystems, for example, "slash and burn" destruction of forests, and colonization of the hillsides bringing soil erosion. Hunger is a manifestation of extreme poverty. The poorest of the poor, without the money to go to markets for their most basic needs, require special attention. Intermediarv institutions, such as the Grameen Bank in Bangladesh, have shown that micro-credit can be a viable instrument to empower the very poor.

Efforts by the donors and the international financial institutions should be deployed to find ways of replicating such schemes on a large scale, as a complement to their support for broad-based pro-growth and anti-poverty macro-policies. The recently proposed Consultative Group to Assist the Poorest (CGAP), which provides such small loans, is a promising step in that direction.

Access to Markets

An essential part of the mobilization of resources in developing countries is going to be their ability to export their products to OECD markets. The Uruguay Round accords will go some way in facilitating this, but the poorest countries, especially Sub-Saharan Africa (SSA), will not benefit adequately, and considerable distortion in international agricultural markets will remain upon implementation of the Agreement on Agriculture. Further, some countries that had preferential treatments cannot fully use them. Obstacles to their exports include domestic institutional, infrastructure and market failures but also restrictions in access to OECD markets.

Addressing these deficiencies, especially in SSA, will be an integral part of strengthening the access of the very poor countries to international trade. Donors should target some of their assistance to smashing these bottlenecks and hurdles to trade, in parallel with opening their markets to exports from poor countries. These bottlenecks also restrict the internal flow of goods and services within the countries and limit their ability to accelerate their economic growth.

Capital Flows

A most notable feature of the last four years has been the quadrupling of private capital flows to developing countries. These today represent over $170 billion, over three times the total OECD ODA flows of about $55 billion. These capital flows comprise portfolio investments, foreign direct investment (FDI) and some private capital loans to governments and enterprises.

The bulk of these flows, however, are concentrated in about 20 countries. A number of these 20 countries have an excessively high proportion of portfolio investment which can be extremely volatile as was recently demonstrated in Mexico. It is important that an increasing proportion of private capital flows come in the form of FDI and to that end, governments should design their incentive structures and their trade regimes with a view to encourage FDI rather than obtaining private loans or portfolio flows.

To draw private capital into financing long-term investments, special efforts by LDC governments and international financial institutions as well as donors will be required. The creative use of guarantees and other mechanisms should be explored.

A more careful calculation of the real costs and benefits of investments that takes into account environmental, social and human costs, as well as benefits, should be made in order that the apparent investment does not, in fact, turn out to be destructive to the long-term economic or environmental prospects of the country concerned. This is the case where a number of poor countries have subsidized extractive industries for export (such as mining, tropical hardwoods) but have not factored in the costs of reforestation, soil erosion and other aspects euphemistically treated as "externalities" in assessing investments. Issues like these will be particularly important, as the expansion of agricultural production necessary to meet rising food needs will be increasingly financed by internal private sources. Debt remains an issue for many of the poorest countries. Special efforts to reduce the stock of debt and the burden of debt service will be needed. Multilateral non-concessional debt should be retired and/or concessionalized under agreed performance criteria. Debt reduction, however, must be 'carefully managed so as not to impede the access of poor countries to credit markets, especially for trade finance.

Farm Subsidies and Food Aid

Under the Uruguay Round agreement on agriculture, farm subsidies will be reduced in the OECD countries. Food surpluses, especially in the EU, will be reduced and be less available as food aid. It is our view that non-crisis food aid has been sometimes counter-productive, since it has tended to undercut domestic production by poor farmers and frequently creates a level of dependency that cannot be sustained. The removal of farm subsidies in the North will create opportunities for Southern countries to sell farm products in which they have comparative advantage. Such opportunities should be pursued.

Preliminary estimates of the likely impact of freer world trade in food and other commodities indicate a likely benefit to most countries and especially to net food exporters. SSA, being a net food importer for some time to come, is likely to find its import bill increase, and will therefore require special compensatory programs to be implemented by donors, especially by food exporting countries, so that they can gain recompense from a scheme that will benefit the rest of the world. To the extent that some other very poor countries (e.g., Haiti) are also likely to suffer as a long-term net food importers, they too should benefit from such compensatory programs.

Need for Sustainable Development

Responding to Population Pressures

- Over the last two centuries the developed world has experienced an historic demographic transition from high to low birth and death rates, resulting in massive population growth. This demographic transition is now being experienced by the developing regions of the world. South Asia and Africa in particular are experiencing unprecedented increases in population. It is crucial for the social and economic development of these regions that this population growth does not exceed sustainable levels.

- One way to encourage sustainable population growth is through family planning programmes. Along with this, attention also needs to be given to the availability of food for a significantly increasing population.
- There are already about 800 million malnourished people in the world. If current rates of population growth continue, the present population in developing countries is expected to be nearly 50 percent higher by the year 2020. Future global food production will need to dramatically increase to provide adequate food for everyone. The availability of land for food production, however, is under growing pressure because of spreading urbanization.
- For these reasons, the increase in agricultural productivity required to meet a growing world population will need to come primarily from technological innovation and intensified production methods. There are, however, serious problems of bio-diversity associated with the substantial intensification of agricultural production. Therefore, it will be essential to ensure that intensified food production is carried out in an environmentally sustainable manner.
- Sustainable development means meeting the needs of the present generation without compromising the ability of future generations to meet their needs. A central aspect of sustainable development is preserving the natural environment. The working group notes that there is considerable scope for improving food production, using currently available technologies, without causing irreparable damage to the environment.

Productivity and Environment

Agricultural and industrial intensification will inevitably produce certain by-products and side effects that are unfriendly to the environment. Ways must be found to minimize the effects of these by-products and side effects on the quality of soil, water, and the atmosphere. To this end, research on environmentally sound farming techniques should be increased. We also need to strengthen the ability to monitor the impact of production on the environment.

Achieving sustainable agricultural production growth in most countries will also require higher rates of savings. This can be achieved by reducing present levels of consumption in favour of future consumption, Investing in technological improvements and other production infrastructure will help improve productivity as well as the versatility of available resources.

To oversee this transformation in production, existing institutions will need to be refocused, or new institutions designed, to ensure that individuals, organizations, and societies in general manage resources and the environment in a compatible manner. This should aim to minimize the negative impact that the production activities of one operation has on the activities of other operations, both within the same country and abroad.

Interaction Between Developed and Developing Countries

Developed countries and a growing number of developing countries have accumulated knowledge, technology, and capital necessary for improving food productivity. The transfer of these assets to other developing countries should be facilitated through appropriate bilateral and multilateral arrangements. In particular, the experience of some countries in East Asia in coping with high density populations could provide valuable lessons to less developed countries and regions. Such assistance to developing countries is important not only to meet immediate critical needs, but also to encourage self-reliance in future food security as a major goal of national policies.

At the same time, developed countries should make further efforts to reduce inequalities between rich and poor countries, particularly in regard to food and nutrition. Technology and resources available in the advanced industrial countries in North America and Western Europe combined with those of successful countries in East and Southeast Asia and elsewhere should be utilized to assist the lesser developed countries to increase their food productivity and meet the needs of a growing population. In this sense, agricultural development in East Asia, North America and Western Europe may provide valuable lessons for developing countries in the development of sustainable food production strategies. To underscore an effective transfer of technology, improved interaction and dialogue are necessary between developed and developing countries, especially at the levels of policy-making and research.

Role of Political Leadership in Developing Countries

Whatever happens at the global level, social and economic advances in developing countries will depend primarily on their own peoples and their own leaders. The quality of governance, institutional responsiveness, commitments to justice and equity will be critical. Farsighted political leadership is absolutely essential.

Population Growth and Vehicular Emissions in Delhi, India

Air pollution is a growing issue of concern all over the globe, particularly in developing countries that are undergoing rapid urbanization. Growing populations increase the strain on the environment. We will start with a brief overview of the country of India as a whole, and then slowly narrow to focusing just on one city, Delhi, India. There, we will focus on some of the trends in population as well as pollution and try to show a relationship and support our hypothesis.

India is the world's seventh largest country. However, in terms of population, it falls second to China in its population. The total population ofIndia is expected to exceed 1.6 billion by the year 2050 (Oldenburg 2005). This rapidly expanding population, especially in urban areas, is one of the main reasons for environmental concerns in the country. This problem can be narrowed to many of the large cities in India. As the seventh most populous metropolis in the world, Delhi 's population was listed at 13.8 million (Kathuria 2006). Between the years of 1997 and 2020 the population ofIndia's second largest city (Delhi) is expected to grow 1.9 times, almost doubling (Bose 1997).

Following the trends of Delhi 's urbanization, people buying more vehicles for personal use have perpetuated an increase in vehicles. The amount of registered vehicles in Delhi have increased fifty-one times over a thrity year period (Goyal 2003). Today, between 370 and 600 new vehicles are registered daily (Kathuria 2002). With more people working in the city, commuting has added to the demand for personal vehicles. The increased trend in transport of goods and services has also contributed to this demand. The vehicle stock in Delhi is expected to almost quadruple by the year 2020 (Ramanathan 2000). This increase in vehicles, as well as the presence of other motorized forms of transportation (taxis, autos, trains, buses, etc.), will ruther contribute to the already large amounts of vehicular emissions containing pollutants such as sulfur dioxide, nitrogen oxides, carbon monoxides, lead, ozone, benzene, and hydrocarbons (Goyal 2005).

Delhi is the fourth most polluted city in the world. The top-contributing factor to the air pollution in Delhi is transportation. The transprot sector of Delhi has been responsible for rates as high as 72% of the total amount of air pollution (Goyal 2005). Recently, the air quality in Delhi has exceeded air quality standards set by the World Health Organization (Gurjar 2006). This calls for a change in the way people in the city are living. This is why we chose this topic for our project. This is a problem not only in Delhi, but all over the world, especially in major cities and in cities of developing countries (Ramanathan 2000).

We will narrow our research and focus on one extreme case in the city of Delhi, India. We were able to gain a real understanding of some of the main causes as well as some preventative measures that can be taken and are trying to be implemented today. We believe that the number of motorized vehicles in the city is positively related to the growing population of this expanding city. Since emissions from vehicles are one of the leading causes of Delhi's pollution, we hypothesize that the growing population has an indirect effect on the increasing levels of air pollution in Delhi.

Methods

We will be looking at one case study exploring the concepts of population growth and the growth of the number of vehicles within the city ofDelhi. We will also look at two other case studies regarding the effectiveness of current and possible future policies aimed at reducing air pollution inDelhi. With this information, we will talk about the effect of the number of vehicles on air pollution, and how it has affected the city as a whole. Along with these case studies, we will look at graphs and tables with information on rates of vehicular use, vehicular emissions, and population growth inDelhi, India.

The first case study, we'll refer to this as Case Study 1, was started in 1997 and examines the current transport situation in Delhi. It talks about the growth in vehicles and the demand of travel through the year 2020 assuming a constant population growth. In large cities, such as Delhi, the urban transport system is one of the most important infrastructures. With the population rapidly increasing, Delhi 's urban transport system has proven to be inadequate. There has been a significant increase in the demand of personal vehicles which has led to more congestion, longer travel time, high consumption rates of energy; all leading to higher amounts of pollution. This case study estimates the energy demand and emissions inDelhi from several models (econometric, spread sheet, long range energy alternative planning) to project the vehicle stock, the travel demand, and the energy demand from the transport system. It also looks at three scenarios including "business as usual (BAU)," "high GDP growth rate (HGS)," and "low GDP growth rate (LGS)."

Case Study 2, by Vinish Kathuria, concerns vehicular pollution control and the different current policies implemented in Delhi . In order to restore the air quality in the city, a large number of policy instruments have been applied. This case study investigates whether or not these policies have improved the air quality in the city or if they have not been effective. The final case study (Case Study 3), by Ranjan Bose and V. Srinivasachary, analyzes factors contributing to consumption of energy and emission levels in Delhi as relating to the transport system and future policies that could help decrease the damaging effects of vehicular emissions on air pollution. The study aims to reach an optimal transport policy limiting dual consumption and polltion.

Results and Discussion

Case Study 1 shows that the population in Delhi is expected to almost double by 2020 and the GDP and the vehicle stock is expected to increase by about 3.7 times in that same period. The case study also projected that travel demand in Delhi would increase from 73 billion passenger kilometres in 1997 to 253 billion passenger kilometres in 2020. Below is a graph exhibiting this increase in vehicular stock in Delhi .

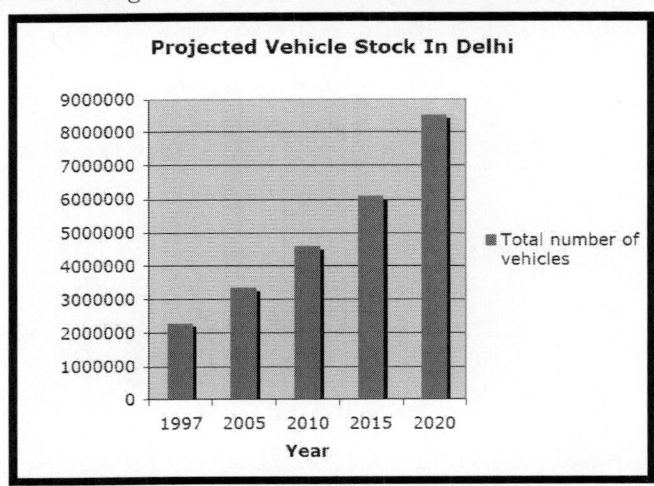

Source: *Das 1997*

The energy demanded by the transportation sector in Delhi is expected to grow by 2.7 times with this increase in travel demand. Regarding emissions, the case study shows a table in which expected rates of CO2 will increase from 3,646,000 metric tons in 1997 to 9,364,000 metric tons in 2020. Below is a graph that demonstrates this increase over this period of time.

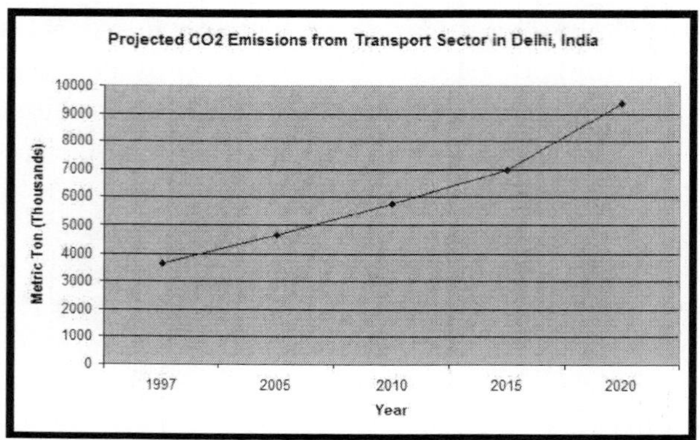

Source: *Das 1997*

Cities undergoing rapid urbanization typically demonstrate rapidly growing economies. As the GDP of a city increases, the vehicular demand will increase as well because the population has a larger amount of money. This is shown by this case study. For example, in the HGS scenario, as GDP increases the vehicle stock increases by approximately six times and the energy demand is about 1.67 times higher than in the BAU scenario. These results are the opposite for the LGS scenario (Das 1997). Below is a graph representing the different scenarios and their effects on travel demand inDelhi.

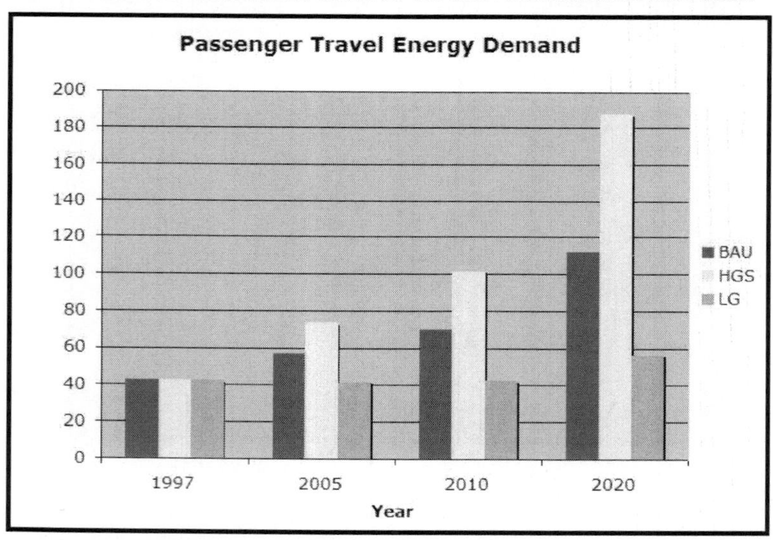

Source: *Das 1997*

Delhi has implemented numerous policies to help reduce vehicular emissions in the city. These policies include the removal of leaded-petrol, the phasing out of commercial vehicles older than fifteen years old, replacement of all autos and taxis made before 1990 with new vehicles using cleaner fuel, switching all buses to compressed natural gases (CNG) or other forms of cleaner fuels, and increasing the number of buses in the city for public transport from 6600 to 10,000 (Kathuria 2002). These policies, as well as several others, are examined in Case Study 2. The amounts of air pollution are taken from the busiest traffic intersection in Delhi, and data collected for this is from the period of June 1999 to June 2001. Even with these policies having been implemented, the levels of pollutants have stayed relatively the same. The following graphs, taken from Case study 2 illustrate this.

Weekly Trends in Air Quality, June 1999 to June 2001:

Case Study 3 (1997) examines five different scenarios regarding the possible implementation of future policies to reduce air pollution. The first scenario is "business as usual (BAU)," with a continual growth of vehicle population. In this scenario if the vehicular population remains the same as it was in 1990-91, the fuel consumption will more than double by 2010. The second scenario examines the effect of traffic management measures and increases the average speed of all types of vehicles to 40 km/hr from the present speed of 20 km/hr. It shows that there will be an overall conservation of 27% by 2010. The third scenario estimates the total energy demand if the total stock of buses increases 6%. This model predicts that although the dependence on diesel fuel will increase, the reduction in the demand for gasoline will be reduced by 19% in 2010. The fourth scenario deals with the Mass Rapid Transit System (MRTS) that Delhi was expected to have by 2005. It is estimated that this transit system will accommodate 12% of the total passenger travel demand. The total energy reduction will be about 24% by 2010. The fifth, and final scenario, assumes scenarios 2, 3, and 4, are implemented in different phases, but all by the year 2005. In this scenario, there will be about a 50% decrease in total energy demand by 2010 (Bose 1997).

Solutions

As the second case study we examined showed us, the government of Delhi has implemented numerous policies regarding vehicular emissions to improve the air quality of the city. However, this case study also proved that the instruments to improve the pollution situation in the city have not led to an improvement of the air quality. If policies and the overall approach to control vehicular emissions are not changed within the city, Delhi will continue to suffer the growing effects of the large amounts of vehicular emissions. The issue of air pollution levels from vehicular emissions is not being addressed adequately in the city. One thing that could help this augmenting problem is creating a greater sense of awareness through education. Having society be aware of the problem is the first step to taking further action. Furthermore, it is society's responsibility to be active in the containment of the problem. The population should be aware of their effects on the environment and should be taught how to change their everyday habits. Even if these changes made are small, they could make a huge difference in the city. School-sponsored programs could also be initiated in order to teach the young population how to prevent pollutant habits.

Research in areas of fuel-efficient transportation and alternative resources could prove to be very beneficial to Delhi and other urbanizing cities throughout the world in the near future. However, turning toward research and development of new resources may be extremely costly, and the effects may not be seen in Delhi for years. Rather than devotign efforts toward technological advance, many major cities across the globe have been focusing their efforts directly on the externalities of transport systems, such as congestion and traffic accidents (Kathuria 2002).

We think that Delhi should direct more of its efforts to contain air pollution on these externalities of the current transportation situation. Not only will the quality of the air improve, but the entire system of transport in the city will become more efficient. The creation of new roads and widening of existing roads, for example, will alleviate the problems associated with congestion, the flow of traffic open, and vehicular emissions will be decreased. Probably the most effective approach to containing vehicular emissions would be an integrative approach, focusing efforts on new developments through technology, and directing more attention to the externalities that will quickly lessen the amount of air pollution emitted. Through examining various case studies and conducting further research, we have found that the rapid growth in the population in Delhi has had a large amount of stress on the environment, particularly on the quality of air. As the population continues to grow, the demand for motorized vehicles will increase, as well. The increasing number of vehicles on the road will emit thousands of tons of pollutants into the atmosphere each year, affecting not only the city, but the entire globe. The city of Delhi has implemented numerous policies regarding vehicular emissions, but these have had little, if any, affect on the quality of the air. Other solutions have been considered, which hopefully once active, will reduce the amount of vehicular emissions released each year. From our research, it can be clearly seen that something different needs to be done in Delhi, and probably developing cities throughout the world. Until the human population is able to decrease the amount of pollution released into the air, the globe will continue to suffer its growing effects that are increasing in severity partly becasue of the rapid population rates.

Population and Family Planning Policy in India

Population growth has long been a concern of the government, and India has a lengthy history of explicit population policy. In the 1950s, the government began, in a modest way, one of the earliest national, government-sponsored family planning efforts in the developing world. The annual population growth rate in the previous decade (1941 to 1951) had been below 1.3 percent, and government planners optimistically believed that the population would continue to grow at roughly the same rate.

Implicitly, the government believed that India could repeat the experience of the developed nations where industrialization and a rise in the standard of living had been accompanied by a drop in the population growth rate. In the 1950s, existing hospitals and health care facilities made birth control information available, but there was no aggressive effort to encourage the use of contraceptives and limitation of family size. By the late 1960s, many policy makers believed that the high rate of population growth was the greatest obstacle to economic development. The government began a massive program to lower the birth rate from forty-one per 1,000 to a target of twenty to twenty-five per 1,000 by the mid-1970s. The National Population Policy adopted in 1976 reflected the growing consensus among policy makers that family planning would enjoy only limited success unless it was part of an integrated program aimed at improving the general welfare of the population. The policy makers assumed that excessive family size was part and parcel of poverty and had to be dealt with as integral to a general development strategy. Education about the population problem became part of school curriculum under the Fifth Five-Year Plan (FY 1974-78). Cases of government-enforced sterilization made many question the propriety of state-sponsored birth control measures, however.

During the 1980s, an increased number of family planning programs were implemented through the state governments with financial assistance from the central government. In rural areas, the programs were further extended through a network of primary health centers and subcenters. By 1991, India had more than 150,000 public health facilities through which family planning programs were offered (see Health Care, this ch.). Four special family planning projects were implemented under the Seventh Five-Year Plan (FY 1985-89). One was the All-India Hospitals Post-partum Programme at district- and subdistrict-level hospitals. Another program involved the reorganization of primary health care facilities in urban slum areas, while another project reserved a specified number of hospital beds for tubal ligature operations. The final program called for the renovation or remodelling of intrauterine device (IUD) rooms in rural family welfare centers attached to primary health care facilities. Despite these developments in promoting family planning, the 1991 census results showed that India continued to have one of the most rapidly growing populations in the world. Between 1981 and 1991, the annual rate of population growth was estimated at about 2 percent. The crude birth rate in 1992 was thirty per 1,000, only a small change over the 1981 level of thirty-four per 1,000. However, some demographers credit this slight lowering of the 1981-91 population growth rate to moderate successes of the family planning program. In FY 1986, the number of reproductive-age couples was 132.6 million, of whom only 37.5 percent were estimated to be protected effectively by some form of contraception. A goal of the seventh plan was to achieve an effective couple protection rate of 42 percent, requiring an annual increase of 2 percent in effective use of contraceptives.

The heavy centralization of India's family planning programs often prevents due consideration from being given to regional differences. Centralization is encouraged to a large extent by reliance on central government funding. As a result, many of the goals and assumptions of national population control programs do not correspond exactly with local attitudes toward birth control. At the Jamkhed Project in Maharashtra, which has been in operation since the late 1970s and covers approximately 175 villages, the local project directors noted that it required three to four years of education through direct contact with a couple for the idea of family planning to gain acceptance. Such a timetable was not compatible with targets. However, much was learned about policy and practice from the Jamkhed Project. The successful use of women's clubs as a means of involving women in community-wide family planning activities impressed the state government to the degree that it set about organizing such clubs in every village in the state. The project also serves as a pilot to test ideas that the government wants to incorporate into its programs. Government medical staff members have been sent to Jamkhed for training, and the government has proposed that the project assume the task of selecting and training government health workers for an area of 2.5 million people.

Another important family planning program is the Project for Community Action in Family Planning. Located in Karnataka, the project operates in 154 project villages and 255 control villages. All project villages are of sufficient size to have a health subcenter, although this advantage is offset by the fact that those villages are the most distant from the area's primary health centers. As at Jamkhed, the project is much assisted by local voluntary groups, such as the women's clubs. The local voluntary groups either provide or secure sites suitable as distribution depots for condoms and birth control pills and also make arrangements for the operation of sterilization camps. Data provided by the Project for Community Action in Family Planning show that important achievements have been realized in the field of population control. By the mid-1980s, for example, 43 percent of couples were using family planning, a full 14 percent above the state average. The project has significantly improved the status of women, involving them and empowering them to bring about change in their communities. This contribution is important because of the way in which the deeply entrenched inferior status of women in many communities in India negates official efforts to decrease the fertility rate.

Studies have found that most couples in fact regard family planning positively. However, the common fertility pattern in India diverges from the two-child family that policy makers hold as ideal. Women continue to marry young; in the mid-1990s, they average just over eighteen years of age at marriage. When women choose to be sterilized, financial inducements, although helpful, are not the principal incentives. On average, those accepting sterilization already have four living children, of whom two are sons.

The strong preference for sons is a deeply held cultural ideal based on economic roots. Sons not only assist with farm labor as they are growing up (as do daughters) but they provide labor in times of illness and unemployment and serve as their parents' only security in old age. Surveys done by the New Delhi Operations Research Group in 1991 indicated that as many as 72 percent of rural parents continue to have children until at least two sons are born; the preference for more than one son among urban parents was tabulated at 53 percent. Once these goals have been achieved, birth control may be used or, especially in agricultural areas, it may not if additional child labor, later adult labor for the family, is deemed desirable. A significant result of this eagerness for sons is that the Indian population has a deficiency of females. Slightly higher female infant mortality rates (seventy-nine per 1,000 versus seventy-eight per 1,000 for males) can be attributed to poor health care, abortions of female fetuses, and female infanticide. Human rights activists have estimated that there are at least 10,000 cases of female infanticide annually throughout India. The cost of theoretically illegal dowries and the loss of daughters to their in-laws' families are further disincentives for some parents to have daughters. Sons, of course continue to carry on the family line (see Family Ideals, ch. 5). The 1991 census revealed that the national sex ratio had declined from 934 females to 1,000 males in 1981 to 927 to 1,000 in 1991. In only one state—Kerala, a state with low fertility and mortality rates and the nation's highest literacy—did females exceed males. The census found, however, that female life expectancy at birth had for the first time exceeded that for males. India's high infant mortality and elevated mortality in early childhood remain significant stumbling blocks to population control (see Health Conditions, this ch.). India's fertility rate is decreasing, however, and, at 3.4 in 1994, it is lower than those of its immediate neighbors (Bangladesh had a rate of 4.5 and Pakistan had 6.7). The rate is projected to decrease to 3.0 by 2000, 2.6 by 2010, and 2.3 by 2020.

During the 1960s, 1970s, and 1980s, the growth rate had formed a sort of plateau. Some states, such as Kerala, Tamil Nadu, and, to a lesser extent, Punjab, Maharashtra, and Karnataka, had made progress in lowering their growth rates, but most did not. Under such conditions, India's population may not stabilize until 2060.

Population, Migration, and Globalization

Globalization is not internationalization, but the effective erasure of national boundaries-opening the way not only to free mobility of capital and goods but also, in effect, to free movement (or uncontrolled migration) of vast labor pools from regions of rapid population growth. The impacts on national economies could be tragic. The trend toward globalization (free trade, free capital mobility) is not usually associated with migration or demography. If globalization were to be accomplished by free mobility of people, then demographers would certainly be paying attention. However, since globalization is being driven primarily by "free migration" of goods and capital, with labor a distant third in terms of mobility, few have noticed that the economic consequences of this free flow of goods and capital are equivalent to those that would obtain under a free flow of labor. They are also driven by the same demographic and economic forces that would determine labor migration, if labor were free to migrate.

The economic tendency resulting from competition is to equalize wages and social standards across countries. But instead of cheap labor moving to where the capital is, and bidding wages down, capital moves to where the cheap labor is, and bids wages up-or would do so if only there were not a nearly unlimited supply of cheap labor, a Malthusian situation that still prevails in much of the world. Yet wages in the capital-sending country are bid down as much as if the newly employed laborers in the low-wage country had actually immigrated to the high-wage country. The determinant of wages in the low-wage country is not labor "productivity," nor anything else on the demand side of the labor market. It is entirely on the supply side-an excess and rapidly growing supply of labor at near-subsistence wages. This demographic condition-a very numerous and still rapidly growing underclass in the third world-is one for which demographers have many explanations, beginning with Malthus.

Globalization, considered by many to be the inevitable wave of the future, is frequently confused with internationalization, but is in fact something totally different. Internationalization refers to the increasing importance of international trade, international relations, treaties, alliances, etc. Inter-national, of course, means between or among nations. The basic unit remains the nation, even as relations among nations become increasingly necessary and important. Globalization refers to the global economic integration of many formerly national economies into one global economy, mainly by free trade and free capital mobility, but also by somewhat easier or uncontrolled migration. It is the effective erasure of national boundaries for economic purposes. What was international becomes interregional.

The word "integration" derives from "integer," meaning one, complete, or whole. Integration is the act of combining into one whole. Since there can be only one whole, it follows that global economic integration logically implies national economic disintegration. As the saying goes, to make an omelette you have to break some eggs. The dis-integration of the national egg is necessary to integrate the global omelette. It is dishonest to celebrate the benefits of global integration without counting the consequent costs of national disintegration.

Forgotten Root

Those costs are significant. It is not for nothing that the population explosion in the third world has only recently affected wages in the industrial world. The British did not allow colonial India, for instance, to compete in global markets with its cheap labor, nor did the Chinese seek to do so under the isolation policies of Chairman Mao. Only in the last 30 years has the World Bank become converted to the now "incontestible" orthodoxy of export-led development based on foreign investment as the key part of structural adjustment. But although "free trade" is the new mantra, it now means something very different from what it meant in the early nineteenth century, when English economist David Ricardo gave it the enduring blessing of his comparative advantage argument.

In the classical nineteenth-century vision of Ricardo and Adam Smith, the national community embraced both national labor and national capital. These classes cooperated (albeit with conflict) to produce national goods, which then competed in international markets against the goods of other nations produced by their own national capital/labor teams. This was internationalization, as defined above.

However, in the globally integrated world of the twenty-first century, both capital and goods are free to move internationally-and capital, or at least money, can be shifted electronically with almost no effort at all. But free capital mobility totally undercuts Ricardo's comparative advantage argument for free trade in goods, because that argument is explicitly and essentially premised on capital (and other factors) being immobile between nations. Under the new globalization regime, capital tends simply to flow to wherever costs are lowest-that is, to pursue absolute advantage.

Nevertheless, the conventional wisdom seems to be that if free trade in goods is beneficial, then free trade in capital must be even more beneficial. However, you cannot use the conclusion of an argument to deny one of its premises! In any event, it no longer makes sense to think of national teams of labor and capital in the globalized economy. There are competing global capitalists, and national laborers thrown into global competition by mobile capital.

Back, finally, to the costs mentioned above. What are the consequences of globalization for national community? Here in the United States, we have seen the abrogation of a basic social agreement between labor and capital over how to divide up the value that they jointly add to raw materials (as well as the value of the raw materials themselves, i.e., nature's often-uncounted value added). That agreement has been reached nationally, not internationally, much less globally. It was not reached by economic theory, but through generations of national debate, elections, strikes, lockouts, court decisions, and violent conflicts. That agreement, on which national community and industrial peace depend, is being repudiated in the interests of global integration. That is a very poor trade, even if you call it "free trade."

Stresses and Strains

At a deeper level, what if globalization began to entail the overt encouragement of free migration? Even some free trade advocates might recoil from the radical cosmopolitanism of such a policy. Perhaps they can see that it would lead to massive relocation of people between world regions of vastly differing wealth, creating a tragedy of the open access commons. The strain on local communities, both the sending and the receiving, would be enormous. In the face of unlimited migration, how could any national community maintain a minimum wage, a welfare program, subsidized medical care, or a public school system? How could a nation punish its criminals and tax evaders if citizens were totally free to emigrate? Indeed, one wonders, would it not be much cheaper to encourage emigration of a country's poor, sick, or criminals, rather than run welfare programs, charity hospitals, and prisons? (Fidel Castro took precisely this course of action in opening Cuba's jails in 1980. His policy encouraged migration of prisoners and others that became part of the wave of "marielito" immigrants to the United States.)

Further, one might reasonably wonder how a country could reap the benefit of educational investments made in its own citizens if those citizens are totally free to emigrate. Would nations continue to make such investments in the face of free migration and a continuing "brain drain"? Would a country make investments in education if it experienced massive immigration pressures, which would dilute the educational resources of the nation? Would any country any longer try to limit its birth rate, since youths who migrate abroad and send back remittances can be a good investment, a fact that might increase the birth rate? (With unfettered migration, a country could never control its numbers anyway, so why even talk about the controversial issue of birth control?)

To some this skepticism will sound like a nationalistic negation of world community. It is not. It is the view that world community should be viewed as a "community of communities," a federation of national communities rather than a cosmopolitan world government lacking any historical roots in real communities. A "world with no boundaries" makes a sentimental song lyric, but community and policy cannot exist without boundaries. For mainstream-neoclassical-economists, only the individual is real; community is just a misleading name for an aggregate of individuals. From that perspective, national communities impose "distorting" interferences upon the individualistic free market, and their disintegration is not a cost but something to be welcomed. To the contrary, I would argue, this aspect of globalization is just another way in which capitalism undermines the very conditions it requires in order to function. Few would deny that some migration is a very good thing-but this discussion concerns free migration, where "free" means deregulated, uncontrolled, unlimited, as in "free" trade, or "free" capital mobility, or "free" reproduction. One must also be intensely mindful that immigrants are people, frequently disadvantaged people. It is a terrible thing to be "anti-immigrant." Immigration, however, is a policy, not a person, and one can be "anti-immigration," or more accurately "pro-immigration limits" without in the least being anti-immigrant. The global cosmopolitans think that it is immoral to make any policy distinction between citizen and noncitizen, and therefore favour free migration. They also suggest that free migration is the shortest route to their vision of the summum bonum, equality of wages worldwide. Their point is fair enough; there is some logic in their position-so long as they are willing to see wages equalized at a low level. But those who support free migration as the shortest route to equality of wages worldwide could only with great difficulty try to contend with problems of an open-access commons, the destruction of local community, and other issues raised above.

A more workable moral guide is the recognition that, as a member of a national community, one's obligation to non-citizens is to do them no harm, while one's obligation to fellow citizens is first to do no harm and then try to do positive good. The many dire consequences of globalization (besides those mentioned above)-over-specialization in a few volatile export commodities (petroleum, timber, minerals, and other extractive goods with little value added locally, for instance), crushing debt burdens, exchange rate risks and speculative currency destabilization, foreign corporate control of national markets, unnecessary monopolization of "trade-related intellectual property rights" (typically patents on prescription drugs), and not least, easy immigration in the interests of lower wages and cheaper exports-amply show that the "do no harm" criterion is still far from being met.

Some feel that U.S. economic policies have harmed third-world citizens, and that easy immigration to the U.S. is a justified form of restitution. I have considerable sympathy with the view that U.S. policies (precisely those of globalization) have harmed third-world citizens, but for reasons already stated, no sympathy with the idea that easy immigration is a fair or reasonable restitution. For restitution I would prefer a series of small grants (not large interest-bearing loans), accompanied by free transfer of knowledge and technology.

Free Trade's Hidden Shackles

Free trade, specialization, and global integration mean that nations are no longer free not to trade. Yet freedom not to trade is surely necessary if trade is to remain voluntary, a precondition of its mutual benefit. To avoid war, nations must both consume less and become more self-sufficient. But free traders say we should become less self-sufficient and more globally integrated as part of the overriding quest to consume ever more. We must lift the laboring masses (which now include the formerly high-wage workers) up from their subsistence wages. This can only be done by massive growth, we are told. But can the environment sustain so much growth? It cannot. And how will whatever growth dividend there is ever get to the poor, i.e., how can wages increase given the nearly unlimited supply of labor? If wages do not increase then what reason is there to expect a fall in the birth rate of the laboring class via the "demographic transition"? How could we ever expect to have high wages in any country that becomes globally integrated with a globe having a vast oversupply of labor? Why, in a globally integrated world, would any nation have an incentive to reduce its birth rate?

Global economic integration and growth, far from bringing a halt to population growth, will be the means by which the consequences of overpopulation in the third world are generalized to the globe as a whole. They will be the means whereby the practice of constraining births in some countries will be eliminated by a demographic version of the "race to the bottom," rather than spread by demonstration of its benefits. In the scramble to attract capital and jobs, there will be a standards-lowering competition to keep wages low and to reduce any social, safety, and environmental standards that raise costs.

Some are seduced by the idea of "solving" the South's population problem and the North's labor shortage problem simultaneously-by migration. However, the North's labor shortage is entirely a function of below-equilibrium wages. The shortage could be instantly removed by an increase in wages that equated domestic supply and demand-simply by allowing the market to work. But the cheap-labor lobby, in the United States at least, thinks we must import workers in order to keep wages from rising and thereby reducing profits and export competitiveness. Of course this also keeps 80 percent of our citizens from sharing in the increased prosperity through higher wages. But never mind! They will still benefit, because importing workers is the key to saving Social Security-which, we are told, will collapse without growth in the cohort of working-age people provided by immigration. And when the large cohort of worker-immigrants retires? Well, we will just repeat the process. The real solution to the Social Security imbalance is to raise the age of retirement and lower the benefits. The real solution to the South's problem is for those countries to lower their birth rates and to put their working-age population to use at home producing necessities for the home market. And the reply to the half-truth that the United States is really more overpopulated than India because each American consumes so much more than each Indian, is that the United States needs mainly to lower its per capita consumption (and secondarily its population growth), while India and

China need primarily to lower their population growth, and are in no position to lower per capita consumption, except for the elite. Serious efforts to reduce birth rates in these countries are sometimes condemned, because, with the advent of ultrasound technology that can determine the gender of the fetus, the cultural preference for males has led to selective abortion of females. The problem here is neither birth control nor ultrasound but the immoral preference for males and indifference to the social costs of a gender imbalance a generation hence.

Demographers and economists have understandably become reluctant to prescribe birth control to other countries. If a country historically "chooses" many people, low wages, and high inequality over fewer people, higher wages, and less inequality, who is to say that is wrong? Let all make their own choices, since it is they who will have to live with the consequences. But while that may be a defensible position under internationalization, it is not defensible under globalization. The whole point of an integrated world is that these consequences, both costs of overpopulation and benefits of population control, are externalized to all nations. The costs and benefits of overpopulation under globalization are now distributed by class more than by nation. Labor bears the cost of reduced wage income; capital enjoys the benefit of reduced wage costs. Malthusian and Marxian considerations both seem to foster inequality. The old conflict between Marx and Malthus, always more ideological than logical, has now for practical purposes been further diminished. After all, both always held that wages tend toward subsistence under capitalism. Marx would probably see globalization as one more capitalist strategy to lower wages. Malthus might agree, while arguing that it is the fact of overpopulation that allows the capitalist's strategy to work in the first place. Presumably Marx would accept that, but insist that the overpopulation is only relative to capitalist institutions, not to any limits of nature's bounty, and would not exist under socialism. Malthus would disagree, along with the post-Mao Chinese communists. I confess that my sympathies lean more toward Malthus, and that I lament the recent tendency of the environmental movement to court "political correctness" by soft-pedaling issues of population, migration, and globalization.

Chapter 10

Economics and Population

Until now most economic study has been preoccupied with the reasons one country's economy is healthier than another's. The comparisons help us discover the best practices. Over the years, we've improved economies by learning from each other and adopting the models that are most successful. On the whole, the evidence has demonstrated that nations with market-directed economies are more successful than those with centrally planned economies. The big centrally planned economies of China and the former Soviet Republics have, over the last few decades, converted to more market-driven systems. And they have found new prosperity.

Economists have paid a lot more attention to the relative success or failure of national economies than to the larger dynamics of the world's economy. Students of economics understand the reasons why one nation outperforms another better than they understand the fundamental forces that direct the human economy as a single entity or the symbiotic relationships that support groups of national economies. Likewise we find it hard to track economics across long periods of time. What events occurred in the 19th century that made some nations prosperous in the 20th century? Are events occurring today that might undermine our economic health 30 years from now? We're pretty comfortable looking at one national economy and its condition today. When we aggregate more than one national economy and then try to track economic trends over time, the equation's complexity increases by orders of magnitude. It's difficult for the economist to get his or her arms around the global economy as it evolves across the decades.

Economists are aware of this gap in understanding. They recognize the complexity of their subject matter. They make allowances for what they call "externality." In economics, "externality" refers to the effects of an economic event on parties not directly involved – people in faraway places, in the past or in the future. The most vivid illustrations of externality, these days, come from the environmental realm. The carbon we've added to the atmosphere by burning fossil fuels has had relatively little effect on the people who pumped the oil, sold the oil or burned the oil. Most economic studies quantify our reliance on fossil fuels as a logical reliance on a relatively abundant natural resource. Viewed in this way, fossil fuels have been a precious resource fueling prosperity and innovation for more than 100 years with almost no bad effects. If negative environmental consequences are not felt within the economy where the petroleum is produced or where it is burned, then those consequences are "externalities." It is increasingly evident, however, that burning fossil fuels has a generalized effect on the health of the planet overall and that it will have an effect on the health and welfare of future generations.

Those effects are External to Most Economic Models, and it's Hard to Quantify Them

Economists are attempting to measure the effects of externalities like long-term environmental consequences. Economies that accurately evaluate the costs of their products are more efficient. If oil were taxed to pay reparations for the long-term environmental consequences of its extraction and consumption, then governments could use the additional revenues to mitigate the damage. Consumers might use less oil because it would be more expensive. Either way, the "externality" of environmental damage would be a measured factor in the economic equation. We would at least be aware of the true economic effects of our behaviour. Nigeria's birthrate would be external to most equations measuring economic growth in the United States even though Nigerian labour provides a lot of affordable oil to Western industrialized nations, and lots of Nigerians emigrate to wealthy countries where they provide high-quality, low-cost labour. Africa's population increase is not routinely measured as a factor in the economics of England, France or the United States. But effects are felt nonetheless in both negative and positive ways.

Some economists conclude that stable populations are good for national economies because the most prosperous nations record the lowest birth rates – the demographic-economic paradox again. Though we can speculate on the effects of stable population on economies, the fact is we don't have any real-world knowledge to draw on. A few nations have stabilized their populations, but they depend on population growth in other parts of the world to supply cheap labour and new consumers.

Every nation in Western Europe is supplementing its population with immigrants. In 2005, the most recent year for which I could find a firm number, 1.8 million new people moved to Europe from elsewhere. Somewhere between 45 million and 60 million people living in the United States today are in first-generation immigrant households. About 17 percent of people living in the United States are immigrants.

Bluntly, we have no examples of economic growth occurring in the absence of human population growth. The expansion of our species has always supported the expansion of our economies for as long as we've been keeping track, yet wealthy nations generally ignore the growth in foreign populations when they measure their own prosperity. It appears that the United States is an economic success story standing on its own two feet, but to what extent does our prosperity depend on a steady stream of ambitious immigrants? On the other hand, how prosperous will we be when North America's population reaches a billion people? Population growth is a Ponzi scheme and we're setting up future generations as its victims. We are paying into the base of the pyramid with our natural resources.

Overcoming the Problems of Population Growth

Implementing any human development programme has become a daunting challenge due mainly to the increasing population. Demographic transition over time paints an alarming picture of the state of population. The country's population growth has been showing an alarming trend over a couple of decades and has now reached the height of overpopulation with 14.45 people. If there is no attempt to arrest the growth of population the total population will double. With this growth of population it has become difficult to meet the nutritional demands of the citizens. With the growing number of poor, it has become even more difficult to get them within the reach of development programmes. The reproductive health sector is also deficient.

The dire consequences of rapid population growth is the depletion of natural resources. We now see devastation of resources caused by non-ecological human behaviour. Demographic imbalance, unplanned settlements and economic growth tend to harm the natural order of things dismantling ecological settings.

Public policy through resource mobilisation and allocation cannot do much in determining which way things should move unless the government plans to combat overpopulation. Only observing population day on 11th July is not enough. Of course this day is a reminder to all the citizens thinking rationally at the level of awareness with the global policy community reaffirming its commitment to sustainable level of population growth. There can hardly be any argument with the fact that a swelling population threatens to put at risk all implementation strategies of development in the substantive areas of public policy. Even a high budgetary allocation against any policy moves for a change can hardly be implemented in a country with a rising population.

The policymakers may look at demographic transition over time — bulge and decline of population on a comparative scale in all groups respective of age, sex, class, religion and sect or location. Time series data is available to surmise population growth at various levels. Nevertheless it is more important to probe the fact that we are lagging behind the western countries as far as population control measures are concerned. With advances in science and technology come new challenges. In fact tangible progress of the nation requires institutional capacity to combat them. It has been increasingly important for the state to comply with fiscal demands of the increasing number of young people and their share in economic participation. The energetic youth can be used to deal with birth control measures if it can be put into a productive force.

The current development intervention does not incorporate any concern about maintaining demographic balance through a streamlined population policy and conserving environmental resources. When the population base is extremely high it harms 'per capita well being' and per capita consumption. The fundamental condition for resilient economic growth is population growth at the desired level. It cannot be done only by allocation on reproductive health. The government has a plan to formulate a 'pragmatic population policy' realising the weaknesses in the family planning intervention. Its new policy move is to increase the contraceptives prevalence rate upto 80 per cent by 2021. The government has earmarked Tk.498 crore, development and non-development combined, for the procurement of birth control related materials and equipment.

The theme of Population Day this year (2009) is 'Responding to the Economic Crisis: Investing in women is a Smart Choice.' The comment of the UNFPA representative, Bangladesh, deserves mention: "In time of economic hardship women in developing countries are likely to be disproportionately affected which in turn inversely impacts their children and communities That's why it is so important that people's basic needs, including for reproductive health and family planning are being addressed even more urgently..." The situation of women nowadays presents the world with an opportunity to generate income and reduce poverty. Because of human development achievements of the past decades many young daughters are going to schools and combating childhood diseases. But to succeed in competitive global economy they should be equipped with better skills. Despite rising awareness about gender equality and birth control resulting in lower fertility rates in many developing countries the family planning movement has yet to attain any remarkable success. It still remains to be seen how population control measures are being managed in patriarchal societies. There is a need to test the level of acceptability of birth control methods considering the variables of sex, class and outlook.

Family planning in Bangladesh needs to be strengthened as a movement involving a large number of rural and urban women as activists. Fiscal demands for reproductive health for mother and child, education for the vulnerable and employment should be redeemed all within a broad brush of social security net. What is urgently needed is persuasion through motivation. It's high time to enhance social security of the disadvantaged group. The state should compensate those women who cannot have children. The state should also provide all logistics and support including allowances and social insurance for health, education and old age to the parents blessed with only one baby. Confidence building measures to be institutionally dealt with of course has a positive impact on the married couples willing to take contraceptives. The new health policy may incorporate a special section on family planning with indices like reproductive and protective health services including safe birth, safe abortions and prenatal and antenatal services in clinics and proper nursing of the newborn baby. There should have been a provision for the prevention of early marriage and premature pregnancy. I think with well thought measures of birth control in the proposed health policy voluntary family planning movement will be reinforced.

Ending Population Growth: Why Family Planning is Key to a Sustainable Future

The widespread assumption that world population, now at 6.9 billion, will inevitably grow to 9 billion by midcentury is wrong. The equally widespread belief that an earlier, lower population peak would require coercive "population control" is also incorrect. Population growth rates and average family size worldwide have fallen by roughly half over the past four decades, as modern contraception has become more accessible and popular. Population could peak before then and at a lower level, ameliorating environmental risks associated with climate change, water scarcity, biodiversity loss, and food and energy insecurity. Don't Take Demographic Projects At Face Value. Those who ponder humanity's future in the twenty-first century generally take at face value demographic projections suggesting that the world population will reach something like 9 billion around 2050 and will then stabilize at about that level. The widespread belief that this 30 percent increase from today's 6.9 billion people is inevitable undermines consideration of the role of population size in climate change, water scarcity, biodiversity loss, rising energy prices, and food security. Contributing to this is the related view that efforts to prevent population growth would require coercive government policies that constrain couples from having the children and the family sizes they want. While some analysts are confident that the world can feed, house, and otherwise support 9 billion or more people, others are less certain, and voices of caution about population growth are heard more often than in the past. A logical application of the precautionary principle in the face of current environmental problems would suggest that humanity could more easily accomplish these feats in an environmentally sustainable manner with a smaller population.

In a joint statement in 1993, representatives of 58 national scientific academies stressed the complexities of the population-environment relationship but nonetheless concluded, "As human numbers increase, the potential for irreversible changes of far-reaching magnitude also increases. ... In our judgment, humanity's ability to deal successfully with its social, economic, and environmental problems will require the achievement of zero population growth within the lifetime of our children." In 2005, the United Nations' Millennium Ecosystem Assessment identified population growth as a principal indirect driver of environmental change, along with economic growth and technological evolution.

In October 2010, a group of US and European climate and demographic researchers published findings from an integrated assessment model calculating the impact of various population scenarios on fossil-fuel carbon dioxide emissions over the coming century. If world population peaked at close to 8 billion rather than 9 billion, along the lines described in a low-fertility demographic projection published by the UN Population Division, the model predicted there would be a significant emissions savings: about 5.1 billion tons of carbon dioxide by 2050 and 18.7 billion tons by century's end. What if we could prove wrong the popular conviction that a future with 9 billion people and a growing population is inevitable? Suppose we could demonstrate that world population size might peak earlier and at a lower level if government policies aimed not at reproductive coercion but at individual reproductive freedom? Suppose such policies aimed to help all women and girls prevent unwanted pregnancies and conceive only when they want to bear a child? This article presents new data on births resulting from women's active intentions to become pregnant.

The hypothesis it probes may appear counterintuitive: if, starting at any moment, all pregnancies in the world resulted from each woman's intent to give birth, human population would immediately shift course away from growth towards decline within a few decades.

Key Concepts

- Even though most women of reproductive age now use contraception, we are far from a world in which all births result from intended pregnancies. Based on survey data, approximately 40 percent of pregnancies are unintended in developing countries, and 47 percent in developed ones.
- More than one in five births worldwide result from pregnancies women did not wish to occur.
- An estimated 215 million women in developing countries have an unmet need for family planning: they are sexually active, don't want to become pregnant, and yet for various reasons—including lack of access—are not using contraception.
- If all births resulted from women actively intending to conceive, fertility would immediately fall slightly below the replacement level; world population would peak within a few decades and subsequently decline.
- Assuring that all women are fully in control of the timing and frequency of childbearing is not expensive. Religious, cultural, and political opposition to contraception or the possibility of population decline is the key obstacle to such assurance. More research and a public better educated about sexuality and reproduction could engender a global social movement that would make possible a world of intended pregnancies and births.
- *Total Fertility Rate*: Refers to the average number of children a woman would bear over her lifetime if at each point in her reproductive age she had the number of live births typical of women at that age. Note that the total fertility rate differs from the population growth rate, which is the percentage by which a population grows each year, and from the birthrate, which is the number of live births each year per thousand people in the population. The global total fertility rate currently stands at 2.53 children per woman.
- *Replacement Fertility Rate*: Refers to the total fertility rate in a population that, if held steady over time and absent net migration, would result in a nonchanging population. This rate is often mischaracterized as uniformly and precisely 2.1 children per woman, but not all children survive to reproductive age,

and the proportion of those who do not varies over time and by population. For the world as a whole, with many low-income regions still experiencing high death rates among young people, the replacement fertility rate currently stands at 2.35 children per woman. Surprisingly, the gap between global total fertility and replacement fertility is now less than one-fifth of one birth.

Even achievement of global replacement fertility would not stop population growth for several decades, due to population momentum. This is the tendency of a population, influenced by its age structure, to continue its current growth dynamic even as fertility changes. Because there are so many young people of reproductive age in any population that has had above-replacement fertility for some time, for example, even low fertility can produce an overall number of births that statistically overwhelms deaths among the smaller cohorts of older individuals. It can take decades before subreplacement fertility actually halts growth. If total fertility falls well below replacement however, this momentum is weakened and a peak in population will come sooner, followed by a decline. These demographic phenomena are evident in Japan, with a total fertility rate of 1.3 children per woman and a population that has already peaked and is now slowly shrinking.

An Ethical Basis for Action to Slow Population Growth

What can societies that value democracy, self-determination, human rights, personal autonomy, and privacy do to include demographic change among strategies for environmental sustainability? An important answer may lie in a relatively untested set of principles adopted by almost all the world's nations at a 1994 UN conference held in Cairo. The third of three once-a-decade governmental conferences on population and development, it produced a programmer of action that abandoned the strategy of "population control" by governments in favour of a focus on the health, rights, and well-being of women.6 An operating assumption of this programmer is that when women have access to the information and means that allow them to choose the timing of pregnancy, the intervals between births lengthen, average family size shrinks, and teen births become less frequent. All of these improve maternal and child survival and slow population growth.

Experts disagree on how reproductive autonomy compares with other strategies in slowing that growth. Some assume economic growth is the most effective means, although birthrates rose along with prosperity in many countries after World War II and remain relatively high in several wealthy oil-exporting nations in which women have fewer rights and lower status than men. Moreover, some analysts argue that the arrow of causation operates more in the other direction, with low fertility stoking economic growth.

There is a more robust and demonstrable correlation between female educational attainment and fertility. Worldwide, women with no schooling have an average of 4.5 children, while those who have spent at least a year or more in primary school have just three. Women who complete at least a year or two of secondary school have 1.9 children—well below replacement fertility rates. With one or two years of advanced education for women, average childbearing rates fall even further, to 1.7. On this basis alone, those interested in depressing population growth rates might want to focus on improving women's educational attainment.

Questions remain about whether education alone can bring about declines in fertility without other supporting conditions, especially easy, affordable access to a range of contraceptive options. Similar uncertainties cloud understanding of exactly how improved child survival and the empowerment of women affect fertility. Improving both factors certainly contributes to later births and smaller families and is valuable regardless of its demographic impacts. But without clear data on the magnitude of these influences, interventions related to schooling, child survival, and women's empowerment are rarely seen as core aspects of governmental population policy.

This brings us to family planning. Access to safe and reliable contraception has exploded since the mid-twentieth century. An estimated 55 percent of all heterosexually active women worldwide now use modern contraceptive methods, while an additional seven percent use less reliable traditional methods. As the use of birth control has spread, fertility has plummeted from a global average of five children per woman in 1950 to barely more than 2.5 today.

While not necessarily sufficient to depress fertility on a population-wide basis, family planning is essential to the phenomenon. Women may begin sexual activity later in life and may resort to abortion to terminate unwanted pregnancies. But humanity's average family size could not have plummeted simply because women had diplomas, contractual rights, or confidence that their children would survive. To have small families, heterosexually active women and their partners need safe and effective contraception—modern birth control.

Lessons from history suggest that women have sought and employed contraceptives since ancient times to avoid unwanted pregnancy when circumstances were inauspicious for the 15 to 18 years of parental commitment a new birth entails. Egyptian papyri that date back 4,000 years describe pessaries, ancient precursors to the diaphragm, made of acacia oil and crocodile dung. Literature from Asia to North America documents herbs used for centuries as emmenagogues, substances that induce immediate menstruation and hence expel recently fertilized eggs. In the Mediterranean, in the ages of ancient Greece and Rome, a booming trade in the contraceptive, or possibly abortifacient, silphium helped drive its source, a wild giant fennel, into extinction. And an ecclesiastical court record from 1319 preserves the personal account of a young widow in southwestern France who provided details of her use of an herbal contraception during an extended affair with a priest.

We know, too, that women and their partners historically have moderated their reproduction in response to their external environments, natural and economic. (Until modern times, these were generally the same thing.) In eighteenth- and nineteenth-century Sweden, for example, birthrates neatly tracked the price of grain crops with a roughly nine-month delay. The Japanese population during the eighteenth-century Tokugawa shogunate declined during several decades of food scarcity—until a government propaganda campaign against infanticide (the dominant method of family-size control at the time) pushed fertility well above replacement levels in the nineteenth century, restoring demographic growth.

Similar responses of fertility to external circumstances are evident today. The high cost of housing in Japan is prominent among the reasons offered by young people for delaying marriage and childbearing. In the United States, a two percent decline in the country's birthrate in 2008 was attributed largely to the deterioration of the economy.

Implications of Personal Fertility-Management Aspirations

History and recent fertility phenomena thus suggest the likelihood that the interest in safely and effectively managing the timing of pregnancy and childbirth may be nearly universal among women. Lack of education, affluence, and equality may simply be barriers—along with others related to patriarchal, pronatalist, and even medical cultural norms—to existing aspirations to avoid unwanted pregnancies.

Data exist for the likely demographic impact of establishing conditions worldwide that would facilitate women's choices about the timing of pregnancy. According to the Guttmacher Institute, a US reproductive health-care research organization, an estimated 215 million women in developing countries have an "unmet need for family planning." This applies to women who are sexually active and express the desire to avoid pregnancy yet are not using contraception. Estimates of their number derive from demographic and health surveys conducted in certain developing countries every few years. Many women in developed countries may be in the same circumstances, but data are insufficient in most cases to suggest their numbers. In early 2010, researchers with the Futures Group in Washington, DC, estimated the demographic impact of meeting unmet family-planning demand in 99 developing countries and one developed one. The researchers excluded China, on the assumption that government population policies aimed at limiting most families to a single child rule out births from unintended pregnancies. And they supplemented their country list with the United States, the world's most populous developed county and one for which there is some data suggesting the magnitude of unmet need. Using accepted models for the impact of rising contraceptive prevalence on birthrates, the researchers concluded that satisfying unmet need for contraception in these 100 countries—with a cumulative 2005 population of 4.3 billion—would produce a population of 6.3 billion in 2050. Under the United Nations' medium projection, the countries' population would be 400 million higher, at 6.7 billion. Average global fertility at midcentury would be 1.65 children per woman, well below the population replacement fertility level—and would continue to fall. This conclusion, if backed up by further research, is momentous. By implication, simply providing safe and effective contraceptive options to all sexually active women who do not want to become pregnant would end and then reverse world population growth. The effect is independent of any further fertility reductions that might occur as a result of greater educational attainment for women, improved child survival, women's empowerment, and general economic advancement.

To some experts the idea that simply facilitating women's childbearing intentions would end population growth, without significant demand creation for family planning through cultural shifts and other means, goes against survey findings from many African and some Asian countries. These findings suggest that in parts of these continents women's average desired family size is as high as six or seven children. Wouldn't facilitating these women's childbearing intentions undermine any hope of ending world population growth? Not necessarily. For one thing, women expressing such high desired family sizes are at most a relatively small proportion of the world's population (albeit significant in Africa's). But the more important point is that a high desired family size can easily coexist with high levels of unintended pregnancy that, if prevented, would result in significantly lower birthrates than if not prevented.

The reason for this is not hard to understand: women's individual reproductive decisions arrive at their desired family size, if at all, only cumulatively. Decisions about the desirability of pregnancy are made singly, in individual acts of sexual intercourse in which conception is possible. Whatever one's hopes for an eventual number of children, pregnancy decisions occur in the context of current personal, economic, and social circumstances. Desired family size can be compared to house size and the number of cars owned. We may wish to have a large house and many cars, but our circumstances may not allow for us to have either without endangering our finances and well-being. We decide moment by moment whether working towards that goal makes sense for us. So it is with reproductive intentions; every step of a woman and her partner's reproductive lives is governed by their immediate circumstances.

It seems likely that even in countries where women respond in health surveys that they desire six or seven children, they would end up with fewer, possibly many fewer, if at each step of their reproductive lives they were able to choose precisely when to become pregnant. In some developed countries with low fertility, women express a desire to have two children yet have closer to one on average. With the right partner, the right job, the right apartment, and the right economic and social-support systems, a woman in Japan, for example, might have the two children she desires. But with options to prevent or terminate pregnancies, many Japanese women have one child or none; the national average is 1.3.

All of this suggests the value of developing and testing the hypothesis that meeting the needs of women and their partners for personal control of pregnancy could lead to the end of population growth. Physician and reproductive specialist Malcolm Potts has found that in all countries where women can choose from a range of contraceptive options, backed by access to safe and legal abortion services, total fertility rates are at or below replacement fertility levels.

If these findings can be borne out consistently by additional research, those who worry about the impact of global population growth on environmental and social sustainability might usefully advocate for worldwide universal access to family-planning services. The need for such access is enshrined in the second target of the fifth UN Millennium Development Goal, which calls for developing countries to "achieve, by 2015, universal access to reproductive health." This concept embraces more than family planning, including a holistic state of sexual and reproductive well-being that encompasses maternal and child health, prevention of AIDS and other sexually transmitted infections, access to safe abortion services (where these are legal), and post-abortion care.

A Thought Experiment With Data

The Futures Group study has not yet gained the widespread attention its findings merit. Among the reasons for this may be that the concept of "unmet need" for contraception is not widely understood among the public, news media, and policymakers. Moreover, because of lack of data the study excluded not only China, with a fifth of the world's population, but dozens of other developing countries—and all the world's industrialized countries other than the United States.

Newly available data on unintended pregnancy in many countries, assembled by the Guttmacher Institute, support an alternative research approach to the question of the demographic impacts of births that result from pregnancies women never sought or wanted to have. These data, based on a range of surveys worldwide, provide the basis for beginning to answer an intriguing and valuable question: What would happen to world population growth if every pregnancy worldwide, starting tomorrow, were the outcome of a woman's active intention to become pregnant and bear and help raise a child? If no pregnancies were unintended, in other words, how many births would there be compared to current births, and how would this new birthrate affect the future of human population?

Averaged over the 73 countries for which data exist, and comprising 83 percent of the world's births, just under ten percent of births result from pregnancies occurring among women who never wanted to have another child. Even under the most conservative scenario—extrapolated globally, with all births from pregnancies that are merely mistimed considered equivalent to births from intended pregnancies—a hypothetical world population in which women only become pregnant when they want to would reduce today's global total fertility rate to 2.29 births per woman. That figure is slightly below today's global replacement fertility rate—placing world population on a direct path towards future decline, albeit at a very slow pace given population momentum (and assuming neither future fertility decline nor improvement in mortality among young people). Under the less conservative assumption that one-quarter of births from mistimed pregnancies are equivalent to unwanted pregnancies, the total fertility rate sinks lower, to 2.22 births per woman—resulting in a somewhat faster track towards a human population peak, even with no future fertility decline. These calculations are, at best, first-order analyses of the impact on world population growth of an idealized scenario in which all births are the outcomes from intended pregnancies. As noted, they do not take into account the possibility that global fertility would continue its decline once all births resulted from intended pregnancies.

More survey research and data on pregnancy intention among individual women in all countries would be needed to make a more robust determination of demographic impacts. But the essence of research on this question remains hopeful—and little known: a successful global effort that assured all women the capacity to decide for themselves whether and when to become pregnant would also place world population on a path towards a reasonably imminent peak followed by slow demographic decrease. Additional efforts to see that women have the educational, economic, legal, and political opportunities they deserve would accelerate this transition.

Toward a World of Intended Pregnancies and Wanted Children

Given the feasibility of such a transition, why isn't it happening today? Why aren't higher proportions of births the result of intended pregnancies? And what might we do to overcome the obstacles and actually bring that world about?

Popular as it is with women and couples, contraception remains a deeply sensitive issue for much of the public. Vehemently opposed by the Catholic Church and regarded with suspicion by many other Christian, Islamic, and even some Jewish religious leaders, open advocacy for contraceptive availability and use inevitably risks stoking religious opposition. Influence of the Catholic Church hierarchy has blocked efforts in the Philippines, for example, to include access to modern contraception in the country's government health system. Opposition from the Holy See, which has permanent observer status within the UN system, led to silence on reproductive health in the UN Millennium Development Goals when they were forged in 2000—even though representatives of the world's governments had pledged to achieve universal access to reproductive health by 2015 at the UN conference in Cairo in 1994. Only in 2007 was language aiming at that reproductive health access target added to Millennium Development Goal number five. Seven years of opportunities to achieve the target had been squandered.

Perhaps more destructive than religious opposition is a relative denigration in most cultures of concerns that lie principally in the sphere of women. Access to contraception is clearly one such concern, since women bear the babies and undergo most of the risks to life and health associated with reproduction. At least since the rise of agricultural, urban, and hierarchical societies, male interests in reproduction have differed markedly from those of women. Men are often anxious to produce a multitude of future heirs, soldiers, labourers, farmers, and followers. Women tend to be strategically concerned with the survival and well-being of each of their children. These gender differences are anything but ironclad, and in many cultures the gender gap in attitudes has narrowed in recent decades, especially as women's status has risen relative to men's. In other cultures, however, the gap not only remains wide, it demands the subjugation of women, sex, and reproduction to male needs.

Beyond male reproductive dominance lies the conviction among neoclassical economists that endless economic growth is possible and that it requires endless population growth. Politicians often measure their self-worth based on the size of their electorates. They happily side with economists on the idea that endless economic and demographic growth is both possible and desirable. With all these factors in play, it is not surprising that the world's governments are nowhere close to allocating the resources the Cairo conference had estimated would be needed for all women in developing countries to have reasonable access to decent family-planning services. This was roughly \$18 billion for the year 2010, a third of which was to be contributed by industrialized-country governments (the 1993 dollars in the UN document are here converted to current dollars). Despite that commitment—and an increase in the population of reproductive-age people in developing countries, from 2.3 to 2.9 billion—actual expenditures from these governments on international family-planning assistance fell from \$723 million in 1995 to \$338 million in 2007. Assistance has changed little since the latter year.

A global social movement is needed to pressure policymakers and influential cultural and thought leaders to reverse this dismal trend. Raising \$9 billion a year from wealthy governments that currently spend just a few hundred million on international family-planning assistance shouldn't be as difficult as it is. As much money is allocated for a few days worth of military activities worldwide. A comparable or greater amount probably would be needed to assure that the vast majority of pregnancies in wealthy countries are intentional, but this sum has never been estimated. Significant investments in all countries in education on sexuality and reproduction are also needed, but what these should be is unknown as well.

Still, the point undoubtedly still holds: a world in which almost all births result from intended conceptions would not be prohibitively expensive or difficult, aside from cultural barriers, to bring about. Yet due to contraception's sensitivity—complicated by a history pockmarked with episodes of contraceptive coercion in China, India, Peru, and a few other countries—environmentalists and advocates for women's rights and health have never succeeded in forging an activist alliance capable of raising the modest sums needed for all to have access to family planning. Several elements are needed if a global social movement to promote family planning and intentional pregnancy is ever to have its own birth. One is more research about the likely population and environmental outcomes of a world of fully intended pregnancies—and the policies, programmes, and costs that could lead to such a world. Another is agreement that any such policies and programmes must be based on reproductive rights rather than on coercion, and therefore on the intentions of women and their partners rather than on those of anyone else. And a third is the creativity to shape—or the courage to stand up to—the religious, economic, and other cultural forces that promote population growth and oppose the gender and reproductive health conditions that undermine it.

There is nothing fated about a world of 9 billion people—in 2050, or ever. While true control of population is beyond our aspirations and capacities, policy choices are available that will nudge our numbers closer to environmentally and socially sustainable levels. The choices are rooted in human development and human rights, specifically the right of all, and most directly of women, to decide for themselves when it is the right time to bring a new child into the world.

Population Growth and Food Security in the Horn of Africa

The current food crisis in the Horn of Africa has fast become a humanitarian disaster. According to World Vision UK, the crisis has affected in excess of 6 million people in Ethiopia, 2 million in Uganda, 3 million in Somalia and 10 million in Kenya.

The ongoing effects of the food crisis are devastating. In northern Kenya, the impact of the drought and rising food costs has been largely felt amongst the pastoralist community, where in excess of 70% of people's livelihoods have been affected. In Turkana, for example, one in four children suffer from acute malnutrition. Across Ethiopia, the cost of food has increased by more than 50% and in the Karamoja region of Uganda, 70% of residents are receiving food aid following insufficient rains over three consecutive years. In Somalia, a country that has existed without a formal government for the past 18 years, increased fighting and instability has resulted in a steep increase in the price of food and water, a problem compounded by the inability of aid agencies to deliver vital supplies. In some regions water costs have increased by 1,000% in recent months. With widespread malnutrition across the country, it is currently estimated that one in six Somali children are acutely malnourished.

Multiple Factors

There is not one single catalyst for the current food crisis. A myriad of factors including drought, poverty, rising food prices, unemployment, landlessness, lack of drinking water and civil conflict are all commonly cited as contributing factors. The impact of population growth on food crises, however, is commonly overlooked.

The countries currently affected by the food crisis in the Horn of Africa have all witnessed a decrease in fertility rates over recent decades. In spite of this decrease, population momentum, where high fertility in the previous generation has resulted in a large portion of the population being of childbearing age, means that the populations of these countries continue to grow rapidly. In Kenya, for example, where according to the US Census Bureau fertility has decreased from 7.6 in 1980 to its current rate of 4.2, the country's population continues to increase at a rate of 2.6% per year. The sustained and rapid population growth occurring in the Horn of Africa raises serious concerns over food supply. According to the Principal Policy Analyst at the Kenya Institute for Public Policy Research and Analysis, John Omiti, "population growth is higher than our ability to produce food. We need to address the demographic challenge to balance supply and demand."

A Malthusian Trap?

Although food production was largely able to cater for the exponential growth in world population that occurred during the 20th century, population growth within Africa is beginning to outpace food supply. Between 2007 and 2025, food production in Africa must increase from its current production level of 2.2 billion tonnes to 3 billion tonnes to keep up with population growth. In light of this and the recent food crisis, the question arises: are we heading towards the Malthusian trap, whereby population growth will outstrip food supply? Due to trade, aid and increased technological innovation as a result of the Industrial Revolution, it is unlikely that Malthus' visions will be felt on a large scale. It is plausible, however, to suggest a strong correlation between high fertility and food insecurity. Continuously high rates of fertility amongst subsistence farmers and the associated increase in population density result in the further sub-division of family plots, thereby placing increased pressure on the success of crops. When food shortages do occur, moreover, it is the poor who are most affected. With decreases in food supply, those already forced to live on the smallest of rations are confronted with a simultaneous increase in the price of food. Food affordability therefore becomes a major concern, as the poorest members of society already spend 50-70% of their incomes on food.

High fertility as a barrier to development

With poverty inextricably linked to hunger, high fertility rates in the countries of the Horn of Africa have proven a major hurdle to economic prosperity and therefore food security. The persistence of high fertility in the Horn of Africa has precluded the countries in the region from capitalising on what is commonly referred to as the "demographic dividend". This occurs in countries in transition from high to low fertility, where there is a window of opportunity to achieve economic growth via an increased ratio of workers to non-workers. When coupled with government initiatives and increased foreign investment, a demographic dividend can induce economic growth and increase government revenue via the collection of income tax. A decrease in the number of dependents not only minimises the impact of sub-dividing land within families, it also reduces constraints to family savings that can in turn provide families with a valuable safety net. Although Malthus's grand claim that unchecked population growth will inevitably result in widespread food shortages remains unproven, high fertility rates do provide a significant obstacle to food security. A decrease in fertility would therefore go some way to minimising the risk of future food crises.

Population and the Environment

Stress on the environment and the depletion of natural resources both reinforce and are exacerbated by gender inequality, poor health and poverty, the Cairo conference emphasized. Environmental stress is increasing, due to both "unsustainable consumption and production patterns" (including high resource consumption in wealthy countries and among better-off groups in all countries) and demographic factors such as rapid population growth, population distribution and migration.

Affirming that "meeting the basic human needs of growing populations is dependent on a healthy environment", ICPD Programme of Action(1) addressed the interrelationships among population, economic growth and protection of the environment, reiterating principles of Agenda 21, adopted by the United Nations Conference on the Environment and Development in Rio in 1992.

A Virtuous Circle

Efforts to slow down population growth, to reduce poverty, to achieve economic progress, to improve environmental protection, and to reduce unsustainable consumption and production patterns are mutually reinforcing. Slower population growth has in many countries increased those countries' ability to attack poverty, protect and repair the environment, and build the base for future sustainable development.

At both the Cairo conference and its five-year review, the global community affirmed that greater equality between men and women is an essential component of sustainable development, including environmental protection. Boosting the status of women is now accepted as a prerequisite for lowering fertility and ensuring sound management of natural resources. And awareness is increasing of the need to address environmental crises, demographic realities, gender inequity and rising consumption amid persistent poverty in a holistic manner.

At both the Cairo conference and its five-year review, the global community affirmed that greater equality between men and women is an essential component of sustainable development, including environmental protection. Boosting the status of women is now accepted as a prerequisite for lowering fertility and ensuring sound management of natural resources. And awareness is increasing of the need to address environmental crises, demographic realities, gender inequity and rising consumption amid persistent poverty in a holistic manner. The 2003 UNFPA global survey found that countries have made progress in addressing population issues within the context of poverty, environment, and decentralized planning processes. One hundred and twenty-two countries reported developing plans or strategies on population-environment linkages. Forty countries have developed specific policies, and 22 have put in place laws or legislation on population dynamics and the environment. Still, the stakes are high, as human activity continues to alter the planet on an unprecedented scale. More people are using more resources with more intensity and leaving a bigger "footprint" on the earth than ever before.

Signs of Ecological Change

Over the past century and especially over the past 40 years, people have effected vast changes in the global environment. Those most directly affected by environmental challenges, from water pollution to climate change, are also the poorest—and least able to change livelihoods or lifestyles to cope with, or combat, ecological decline. Some snapshots:

- Farmers, ranchers, loggers, and developers have cleared about half the world's original forest cover, and another 30 per cent is degraded or fragmented.
- Over the last half century, land degradation has reduced cropland by an estimated 13 per cent and pasture by 4 per cent. In many countries, population growth has raced ahead of food production in recent years. Some 800 million people are chronically malnourished and 2 billion lack food security.
- Three quarters of the world's fish stocks are now fished at or beyond sustainable limits. Industrial fleets have fished out at least 90 per cent of large ocean predators —including tuna, marlin and swordfish—in the last 50 years.
- Since the 1950s, global demand for water has tripled. Groundwater quantity and quality are declining due to over-pumping, runoff

from fertilizers and pesticides, and leaking of industrial waste. Half a billion people live in countries defined as water stressed or water-scarce; by 2025, that figure is expected to surge to between 2.4 billion and 3.4 billion.

- Climate change. As a result of fossil fuel consumption, carbon dioxide levels today are 18 per cent higher than in 1960 and an estimated 31 per cent higher than at the onset of the Industrial Revolution in 1750. Accumulation of greenhouse gases in the atmosphere, including carbon dioxide, is tied to rising and extreme change in temperatures, and more severe storms.
- Sea level has risen an estimated 10-20 centimetres, largely as a result of melting ice masses and the expansion of oceans linked to regional and global warming. Small island nations and low-lying cities and farming areas face severe flooding or inundation.

Population's Impact on Resource Use

Numbers alone do not capture the impact of the interactions between human populations and the environment. The size and weight of the environmental footprint each person plants on Earth is determined by the ways people use resources, which affects the quantities they consume. For instance, a vegetarian who primarily uses a bicycle has a much smaller impact than someone who eats meat and drives a sport utility vehicle. The ecological footprint of an average person in a high-income country is about six times bigger than that of someone in a low-income country, and many more times bigger than in the least-developed countries. The combined footprints of people in a region determine the prospects for saving or permanently losing the biological diversity found there.

Many economists and environmentalists use an equation that ties together population, consumption and technology to describe their relative impacts (I=PAT: Impact=Population x Affluence x Technology).

As birth rates fall, consumption levels and patterns (affluence), coupled with technology, will take on new importance in determining the state of the global environment. But population will remain the critical factor where lack of access to reproductive health services and family planning, shortfalls in education for girls and women, poverty and women's limited power relative to men continue to fuel high fertility. Global Consumers And Persistent Poverty. A rapidly growing global consumer class, now around 1.7 billion people, accounts for the vast majority of meat eating, paper use, car driving, and energy use on the planet, as well as the resulting impact of these activities on its natural resources. This class is not limited to industrialized countries; as populations surge in developing countries and as the world economy becomes increasingly globalized, more and more people have the means to acquire a greater diversity of products and services than ever before. Meanwhile, 2.8 billion people—two in five—still struggle to survive on less than $2 a day. In 2000, 1.1 billion people did not have reasonable access to safe drinking water, and 2.4 billion people worldwide lived without basic sanitation. Lack of access to clean water and sanitation in the developing world led to 1.7 million deaths in 2000.(3). Differential Impacts. Where population growth and high levels of consumption coincide, as they do in some industrial nations, the impact of growth is significant. For instance, even though the United States' population is only a fourth as large as India's, its environmental footprint is over three times bigger—it releases 15.7 million tons of carbon into the atmosphere each year compared with India's 4.9 million tons. Hence the impact of the current 3 million annual population increase in the United States is greater than that of India's 16 million increase.

Environmental impact can continue to grow even as population growth levels off. In China, population growth has slowed dramatically, but consumption of oil and coal and the resulting pollution continues to rise. While the Chinese Government is promoting greater fuel efficiency for cars, it is not promoting increased use of public transportation, biking and walking, or efficient urban planning so people would not have to drive.

Besides reducing overall resource use, governments can reduce the environmental impacts of increased consumption by promoting appropriate technology that uses resources more efficiently. Industrial countries can help the developing world by assisting with the dissemination and adoption of cleaner technologies. Other demographic trends intersect with consumption in surprising ways. As a result of rising incomes, urbanization, and smaller families, the average number of people living under one roof declined between 1970 and 2000—from 5.1 to 4.4 in developing countries and from 3.2 to 2.5 in industrial countries—while the total number of households increased. Each new house requires land and materials. And with fewer people in each household, savings from shared use of energy and appliances are lost. A one-person household in the United States, for example, uses 17 per cent more energy per capita than a two-person household.

Even in some European nations and in Japan, where population growth has stopped, changing household dynamics are important drivers of increased consumption.

Economic Impact of Population Dynamics

There is clear evidence that enabling people to have fewer children, if they want to, helps to stimulate development and reduce poverty, both in individual households and at the macro-economic level. Family Size And Well-being. Recent research supports the premise that having many (and unplanned for) children imposes a heavy burden on the poor, while smaller families have higher upward economic mobility.

Fertility impacts on a family's poverty in several ways:

- Smaller families share income among fewer people, and average income per capita increases. A family of a certain size may be below the poverty line, but with one less member may rise above the poverty threshold.
- Fewer pregnancies lead to lower maternal mortality and morbidity, and often to more education and economic opportunities for women. A mother's death or disability can drive a family into poverty. Her ability to earn income can lead the family out of poverty.
- High fertility undermines the education of children, especially girls. Larger families have less to invest in the education of each child. In addition, early pregnancy interrupts young women's schooling, and in large families mothers often remove daughters from school to help care for siblings. Less education typically implies increased poverty for the family as well as the inter-generational transmission of poverty.
- Families with lower fertility are better able to invest in the health of each child, and to give their children proper nourishment. Malnourishment leads to stunted growth, cerebral underdevelopment and subsequent inability to achieve high levels of productivity in the labour force.

MACRO-ECONOMIC IMPACT. High fertility impedes development in a variety of ways. The World Health Organization (WHO) Commission on Macroeconomics and Health noted in 2001, "At the societal level, rapid rural population growth in particular puts enormous stress on the physical environment and on food productivity as land-labour ratios in agriculture decline. Desperately poor peasants are then likely to crowd cities, leading to very high rates of urbanization, with additional adverse consequence in congestion and in declining urban capital per person." Lower fertility, on the other hand, is linked to economic gains. A 2001 study of 45 countries found that if these countries had reduced fertility by 5 births per 1,000 people in the 1980s, the average national incidence of poverty of 18.9 per cent in the mid-1980s would have been reduced to 12.6 per cent between 1990 and 1995. At the time of Cairo, econometric proof of this "population effect" on economic growth was difficult to obtain, and mainstream economists tended to dismiss it or play down its importance. A 1986 study by the National Research Council in the United States. concluded that population growth had little or no effect on overall economic growth, despite its important effects at the household level; but it relied on data from the 1960s and 1970s, when many developing countries were early in their demographic transition.

The Demographic Window. A new round of research in the mid-1990s, using data from longer periods, showed clearly that falling fertility opens a "demographic window" of economic opportunity. With fewer dependent children relative to the working age population, countries can make additional investments which can spur economic growth and help reduce poverty. This window opens only once and closes as populations age and the ratio of dependants (children and the elderly) eventually starts to rise again.

Several countries in East Asia—the so-called Asian Tigers—and a few others have taken advantage of this economic bonus. China has seen a dramatic drop in the incidence of poverty. One study estimated that declining fertility in Brazil has raised the annual growth of GDP per capita by 0.7 percentage points. Mexico and other Latin American countries have registered similar effects. On the other hand, some countries have largely squandered the opportunity for a one-time "windfall" because of a lack of good governance or policies that have led to unproductive investments. In the poorest countries where fertility remains high, the demographic window will not open for some time, but investments now—particularly in improving reproductive health service delivery—could hasten its arrival and ensure future dividends.

The world's regions are at different stages of the demographic transition. South Asia will reach its peak ratio of working-age to dependent-ages between 2015 and 2025. In Latin America and the Caribbean, the proportion in working ages started to increase earlier than in East Asia and will peak during 2020-2030, but the proportional change has been less marked, and the economic bonus will be correspondingly less sudden and less intense. Some Arab and Central Asian countries will approach their demographic opportunity within two decades, while others are farther away. In much of sub-Saharan Africa the demographic bonus is still a long way off. The population is still very young and the proportion in working ages relatively low. Many countries are just beginning the demographic transition, and others have not even started. Only 11 countries are projected to reach their maximum working-age proportion before 2050. Unmet need for contraception in the region is high, however, suggesting the expansion of quality programmes could hasten the arrival of the bonus.

Inequality In Reproductive Health Fosters Poverty

The ICPD recognized that ill health and unplanned births can determine whether a family falls into or escapes poverty, as the poor themselves have long known. But policy makers have been slow to address the inequitable distribution of health information and services that helps keep people poor. An analysis of data on access to reproductive health among different income groups in 56 countries shows that the poorest groups are clearly disadvantaged, in a number of ways: · The biggest gap between richer and poorer populations is in delivery by a skilled attendant, the most expensive of the reproductive health services;Adolescent fertility showed the next largest differential—poorer women have children at younger ages.

Wealth-based health inequities are greater for safe motherhood, adolescent fertility, contraceptive use and total fertility than for infant mortality; Poor women have more children throughout their lives than wealthier women; Poor countries have a heightened risk of maternal, infant and child death and illness, and poor women in all countries face higher risks than others; Use of family planning, particularly of modern methods, is higher in richer segments of society. These findings corroborate those presented in The State of World Population 2002 which examined data from 44 countries. Shortages of resources, skills, opportunities and outreach deprive the poor of access to reproductive health information and services and the effects are apparent. The information and service deficits result from various factors: Poor women and couples have less access to information and to the skills education provides to expand their knowledge; Poor individuals and communities are riskaverse —less likely to try new behaviours— since their room for error is so small; Costs for information and services (formal and informal monetary costs, and transport and opportunity costs) are more daunting for the poor; When addressing the poor, service providers are less willing or able to interact as closely as is required to exchange information and support about sensitive topics; Services are not in locations or open at times accessible to the poor. Richer populations are more skilled at working with formal institutions and receiving a responsive hearing. In 2000, only 3 per cent of gross domestic product was devoted to the health sector in developing countries; in the least-developed countries the figure was even lower. Expenditures in many countries still tend to favour hospitals and medical facilities in the capital city, and there has been little progress towards more equitable distribution of resources at local levels: the percentage of national health expenditures devoted to local health services has stagnated in developing countries and decreased in the least developed.

Global Resources and Population

In his famous text *An Essay on the Principle of Population* (1798), English clergyman Thomas Malthus argued that the human population tends to increase more rapidly than food supplies and that population growth would ultimately lead to disease, starvation, and war. Malthus's argument remained popular for decades, and his ominous forecasts are currently mirrored in various predictions that the human population will be unable to sustain itself in the future. Many researchers and scientists calculate that because the world's population could double to more than ten billion as early as the year 2050, increased human consumption and activity will rapidly deplete or exhaust the earth's vital natural resources. Others disagree, arguing that human activity is not critically reducing supplies of global resources. They contend that due to frequent discoveries of new reserves, known supplies of many resources are in fact increasing.

Some researchers blame industrial societies, particularly the United States, for extensive resource depletion. Dartmouth College environmental studies professor Donella Meadows states, "If everyone on Earth lived like the average North American and we utilized fully every productive acre (leaving no wilderness), we would need three Earths to support the present world population." According to these experts, humanity's growing impact on land and natural resources is straining the world's ability to support its increasing population. University of British Columbia planning professor William Rees calls this effect the "ecological footprint."

Many observers warn that humanity's ecological footprint is growing at a dangerous pace. Stanford University professor of population Paul R. Ehrlich and his wife, Stanford biologist Anne H. Ehrlich, maintain that the "explosion of human numbers has been combined with a four-fold increase in consumption per person. The result is a twenty-fold escalation since 1850 of the pressure humanity places on its environment." The Ehrlichs are among those who contend that population increases will exert more pressure on land, soils, forests, water, and other resources. As Princeton University sociologist and demographer Charles F. Westoff writes, "Growing populations multiply whatever environmentally destructive behaviour is present."

Beginning in 1970, Meadows and others at the Massachusetts Institute of Technology administered a computer simulation model called World3 that studied such variables as population, pollution, and the use of energy and other resources. In their 1972 book *The Limits to Growth*, these researchers cautioned that humanity was fast approaching the limits—especially the environmental limits—to the rapid growth of civilization and its consumption of global resources. They maintained that if increases in population, industrialization, and resource depletion continued unabated, limits to growth would be reached early in the twenty-first century, causing drastic declines in energy use as well as food and industrial production. The preface to their 1992 update, Beyond *the Limits to Growth,* notes that "the world has already overshot some of its limits, and if present trends remain unchanged, we face the virtually certain prospect of a global economic collapse."

However, other observers disagree with these predictions. They argue that although human consumption of global resources has increased, the supply of resources is not in jeopardy and remains abundant. These experts note that because of technological advances, more supplies of global resources are being discovered or conserved. Some maintain, for example, that raw materials such as lead, tin, wood, and zinc, which are used in manufacturing, are being conserved due to the increased use of other materials, including aluminum, glass, plastic, and rubber. Also, new mining methods use bacteria, electricity, and foaming agents to recover copper, gold, and other minerals from low grade ores that would otherwise be discarded. Economist Julian L. Simon asserts that the prices of most resources are decreasing, suggesting that they are in ample supply. In Simon's words, "The real prices of food and of every other raw material are lower now than in earlier decades and centuries, indicating a trend of increased natural-resource availability rather than increased scarcity."

Simon and others also contend that since the known supplies of many global resources are increasing, humanity will not be hindered by limits to growth. As Cato Institute economist Stephen Moore writes, "The introduction of new technologies and innovations, which make us more efficient in consuming and producing natural resources, has meant that the earth's resources have continually become less of a limit to growth over time rather than more so." The downward trend in resource prices, Moore and others maintain, proves that resources are abundant and disproves the findings of the World3 model, which they claim did not use accurate data as input. Simon points out that the Club of Rome, an organization that sponsored the World3 model, later disavowed the Limits *to Growth* report for exaggerating the extent of resource depletion. Furthermore, according to *Eco-Scam* author Ronald Bailey and researchers Michael Sanera and Jane S. Shaw, the dire predictions of The *Limits to Growth* have not come true since the book's publication. Sanera and Shaw write, "Oil is plentiful and cheap. The world did not run out of gold by 1981, or zinc by 1990, or petroleum by 1992, as the book predicted." Bailey adds, "America's population has risen 22% and its economy has grown by more than 58%." He notes that "humanity hasn't come close to running out of any mineral resource." Even if some resources do become more scarce over time, Sanera and Shaw assert, price increases will cause producers to seek cheaper substitute materials, thus maintaining consumers' access to products and services. In their words, "The resources that we use will change over time. Materials that were previously unknown or neglected will provide the services we want."

The debate over the effects of population growth on the availability of global resources is a main theme in *Global Resources: Opposing Viewpoints*, which poses arguments on resource scarcity in the following chapters: Are Global Resources Being Depleted? What Agricultural Policies Should Be Pursued? What Energy Sources Should Be Pursued? How Can Global Resources Be Protected? The contributors in this anthology examine the availability of and dependence on the world's vital natural resources.

Population Growth and Future Energy Consumption

At the UN conference on environmental and developmental issues in June 1992, it became clear that population growth and increasing resource consumption are closely linked with economic and social development. The previous chapters emphasised the fact that the industrial countries produce by far the greatest portion of greenhouse gas and are thus responsible for its accumulation in the atmosphere. For this reason, the developing countries should be given the chance to catch up on the development of the industrialised countries. At the Rio conference, it was the first time that this was officially confirmed and agreed upon. The people of the developing countries suffer most from the consequences of the climate change, without contributing to it. We, living in the rich countries, are still worsening and destroying the basic conditions of existence in the third world by our way of life.

This is particularly true with regard to some island states which are directly endangered by the rise of the sea level, but also for most of the other developing countries which are plagued by risk factors such as dry or half dry soil, water shortage or high population density in areas threatened by flooding. The population of the poorer countries, due to the economic circumstances and to the lack of an institutionalised infrastructure, are to a higher degree defenceless against the consequences of drought, infectious decease, catastrophic floods and so on.

Prof. Klaus Meyer-Abich, once a member of the enquete commission of the German Bundestag on the protection of the atmosphere, rejects the opinion that the growing number of people in the developing countries overburdens the ecosystem of the earth by resuming "It would be the best development aid if we would stop harming the environment of the developing countries". Referring to te argument that the growing demand for fossil energy in the developing countries could only be satisfied by using nuclear energy in the industrialised countries, he says: "This argument serves only to justify the development in our countries by claiming its beneficiality for the developing countries while at the same time it blocks alternative solutions for our economy".

The overall aim must be to develop an alternative to the current way of running our economy, as the respected Wuppertal Institut in

Germany has done, for instance, with the study "Zukunftsfähiges Deutschland (Sustainable Germany)" or as Prof. Ernst-Ulrich v. Weizsäcker, Amory B. Lovins and L. Hunter Lovins have presented with their book 'Faktor 4 (Factor 4)'. If we in the industrialised countries take in account not only the population growth in the developing countries but also their dynamic economic growth, then we can no longer entertain the illusion that we can just go on without changing anything.

Although, in 1990, nearly 80% of the world's population lived in developing countries, their proportion of the world's energy consumption was only 1/3. This proportion will grow to over 50% according to the studies explained in detail below. The current economic growth alone is causing a rapid rise of CO_2-emissions. This is due to the following factors (among others):

- People tend to use less 'traditional' fuel and more fossil fuel from the official market.
- The rise of the average personal income leads to an increase of consumer goods sales (such as refrigerators, air condition, cars and so on).
- Industries with high energy consumption are on the increase while subsistence farming is on the decline

The population growth is the second important factor which, in combination with the other factors described in the studies presented below, has an impact on the future energy use and by that on the CO_2-emissions. The global population has doubled in the period from 1950 to 1990, that is from 2.52 Billion to 5.28 Billion people in only forty years. During this period the increase of population growth was rising every year; in 1989 with 88.6 Millions an all-time peak was reached. Although the growth rates are strongly variable (in 1990 it was only 1.69%), the total number of people is still rising in absolute numbers.

According to UN-scenarios (World Population Prospects 1950-2050) the world's population will increase further, despite falling birth rates. One reason for this is the age pyramid where younger generations are prevailing and the other reason is the rising life expectancy or decreasing mortality. This kind of dynamic influencing the population growth is called momentum by demographic experts. The momentum is so strong that it is hardly alterable.

The 'medium-growth' scenario, which is currently regarded as the most likely one, forecasts that the annual population growth will reach its highest value of 88.7 Million people already in 1998. However, in 2050 the population will still grow annually by 48.2 Millions and will have increased then by 86% compared to 1990. According to the 'high-growth' scenario, the increase is said to be 125%, whereas the 'low-growth' scenario expects the population to reach its maximum number of 7.97 Billion people in 2043 and predicts that it will start to decrease after that. The 'low-growth' scenario, however, is not seen as very likely to become reality. Estimations about the future energy demand and the future CO_2-emissions are mainly based on the above mentioned assumptions about the population growth (mainly in the UN-scenarios) and the following factors:

- The global economic growth
- The rate at which innovational changes occur (e.g. more efficient use of energy)
- The rate at which new energy-saving technologies are implemented
- The relative availability and price of fossil and nuclear fuel vs. renewable energy sources (amount of known energy resources, future energy price)

It follows a presentation of the studies mentioned in the WRI report, which are: the World-Energy-Council study (WEC, prognosis until 2020), the study of the International Energy Agency (IEA, prognosis until 2010) and the US-Department-of-Energy study (DOE, prognosis until 2010). The results are summarised. Further information about the different prognoses can be found in the passage under the header 'Projecting Future Energy Use' sea box 12.2 of the WRI report. All three prognoses predict a considerable increase of the energy consumption and of the CO_2-emissions over the next 20 to 30 years. In the WEC reference scenario the energy demand rises by 50% until 2020. The IEA and the DOE prognoses, which cover a shorter period, predict an increase by 34 to 44 per cent until 2010.

Similar findings show the prognoses of the International Institute for System Analysis (ILASA) in Laxenburg near Vienna and the scenario analyses by Wilfrid Bach (member of the enquete commissions of the 11th and 12th German Bundestag). The ILASA study forecasts, under the assumption of high economic growth, an increase of the energy consumption to 273% (current value=100 percent), for moderate economic growth to 220% and for a radically ecological scenario, which is regarded as unlikely, to 158%. The third scenario is to show mainly what would be technologically feasible in the direction of ecological innovations under extreme conditions. Thinking about these prospects, we could be tempted to draw the conclusion that there is no way of solving the problems. However, this would be the worst kind of reaction and would help only those who profit from this development. Some economic experts claim that an active climate policy would allegedly cost appr. 850 billion DM, for Germany alone, of course connected with rising unemployment figures.

The WRI has made the interesting observation that the results of so-called bottom-up analyses , which are based on detailed lists of engineering costs for different technologies and on detailed assessments of energy consumption, are much more optimistic in regard to the costs and benefits of a change than the so-called top-down studies, which are preferred by the economic experts. The latter kind of analyses is based on macroeconomic figures which are generalised mean values extrapolated from past periods. With bottom-up studies the result is that the costs of a reduction of the emissions by 20%, below the value of 1990, would be negligible or even negative over a period of some decades. In the long-term perspective, reductions by 50% are possible without increasing the costs of the energy supply system as a whole, because some of the improvements will pay through their energy saving function alone.

In this context please test our Java-based simulation tool Energy Tool. The development of wind and solar energy generation in Germany (tripling of applications for photovoltaic systems in 1996) gives rise to hope and shows that with persistence a change can be brought about. Many reputable research institutes, like the World Watch Institute or the National Renewable Energy Laboratory (NREL in Colorado), who have been in touch with the technological development for a long time, are convinced that the development on the energy market will enjoy a boom similar to the one in the telecommunications market.

In addition, the WRI points out that the above mentioned studies are based on current trends of energy demand and do not consider the prospect of a more tangible course correction, united international efforts, for instance, to make a move towards renewable and other non-fossil energy sources.

The clear signs of the significant and damaging effects caused by the man-made climate change could lead to a worldwide consensus and thus to a widespread support for a strengthened global convention on climate. By putting into practice such an agreement the availability of money for investment in alternative energy sources should improve considerably. This would turn around the whole energy system in the direction of a new climate-neutral technology, which is to a large degree available at present. Despite their lobbying of the fossil energy sources, the industry is preparing the ground for the day, when the renewable energy sources will replace the other sources. The WRI points out that the move away from fossil energy sources is necessary to avoid the dangerous risks of a climate change. Of the non-fossil forms of energy, wind and solar energy have the best long-term prospects.

Bibliography

Adhikari D S : *Population Challenge and World Crisis : Documents and Case Studies*, Cyber Tech, Delhi, 2008.

Ahuja, N.: *Evolution and Population Genetics*, Pearl Books, Delhi, 2008.

Ayala, F. J.: *Evolution*, W.H. Freeman & Co., California, San Francisco, 1977.

Balshaw, Maria, and Liam Kennedy: *Urban Space and Representation*. Pluto Press, Sterling, VA, 2000.

Banerjee, Anuradha: *Environment Population and Human Settlements of Sundarban Delta*, Concept, Delhi, 1998.

Burrough, P.A. and McDonnell, R.A. : *Principles of Geographical Information Systems*, Oxford University Press, Oxford, 1998.

Chandra, Amitabh : *Population Challenge and World Crisis*, Alfa Pub, Delhi, 2008.

Chaurasia, Alok Ranjan: *India: The State of Population 2007*, Oxford University, Delhi, 2008.

Christophe, Z. Guilmoto : *Essays on Population and Space in India*, Institut Francais De Pondichery, Delhi, 2000.

Cronon, William: *Changes in the Land: Indians, Colonists, and the Ecology of New England*. Hill and Wang, New York, 1983.

Datta, K.B.: *Dynamics of Gender Planning and Population : Issues and Challenges*, Akansha Pub, Delhi, 2002.

Devi D. Uma and Reddy P. Adinarayana: *Environment Education for Rural Population*, Discovery, Delhi, 2007.

Dyson, Tim: *Population And Development : The Demographic Transition*, Rawat, Delhi, 2011.

Jain, Prakash C. : *Population and Society in West Asia : Essays in Comparative Demography*, National Publishing House, Delhi, 2001.

Kimura, Motoo : *An Introduction to Population Genetics Theory*, Scientific Pub, Delhi, 2010.

Ksheerasager, Surekha F. : *Instructional Module : On Teaching Population Education*, Current Publications, Delhi, 2008.

Kumar, A.K. Shiva : *Handbook of Population and Development in India,* Oxford University Press, Delhi, 2010.

Kumar, Aditya Patra : *Population and Health,* Discovery, Delhi, 2010.

Lakshmanasamy T. : *Population Dynamics and Human Development,* Bookwell, Delhi, 2010.

Lewis, Earl. *In Their Own Interests: Race, Class, and Power in Twentieth-Century Norfolk, Virginia.* University of California Press, Berkeley, 1990.

Lewis, Peirce: *New Orleans: The Making of an Urban Landscape.* Ballinger Publishing Co., Cambridge, MA, 1976.

Macbeth Helen : *Human Population Dynamics: Cross-Disciplinary Perspectives,* Cambridge Univ Press, 2003.

Malthus Thomas: *An Essay on the Principle of Population,* Atlantic Pub, Delhi, 2011.

Mitra, K.C. : *Handbook of Population Studies,* Wisdom Press, Delhi, 2012.

Mittal, A. C.: *Population and Sustainable Development,* Vista International Pub, Delhi, 2008.

Murty, S. : *Female Ageing Population : Problems and Prospects,* RBSA, Delhi, 2008.

Narasaiah, M Lakshmi : *Population and Biodiversity,* Discovery Pub, Delhi, 2006.

Prakasam, C.P. : *Population and Environment Linkages,* Rawat, Delhi, 2007.

Rahman, A. Atiq : *Exploding the Population Myth : Consumption Versus Population,* The University Press, Delhi, 1998.

Reddy, M.M. Krishna : *Marriage, Population and Society : Demographic Perspectives of a Social Institution,* Kanishka, Delhi, 1998.

Santilata, Patnaik : *Adult Attitude Towards Population Education* , Discovery, Delhi, 2003.

Sharma, Rajendra K : *Demography and Population Problems,* Atlantic, Delhi, 2007.

Shimray, U.A. : *Naga Population and Integration Movement : Documentation,* Mittal Pub, Delhi, 2007.

Singh, Sudhir Kumar: *Population and Sustainable Development in India,* Authorspress, Delhi, 2006.

Sinha Smita and Gupta Abha : *At Risk Population : Sociolinguistic and Educational Issues,* Dominant, Delhi, 2006.

Srinivasan K.: *India: Towards Population and Development Goals,* OUP, Delhi, 1997.

Verma N.K. : *Population and Poverty,* Sumit Enterprises, Delhi, 2006.

Walter M.: *Encyclopaedia of Population and Development,* Sarup, Delhi, 2002.

Index

❑❑❑